LEGO NINJAGO
Masters of Spinjitzu

BUILD YOUR OWN ADVENTURE
GREATEST NINJA BATTLES

CONTENTS

MEET NYA

Nya is one of the six ninja who protect Ninjago City from evil. Quick thinking and very brave, Nya is an essential part of the team. She knows that being a ninja is not just for boys and is determined to prove it with every chance she gets.

CHECK OUT MY NINJA GEAR!

Tenugui headband

Crossed obi sash

Kyahan leg wraps

Tabi boots

THE NINJA

The six ninja are Nya, the Master of Water; Nya's brother, Kai, the Master of Fire; Lloyd, the Master of Energy; Cole, the Master of Earth; Jay, the Master of Lightning; and Zane, the Master of Ice. They are all experts in the martial art of Spinjitzu.

THE NINJA'S FOES

The ninja have battled many enemies. They look back proudly on their victories, but there are still some villains they would rather forget. With each new foe they defeat, they learn more about themselves and about one another. Maybe that's why they love to tell stories about their battles!

THE ANACONDRAI
The snakelike Anacondrai were the most fearsome of the five Serpentine tribes that once ruled Ninjago Island. They were banished long ago, but Pythor, their leader, came back with plans to rule the world and bring the Anacondrai back to life.

WE STILL HAUNT THE NINJA!

THE GHOST WARRIORS
The ghoulish Ghost Warriors were spirits that had escaped from the Cursed Realm. They went on a mission to make Ninjago as horrible as their haunted home and possessed minds in order to do so. They terrorized the city of Stiix.

I WILL HAVE MY REVENGE!

THE SKY PIRATES
A band of crooks led by Captain Nadakhan, the Sky Pirates were tricked into serving their captain. When Nadakhan swore revenge on the ninja for accidentally destroying his home, the Sky Pirates had no choice but to obey!

THE VERMILLION
The Vermillion were born out of the eggs of a monster serpent. They could change from people into swarms of snakes! Under the leadership of the evil Time Twins, they set out to attack and devour everything in their path.

THE SONS OF GARMADON
The Sons of Garmadon are the latest threat to Ninjago City. A ruthless biker gang, they are trying to get their hands on three ancient Oni Masks. When they have all three masks, they plan to use them to revive their idol, Lord Garmadon!

OUR TIME WILL COME AGAIN

NYA'S HOVER-BIKE

The Elemental Master of Water rides a bike that can race like a river and float like a mist! In ground mode, its wheels look like a waterfall. In hover mode, they can spin like whirlpools. Wherever it goes, it can fire missiles from its missile launchers.

Nya stands up at the controls

Two katana swords can be stored at the back

Fire 1x1 round tiles using these stud shooters

Smooth plate provides a step down when wheels are in hover mode

Wheels fold together for ground mode

GOTTA FLY!

HOVER MODE

When Nya activates her bike's hover mode, its two wheels pull apart to become four antigravity pads! On water, she can quickly cross any terrain and take on any opponent, no matter where they go!

Wheels in hover mode

BUILDING INSTRUCTIONS

1x

1

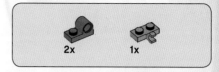

2x   1x

3

1x

2

1x

4

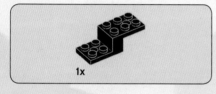

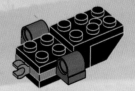

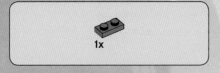

5

7

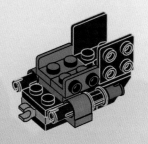

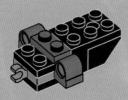

6

8

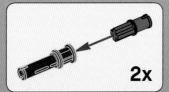

2x

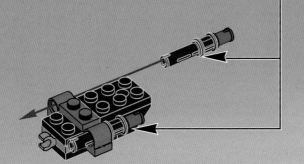

2x

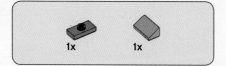

1x 1x

9

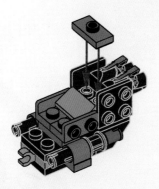

1x 1x

10

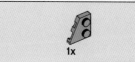

1x

11

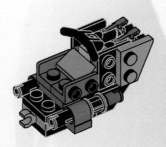

1x

12

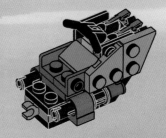

13

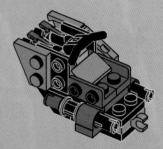

14

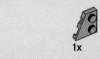

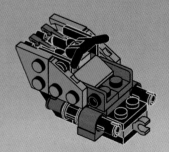

15

16

1x 1x

17

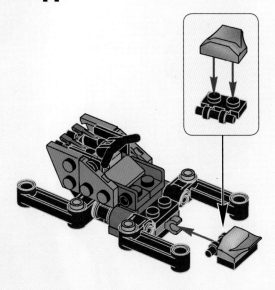

4x 4x 4x

18

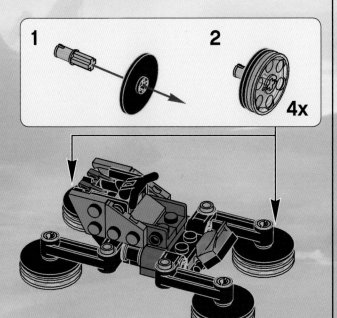

1 2 4x

2x

19

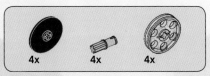

2x

20

21

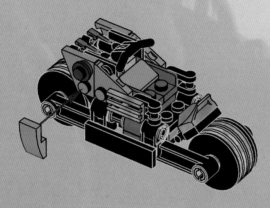

22

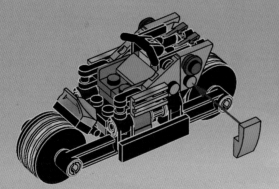

23

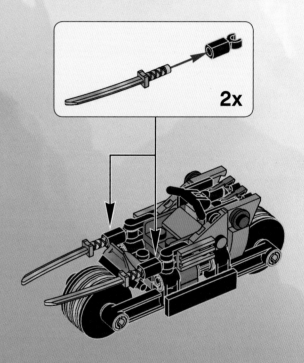

2x

4x

24

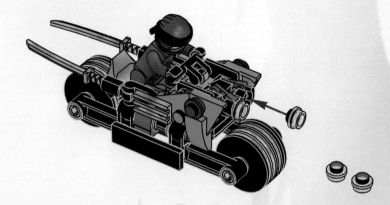

BUILD YOUR OWN ADVENTURE

In the pages of this book, you will discover an exciting LEGO® NINJAGO® adventure. You will also see some clever ideas for LEGO NINJAGO models that might inspire you to create your own. Building LEGO models from your imagination is creative and endlessly fun. There are no limits to what you can build. This is your adventure, so jump right in and start building!

BE CREATIVE!

HOW TO USE THIS BOOK

This book will not show you exactly how to build the models, because you may not have the same bricks in your LEGO collection. It will give you lots of ideas and show you some useful building tips and model breakdowns that will help you when it comes to building your own models. Here's how the pages work...

Sometimes, different views of the same model are shown

"What will you build?" flashes give you even more ideas for models you could make

SEWER MYSTERY
When he sees his special signal, Kai follows it to its source. In the swamp, he finds more giant eggs, and a Vermillion sentry keeping an eye on them from a lookout. Kai knows that if the eggs hatch, they will turn into more evil Vermillion warriors!

I'M ON THE LOOK-OUT FOR LOOKOUTS!

OPEN VIEW

A-plate

Plate with bar

6x6 round plate with hole

HISS!

Half-snake fits into plate with top clip

I CAN SEE THINGS MILES AWAY!

A stack of different-shaped bricks makes a ruined tower.

What will you build?
• Vermillion spy plane
• Sewer system
• Giant snake
• Rusty railings

Plate with bar

2x2 corner slope

Tall Vermillion egg piece

Telescope is made from a telescope piece and 1x1 round plate

LOOKOUT TOWER
The Vermillion sentry can see across the entire swamp from this tall lookout. Its tall sides protect him from attack, and the ladder to the top is guarded by a scary snake!

Decorative wings connect to LEGO Technic pins

Spider-leg pieces slot into plates with rings

2x2 round brick

Ladder with clips

LUCKY I'M RIGHT HERE, THEN!

HIDDEN EGG
Kai finds the biggest egg hidden by vines at the base of an ornate sewer outlet. This one is clearly very important to the Vermillion, and Kai is determined to keep an eye on it!

Brick with hole

Horn piece

1x2 jumper plate

Textured wall brick

Plate with ring

Brick with side stud

BEHIND THE FENCE
The tumbledown fence is made from smooth plates attached to bricks with side studs. The half-snake piece pokes through on a plate with a ring.

The ooze from the sewer pipe is attached to the base.

See giant pieces fit onto sideways plates with top clips

4x4 round plate

3x3 angled plate

Breakdowns of models feature useful build tips

Special features or elements on models are annotated

MEET THE BUILDER

Barney Main is a LEGO fan and super-builder, and he made the inspirational LEGO models that can be found in this book. To make the models just right for the LEGO® NINJAGO® world, Barney worked with the LEGO NINJAGO team at the LEGO Group headquarters in Billund, Denmark. Use Barney's creations to inspire your own models!

HAPPY BUILDING!

BEFORE YOU BEGIN

Here are five handy hints to keep in mind every time you get out your bricks and prepare to build:

Organize your bricks
Organizing bricks into colors and types can save you time when you're building.

Make your model stable
Make a model that's sturdy enough to play with. You'll find useful tips for making a stable model in this book.

Be creative
If you don't have the perfect piece, find a creative solution! Look for a different piece that can create a similar effect.

Research
Look up pictures of what you want to build online or in books to inspire your ideas.

Have fun
Don't worry if your model goes wrong. Turn it into something else or start again. The fun is in the building!

LET'S GET BUILDING!

Did you know that LEGO® builders have their own language? You will find the terms below used a lot in this book. Here's what they mean:

TILE

When you want a smooth finish to your build, you need to use a tile. Printed tiles add extra detail to your models.

1x6 tile

2x2 tile

2x2 tile with pin

1x1 printed tile

2x3 shield tile

STUD

Round raised bumps on top of bricks and plates are called studs. A chain has a single stud at each end. Studs fit into "tubes," which are on the bottom of bricks and plates.

2x2 corner plate

Chain

MEASUREMENTS

Builders describe the size of LEGO pieces according to the number of studs on them. If a brick has 2 studs across and 3 up, it's a 2x3 brick. If a piece is tall, it has a third number that is its height in standard bricks.

2

3

2x3 brick

1x1x5 brick

CLIP

Some pieces have clips on them. You can fit other elements into these clips. Pieces such as ladders fasten onto bars using built-in clips.

1x1 plate with clip

1x1 plate with clip

2x3 tile with clips

HOLE

Bricks and plates with holes are very useful. They will hold bars or LEGO® Technic pins or connectors.

1x1 brick with hole

2x3 curved plate with hole

2x2 round grooved brick

4x4 round brick

SIDEWAYS BUILDING

Sometimes you need to build in two directions. That's when you need bricks or plates like these, with studs on more than one side.

1x4 brick with side studs

1x1 brick with two side studs

1x2/2x2 angle plate

1x1 brick with one side stud

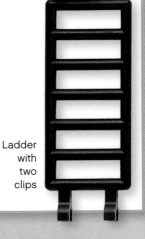

Ladder with two clips

BRICK

Where would a builder be without the brick? It's the basis of most models and it comes in a huge variety of shapes and sizes.

2x2 brick

1x2 textured brick

1x1 headlight brick

1x2 grooved brick

2x2 domed brick

1x1 round brick

PLATE

Like bricks, plates have studs on top and tubes on the bottom. A plate is thinner than a brick—the height of three plates is equal to one standard brick.

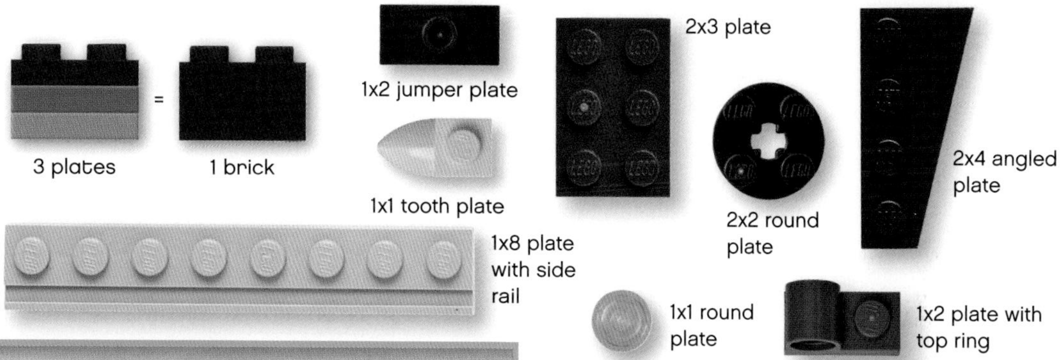

3 plates = 1 brick

1x2 jumper plate

1x1 tooth plate

1x8 plate with side rail

2x3 plate

2x2 round plate

2x4 angled plate

1x1 round plate

1x2 plate with top ring

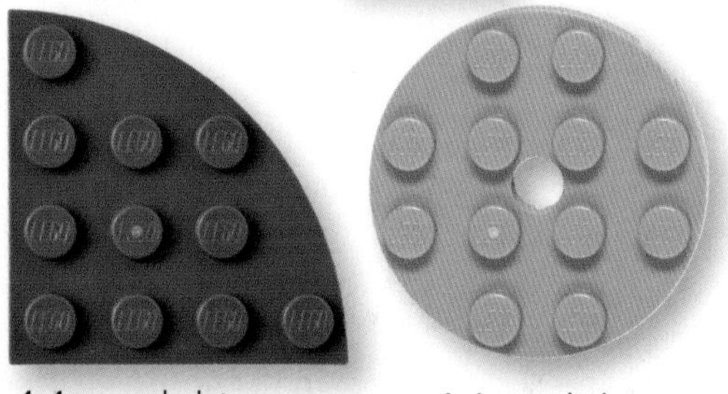

4x4 curved plate

4x4 round plate

SPECIAL PIECES

Special pieces are used to create specific structures, or to link the build to a LEGO theme.

1x1 slope

4x4 rocky angled slope

4x4 angled slope

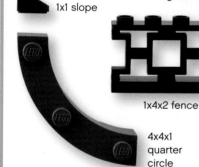

1x4x2 fence

4x4x1 quarter circle

4x4 printed radar dish

SLOPE

Slopes are bigger at the bottom than on top. Inverted slopes are the same, but upside down. They are smaller at the bottom and bigger on top.

1x2 slope

1x2 Inverted slope

HINGE

If you want to make a roof that opens or give a creature a tail that moves, you need a hinge. A ball joint does the same job, too.

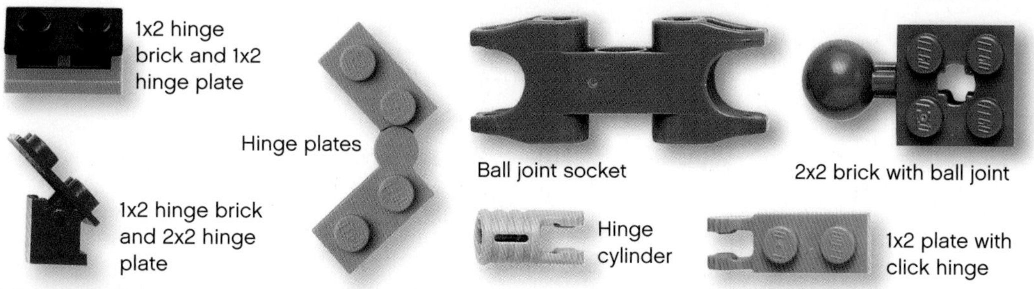

1x2 hinge brick and 1x2 hinge plate

1x2 hinge brick and 2x2 hinge plate

Hinge plates

Ball joint socket

Hinge cylinder

2x2 brick with ball joint

1x2 plate with click hinge

AT THE NOODLE BAR

The ninja have found an Oni Mask, which they must keep safe from their enemies. To celebrate their discovery, they visit their favorite noodle joint in Ninjago City. Over bowls of ramen, they compare stories about some of their most exciting and past adventures.

OK, GUYS, TELL YOUR TALES!

Upside-down dome

Placemats are round tiles with holes

Each leg is a small round table

The bowl and plate fit onto placemats made from round tiles with holes.

RESTAURANT BOOTHS

The ninja get together in their favorite booth, which has room to seat all six of them. They share stories across a large table with room for plates, bowls, and ice cream sundaes!

SO, THIS ONE TIME I WAS...

What will you build?
- Drink dispenser
- Robot waitstaff
- Platter of sushi
- Dining chair

1x1 slope

WAIT UNTIL YOU HEAR HOW I...

FRONT DESK

The ninja hang up the Oni Mask at the front desk, near their booth. It should be safe beside the cat statue, which is a traditional good-luck charm.

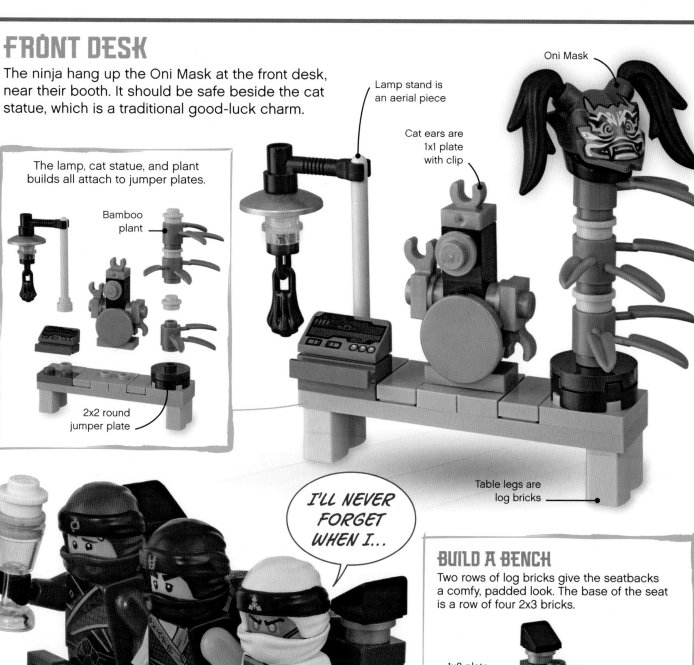

Oni Mask

Lamp stand is an aerial piece

Cat ears are 1x1 plate with clip

The lamp, cat statue, and plant builds all attach to jumper plates.

Bamboo plant

2x2 round jumper plate

Table legs are log bricks

I'LL NEVER FORGET WHEN I...

2x3 brick

2x8 plate

1x8 plate

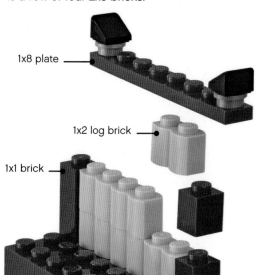

BUILD A BENCH

Two rows of log bricks give the seatbacks a comfy, padded look. The base of the seat is a row of four 2x3 bricks.

1x8 plate

1x2 log brick

1x1 brick

CHAPTER 1
ANACONDRAI ATTACK

INTO THE JUNGLE

First, Lloyd and Zane tell their tale of defeating the Anacondrai in the jungle... It begins with Lloyd tracking the Anacondrai to find their base when he suddenly falls into a quicksand trap! The Anacondrai notice him and quickly flee in their speedy flying machines.

FOOLISH NINJA!

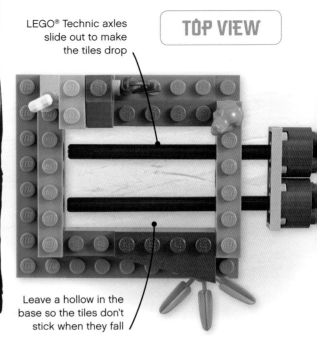

LEGO® Technic axles slide out to make the tiles drop

Leave a hollow in the base so the tiles don't stick when they fall

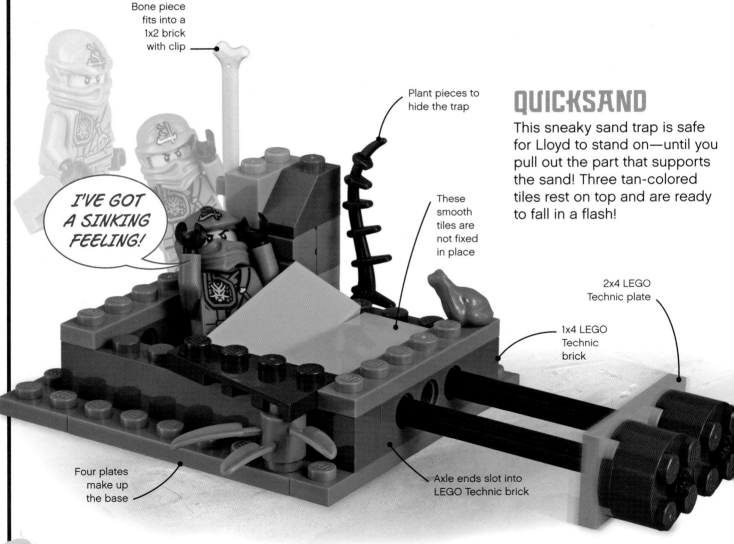

Bone piece fits into a 1x2 brick with clip

Plant pieces to hide the trap

These smooth tiles are not fixed in place

I'VE GOT A SINKING FEELING!

QUICKSAND

This sneaky sand trap is safe for Lloyd to stand on—until you pull out the part that supports the sand! Three tan-colored tiles rest on top and are ready to fall in a flash!

2x4 LEGO Technic plate

1x4 LEGO Technic brick

Four plates make up the base

Axle ends slot into LEGO Technic brick

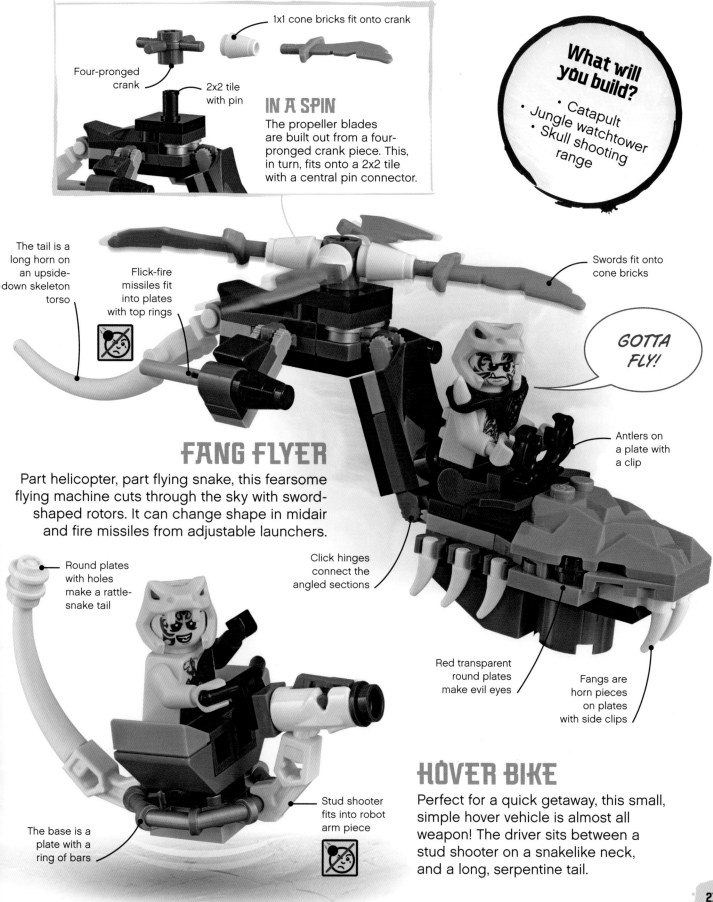

1x1 cone bricks fit onto crank

Four-pronged crank

2x2 tile with pin

IN A SPIN
The propeller blades are built out from a four-pronged crank piece. This, in turn, fits onto a 2x2 tile with a central pin connector.

What will you build?
- Catapult
- Jungle watchtower
- Skull shooting range

The tail is a long horn on an upside-down skeleton torso

Flick-fire missiles fit into plates with top rings

Swords fit onto cone bricks

GOTTA FLY!

Antlers on a plate with a clip

FANG FLYER

Part helicopter, part flying snake, this fearsome flying machine cuts through the sky with sword-shaped rotors. It can change shape in midair and fire missiles from adjustable launchers.

Click hinges connect the angled sections

Round plates with holes make a rattle-snake tail

Red transparent round plates make evil eyes

Fangs are horn pieces on plates with side clips

Stud shooter fits into robot arm piece

HOVER BIKE

Perfect for a quick getaway, this small, simple hover vehicle is almost all weapon! The driver sits between a stud shooter on a snakelike neck, and a long, serpentine tail.

The base is a plate with a ring of bars

23

UNDER ATTACK

Using all his strength, Lloyd breaks free from the quicksand and leaps into his blade-dozer. He races after the Anacondrai and catches up with them in a jungle clearing. When they start to fire missiles at him, he knows he must be close to their main base!

I'M ON YOUR TAIL, SNAKES!

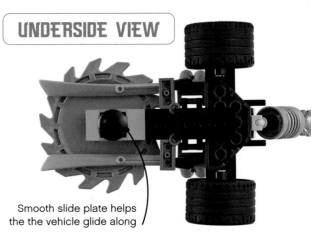

Smooth slide plate helps the the vehicle glide along

LLOYD'S BLADE-DOZER

Lloyd can cut through the jungle undergrowth in this turbocharged two-wheeler. The huge spinning blade at the front carves a path straight to the Anacondrai—and keeps them from coming too close!

Exhaust is made from two wheel rim pieces back to back

I'LL BE THERE IN A MOW!

Exhaust pipes are angled on plates with bars attached to plates with clips

The spinning saw blade turns on a 2x2 tile with a pin.

Circular saw piece

2x2 tile with pin

The katana blades are angled on hinge plates

JUNGLE PLANTS

Tall trees and trailing vines surround the clearing where Lloyd finds the Anacondrai. They can try to hide in the undergrowth, but nothing will stop the blade-dozer!

Upside-down sea grass piece fits into a leaf piece to make vines

Round bricks alternate with bamboo plants

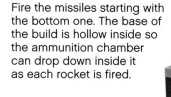

I'LL JUST CHECK ON OUR GUEST...

What will you build?

- Ninja-eating plants
- Giant flowers
- Overgrown ruins
- Jungle tree house

Radar dishes make stable bases for tall trees

Missile chamber is a LEGO Technic beam

Each missile is a LEGO Technic half pin with a bar

READY, AIM, FIRE!

MISSILE CHAMBER

Fire the missiles starting with the bottom one. The base of the build is hollow inside so the ammunition chamber can drop down inside it as each rocket is fired.

Brick with side stud

The sides are made from six 1x3 bricks

MISSILE LAUNCHER

The Anacondrai have weapons all over the jungle, including this missile launcher. It can fire four missiles in quick succession—all aimed at the same height, as the chamber drops down with each shot.

Snake helmet on a plant is a warning to intruders!

RESCUING ZANE

Powering through the missiles, Lloyd reaches the Anacondrai's lair and finds Zane is being held prisoner there! He uses his blade-dozer to cut down Zane's cage, which smashes as it hits the ground, freeing Zane to help Lloyd fight the Anacondrai in their lair.

WHAT TOOK YOU SO LONG?

ZANE'S CAGE

Even the mighty Zane can't break out of this bony prison on his own! Clips hold it together all the way around, and it hangs from a tall, sturdy-looking column.

Short LEGO Technic axle

Axle connector

Brick with cross hole

Claw piece

BUILD TIP

Build a sturdy beam to take the weight of the cage using short LEGO Technic axles and axle connector tubes.

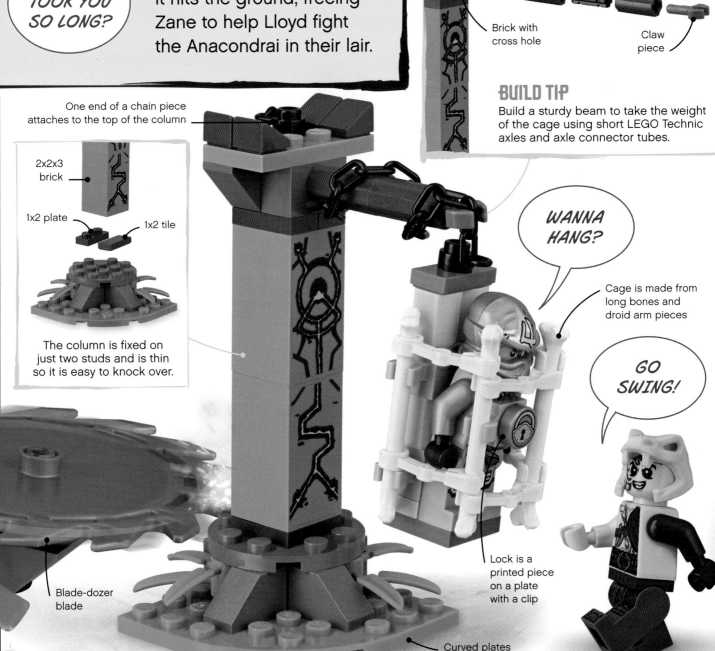

One end of a chain piece attaches to the top of the column

2x2x3 brick

1x2 plate

1x2 tile

The column is fixed on just two studs and is thin so it is easy to knock over.

WANNA HANG?

Cage is made from long bones and droid arm pieces

GO SWING!

Blade-dozer blade

Lock is a printed piece on a plate with a clip

Curved plates

ANACONDRAI LAIR

Deep in the jungle, the Anacondrai's base is devoted to venom and villainy. It is full of special weapons that only the greatest Anacondrai warriors are allowed to use.

Slope pieces add an interesting shape to the structure

Purple plates secure columns of round bricks

A single 2x10 brick makes a strong top section

Tooth pieces slot into headlight bricks

An arch makes a secret hiding place!

Combine small pieces to make unusual weapons.

Bone piece

1x1 plate with clip

Jumper plate

Round textured bricks look like bamboo wood

Bamboo plant

1x1 gray cone

What will you build?

• Skull storage
• Punch bag
• Weight-lifting bench

NINJA TEAM-UP

After Zane thanks Lloyd for freeing him, they plot together to teach the Anacondrai a lesson. The crafty pair decide to set a couple of traps for the villains. One ends up in a giant spiderweb and the other under a net. Teamwork wins the day!

I'VE GOT A GREAT IDEA!

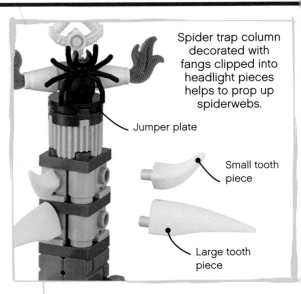

Spider trap column decorated with fangs clipped into headlight pieces helps to prop up spiderwebs.

Jumper plate

Small tooth piece

Large tooth piece

SPIDER TRAP

The Anacondrai get along well with creepy-crawlies and have trained big jungle spiders to make giant, sticky webs to catch their enemies. But they're just as good at catching Anacondrai warriors, too!

A Djinn sword hilt makes a scary skull sculpture

HELP! I'M NOT A FLY!

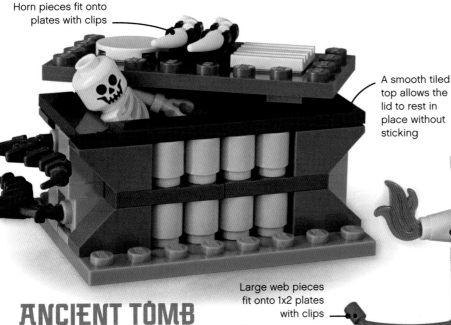

Horn pieces fit onto plates with clips

A smooth tiled top allows the lid to rest in place without sticking

ANCIENT TOMB

Take a look inside this tomb and you will come face-to-face with a scary skeleton! Lloyd wastes no time in setting the bony brute free, so it can wreak havoc around the Anacondrai base. The villains are so surprised, they run straight into traps.

Large web pieces fit onto 1x2 plates with clips

The launch mechanism moves back and forth through a LEGO Technic brick.

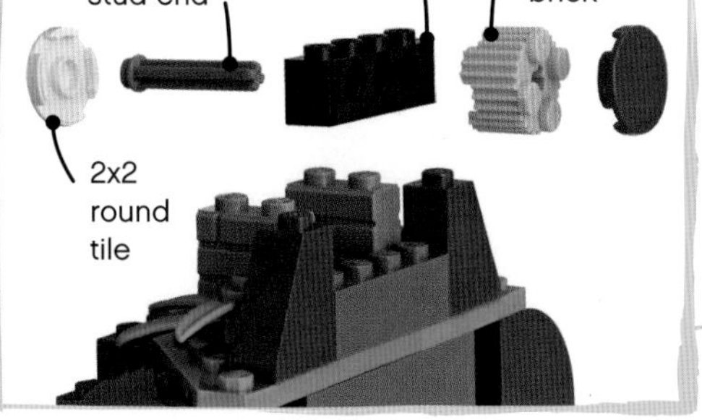

LEGO Technic axle with stud end

1x4 LEGO Technic brick

Textured round brick

2x2 round tile

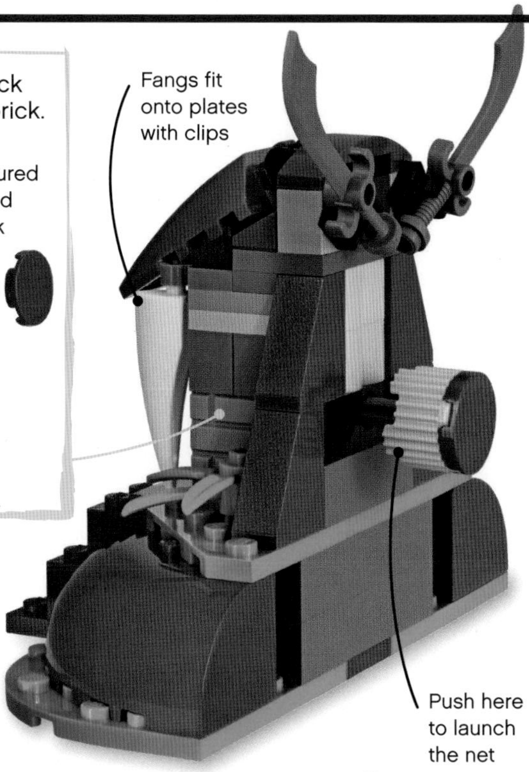

Fangs fit onto plates with clips

HINGED HEAD

The top of the snake's head is a curved slope piece, angled downward on a hinge made from a plate with clips and a plate with a bar.

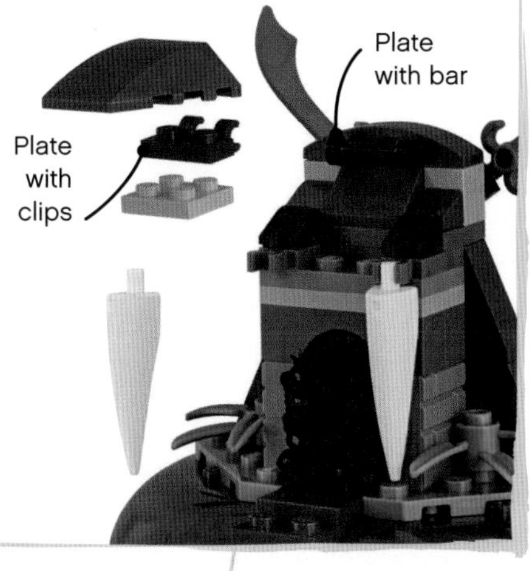

Plate with bar

Plate with clips

REAR VIEW

NET TRAP

Looking like a huge, coiled snake, this trap is scary enough to keep most intruders away. But if that doesn't work, a net can easily be triggered from behind the snake's head.

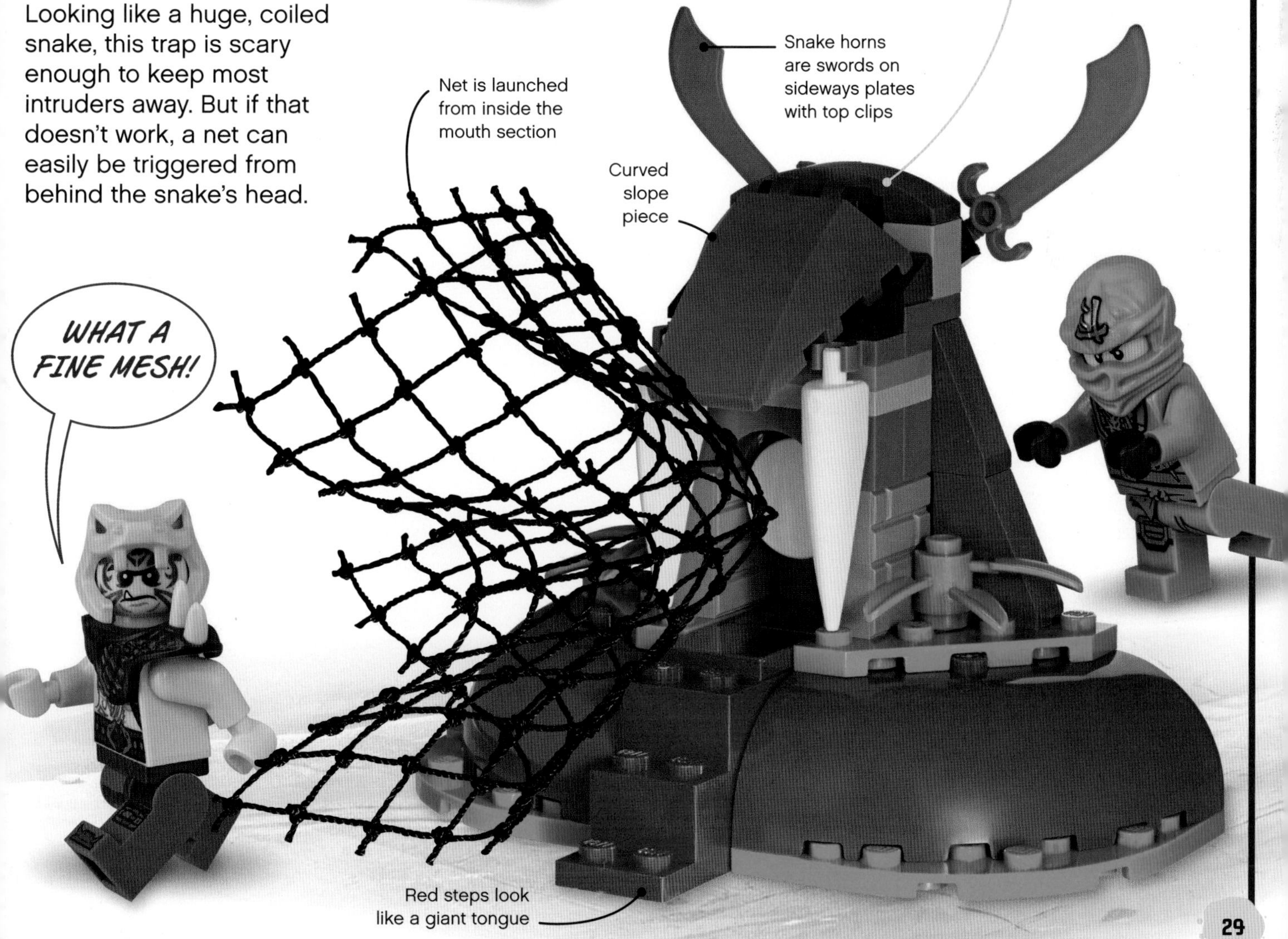

Push here to launch the net

Snake horns are swords on sideways plates with top clips

Net is launched from inside the mouth section

Curved slope piece

WHAT A FINE MESH!

Red steps look like a giant tongue

CHAPTER 2
GHOST ARMY

SPOOKY STREET

The next hero to tell his story is Cole. He recalls how he fought the Ghost Warriors from the Cursed Realm without help from a single soul... It all starts one night in a forgotten corner of Ninjago City, where a strange voice calls out from near an abandoned store.

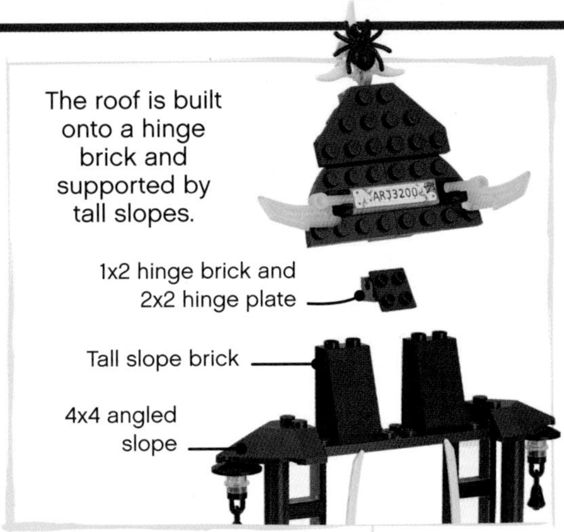

WHO LIKES GHOST STORIES?

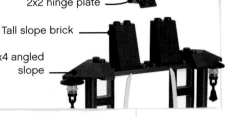

The roof is built onto a hinge brick and supported by tall slopes.

1x2 hinge brick and 2x2 hinge plate

Tall slope brick

4x4 angled slope

GATEWAY

There's a grand gateway on this empty shopping street. It used to be bustling until rumors of ghosts scared people away. Cole is walking past the gate when he hears something strange.

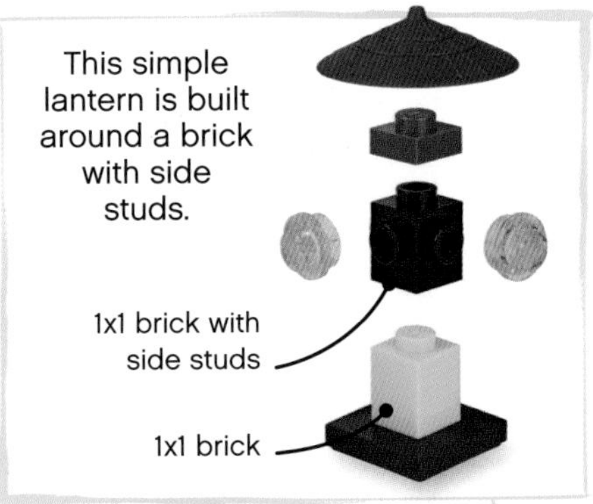

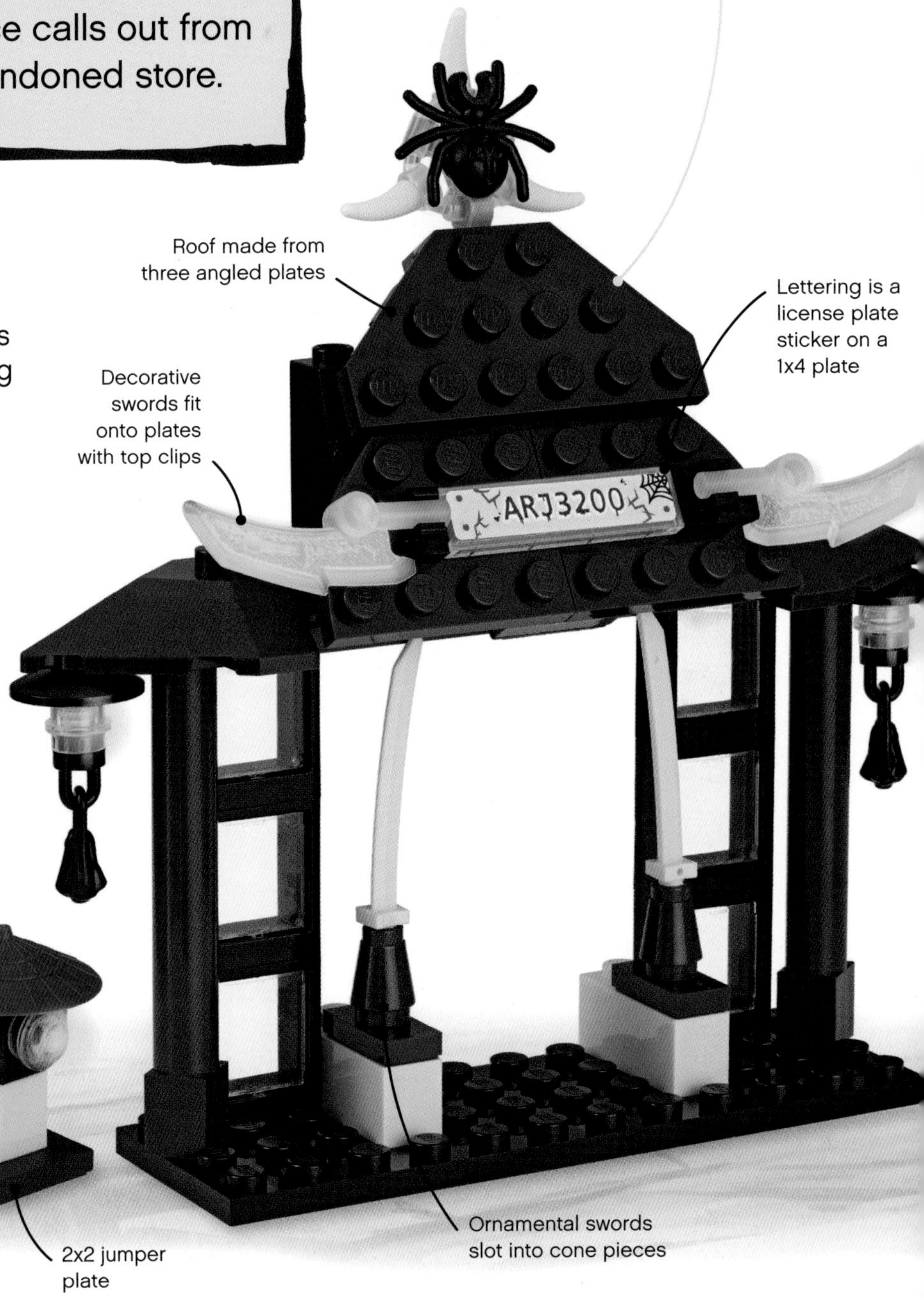

This simple lantern is built around a brick with side studs.

1x1 brick with side studs

1x1 brick

Roof made from three angled plates

Decorative swords fit onto plates with top clips

Lettering is a license plate sticker on a 1x4 plate

ARJ3200

COME IIIN, COLE!

2x2 jumper plate

Ornamental swords slot into cone pieces

ABANDONED STORE

This spooky storefront is packed full of details. Different angles of slope brick give it a creepy, uncared-for look.

These green bricks show through the crack in the front

Transparent rock crystal piece

Horn pieces slot into the top of inverted slope bricks

Small transparent slopes look like jagged broken glass

An 1x3 inverted slope and a 1x2 slope make a big crack in this wall

L-shaped bar slots into a brick with a side stud

Plate with clips

2x4 plate

Fit the shop sign at an angle to make it look broken.

A sideways plate with a clip looks like a padlock

Gray textured bricks look like a shuttered storefront

Locked door is a stack of three fence pieces

WHO'S THERE?

33

TARGET TEST

Bravely stepping through the creepy entrance, Cole finds himself in a ninja training area like nothing he has ever seen before. This dojo has been built by Ghost Warriors to test him. First up, he has to face the Soul Archer in an epic target-shooting contest!

G-G-G-GHOST WARRIORS!

STRAIGHT DOWN THE MIDDLE

The spring shooter is fixed on a cart base using four jumper plates. It is triggered by pushing down the missile, firing it out of the spring.

1x1 ring plate

1x3 tile

Missile in spring shooter

Row of 1x2 jumper plates

ARROW CART

Cole has to hit the targets by firing missiles from this cannon. It is built around a spring shooter brick. A flame piece shows where Cole has lit the fuse to fire it!

Flame piece

Fang pieces on front ward off attackers

I AIM TO WIN!

Wheels connect to 1x4 axle plate

BULLSEYE

The Soul Archer never misses his target, but can Cole hit it, too? Striking the red ring is fine for a beginner, but a skilled ninja should get the bullseye every time!

A LEGO® Technic angled connector is the key to this build.

L-shaped bar

Brick with hole

Angled connector

Aim for this shield

Bullseye is a 2x2 round tile

A round brick, radar dish, and clipped-on bow make a dummy archer

Flag clips onto LEGO Technic T-bar

Base is a 3x8 angled plate

Tube with clip

Base is made from curved plates

Skeletal spider-leg pieces fit onto plates with clips

FLIPPER TARGETS

These two flipper targets tip over when hit, and a flag goes up to show Cole has scored a point. They pivot on LEGO Technic pins in bricks with holes.

This red round tile is the target

Horns slot into angle plates on both sides

Start with flag piece flat on ground

3x1 curved slope

Base is broader at the back to stop entire build tipping over

1x2 brick with hole

SCYTHE SURPRISE

When Cole wins the target contest, the Soul Archer disappears, and a door opens ahead of Cole. It leads to a large room where Scythe Master Ghoultar has set another task for the ninja! This time, Cole has to prove his skill with a scythe blade.

THERE ARE TWO SCYTHES TO THIS STORY!

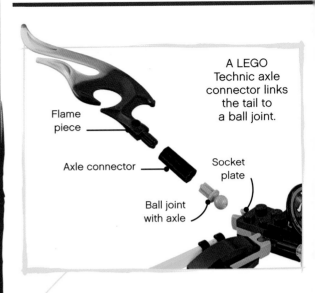

A LEGO Technic axle connector links the tail to a ball joint.

Flame piece

Axle connector

Socket plate

Ball joint with axle

AND NOW FOR YOUR NEXT TEST...

Tail is a giant flame piece

SMALL DRAGON

Ghoultar's assistant rides a ghostly dragon with glinting green eyes. It is built using ball-and-socket joints so that the wings can flap and the scythe-like tail can swish.

Plate with a clip and plate with bar make tilting snou

Green eyes are the ends of chain pieces

Wings are katana swords fixed to plates with clips

SPREAD YOUR WINGS

Each wing is made up of a socket plate and two plates with clips, sandwiched between a curved slope piece and a small angled plate.

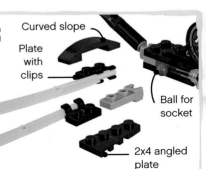

Curved slope

Plate with clips

Ball for socket

2x4 angled plate

The tipping floor is fixed at one end only, using LEGO Technic pins.

2x2 plate with ring below

4x6 plate

LEGO Technic pin

2x1 brick with hole

BARREL STORE

Cole doesn't wait to find out what his challenge is. He grabs a scythe and cuts down the pole supporting some barrels. They tumble down onto Ghoultar!

ACTIVE VIEW

Transparent green plates in each barrel are ghostly slime

Hinge cylinder

The barrels stand loosely on smooth tiles

1x2 brick with hole

This floor tips down when the pole is removed

Pole is not fixed in place

PROVE YOUR SKILL, NINJA!

I HAVE BARREL LOADS OF TALENT!

Each side is one large girder piece

The base of the pole sits in a plate with a hole

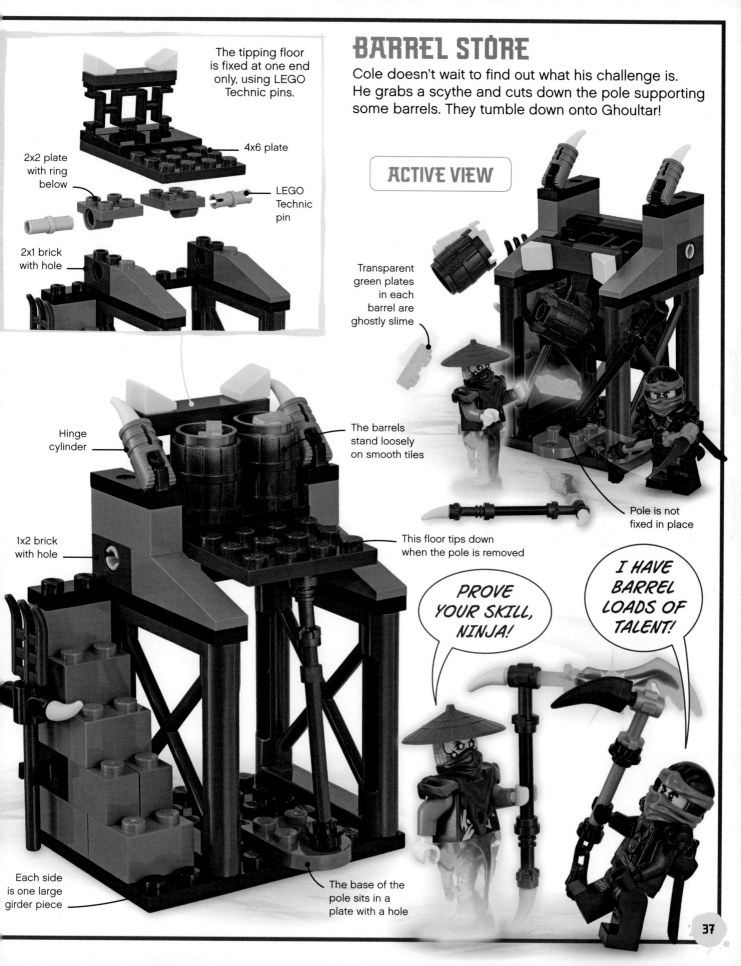

CHAINS CHALLENGE

Leaving Ghoultar behind him, Cole races into the next room, where he meets another Ghost Warrior: Wrayth, the Master of Chains. Wrayth is watching over an obstacle course made from chains that Cole must complete to be allowed out of the dojo.

LET'S HANG OUT!

2x2 brick with pin

The main part of the chandelier is a plate with a ring of bars.

LEGO Technic angle connector

Round plate with hole

Claw piece

Plate with ring of bars

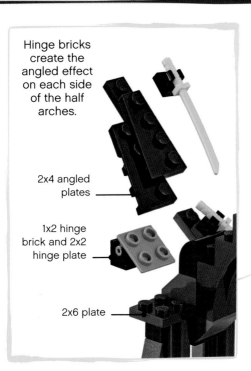

Hinge bricks create the angled effect on each side of the half arches.

2x4 angled plates

1x2 hinge brick and 2x2 hinge plate

2x6 plate

Two large half arches side by side support the chandelier

The chandelier can swing from left to right

Transparent green cone

2x2 inverted slope

THIS IS LIGHT WORK

A base of plates stops the build tipping over

CHANDELIER

Cole's first challenge is to swing across a pit of scorpions on a chandelier! The chandelier is built onto a brick with a LEGO Technic pin, so it can swing through 360 degrees.

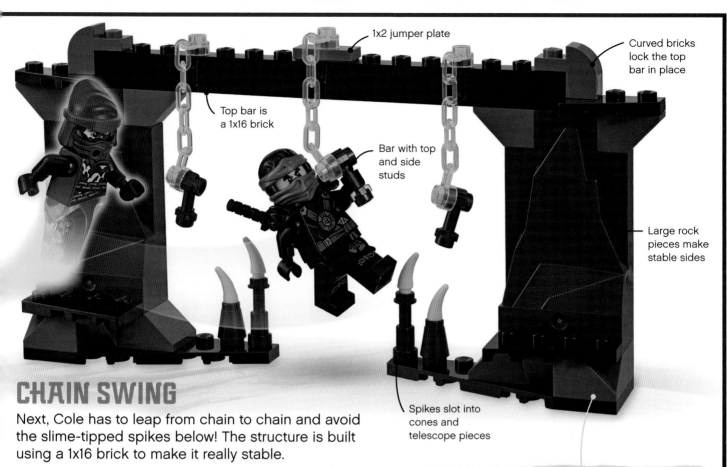

1x2 jumper plate

Curved bricks lock the top bar in place

Top bar is a 1x16 brick

Bar with top and side studs

Large rock pieces make stable sides

CHAIN SWING

Next, Cole has to leap from chain to chain and avoid the slime-tipped spikes below! The structure is built using a 1x16 brick to make it really stable.

Spikes slot into cones and telescope pieces

Scary scorpion decoration

Ghostly torches burn on both sides of the door

DON'T PULL MY CHAIN

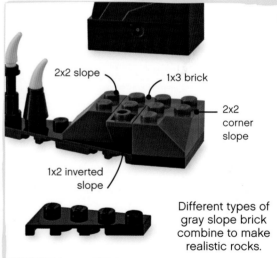

2x2 slope

1x3 brick

2x2 corner slope

1x2 inverted slope

Different types of gray slope brick combine to make realistic rocks.

WAY OUT

Even the door out of this room is part of the assault course! Cole has to break a lock to open the door to escape. Hopefully this is the way out of the dojo!

BLADES BATTLE

Unfortunately, Cole enters yet another room where another challenge awaits. Here, an audience of Ghost Warriors waits for him to do battle with the Blade Master, Bansha! They lock swords for hours, and when Cole wins, the ghosts disappear —and so does the building!

HONESTLY, THAT'S WHAT HAPPENED!

MOVING BLADES

The moving blades pivot on LEGO Technic pins. Each pin connects to a LEGO Technic angle connector and a plate with a ring above.

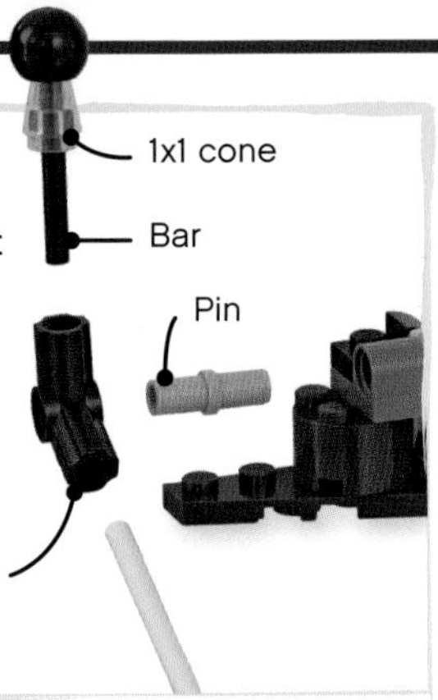

1x1 cone

Bar

Pin

Angle connector

Three-pronged sai weapon fits onto a lightsaber hilt

What will you build?
- Ghostly snack cart
- Winners' podium
- Blade car
- Trophy

Move the swords with a finger on this ball piece

Ladder clips on to upside-down antenna piece

Fence is a sideways ladder

Sideways plate with handled bar

These katana swords can flip up and down

Upside-down antenna fits into brick with clip

BATTLE ARENA

Cole and Bansha meet in a sprawling battle arena. It has fenced sides where the spectators stand and huge chopping blades to keep the contestants on their toes!

Spiders make everything spookier!

The left and right sections are built sideways using angle plates.

2x4 double angle plate

Hinge plate

Top sections are angled on hinge bricks and plates

2x10 plate

Base is built in three hinged sections

Sideways 2x4 angle plate

GO, GHOSTS!

TOUGH CROWD!

Bansha has ghost-style legs

41

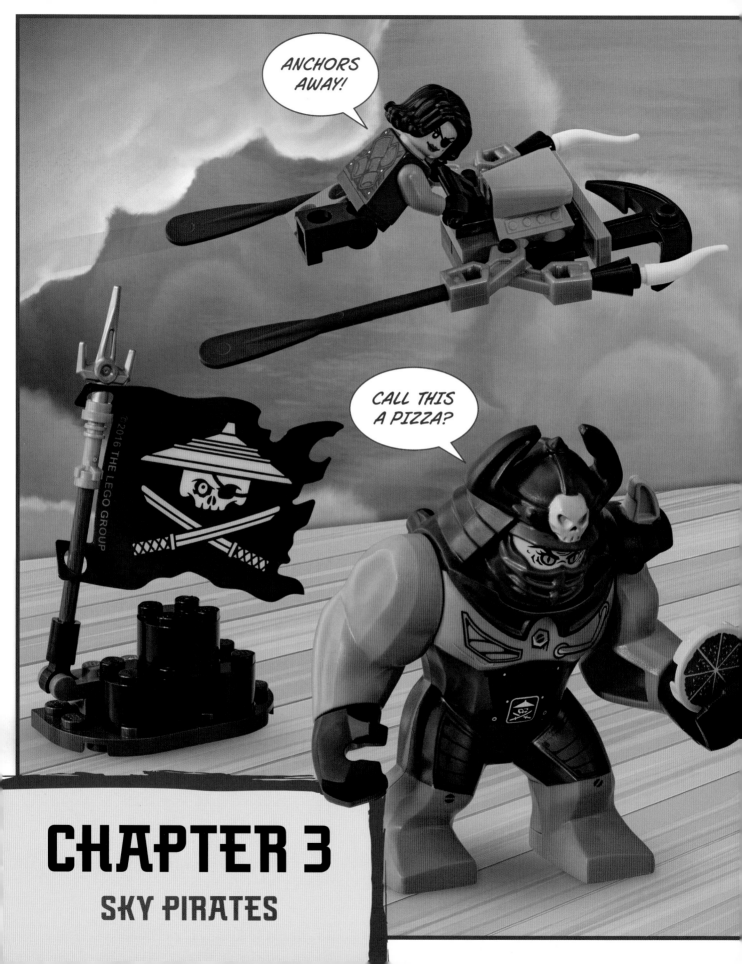

CHAPTER 3

SKY PIRATES

SKYNAPPED!

All eyes turn to Jay as he begins to tell his story of outsmarting the Sky Pirates... It all starts when he sees the Sky Pirates kidnap the ninja's friend, Dareth. Jay speeds after the Pirates' net ship on his glider to save Dareth single-handed!

OPERATION RESCUE DARETH!

TIP OF THE HAT

The gold shield on the front of this structure is one of Master Wu's hats! It fits onto a 1x1 round plate attached to the center of an angle plate.

Wu hat piece

1x2/2x2 angle plate

Long cow horn

1x6 plate

Mug

OUTDOOR DOJO

Dareth is taking a break from a training session in an outdoor dojo when the Sky Pirates grab him. The dojo is a simple structure made from just 15 pieces.

Weapon made from telescope piece and a sword

YOU'RE COMING WITH ME!

HEY, I WAS HAVING A BREAK!

1x4 arch brick

2x2 jumper plate

A chain piece ties the net shut at this end

4x4 plate

A bone weaves through the net to seal in at one end

The net is folded in half to hold a minifigure

JAY'S GLIDER

Jay's solo flyer is little more than an engine with wings! He doesn't need a space to sit—he just holds on to the handlebars and gets pulled along behind!

Engine is one piece

Sword

Angle plate

Plate with angled bar

Robot arm

Plates with angled bars are built into both sides of the glider. The wings clip onto these and can be set at any angle.

Jay's hands grasp the handlebar piece

I'M RIGHT BEHIND YOU!

Sword wings slot into robot arm pieces

Curved slope

The tail fin is a LEGO® BIONICLE® wing piece

SKY PIRATE NET SHIP

The Sky Pirates seize Dareth in a net dragged along behind a small raiding vessel. The scary-looking ship blasts through the air with colossal cannon-shaped engines.

Hinge cylinder

Hinge plate

The cannon engines fit onto a pair of plates with top clips.

Chain fits to a LEGO® Technic cross axle with stud

The front of the ship is a dragon skull!

Tooth plate

CAPTAIN'S QUARTERS

Jay follows the net ship back to the Sky Pirates' flying fortress base, the *Misfortune's Keep*. Inside, he searches for Dareth, but finds the captain's private quarters instead! When he hears someone coming, he has to hide under the captain's bed!

BEING HEROIC IS TIRING!

THE CAPTAIN'S BED

Sky Pirate Captain Nadakhan rarely gets a chance to sleep, but when he does, he sleeps in style! His grand bed has a canopy with a one-eyed pirate's head sculpture on top.

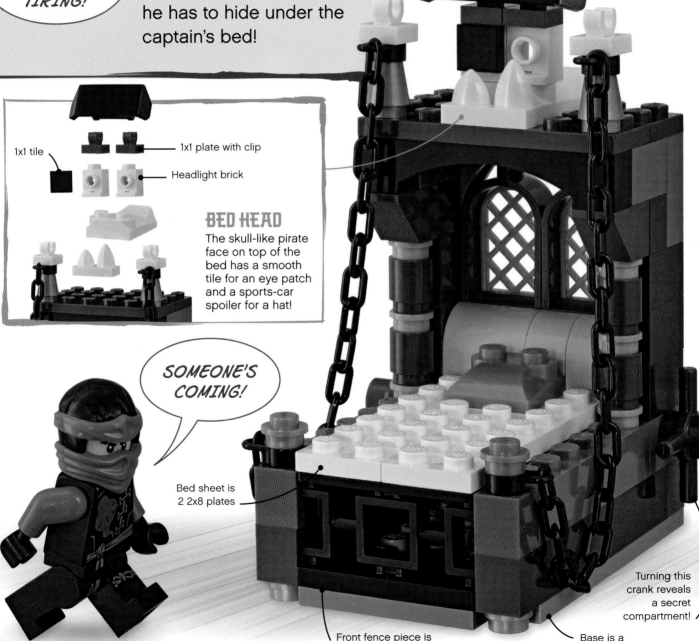

1x1 tile

1x1 plate with clip

Headlight brick

BED HEAD
The skull-like pirate face on top of the bed has a smooth tile for an eye patch and a sports-car spoiler for a hat!

SOMEONE'S COMING!

Spoiler piece

Bed sheet is 2 2x8 plates

Turning this crank reveals a secret compartment!

Front fence piece is not attached to the base

Base is a 6x8 plate

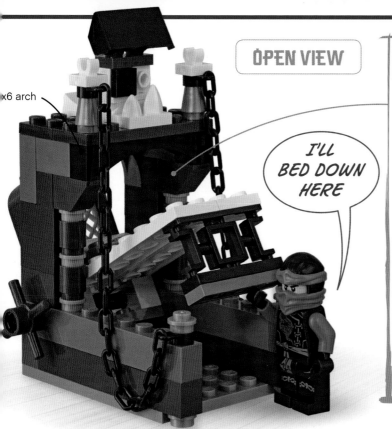

x6 arch

OPEN VIEW

I'LL BED DOWN HERE

UNDER THE BED

Build the moving part of the bed separately from the outer frame. It is not built onto the base, and the two sections only connect at the head end, using a LEGO Technic axle.

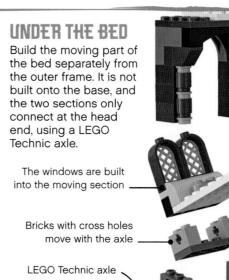

The windows are built into the moving section

Bricks with cross holes move with the axle

LEGO Technic axle

A layer of bricks keeps the moving section clear of the base

MODEL SHIP

The captain keeps an old-fashioned model ship in his quarters. It has tall white sails made from smooth tiles and a plate with a clip.

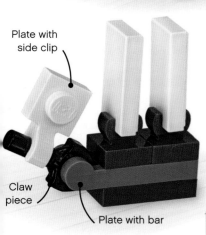

Plate with side clip

Claw piece

Plate with bar

Smooth 1x1 tiles stop the lid from locking shut

TREASURE CHEST

No pirate captain's quarters would be complete without a treasure chest. Nadakhan keeps a stash of pizza locked up inside his!

What will you build?
- Pirate alarm clock
- Parrot perch
- Ship's compass
- Wardrobe

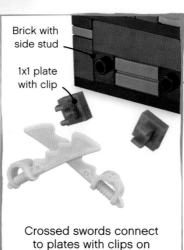

Brick with side stud

1x1 plate with clip

Crossed swords connect to plates with clips on bricks with side studs.

FREEING DARETH

As soon as the coast is clear, Jay puts on a convincing pirate disguise (well, an eye patch) and carries on searching for his friend. He finds Dareth being held captive in the ship's galley. He is being made to wash the dishes by an angry robot chef!

I LOOK JUST LIKE A PIRATE NOW!

GALLEY SINK

A galley is a ship's kitchen, and a ship's crew eats a lot of food! Dareth has lots of dishes to clean—each one made from a small radar dish piece.

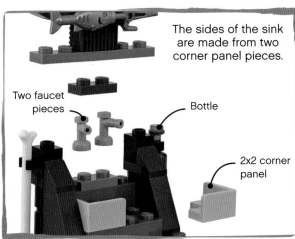

The sides of the sink are made from two corner panel pieces.

Two faucet pieces

Bottle

2x2 corner panel

What will you build?
- Refrigerator
- Knife rack
- Dining table
- Robot rat

THERE YOU ARE!

Inverted curved slopes make a decorative lintel

Mugs and a frying pan make ornamental details

THEY'VE GOT ME WASHING DISHES

Plates are radar dish pieces

Chef hat

Plate with side clip

Gas pump nozzle piece

Motor piece

Tube with clip

Bar

A bar connects the robot's torso to the base of the barrel.

COOKTOP

A stack of different round pieces, starting with a 1x1 round plate, makes the cooktop. The gas flame is an ice blade piece.

LEGO Technic gear ring

2x2 round jumper plate

Medium radar dish

1x1 round plate

STOVE

The galley stove combines an oven and a cooktop. A bright blue gas flame burns out from the cooktop, and is controlled from a panel below the oven door.

Blade piece makes a blue flame

LEGO Technic gear ring

Utensil jar is a transparent round brick

I USED TO BE A DISHWASHER

Shirtfront is a printed tile

Chicken leg

Arms are gas-pump nozzle pieces

Lower body is a barrel piece

ROBOT CHEF

This fierce chef towers over Jay and Dareth and would happily serve them up for dinner! His long arms can move in any direction, so he can grab anything (or anyone) in his kitchen.

Table leg is a small bone fixed to a brick with a clip

WRECK THE DECK

Making their getaway from the galley, Jay and Dareth head up to the top deck to cause some trouble for the Sky Pirates! Jay brings the mast and crow's nest tumbling down, causing chaos on deck, while Dareth looks for a way for the two of them to escape!

WHERE IS THAT NINJA?

I'VE GOT A BAD FEELING ABOUT THIS

CROW'S NEST

The Sky Pirates keep watch from their crow's nest lookout. It is on top of a tall mast that can be made to come crashing down at the turn of a hinge!

The crow's nest is a tub piece

Upside-down curved slopes look like gathered sails

Propeller is two printed round pieces connected with a LEGO Technic axle

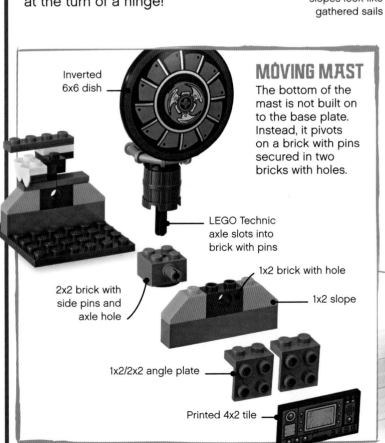

Inverted 6x6 dish

MOVING MAST

The bottom of the mast is not built on to the base plate. Instead, it pivots on a brick with pins secured in two bricks with holes.

LEGO Technic axle slots into brick with pins

2x2 brick with side pins and axle hole

1x2 brick with hole

1x2 slope

1x2/2x2 angle plate

Printed 4x2 tile

HOW'S MY DISGUISE?

6x6 plate

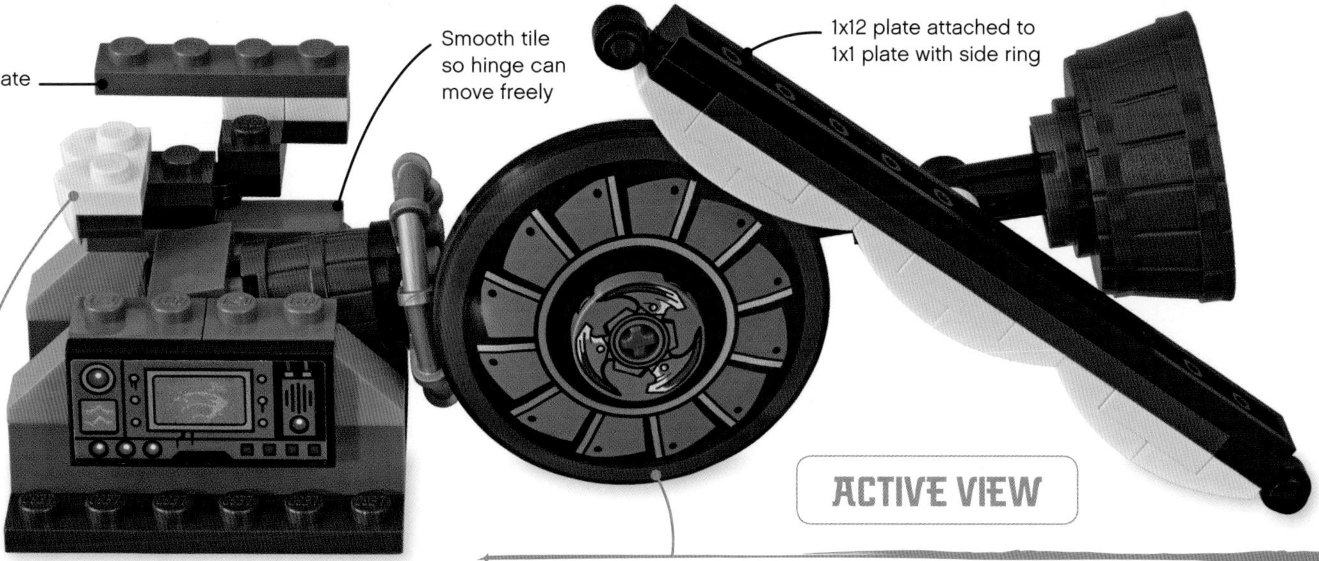

1x4 plate

Smooth tile so hinge can move freely

1x12 plate attached to 1x1 plate with side ring

ACTIVE VIEW

A hinged section locks the mast in place—until you turn it!

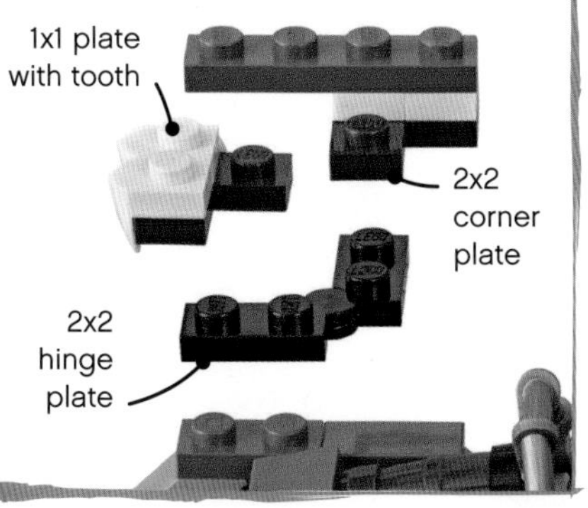

1x1 plate with tooth

2x2 corner plate

2x2 hinge plate

The mast is made out of LEGO Technic elements for strength.

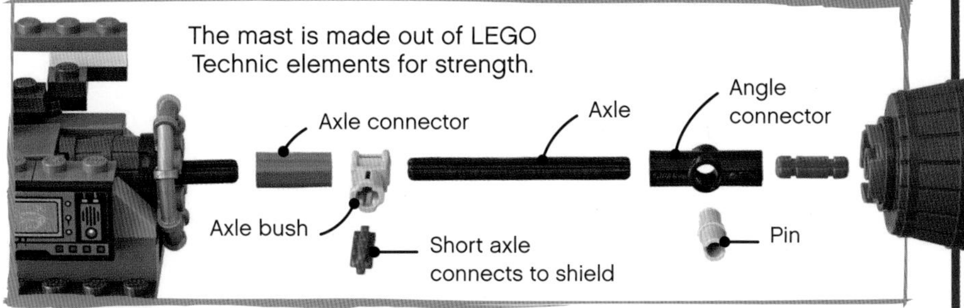

Axle connector

Axle

Angle connector

Axle bush

Short axle connects to shield

Pin

POOP DECK

The poop deck is a raised area at the back of a ship. Like the crow's nest, it is a good place for keeping watch.

THAT PIRATE LOOKS FAMILIAR

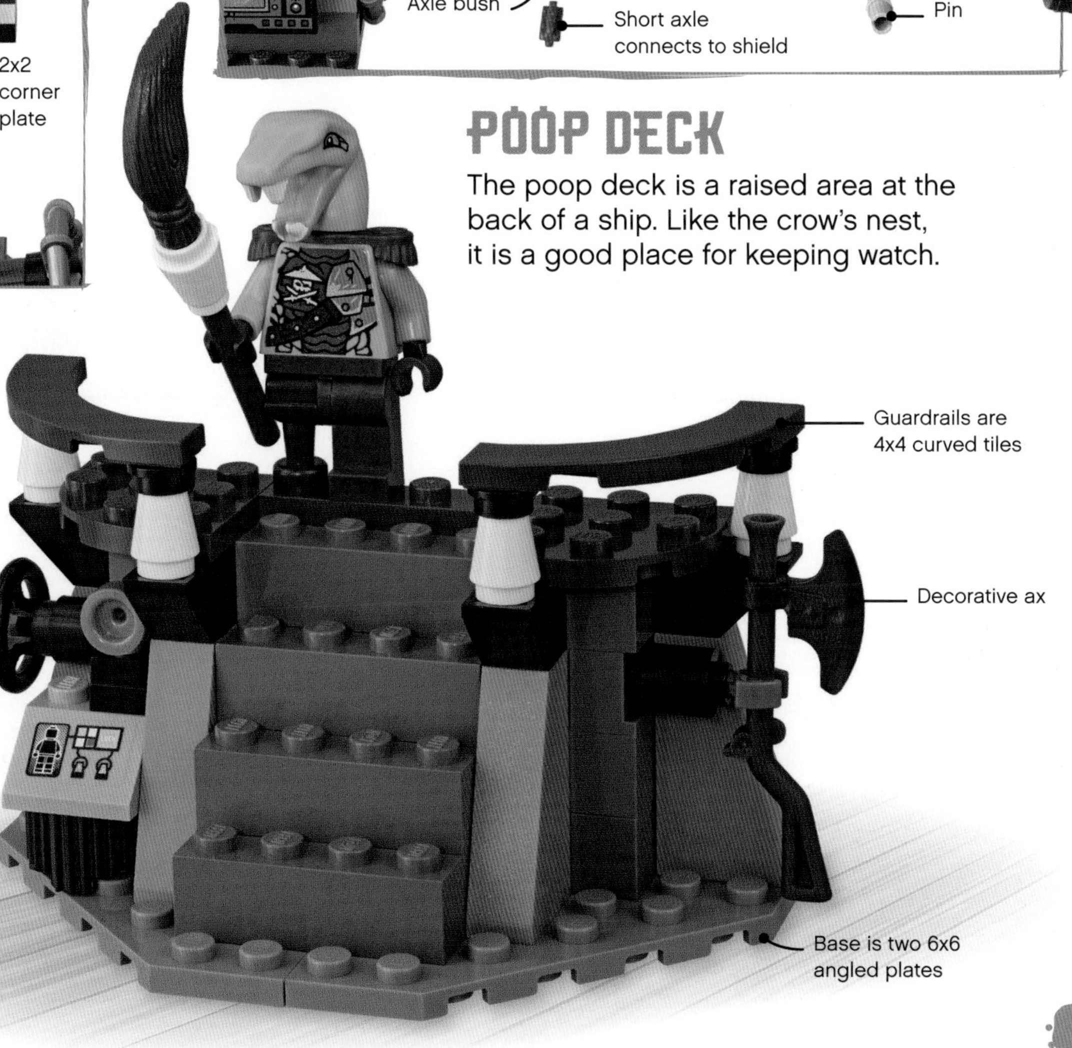

Guardrails are 4x4 curved tiles

Decorative ax

Base is two 6x6 angled plates

EXPLOSIVE ESCAPE

With the Sky Pirates busy fixing their ship's mast, Jay finds a small glider on board that Dareth can use to escape. All that is left for Jay to do is to make his own daring getaway. He does this by convincing the Sky Pirates to fire him out of a massive cannon!

TIME TO MAKE A HEROIC GETAWAY!

Tail slots onto a LEGO Technic axle pin

Push here to fire the cannon

The wheels are made from disc pieces and round plates

The barrel is built sideways with a hole for a LEGO Technic axle.

1x2 bricks

4x4 round plate

LEGO Technic axle with end stop

1x4 plate

CANNON

This huge cannon is big enough to blast a ninja out of its barrel! It is activated by pushing a long LEGO Technic axle though it from behind.

Transparent orange round plate is the cannon's lit fuse

Flame piece slots into telescope piece

Ship's wheels decorate the cannon's sides

GOTTA FLYYY!

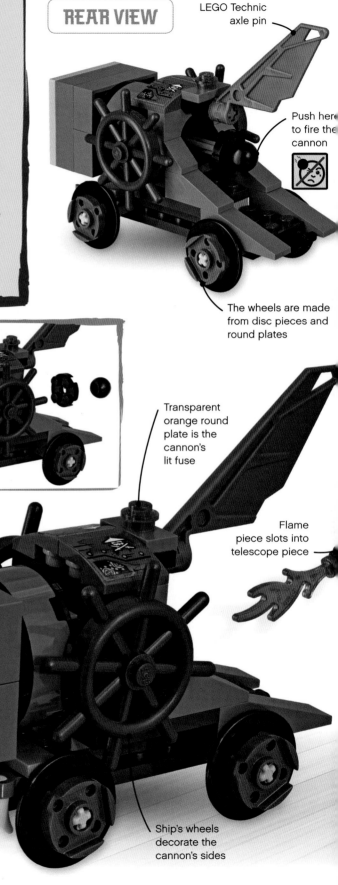

PIRATE GLIDER

The anchor on the front of this glider makes a battering ram for flying through obstacles. Two long horns ward off attackers and can be angled in front or behind.

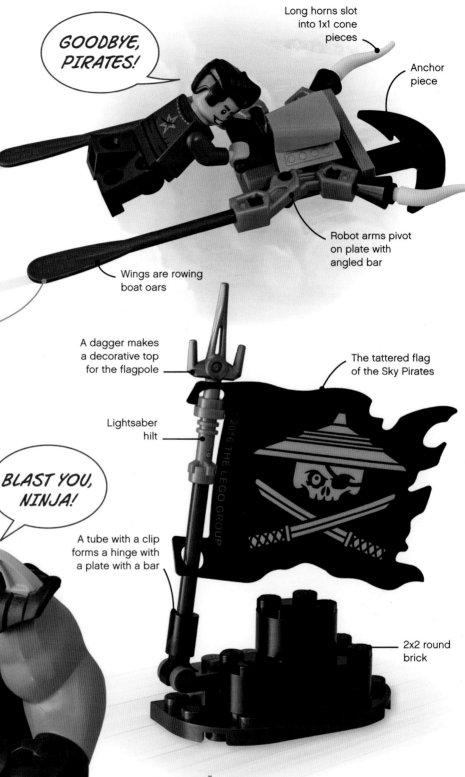

Long horns slot into 1x1 cone pieces

Anchor piece

GOODBYE, PIRATES!

Robot arms pivot on plate with angled bar

Wings are rowing boat oars

Build up the glider by adding special plates to a 2x3 plate.

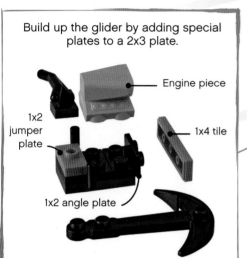

Engine piece

1x2 jumper plate

1x4 tile

1x2 angle plate

A dagger makes a decorative top for the flagpole

Lightsaber hilt

The tattered flag of the Sky Pirates

© 2016 THE LEGO GROUP

A tube with a clip forms a hinge with a plate with a bar

2x2 round brick

Pitchfork

BLAST YOU, NINJA!

CANONBALLS

When there are no more ninja to fire from the cannon, the Sky Pirates go back to using cannonballs. One of these 2x2 round bricks will fit neatly inside the barrel.

CHAPTER 4
THE VERMILLION

CREEPY DISCOVERY

Next, Kai remembers his most heroic adventure... He recalls a group of archaeologists led by Lloyd's mom, Misako, finding some giant snakes' eggs in a creepy swamp. Realizing that this is no ordinary serpent's nest, they call for Kai using a special light-up signal.

WHAT AN EGG-CITING DIG!

MISAKO'S DIGGER

Misako lightly scrapes away layers of earth with her digger to reveal ancient treasures. It has floodlights to help her see what she has found and a digger arm that moves on hinges.

Transparent 1x1 round plate

Floodlights are sidewa saucepan pieces

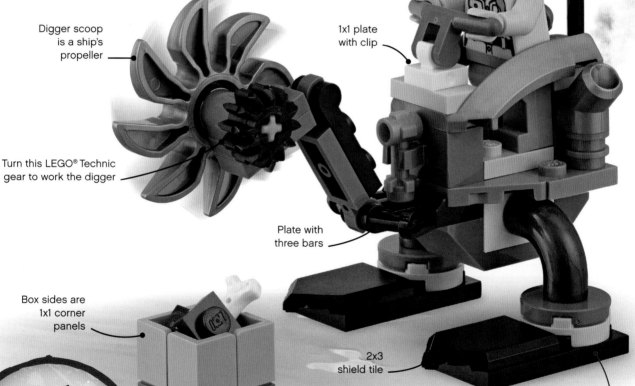

1x1 plate with clip

Digger scoop is a ship's propeller

Turn this LEGO® Technic gear to work the digger

Plate with three bars

Box sides are 1x1 corner panels

2x3 shield tile

What will you build?
- Dinosaur skeleton
- Part-buried ruins
- Laboratory
- Drilling tools

DIGGER LEG

The digger's legs are curved tube pieces with crossholes. They connect to the vehicle's sides and feet using LEGO Technic axle pins.

Curved tube

Brick with crosshole

LEGO Technic axle pin

2x2 round tile with hole

MICROSCOPE

Misako and her team use this microscope to study and identify the small items that they find. It is made from just eight pieces.

Brick with side stud

Lightsaber hilt

2x3 curved plate with hole

Plate with clip

Textured round brick

> I THOUGHT YOU'D BE A GIANT CHICKEN!

MYSTERIOUS EGG

Misako's team gets a nasty surprise when they get closer. One of the eggs is open, and a snake is sticking its hissing head out!

Vermillion egg piece

HISS!

Half-snake piece

Upside-down brick with side stud

An upside-down brick with a side stud holds the snake in place.

THE KAI SIGNAL

The Kai signal projects a bright red light into the sky that can be seen for miles. It tilts to point the light in any direction.

Upside-down slide plate

2x8 plate makes the base

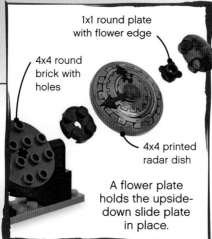

1x1 round plate with flower edge

4x4 round brick with holes

4x4 printed radar dish

A flower plate holds the upside-down slide plate in place.

SEWER MYSTERY

When he sees his special signal, Kai follows it to its source. In the swamp, he finds more giant eggs and a Vermillion sentry keeping an eye on them from a lookout. Kai knows that if the eggs hatch, they will turn into more evil Vermillion warriors!

I'M ON THE LOOK-OUT FOR LOOKOUTS!

OPEN VIEW

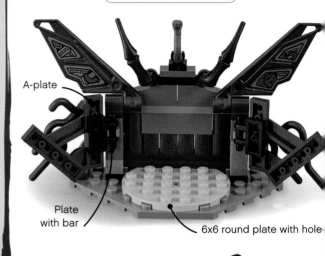

A-plate

Plate with bar

6x6 round plate with hole

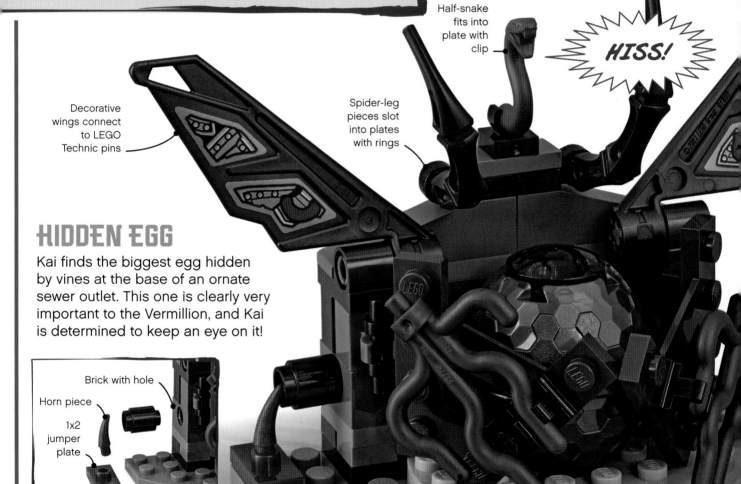

Half-snake fits into plate with clip

HISS!

Decorative wings connect to LEGO Technic pins

Spider-leg pieces slot into plates with rings

HIDDEN EGG

Kai finds the biggest egg hidden by vines at the base of an ornate sewer outlet. This one is clearly very important to the Vermillion, and Kai is determined to keep an eye on it!

Brick with hole

Horn piece

1x2 jumper plate

The ooze from the sewer pipe is attached to the base.

Seagrass pieces fit onto sideways plates with clips

What will you build?
- Vermillion spy plane
- Sewer system
- Giant snake
- Rusty railings

I CAN SEE THINGS MILES AWAY!

A stack of different-shaped bricks makes a ruined tower.

Plate with bar

2x2 corner slope

Tall Vermillion egg piece

Telescope is made from a telescope piece and 1x1 round plate

LOOKOUT TOWER

The Vermillion sentry can see across the entire swamp from this tall lookout. Its tall sides protect him from attack, and the ladder to the top is guarded by a scary snake!

2x2 round brick

Ladder with clips

LUCKY I'M RIGHT HERE, THEN!

Textured wall brick

Plate with ring

Brick with side stud

BEHIND THE FENCE
The tumbledown fence is made from smooth plates attached to bricks with side studs. The half-snake piece pokes through on a plate with a ring.

4x4 round plate

3x3 angled plate

SWAMP CHASE

As soon as the Vermillion lookout sees Kai snooping around the giant eggs, he raises the alarm. Another Vermillion warrior in an unusual vehicle arrives and races away with the biggest egg. Kai jumps onto his blade bike and gives chase!

I'D BETTER POACH THAT EGG!

What will you build?
- Swamp monster
- Vermillion rusty swamp ship
- Ninja airboat

BACK VIEW

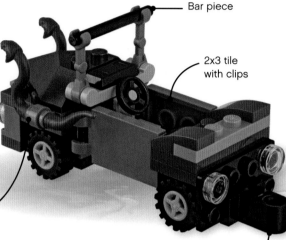

Bar piece

2x3 tile with clips

Half-snake piece slots into headlight brick

LEGO Technic T-beam connects the car to the trailer

EGG TRANSPORTER

This Vermillion vehicle tows a trailer with space for the giant egg. Snakes wind their way through its headlights and side mirrors, giving the whole car a creepy, infested look.

TIME FOR A FAST EGGS-IT!

Windshield sides are droid arms

4x4 angled slope

Plate with ring

Opening door is a 2x3 tile with clips

Back-to-back wheel arches make one big mudguard

BREAKAWAY BLASTER

Kai's cannon is built to be broken off in an instant, with just two studs and a fold-down catch holding it in place.

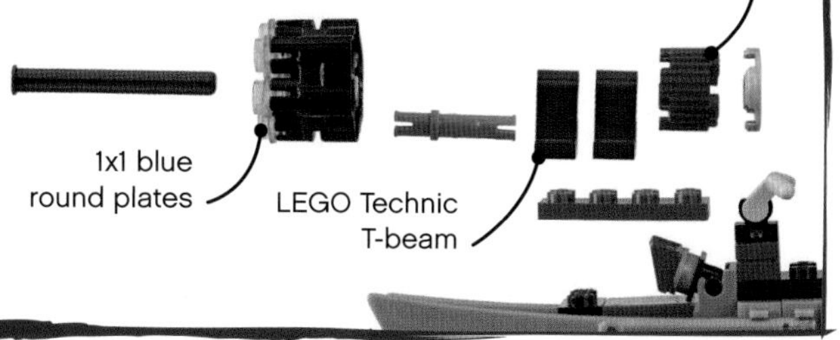

Textured round brick

1x1 blue round plates

LEGO Technic T-beam

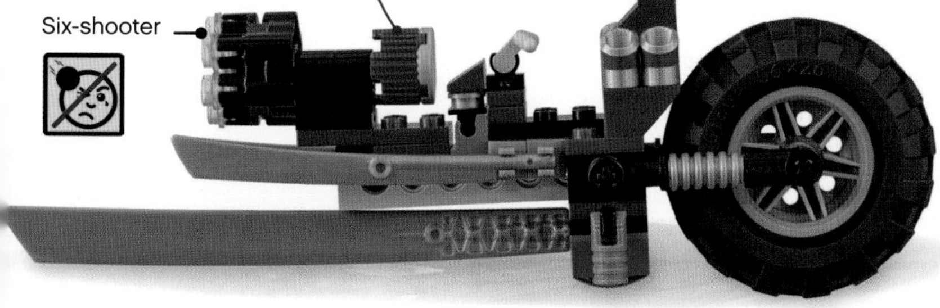

WHEEL CONNECTION

The big wheel on Kai's blade bike is secured on both sides with LEGO Technic elements. These connect to the main build using bricks with crossholes.

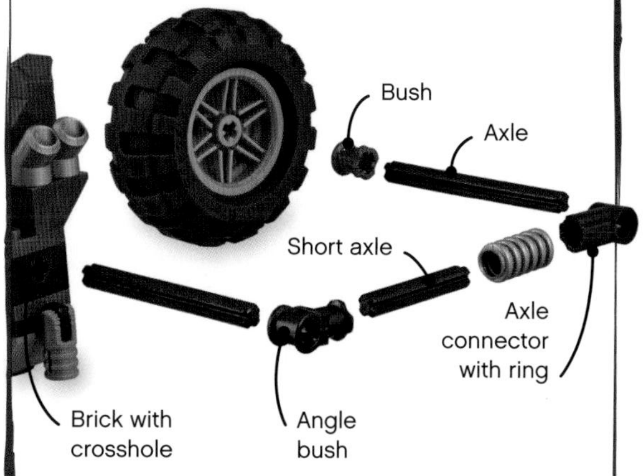

Bush

Axle

Short axle

Axle connector with ring

Brick with crosshole

Angle bush

SIDE VIEW

Six-shooter

Headrest is a plate with bows and a 2x2 slope

KAI'S BLADE BIKE

Propelled by one big wheel at the back, Kai's blade bike uses giant swords to slice through swampy undergrowth. The multi-barrel missile launcher on the front is easy to remove for using separately.

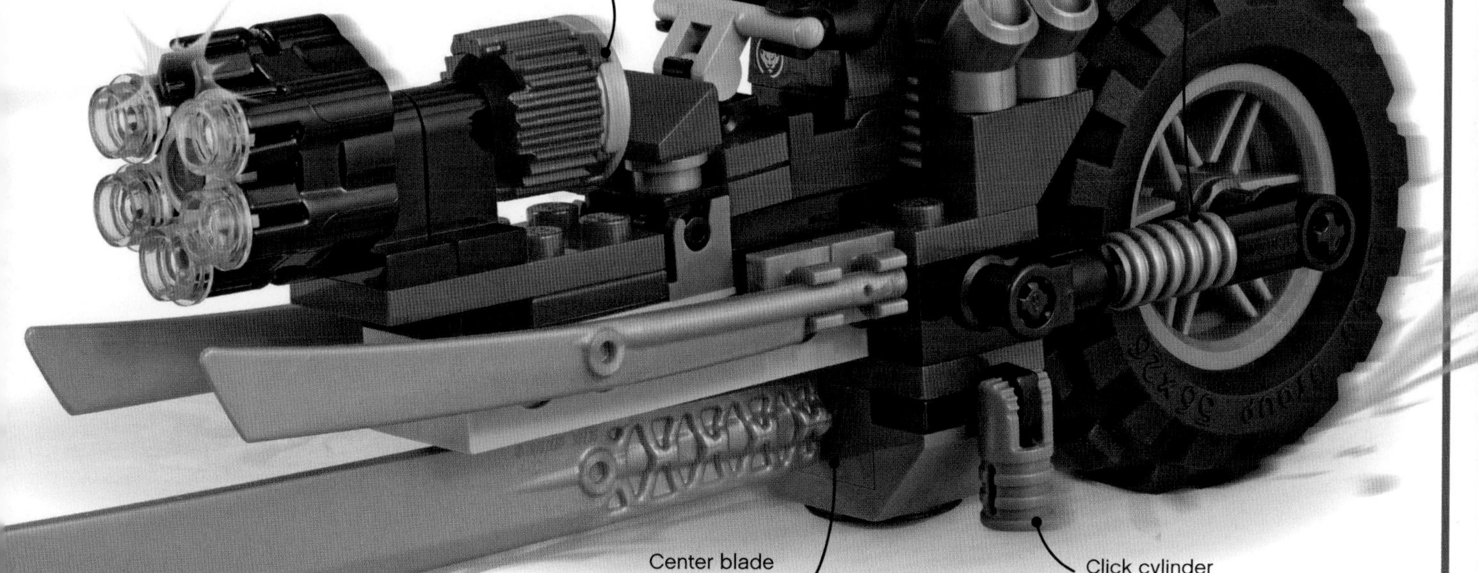

I'M GOING TO SHELL THAT EGG!

Turn this round brick to fire the six-shooter

LEGO Technic ribbed tube looks like chunky suspension

Center blade slots into a brick with a crosshole

Click cylinder makes a kickstand to balance the bike

61

LETHAL LAIR

Before long, Kai finds himself at the Vermillion lair, where the villains have stashed the egg. He fights past a Vermillion warrior at the entrance to their base and launches the egg deep into the swamp before it can spew out hundreds of deadly Vermillion serpents!

I BET THE VERMILLION SEE RED!

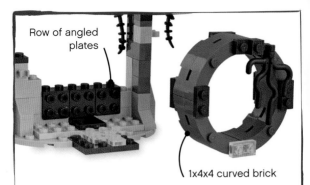

Row of angled plates

1x4x4 curved brick

TUNNEL OPENING

Build the circular sewer entrance on a flat surface using 4x4 curved bricks and 1x2 plates. Then attach it sideways to a row of angle plates.

SEWER ENTRANCE

The way into the Vermillion base is through a stinking sewer tunnel. Green ooze gathers in a pool at the entrance, and a huge snake wraps around the top!

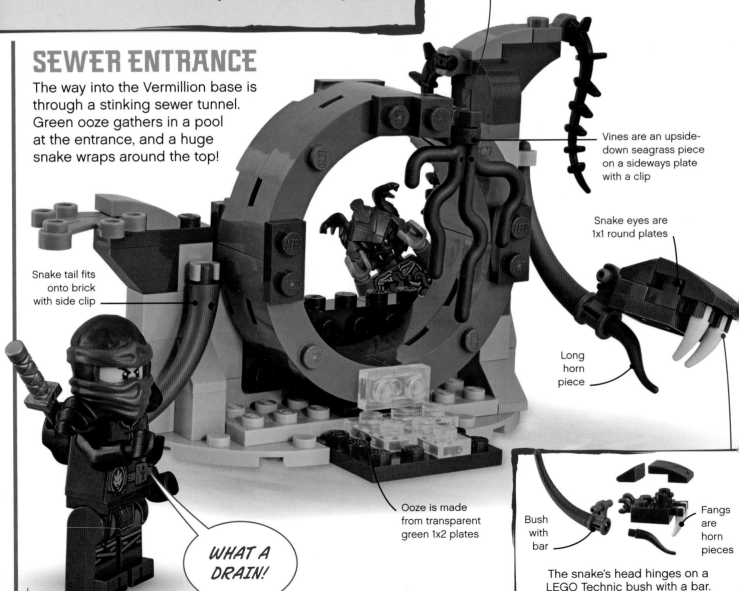

Vines are an upside-down seagrass piece on a sideways plate with a clip

Snake eyes are 1x1 round plates

Snake tail fits onto brick with side clip

Long horn piece

WHAT A DRAIN!

Ooze is made from transparent green 1x2 plates

Bush with bar

Fangs are horn pieces

The snake's head hinges on a LEGO Technic bush with a bar.

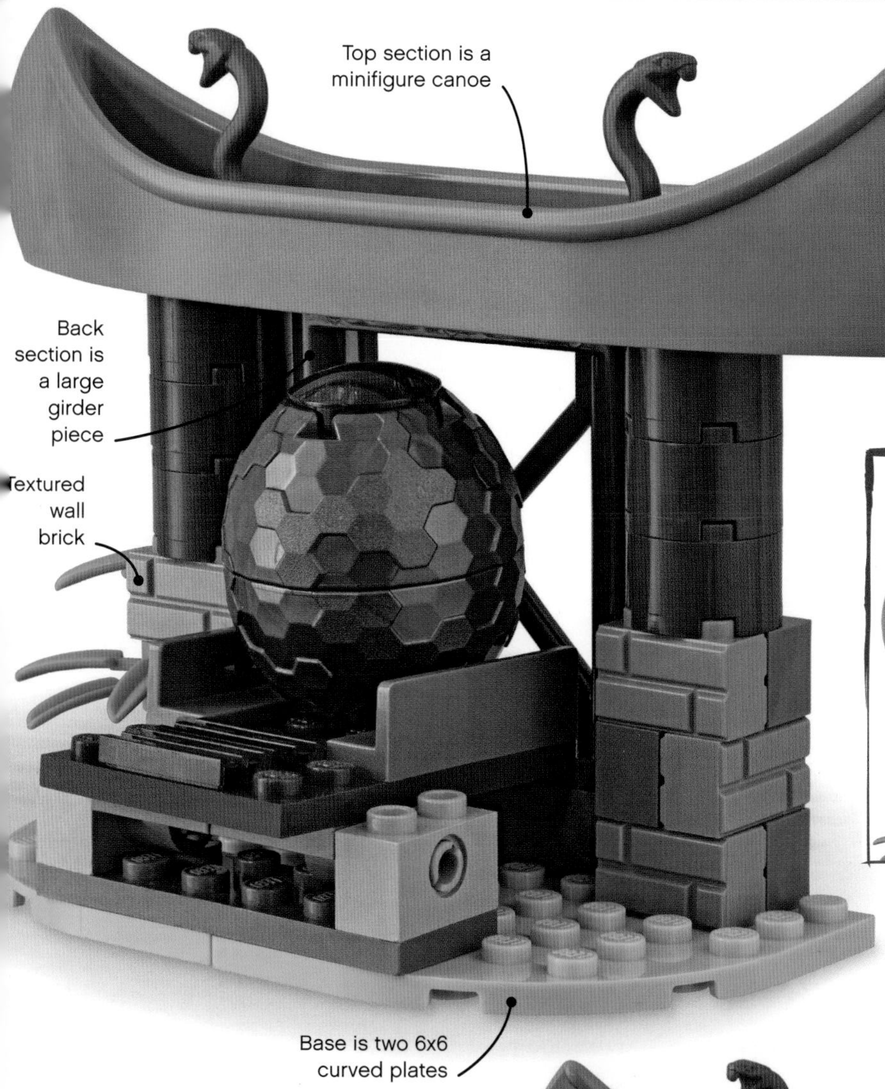

Top section is a minifigure canoe

EGG BASE

This platform tilts forward so that the Vermillion can roll the egg onto it. But if Kai gives the front section a firm strike with his sword, the egg is propelled high into the air!

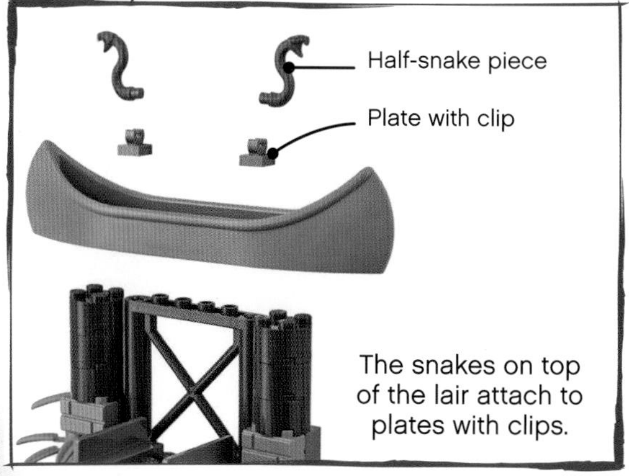

Back section is a large girder piece

Textured wall brick

Half-snake piece

Plate with clip

The snakes on top of the lair attach to plates with clips.

Base is two 6x6 curved plates

ACTIVE VIEW

TIPPING PLATFORM

The egg platform is attached using LEGO Technic pins to create a see-saw pivot. Connect the pins closer to the front than the back.

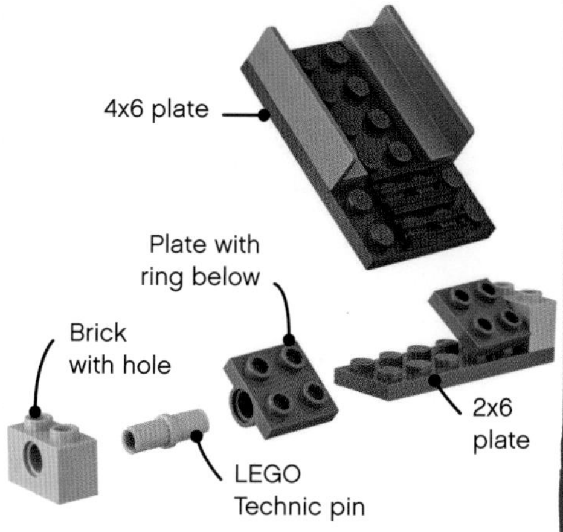

Leaf bricks are built into the ancient walls

4x6 plate

Plate with ring below

Brick with hole

2x6 plate

LEGO Technic pin

YOU'RE FRIED, EGG!

Press here to launch the egg

SNAKE SHOWDOWN

The Vermillion are not at all happy to see their egg sink in the swamp! Their leader, Machia, comes after Kai in a huge snake mech to get revenge. When the ninja gets back to his missile launcher, Machia is forced to crawl back to the Vermillion base!

I FORGOT ABOUT THE SIX-SHOOTER!

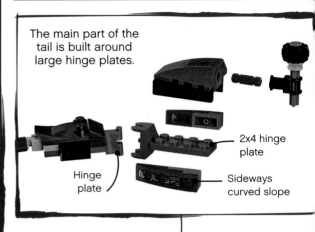

The main part of the tail is built around large hinge plates.

2x4 hinge plate

Sideways curved slope

Hinge plate

What will you build?

- Wheels for six-shooter
- Mech cannon arm
- Weapons store
- Swamp plants

THAT IS ONE WELL-ARMED SNAKE

Turn this brick to fire six round plates

Base is a 4x4 round plate

LEGO Technic axle connector

Angle plate

Axle pin with ball

Tail piece

Ingot piece

FLICKING TAIL

The end of the tail can angle in any direction. It is made using a LEGO Technic axle pin with a ball and a socket plate.

KAI'S SIX-SHOOTER

This is the same weapon that is built onto Kai's blade bike (see page 61). It has been built onto a targeting platform to provide more cover for Kai in battle.

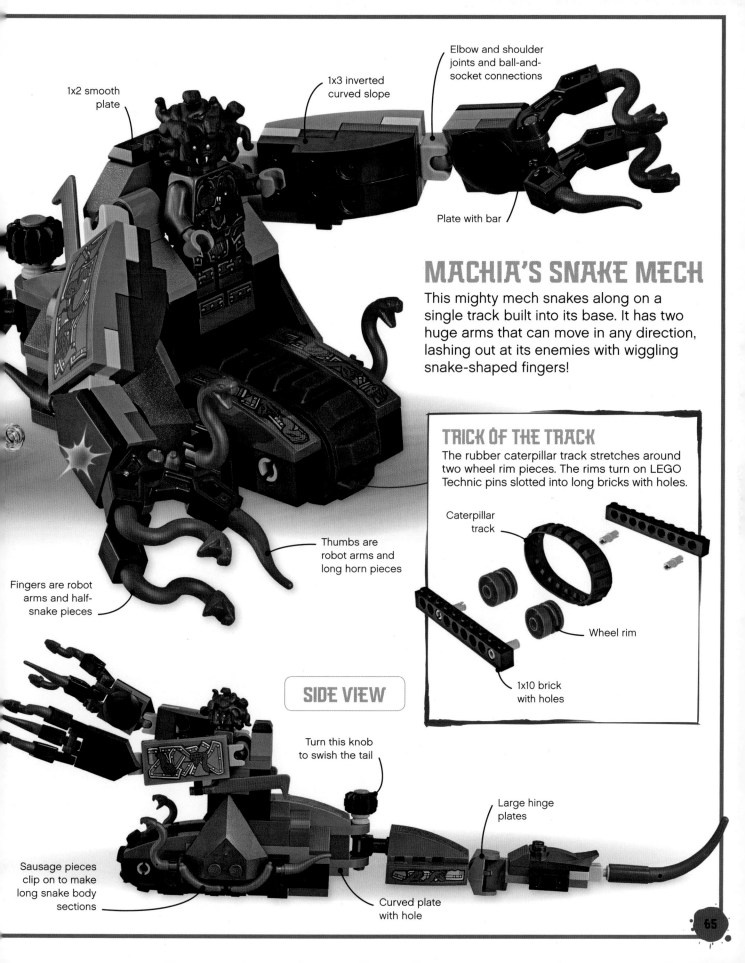

1x2 smooth plate

1x3 inverted curved slope

Elbow and shoulder joints and ball-and-socket connections

Plate with bar

MACHIA'S SNAKE MECH

This mighty mech snakes along on a single track built into its base. It has two huge arms that can move in any direction, lashing out at its enemies with wiggling snake-shaped fingers!

Thumbs are robot arms and long horn pieces

Fingers are robot arms and half-snake pieces

TRICK OF THE TRACK

The rubber caterpillar track stretches around two wheel rim pieces. The rims turn on LEGO Technic pins slotted into long bricks with holes.

Caterpillar track

Wheel rim

1x10 brick with holes

SIDE VIEW

Turn this knob to swish the tail

Large hinge plates

Sausage pieces clip on to make long snake body sections

Curved plate with hole

65

CHAPTER 5
SONS OF GARMADON

MASK THIEVES

At the noodle bar, just as Nya is about to tell her heroic tale, she notices that the precious Oni Mask has gone missing! They rush outside and see the evil Sons of Garmadon biker gang riding away with it. Brave Nya leads the chase to get the mask back!

OH NO! NO ONI!

The steam is made from two curved bricks and a tail piece

Two chopsticks rest in the bowl

The roof is made from four 2x4 ridged slopes

NOODLE BAR

The outside of the noodle bar is built almost flat, but the roof and the porch over the door give it a sense of depth. The sign on top is a steaming bowl of noodles!

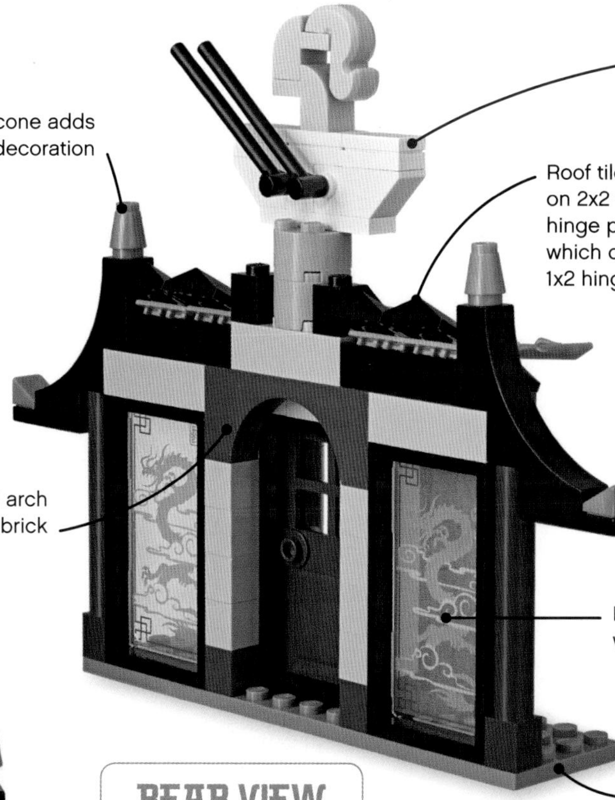

1x1 cone adds decoration

Roof tiles are on 2x2 thin hinge plate, which clips into 1x2 hinge base

BAR SIGN

The chopsticks are L-shaped bars that slot into bricks with side studs.

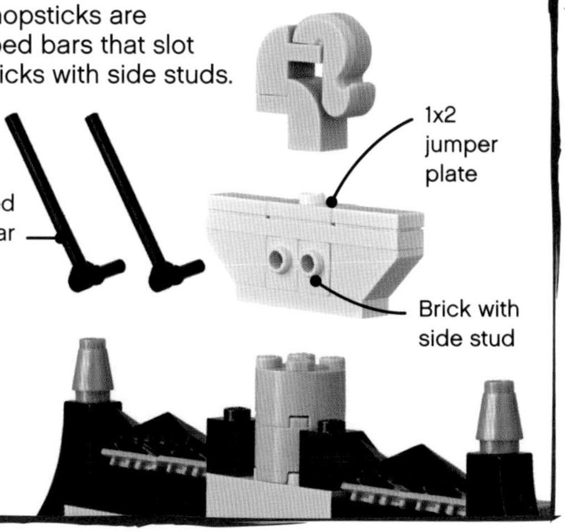

L-shaped bar

1x2 jumper plate

Brick with side stud

1x4 arch brick

Printed windows

REAR VIEW

The base is two 4x8 plates

Beveled curved slope

The front of the bike is made from two beveled curved slopes.

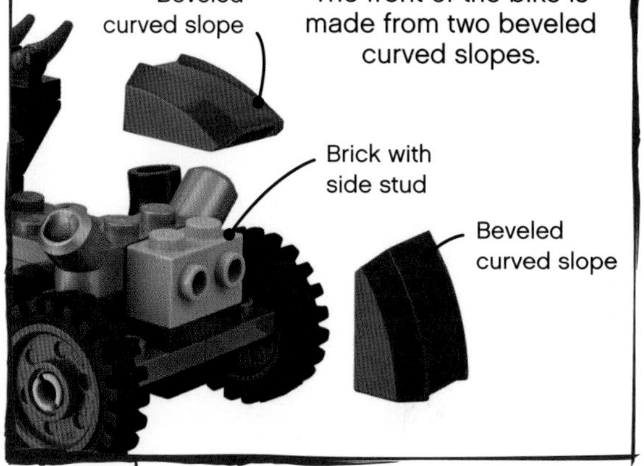

Brick with side stud

Beveled curved slope

Inverted half arches are used for the roof sides

I'VE UNMASKED YOU, NINJA!

Oni Mask rests on the back

SAW SPEEDER

The Sons of Garmadon make their getaway in two-wheeled speeders with chainsaw shooters on the front! There is space at the back for a passenger— or a stolen Oni Mask!

Chainsaw pieces slot into 1x1 ring plates

1x2 plate with stud shooter

MARKET MADNESS

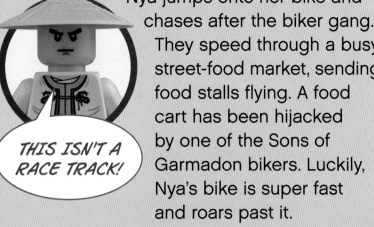

Nya jumps onto her bike and chases after the biker gang. They speed through a busy street-food market, sending food stalls flying. A food cart has been hijacked by one of the Sons of Garmadon bikers. Luckily, Nya's bike is super fast and roars past it.

THIS ISN'T A RACE TRACK!

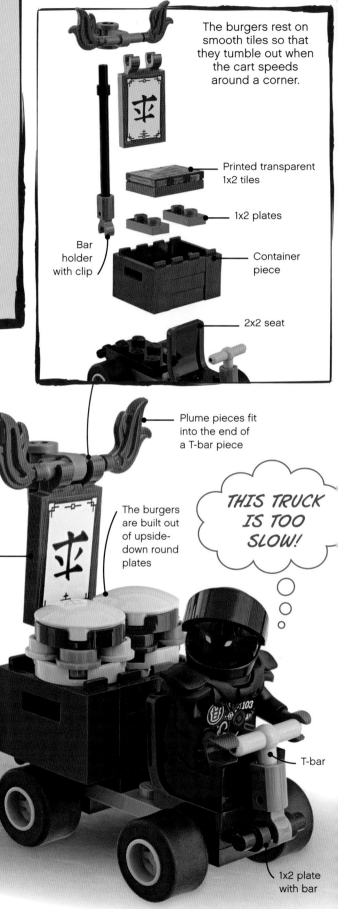

The burgers rest on smooth tiles so that they tumble out when the cart speeds around a corner.

Printed transparent 1x2 tiles

1x2 plates

Bar holder with clip

Container piece

2x2 seat

CALL YOURSELF FAST FOOD?

Plume pieces fit into the end of a T-bar piece

Flag is a 2x3 tile with clips

The burgers are built out of upside-down round plates

THIS TRUCK IS TOO SLOW!

T-bar

1x2 plate with bar

FOOD CART

This little truck is built for moving stock around the market. The flag on the back clips on in the same way as the steering column at the front.

Lantern clips onto a brick with a bar

Eggs are not fixed in place

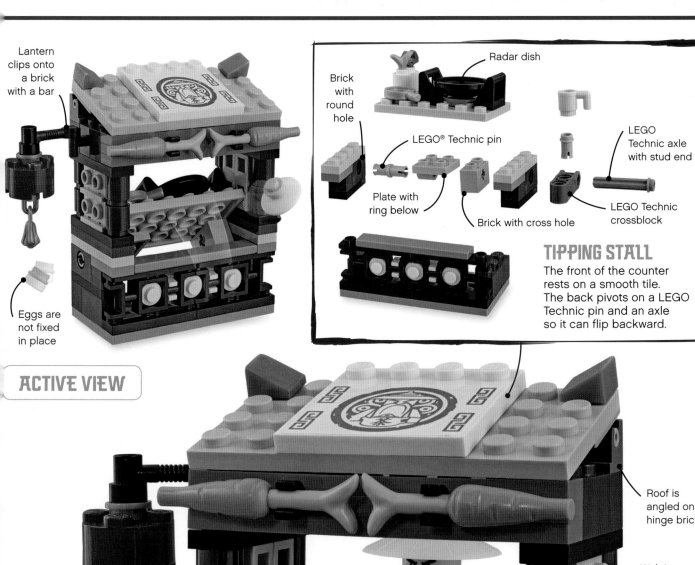

Brick with round hole

Radar dish

LEGO® Technic pin

Plate with ring below

Brick with cross hole

LEGO Technic axle with stud end

LEGO Technic crossblock

TIPPING STALL

The front of the counter rests on a smooth tile. The back pivots on a LEGO Technic pin and an axle so it can flip backward.

Roof is angled on hinge bricks

Wok is an upside-down radar dish on a round tile with a hole

Egg is an upside-down round plate and upside-down round tile

Cup shelf is also a lever for flipping the counter!

FOOD STALL

The fried eggs are about to get scrambled at this market stall! It is built with a counter that flips over, sending the eggs—and anything else that isn't nailed down—flying into the air!

71

AT THE DOCKS

The Sons of Garmadon abandon their bikes when they get to the docks. They cross the water by climbing a huge crane. Nya flips her bike into hover mode and skims across. By now, the other ninja are catching up, with Kai racing into the docks on a jet ski!

I LIKE TO MAKE A SPLASH!

What will you build?
- Fishing rod
- Coastguard station
- Shipping containers
- Fishing boat

A row of smooth tiles allows the crane to slide along the gantry

YOU CAME BY JET SKI?

The sides are made from sturdy girder pieces

I KNOW A SHORTCUT!

KAI'S JET SKI

Kai's water speeder uses swords as skis to slice through the waves. It is mostly built from differently shaped slopes and angled pieces to make it as aerodynamic and aquadynamic as possible!

Handlebars fit onto plate with clip

2x3 plate with bows

Engines are goblet pieces

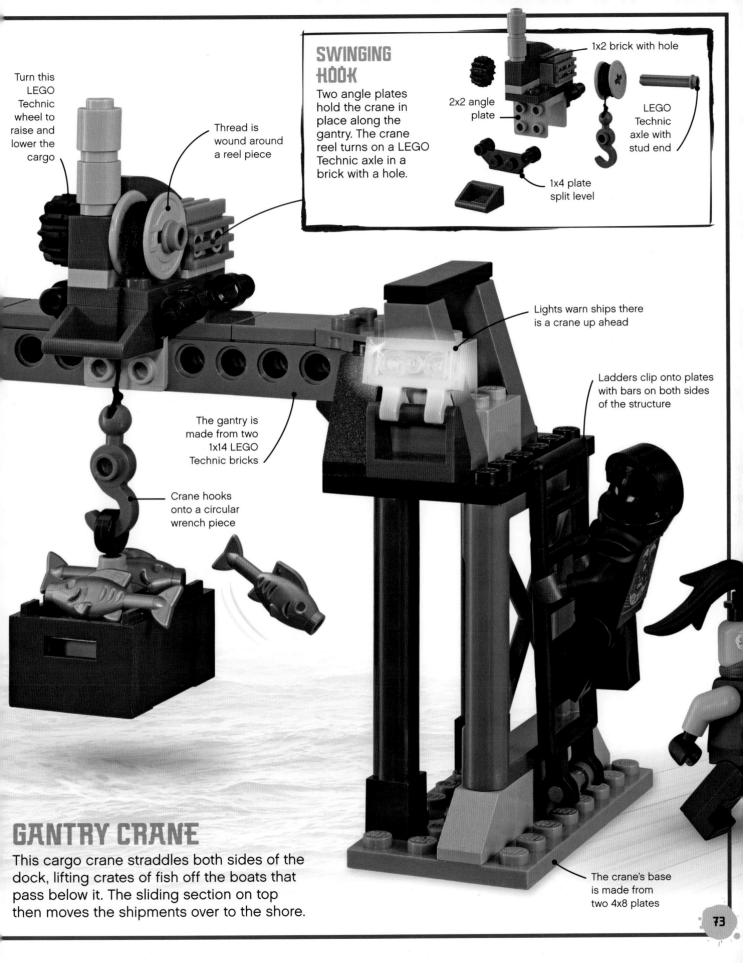

Turn this LEGO Technic wheel to raise and lower the cargo

Thread is wound around a reel piece

SWINGING HOOK

Two angle plates hold the crane in place along the gantry. The crane reel turns on a LEGO Technic axle in a brick with a hole.

2x2 angle plate

1x2 brick with hole

LEGO Technic axle with stud end

1x4 plate split level

Lights warn ships there is a crane up ahead

The gantry is made from two 1x14 LEGO Technic bricks

Ladders clip onto plates with bars on both sides of the structure

Crane hooks onto a circular wrench piece

GANTRY CRANE

This cargo crane straddles both sides of the dock, lifting crates of fish off the boats that pass below it. The sliding section on top then moves the shipments over to the shore.

The crane's base is made from two 4x8 plates

RACE FOR THE FINISH

WHAT ARE YOU DOING HERE?

Beyond the docks, Nya and Kai catch up with the Sons of Garmadon bikers in their garage lair. They are joined by Cole and Zane, who race to be first over the finish line in the garage. Meanwhile, Nya is busy fighting the mighty Kilow. They must get that Oni Mask!

FINISH LINE

How are the Sons of Garmadon so fast? Lots of racing practice! When they race, they use this checkered start and finish line with its bust of their hero, Lord Garmadon, on top.

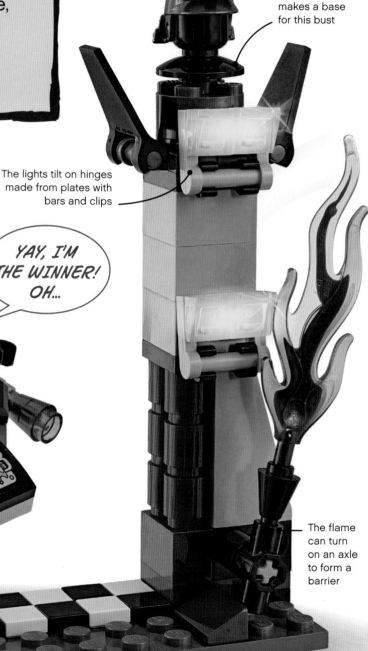

A small radar dish makes a base for this bust

The lights tilt on hinges made from plates with bars and clips

The flame can turn on an axle to form a barrier

COLE'S JET

This sleek flyer is almost flat, apart from its big barrel engines! It is made from just 17 pieces, starting with a 3x6 angled plate that Cole can sit or stand on.

YAY, I'M THE WINNER! OH...

Barrels attach sideways to bricks with side studs

Sword fits onto plate with clip

Both wings are one 3x6 angled plate

Black and white tiles make a checkered start and finish line

ZANE'S SPEEDER

Zane's flying machine has a big, barrel-shaped weapon on the front and a space for him to stand at the back. Its thrusters are mounted on ball-and-socket joints so they can angle in any direction.

IS THAT A GUY OR A TANK?

Horns are a bucket handle piece

1x2 Socket plates are built into both sides of the speeder.

Plate with three bars

Socket plate

Ball plate

Barrel fits sideways on an angle plate

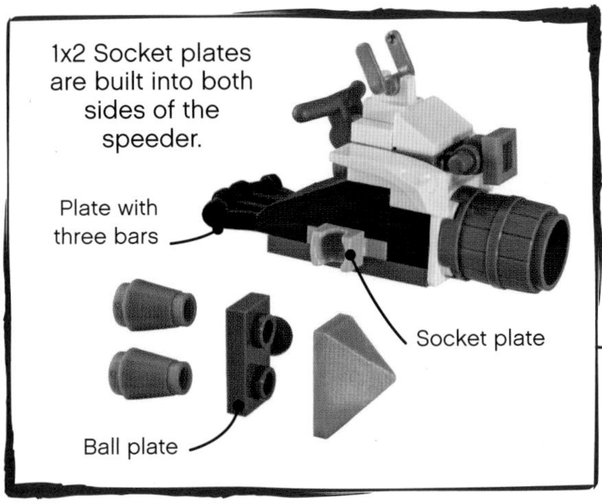

KILOW'S STAFF

A giant villain needs a giant weapon. Kilow grips onto a staff made from a ball joint and axle. It is decorated with red horn pieces.

CALL THAT A WEAPON?

SPEAKER BOX

Kilow likes to listen to very loud music when he works in the garage. This speaker blasts out all his favorite sounds and can also broadcast commentary on race days.

Horn pieces slot into LEGO Technic cross holes

The speakers are radar dishes attached to 1x1 bricks with holes

BATTLE OF THE BIKES

Ultraviolet appears on a huge dragon-shaped bike wearing the stolen Oni Mask. Only Nya and her bike can take them on. She defeats Ultraviolet and decides this battle is even more heroic than the story she was planning to tell the others in the noodle bar!

UH-OH, I'VE MET MY MATCH!

Handlebars are pistol pieces

Click hinges

REAR VIEW

DRAGON BIKE

This bike is actually a trike—with two large wheels at the back and one at the front. A fearsome dragon's head and claws surround the front wheel, and a swordlike tail swishes behind!

I'VE GOT THIS!

Wheel arch 2x4

The eyes are framed by a wheel arch piece

The dragon's nostrils are an exposed angle plate

The dragon's teeth are horn pieces attached to a row of 1x1 plates with clips

LEGO Technic disc

FACE ME, NINJA!

Tooth piece

Horn piece

Blade piece makes the bike look very intimidating

Katana sword at the end of the tail adds extra slashing power!

Curved slope

Katana sword

LEGO Technic beam 1x1

LEGO Technic pin with ball

Ball-and-socket plate

The snaking tail is made from ball-and-socket plates and a LEGO Technic pin.

The front wheel is centred on a LEGO Technic axle and held in place using axle connectors with rings. The claws around it are built on sideways.

Plate with three bars

Robot arm

2x3 shield tile

Senior Editor Victoria Taylor
Senior Designers David McDonald,
Mark Penfound
Designer Sam Bartlett
Pre-Production Producer Kavita Varma
Senior Producer Lloyd Robertson
Project Manager Clare Millar
Managing Editors Sarah Harland, Paula Regan
Managing Art Editor Jo Connor
Art Director Lisa Lanzarini
Publisher Julie Ferris
Publishing Director Simon Beecroft

Written by Simon Hugo
Inspirational models built by Barney Main
Photography by Gary Ombler

Dorling Kindersley would like to thank Randi Sørensen,
Heidi K. Jensen, Paul Hansford, Martin Leighton Lindhardt,
Christopher Leslie Stamp, Li-Yu Lin, Kirsten Hørlyck
Jørgensen, Peter Lønbæk, and Charlotte Neidhardt
at the LEGO Group. Thanks also to Elena Jarmoskaite,
Gema Salamanca, Lisa Sodeau, and James McKeag for
design assistance and Hannah Gulliver-Jones, Joseph
Stewart, and Rebecca Behrens for editorial assistance.

This edition published in 2019
First American Edition, 2018
Published in the United States by DK Publishing
1450 Broadway, Suite 801, New York, New York 10018

DK, a Division of Penguin Random House LLC

012–308288–Aug/19

LEGO, the LEGO logo, the Minifigure, the Brick and Knob
configurations, NINJAGO, and the NINJAGO logo are
trademarks and/or copyrights of the LEGO Group.
©2019 The LEGO Group. All rights reserved. Manufactured
by Dorling Kindersley, 80 Strand, London, WC2R 0RL, UK
under license from the LEGO Group.

A catalog record for this book
is available from the Library of Congress.

ISBN: 978-1-4654-9480-1

Printed and bound in Heshan, China

www.LEGO.com
www.dk.com

A WORLD OF IDEAS:
SEE ALL THERE IS TO KNOW

DEBATING
SEXUAL
CORRECTNESS

DEBATING SEXUAL CORRECTNESS

Pornography, Sexual Harassment,
Date Rape, and the
Politics of Sexual Equality

EDITED AND WITH AN INTRODUCTION BY

ADELE M. STAN

Delta
Trade Paperbacks

A Delta Book
Published by
Dell Publishing
a division of
Bantam Doubleday Dell Publishing Group, Inc.
1540 Broadway
New York, New York 10036

Library of Congress Cataloging in Publication Data

Debating sexual correctness : pornography, sexual harassment,
date rape and the politics of sexual equality / edited and with an
introduction by Adele M. Stan.
p.   cm.
ISBN 0-385-31384-5
1. Sexual harassment of women—United States.
2. Acquaintance rape—United States.   3. Pornography—United
States.   4. Feminist theory—United States.   I. Stan, Adele M.
HQ1237.5.U6D43   1995
305.42—dc20   94-30568
CIP

Manufactured in the United States of America
Published simultaneously in Canada

March 1995

10 9 8 7 6 5 4 3 2 1

BVG

for Megan

ACKNOWLEDGMENTS

As with most book projects, this one has been the beneficiary of more people deserving of thanks than the space herein provides room for, so I ask the forbearance of all those who contributed to this project but whose names do not appear here.

I wish to thank Betsy Bundschuh, my editor at Dell, for conceiving this book and selecting me to put it together. Thanks must also go to Julie Just of *The New York Times,* whose decision to publish my essay, "Women Warriors," on the newspaper's op-ed page and the fine editing that followed led me to this project, and whose editorial judgment is reflected in several of the essays contained herein.

A debt is owed to two friends who indulged me with intellectually rigorous conversations that not only helped shape the ideas contained in the introduction and structure of this book but gave me the courage necessary to explore these ideas in print: Ari Hoogenboom and Anne E. "Obe" O'Brien, who also served as my primary sounding board and responded unfailingly with thoughtful editorial comments. Suggestions from Paul Lipkowitz, Adele Thomas, Stuart Gottesman and Mark W. Palasits added depth to the manuscript.

The enthusiasm and attentiveness of my agent, Loretta Barrett, kept this project in drive when it might otherwise have stalled. Suzanne Braun Levine, editor of the *Columbia Journalism Review,* turned her keen eye to the introduction, gifting me with the editorial insight that so spoiled me when I worked for her at *Ms.* I also enjoyed the support of other former *Ms.* colleagues, particularly editor-in-chief Marcia Ann Gillespie, Letty Cottin Pogrebin, Martha Nelson, Mary Thom, and Mary Kay Blakely.

To my childhood friend Karen L. Hawkins I owe many debts, especially for introducing me to the concept of feminism when we were yet girls, and for her sound business and editorial judgment with regard to this project.

My husband and first reader, Barry Morgan Thomas, provided the support—intellectual, emotional, and material—that made my involvement in this book possible.

Contents

APPENDICES

DEBATING
SEXUAL
CORRECTNESS

Introduction:
Feminism and the
Culture of Sexuality

Adele M. Stan

If, up to this point, the 1990s bear any singular theme, that theme is sex and its place in American life. The decade that opened with a furor over a little buddy film called *Thelma and Louise* went on to give us the date-rape trial of William Kennedy Smith and the volatile public hearings on the nomination of Clarence Thomas to the bench of the Supreme Court, at which the ladylike law professor Anita F. Hill made allegations of sexual harassment against him. Tailhook, the Spur Posse, and the Glen Ridge case have all become household phrases, and the lurid saga of John and Lorena Bobbitt, the tale of a man separated from his privates by his knife-wielding wife, will likely pass into national legend.

On a recent Sunday night, I listened to New York radio personality Vin Scelsa interview Eric Schaeffer, a young filmmaker whose movie, *My Life's in Turnaround,* addresses the complex subject of gender relations. "I mean, what do women want?" he asked Scelsa. "Do they want the penis . . . or do they want to cut it off? I don't know."

As if in answer to the young man's question, twenty-six-year-old bad girl singer-songwriter Liz Phair menaces a male lover in her song "Flower," threatening to do him like a dog and make him like it, promising, "I'll fuck you til your dick is blue." Young women may want the penis, it seems, but some want to both have and hurt it.

At the opposite extreme, we have the media uproar that ensued when a Penn State English professor removed a print of a nude female figure, Goya's "Naked Maja," from her classroom. The remarks elicited from her male students by the titillating masterpiece chilled the classroom climate, said Professor Nancy Stumhofer, making it difficult to teach.[1] Though pundits wildly misreported the story as "The Teacher Who Claimed She Was Harassed by a Painting," other cases have cropped up that border on the absurd, like those in Menlo Park, California, where the complaint of a Seventh-Day Adventist computer operator caused the removal of an art exhibit from a municipal building, and in Oglesby, Illinois, where a WPA mural of loinclothed Native American men was taken down at the behest of a male janitor.

Though sexual ambivalence and fury are nothing new in the land of the free, lately they seem to have reached a fever pitch. America's Puritan roots are never far from the surface, leaving us especially susceptible to a certain dualism, most perfectly illustrated, perhaps, by the lusty reading given a section of the sexually explicit book *The Exorcist*—the part about a pubic hair on a Coke can by Orrin Hatch—the very pious senator from the very Mormon state of Utah, at the Clarence Thomas hearings. Indeed, the recent and long-overdue airing of women's sexual grievances against men has provided the most proper of Americans with a publicly acceptable voyeurism, a sort of folk-medicine antidote to the eighties' backlash against the sexual revolution of the sixties, and the pall that AIDS has cast over sexual freedom.

Our current conundrum over sex and what we want from it stems, in part, from the success of the feminist movement over the last twenty years, ushering in changes in the traditional sexual paradigm. The long-upheld order of man-on-top has been upended, leaving society disoriented, without a proven blueprint for the future. Leaders on both sides of the political scale lament over a nation morally adrift, and many claim feminism to be the cause. On the right, the women's movement is seen as the agent of sexual deviance for its alleged destruction of the nuclear family and its support of gay rights. Among liberals, feminists are increasingly cast as neo-

Victorians who seek to protect women from sexual reality and shower them with privileges of moral purity.

A year or so ago, a lot of dust was kicked up by a young upstart named Katie Roiphe, whose book *The Morning After: Sex, Fear, and Feminism on Campus* claimed that "rape-crisis feminists" were poisoning the sexual atmosphere on college campuses by casting all men as potential rapists and encouraging young women to view sexual experiences that were merely unpleasant as rape.[2] Meanwhile, on the campus of the very liberal Antioch College, a new policy of sexual consent was instituted whereby students (read men) are expected to ask permission of their partners prior to each step of any sexual encounter; a general consent to have sex will not suffice: "May I kiss you?" must be followed by "May I touch your ____?" and on and on. Students who fail to comply with the policy face possible expulsion. All this prompted *Newsweek* to scream on a 1993 cover, SEXUAL CORRECTNESS: HAS IT GONE TOO FAR?

Before we attempt to answer that question, it would be instructive to look at how we got to this place. There once was a time in America when nearly every act of sexual bullying and assault conducted by men against women was tolerated in our society. Acts such as rape, which were always against the law, were made permissible by an onerous burden of proof placed upon the victim and the cultural censure of the accuser. Women felt powerless to halt the sexual aggression of a man, never mind call him to account for his sins. The time of which I write is not some distant past; this is how it was when I came of age, and I remain, however briefly, on the shy side of forty.

When the modern women's movement formed in the late 1960s, feminists sought to liberate women not only from the external oppression heaped upon them in their prescribed roles as mothers and helpmeets, but also from the self-censoring voice within that so often limited women's perceptions of themselves. The flip side of the coin that licensed men to impose their sexual will on women was the stifling of female sexuality to the point where many women were ignorant of their own anatomy, not even knowing where their ticket to orgasm, the clitoris, was located. Feminists became agents of female sexual liberation, asserting a woman's right to sexual pleasure in its myriad forms, both hetero- and homosexual, combating the notion that a woman who liked sex was somehow less than moral.[3] In their most experimental forms, consciousness-raising meetings sometimes included the physical examination by participants of their own anatomy, aided by disposable specula and a mirror. Author Betty Dodson taught women how to masturbate and find their cervixes, while more mainstream women's magazines had us counting climaxes as we sought to fulfill our newly discovered multiorgasmic potential.

But while talk of G-spots and the Big O abounded, assault and harassment continued unabated, and the so-called sexual revolution heaped a double whammy on the old double standard. In the old days, it was assumed that nice girls said no while bad girls said yes; men were free to have sex (as long as it was with women) as they pleased with minimal risk to their reputations. But by the 1960s, with the advent of the Pill, every woman was presumed to want sex with any long-haired man who set himself upon her; to say no was to be "uptight," "unhip," "unliberated," and, most probably, frigid —while saying yes was the groovy, freedom-loving thing to do. Nevertheless you'd most likely be branded "loose" and there for the taking by any number of men once you did the deed.[4] It's important to remember that the sexual revolution was experienced by women who were not raised to be feminists but, rather, a generation that was reared to please men.

So, at the same time that feminists sought to unleash female sexuality, they also called attention to the perils that the sexual construct as we knew it held for women. From the first, a war on degrading sexual imagery was declared, heralded by Gloria Steinem's undercover stint as a Playboy Bunny for *Show* magazine.[5] In the year that fell between the Summer of Love and the Dionysian spectacle that was Woodstock, a group of feminists led by Robin Morgan disrupted the Miss America Pageant with a gutsy protest.[6] Sexual liberation and the war on sexist imagery formed a loosely woven double helix for most in the movement: to be a free agent of one's own sexuality, one's depiction as a whole being, not a mere object, was imperative. Even more pressing was a need to lift the veil of glamor from the rape myth—to declare that women were *not* lusting for abuse, as pornography often showed them to be. The early "women's-libbers" were hardly against sex; they simply sought to seize control of female sexuality from the hands of men.

In 1970 the war on pornography began with a feminist sit-in at the Grove Press, from which a young editor named Robin Morgan, already known as a feminist activist, had just been fired, for apparently political reasons. Although Grove was the darling publishing house of the left, it trafficked in pornographic material as well. Laura Lederer, founding member of San Francisco's Women Against Violence in Pornography and Media (WAVPM), writes that the action "was a manifestation of the growing split between the male radical movement and feminists."[7] Grove's owner, Barney Rossett, called in the police, who arrested the women and threw them in jail for the night where, for their antipornography action, they were strip-searched at the hands of the New York City Police Department.[8]

The focus on female sexuality was only one facet of the women's movement, of course. A major thrust of feminism was to liberate middle-class women from the cloister of the home and to bring economic parity to the workplace. By the mid-seventies, droves of suburban women re-entered the workforce, or enrolled in college, or both. Once back in the world with its attendant dangers, a new awareness formed of the threats nearly all women faced to their physical autonomy, threats that were long endured by single and working-class women in silence.

In 1975 Susan Brownmiller's landmark book *Against Our Will: Men, Women, and Rape,* blew the lid off one of society's dirtiest little secrets—the prevalence of sexual assault against women, and the sociological dynamics that perpetuate it. What made Brownmiller's book particularly controversial was her decision to include co-erced sex within the construct of rape, though she stated forthrightly that verbal sexual coercion "will remain a problem beyond any possible solution of criminal justice." Brownmiller wrote: "It would be deceitful to claim that the murky gray area of male sexual aggression and female passivity and submission can ever be made amenable to legal divination—nor should it be, in the final analysis."[9]

Today Brownmiller's work is often misrepresented by her detractors as a polemic for so-called victim feminism, when in fact she calls upon women to strengthen both their psyches and bodies for the battle against victimization. This single line from her introduction is oft repeated to characterize her complex, groundbreaking analysis: "[Rape] is nothing more or less than a process of intimidation by which *all men* keep *all women* in a state of fear [italics hers]."[10] Though perhaps a tad hyperbolic, this statement was less so in 1975, when it first appeared, a time when virtually no men spoke out against the sexual assault of women, and even those without malicious intent benefited from the climate of fear in which women lived.

The year after *Against Our Will* appeared on the bookshelves, a related issue, sexual harassment, cropped up in the most mainstream of venues, the *Ladies' Home Journal*. There *Ms.* editor Letty Cottin Pogrebin wrote a regular column that served a growing segment of the magazine's readership under the heading "The Working Woman." When Pogrebin gave name to the problem of harassment in the workplace, the magazine was flooded with letters that basically all told the same story—the story of women subjected to all manner of sexual intimidation and demands by employers and coworkers.[11]

Though the campaigns against sexist imagery and sexual violence and intimidation had always overlapped, in the year that followed the Pogrebin article, they became inextricably wed in *Going too Far: The Personal Chronicle of a Feminist* by Robin Morgan. In her angry, literate tome Morgan took the nature of consent one step beyond Brownmiller, arguing that intercourse is rape unless it is "initiated by the woman out of her own genuine affection and desire."[12] Several pages later, she offered the sentence that remains the mantra of the antipornography movement today: "Pornography is the theory, and rape the practice."[13]

As cultural mores loosened, the porn business exploded. By the time of the Watergate scandal, *Playboy*'s circulation was peaking at six million, a figure overtaken several years later by its harder-core rival, *Penthouse*.[14] The appearance of *Hustler* on the newsstands signaled the newfound social acceptability of sexually explicit misogyny; one famous cover featured the image of a naked woman being fed into a meat grinder. As dirty pictures and films took ever more violent forms, the feminist war on pornography grew more vociferous and unruly. Porn bookstores and theaters were picketed and even attacked, while in some locales customers were photographed leaving and entering porno dens.[15] Spurred by the release of the film *Snuff,* which was said to contain the actual sexual murder of a woman, nearly 5,000 women from across the nation turned out for a San Francisco conference sponsored by WAVPM entitled "Feminist Perspectives on Pornography."[16] On the opposite coast, New York's Women Against Pornography (WAP) began offering tours of the city's infamous Forty-second Street smut district. Again 5,000 is the number given by organizers to quantify the crowd that turned out for a march on Times Square led by Gloria Steinem, Bella Abzug, and Susan Brownmiller in October of that year. In the rally that followed the march Andrea Dworkin made her mark in a perfectly constructed speech entitled "The Lie" in which she asserted that the message carried by all pornography is that women want to be hurt, brutalized, and forced to have sex. "To this day," she said, "men believe the pornography and do not believe the women who say no."[17] In other words, pornography is the theory . . .

In 1980 the election of Ronald Reagan to the presidency heralded a grim time for feminism. Hard-won gains in reproductive freedom faced increasingly serious challenges as the Reverend Jerry Falwell's Moral Majority and attorney Phyllis Schlafly's Eagle Forum held sway in the White House. (Schlafly made her name campaigning against the Equal Rights Amendment, and Falwell held feminism responsible for nearly all societal ills.) In that year, Laura Lederer's thoughtful anthology of feminist writing on pornography, *Take Back the Night,* appeared in what may have been the last vestige of feminist cohesion on the topic, though the writers agree that the widespread use and display of pornography created an environment hostile to women, their differing approaches seem more harmonious than dissonant. Here the writing of Wendy Kaminer rests comfortably alongside that of Andrea Dworkin, and writers as diverse as Charlotte Bunch and Gloria Steinem, Susan Griffin and Audre Lorde, Robin Morgan and Alice Walker take their place in a table of contents, united in a cause. Peace on that front would not last long.

The rise of the New Right in the late seventies and early eighties kept feminists busy and on the defensive. Feminist efforts to expand female horizons gave way to the more immediate concerns of protecting the gains already made, especially the legalization of abortion, which suffered a renewed, relentless attack. In this poisonous climate the quest for a politics of pleasure appeared to have fallen by the wayside, especially as the right sought to brand feminists as the immoral destroyers of the nuclear family and the murderers of "unborn babies."

In 1982, a diverse group of feminists attempted to return to an exploration of sexual issues in a conference called "Toward a Politics of Sexuality" held at Barnard College in New York City. The concept paper for the conference, written by the program's academic coordinator, medical anthropologist Carole S. Vance, acknowledged the success the New Right enjoyed in limiting notions of female sexuality to its reproductive function, and urged feminists to seize back the agenda. The conference, part of Barnard's acclaimed "Feminist and Scholar" program, sought to explore the gamut of female sexual experience, including such controversial subjects as "politically incorrect" sex and lesbian "butch-femme" roles. Among those presenting papers were several women known for their critiques of the antipornography movement.

In the anthology *Pleasure and Danger: Exploring Female Sexuality* that emerged from the papers delivered that day, editor Vance tells a harrowing tale of harassment and obstruction that led up to the conference, conducted not by the New Right but by antipornography feminists. According to Vance, antipornography activists alarmed Barnard administrators with accusatory phone calls about the harm that would come to women as a result of the conference, to the point where Barnard President Ellen V. Futter confiscated the conference handbook intended for distribution at this sold-out gathering of some 800 participants. As a result of the controversy, the Helena Rubenstein Foundation dropped its funding for Barnard's Feminist and Scholar series.[18]

On the day of the conference, Vance writes, members of Women Against Pornography leafleted attendees with a flyer that not only decried and mischaracterized the conference but made allegations about the sexual practices of some of the speakers, calling them by name. This action, Vance claims, caused lasting damage to those defamed, derailing careers and causing much grief. "These tactics were McCarthyite," Vance writes. "[They were] cowardly, surrepticious, dependent on slander and sexual panic for their power."[19]

In the wake of the Barnard Conference American feminism appeared poised for a split, and it came the following year with the introduction of a new antipornography statute in Minneapolis by Andrea Dworkin and legal scholar Catharine A. MacKinnon. Years of grassroots organizing among feminists and neighborhood groups paid off in the hearings that led up to the vote on the ordinance, at which a diverse group of academics, health care professionals, women's rights advocates and everyday people testified to a link between pornography and sexual abuse. Women spoke to the harm caused them by pornography, harms Dworkin and MacKinnon would later list to include "dehumanization, sexual exploitation, forced sex, forced prostitution, physical injury, and social and sexual terrorism and inferiority presented as entertainment."[20]

The Minneapolis ordinance addressed pornography as a civil rights issue, allowing anyone who had been harmed by a particular piece of pornography, in accordance with the causes of action specified in the statute, to sue for civil damages. [See Appendix A, "The Dworkin-MacKinnon Antipornography Civil Rights Ordinance (Minneapolis)," items (1) through (o) for specific causes of action.] Arguing that, rather than a form of speech, pornography is something that is done to women, Dworkin and MacKinnon explained, "Under the ordinance, pornography *is* what pornography *does* [emphasis theirs]."[21] Although there was no provision for prior restraint, the ordinance did allow for the removal from stores of material that had been proven harmful.[22] Once the censorship question was called, the double helix of sexual protection and liberation untwined into two strands; the simple mixture of the xx chromosome and a desire for positive change was no longer enough to bind the complex organism the movement had become. Feminists appeared to split into two camps, the so-called protectionists vs. the free speech advocates.

I was a junior editor at *Ms.* magazine when this conflict arose, and it made for some high drama. Dworkin and MacKinnon came to the magazine's offices with several activists (including one who had worked in the sex trade) to make an impassioned presentation before the editorial staff, followed later that day by the women of the Feminist Anti-Censorship Task Force (FACT), led by Carole Vance, writer Lisa Duggan, attorney Nan D. Hunter, and filmmaker Barbara Kerr.

By the time the two sides held their separate teach-ins for the assembled *Ms.* staff, the ordinance had failed in Minneapolis after winning the vote twice in the city council, the result of mayoral vetoes. Soon thereafter an amended version passed into law in Indianapolis, thanks, in part, to the support of a right-wing constituency. Dworkin and MacKinnon took a lot of heat for appearing to make common cause with Indianapolis councilwoman Beulah Coughenhour, described in the pages of *Ms.* as a "Stop-ERA, anti-abortion Eagle Forum member,"[23] who introduced the legislation for vote by the city council. (The Indianapolis statute was ultimately overturned in Federal Court on First Amendment grounds.)

Dworkin and MacKinnon's model ordinance soon took on a life of its own, as politicians more concerned with moral decency than women's rights began tinkering with the model to suit their own purposes, causing alarm among both antipornography and civil libertarian feminists. The most notable example occurred in Suffolk County, New York, where a right-wing county legislator rewrote the ordinance to reflect his political agenda, despite the opposition of both Dworkin and MacKinnon, and the New York chapter of WAP, whose members testified against it. "I don't want to tell anybody what to do as long as they live by the Ten Commandments," asserted Michael D'Andre, sponsor of the Suffolk County measure.[24] A new wariness set in over the right's easy co-option of the pornography issue.

Although the Suffolk measure ultimately failed, at the time each of the warring parties assembled before us in the conference room, the county legislature was considering D'Andre's measure, and the jury was still out on which way the vote would go.

It was one of the most difficult days I ever experienced at *Ms.* As it wore on and we asked more and more questions, the volatility of the issue began to flower, as some women on the staff bravely stated their political discomfort with their own sexual fantasies, and others took emotional objection to the belief stated by one of the FACT members that freedom of expression had to extend to everything in the realm of human experience in order to sustain itself. You see, if you took the Dworkin-MacKinnon position, pornography was not defined simply by its content, as in obscenity law, but by its role as an agent of discrimination against women. MacKinnon's very definition of pornography refers to material that combines "the graphic sexually explicit" with activities that are "actively subordinating, treating unequally, as *less than human,* on the basis of sex [emphasis mine]."[25]

Divisions in the staff became manifest, it seemed, in an instant. Letty Cottin Pogrebin attacked the notion that "anything goes," arguing that although holocaust pornography set in concentration camps may be based on fact, that doesn't mean it belongs in the public consciousness imbued with erotic meaning. Though not present at these discussions, Gloria Steinem, who had long ago made a distinction between erotica and pornography in a much-reprinted article, had already given her blessing to the Dworkin-MacKinnon ordinance. At the helm of the editorial ship Suzanne Braun Levine meditated what at times came close to being a free-for-all. "I'd always believed that on any issue, despite our diversity, that a consensus feminist position could be arrived at, at least within the pages,'' she recently told me, "until this one came along."

Levine had set up the presentations as preparation for the magazine's coverage of the debate. Among ourselves, we handled the issue gingerly, arguing politely with each other, suddenly aware of the potential the pornography problem had to blow us apart. In private, the more libertarian among us (myself included) made cracks about the "feminist thought police," while the debate raged internally in the form of private campaigns waged in the hope of influencing the coverage of this feminist family feud.

The story was assigned to contributing editor Mary Kay Blakely, a thoughtful, mild-mannered reporter who happened to be newly arrived in New York, fresh from the Midwest. The assignment had barely been made before Blakely was cast under a cloud of suspicion by both sides. Dworkin was annoyed that their words would be set into Blakely's narrative. To Blakely the women of FACT seemed convinced that she had been co-opted by the antipornography side in her discussions with Dworkin and MacKinnon, though they had no direct knowledge of her interviews.

Before Blakely wrote a word of her piece, nearly every editor on staff was fielding phone calls from colleagues outside the magazine, as feminists lobbied their contacts for a shot at determining what tack the story would take.

Later, parts of one of Blakely's drafts was leaked out, and the fracas caught fire. The attacks became intensely personal; there wasn't an editor not affected. "Everyone had an agenda," says Blakely, looking back on it now. "There were excesses on all sides."

The resulting cover story, "Is One Woman's Sexuality Another Woman's Pornography?", elicited reams of reader mail, both angry and appreciative. (Even the title of the article was a matter of contention.) The magazine's coverage still angers Andrea Dworkin, who feels that in giving the two sides equal treatment, Blakely's large piece lent FACT, a group of 30 or so New York–based journalists, artists and academics, political legitimacy that was undeserved when compared with the grassroots efforts that brought forth the

Minneapolis and subsequent ordinances.[26] But Vance is quick to point out that events organized by FACT often drew more than 100 participants, and that FACT chapters existed in at least four other cities where antipornography legislation was under consideration.[27]

Pornography was only one among a host of issues that feminists grappled with in the 1980s. Susan Brownmiller's and Robin Morgan's assessments of rape had given rise to a new issue: acquaintance rape, known in the popular lexicon as date rape. In 1975 Brownmiller mentioned, almost offhandedly, that nearly half of all women raped were raped by men they knew, but her analysis of how women were socialized to accept male sexual aggression invited a reassessment of women's sexual experience within her broadened definition of rape.[28]

In 1981 *Ms.* magazine commissioned a study of date rape on college campuses, a study hotly debated even today. Mary P. Koss, a professor of psychology at Kent State University, was engaged to conduct a three-year study of the phenomenon. When preliminary results of the *Ms.* Magazine Campus Project on Sexual Assault appeared in the magazine in 1985, they began with the astounding finding that one in four women studied were victims of either rape or attempted rape. (See Appendix B for selected findings.) Koss's findings were controversial not only for the frequency of male sexual aggression they purported to show, but because she used the Brownmiller definition of rape, which included verbally coerced sex. Furthermore, using a list of indicators, Koss determined herself whether or not her respondents had been raped; 73 percent of those she determined to be rape victims had not identified themselves as such in answering her survey. Within the context of feminist thinking on the subject, Koss's results only affirmed what feminists had been saying for years: that women were not only socialized to be rape victims, but frequently minimized the brutality they suffered at the hands of men as a coping mechanism against the stigma and trauma of rape.[29]

The *Ms.*-Koss study mobilized campus feminists for combat. Students organized "Take Back the Night" events at which date-rape victims were encouraged to offer testimonials of their experience. Rape-crisis centers sprang up on campuses across the country, and "How to Avoid Date Rape" seminars became *de rigueur* in freshman orientation programs.

In the year that followed the conclusion of the *Ms.* study (which was later treated comprehensively in Robin Warshaw's 1988 book *I Never Called It Rape*), the United States Supreme Court handed feminists a victory in the sexual harassment case *Meritor Savings Bank* v. *Vinson,* which determined that sexual harassment, as a form of gender discrimination, was covered by Title VII of the Civil Rights Act of 1964, which bars discrimination in the workplace on the basis of race, sex, religion, and national origin. By unanimous decision the Court ruled that if an "abusive or hostile work environment" was caused by pervasive sexual harassment, it constituted sex discrimination. However, the Court offered little in the way of guidance as to what constituted an abusive or hostile work environment.[30]

The Court's decision in *Meritor* offered feminists one of their few bright spots in a decade that yielded the defeat of the Equal Rights Amendment and a constant assault by the United States Justice Department on *Roe* v. *Wade,* the Supreme Court decision that had legalized abortion. Though the nomination of Geraldine Ferraro to the Democratic vice-presidential ticket was applauded by feminists, it was something less than a triumph; we knew in our hearts that she was a sacrificial lamb, and more than a few of us doubted that we would see another woman grace a presidential ticket for some time once the political climate improved for the Democrats.

Talk of sexual liberation was reduced to whispers once AIDS arose as a major menace that fed too well into the antigay, antisex apocalyptic rhetoric of the Christian right. (Even before the evolution of AIDS as an epidemic, the fast spread of other sexually transmitted diseases such as herpes and chlamydia, diseases especially dangerous to women, had chilled the atmosphere.) It was in this climate that then–attorney general Edwin Meese convened a "blue-ribbon" panel to study the impact of pornography on American life.

While the focus of the Meese Commission was to show how pornography led to the moral degradation of society rather than the specific harm it did to women, antipornography feminists testified before the commission alongside Christian fundamentalists and vice-squad cops. Linda "Lovelace" Marchiano, star of the infamous porn film *Deep Throat,* told her horrific story of having been made to perform for the camera at gunpoint by her manager-husband Chuck Traynor, who went on to play that same role in the life of Marilyn Chambers, another famous porn star of that era. Most eloquent among the witnesses was Andrea Dworkin, whose testimony (included in this collection) was contained in the commission's final report, an honor given no other witness.[31] From the opposing FACT team, Nan Hunter testified in a separate hearing.[32]

Ultimately the Meese Commission failed to adopt the Dworkin-MacKinnon approach, opting instead for an old-fashioned antiobscenity strategy that better served the cause of public decency than it did the well-being of women. Carole Vance argues that antipornography feminists simply played into the hands of the right, which updated its morals campaign with feminist rhetoric and succeeded in demonizing sex itself—not the harm done by sexual aggression.[33] For her participation in the hearings Dworkin was vilified by liberals of many stripes and indeed even heckled from the floor by civil libertarians when she delivered her testimony.[34]

As attacks against feminism continued without respite throughout the late 1980s, the women's movement grew ever more protectionist in strategy. The election in 1988 of the once-moderate George Bush to the presidency only offered more of the same, elected as he was on the promise of continuing the policies of his predecessor.

The Reverends Jim Bakker and Jimmy Swaggart made big news when revelations of their sexual peccadillos emerged, but the fall of these two icons of the Christian right did little to assuage conservatives' obsession with obscenity. In 1989, they turned their focus on the National Endowment for the Arts (NEA), which funded the projects of several controversial artists, most notably a traveling exhibition of photographs—some of homoerotic subjects—by the late Robert Mapplethorpe, who had just recently died of AIDS. The attack against the NEA, led by Senator Jesse Helms of North Carolina, led to the revocation of grants to four performance artists in 1990, two of whom are gay men; the other two, Karen Finley and Holly Hughes, are feminists. (Hughes is also a lesbian.)[35] Congress went so far as to pass a measure that required future grant recipients to pledge that they would not use NEA money to produce works that "might be considered obscene."[36] (After bringing a suit against the agency, the four artists had their grants reinstated in 1994.)

The attack on the NEA in effect constituted an attack on the left, specifically its feminist and gay-rights movements. Although the offensive came from the left's traditional enemies, there was plenty of name-calling and blame-laying within the side under siege over the means by which the NEA was targeted. Many contended that the Meese Commission, with which antipornography feminists had cooperated, provided the ammunition used by Helms to assail the beleagured cultural agency.[37] In the year that followed, as demands for multicultural curricula gained ground in urban school systems and on college campuses, a national campaign against "political correctness" would be joined by many of the forces arrayed against the NEA, as well as some within the left.[38]

In feminism the bunker mentality prevailed until 1991, when George Bush's nomination of the very conservative Judge Clarence Thomas to the Supreme Court took an unexpected turn.

Even before the media received word of Anita Hill's allegations of sexual harassment against the judge, the story of Clarence Thomas's nomination was less than pretty. Still stinging from the Senate Judiciary Committee's rejection of Judge Robert Bork during Reagan's second term, Republicans were determined to stick it to the Democrats on the committee by putting up a nominee who would be ideologically repugnant to the liberals yet impossible for them to reject. In their choice to fill the seat vacated by Justice

Thurgood Marshall, the first black person to sit on the high court, they found their perfect foil in the person of the anti–affirmative action African American Thomas.

Unknown to the public, Anita F. Hill, an obscure law professor (also African American), had alleged to members of the committee that she had been sexually harassed by the judge while in his employ at the Equal Employment Opportunity Commission (EEOC) during the Reagan years. The committee members chose to sit on the allegations, which were subsequently leaked to the press during the course of the confirmation proceedings, raising an immediate clamor for the public airing of Hill's charges before the committee.

The result was the now-familiar tale of one of the most incendiary media dramas in American history—the marathon televised hearing of Hill's accusations, along with corroboration and rebuttal by a number of witnesses before a massive, riveted television audience.

Were the Thomas-Hill hearings merely about sexual harassment and gender relations in the United States, they'd have been compelling enough. That these hearings were about the whole construct of power in our nation made for searing television—the black accuser and accused sitting before a panel of paunchy white men, the drama of a black woman vilified by some members of that panel and hung out to dry by the rest, the sound of a lady being made to speak the filth presumably visited upon her unwelcoming ears, the spectacle of a scandal that is lived every day in the dominant culture being given voice by two handsome, intelligent members of the nation's most oppressed minority group.

The far-reaching implications of the Hill-Thomas hearings are too vast to address adequately in this forum,[39] especially the quandary the incident left African American women in, one of conflicting allegiances to race and gender, which Rosemary L. Bray ponders in this collection. Suffice it to say that the hearings hurled the nation into a heated discussion of race and gender, and set the stage for a feminist comeback. Although polls taken during the course of the hearings and shortly thereafter indicated that more women believed the judge than they did the law professor, a slow burn followed among women who found Hill's tale familiar, culminating in victories for record numbers of female candidates in the ensuing congressional elections. Still, Clarence Thomas sits today on the bench of the nation's highest court.

The issues raised by the Hill-Thomas confrontation shed a spotlight on gender relationships within the workplace. Why had Professor Hill never blown the whistle on Judge Thomas, even after he allegedly regaled her with the plots of pornographic movies and tales of his own romantic conquests? Why had she decided to come forward now, some ten years later? Why did she move with him to his next job, at the Justice Department? Why had she never told him to stop, threatened him with action, or smashed him in the teeth?

As these questions took center stage at dinner tables and cocktail parties nationwide, many were quietly consumed with taking personal inventories of their own experience. Professional women were less inclined than others to question Hill's behavior in the face of harassment by her boss; to charge one's superior with sexual impropriety was a sure-fire way to derail one's career. With no guarantee that her next employer would treat her any differently, the professional woman who toiled in a sexually hostile work environment had little recourse: she could quit and cut her losses, or lodge a complaint that would most likely only impugn her reputation, not his. Either way, she was required to put her achievements, hard-won in a man's world, on the line. So most endured in silence.

On the other hand, many men were gripped with a sense of panic in the wake of the hearings. "That joke I told at the company picnic didn't constitute harassment, did it?" Pundits complained that the uproar over Hill's allegations would kill morale in offices throughout the land. Others suggested that sexual "joking" was part and parcel of doing business in America. Women say they want to be treated as equals, the reasoning went. Well, if they can't take the heat, send them back to the kitchen. Charges of McCarthyism surfaced again, waged at the feminist spoilers perceived to be invading the sacrosanct territory of private conduct. In his *Washington Post* column, E. J. Dionne, Jr., urged all sides to drop the McCarthyism charge, lest the word lose its original, terrifying meaning.[40]

* * *

Nineteen ninety-one proved to be a banner year for gender-war battles. As incidents large and small piled on top of each other in the news media, passions on all sides became increasingly inflamed. On the big screen the film *Thelma and Louise,* the story of two women who kill a would-be rapist, provoked an uproar among men as theaters filled with women who cheered and clapped when Susan Sarandon pulled the trigger.

Two burning feminist tracts published that year upped the ante: Susan Faludi's *Backlash: The Undeclared War Against American Women,* in which the author enumerated the way the media and other institutions manipulated information and imagery to the detriment of women, and Naomi Wolf's *The Beauty Myth: How Images of Beauty Are Used Against Women.* In her much-talked-about book, Wolf asserted that ". . . boys rape and girls get raped *as a normal course of events* [italics hers]," a line that has come back to haunt her as revisionists such as Camille Paglia and Katie Roiphe seek to poke holes in the feminist rhetoric surrounding date rape.[41]

This was also the year that saw the televised date-rape trial of William Kennedy Smith, scion of our nation's royal family, the story that spurred a raging debate over the media's naming of a rape accuser without her consent. Here, too, the Smith-Bowman trial was as much about generalized power as it was about gender relations; this time the prism through which the power-play was viewed was class, not race. The wealthy young man was acquitted of all charges.

In the same year that feminists fed their anger on *Backlash* and *The Beauty Myth,* Camille Paglia's *Sexual Personae: Art and Decadence from Nefertiti to Emily Dickinson* hit the ground running with a breathless and decidedly pro-male assessment of the sexual ethics and excess of Western culture. Paglia's cheeky iconoclasm made her an instant media star, her jokey irreverence welcomed by the mainstream as an antidote to angry feminist polemic. With her exaltation of gay male culture (she claimed lesbians had none), she was unpeggable as a sexual conservative. Calling herself a feminist and celebrating her experience of the sixties, she expressed society's exasperation with feminism's relentless critique of life as we know it.

Stop whining, she cried. Sex has always been dangerous and unfair —get used to it. William K. Smith's accuser was a dope, she added.[42] Speaking for men in a female voice, Paglia told their jokes from behind the mask of the Clown Contessa of Contrarianism.

Despite the appeal of Paglia's nose-thumbing, sensational stories kept cropping up in the media that appeared to validate Naomi Wolf's comment on boys, girls, and rape. Along with the William Kennedy Smith trial, we were served the Mike Tyson date-rape trial, yet another cautionary tale about class, race, and gender, one with a decidedly different outcome than that which greeted Mister Smith. In California a ring of adolescent boys who called themselves the Spur Posse terrorized girls as young as eleven, sometimes through sexual assault, other times by sexual coercion, all the while keeping score of their conquests in a contest with each other.

On the East Coast, the Glen Ridge case and New York City's "whirlpooling"* epidemic highlighted the sexual victimization of girls by gangs of boys. In the ultimate "boys-will-be-boys" case, a convention of naval aviators in Las Vegas gave rise to the Tailhook scandal, when Lieutenant Paula Coughlin blew the whistle on the sexual assault and abuse she and a number of other women endured at the hands of a gang of her fellow officers. Ultimately, not one of the perpetrators was convicted of assault by the military court.

Changing sexual mores and highly publicized battles over the rights and wrongs of sexual conduct had saturated our consciousness by the early nineties. At the 1992 Republican National Convention, the agenda was seized by the Christian right, to the surprising detriment of the G.O.P. The Clarence Thomas drama had left a sour taste in the mouths of the electorate, and conservatives who believed in women's rights, gay rights, or who were members of minority groups saw themselves cast as the enemy by convention speakers. Between the antigay invective of also-rans Pat Robertson and Patrick J. Buchanan, and Marilyn Quayle's shining moment as her party's

---

* "Whirlpooling" is a slang term for the practice, in public swimming pools, of surrounding a girl and sexually assaulting her.

Total Woman (just ignore that law degree, please), the portrait of intolerance rendered by the television cameras served the agenda of those inveighed against.

When Bill and Hillary Clinton ("two for the price of one") moved into the White House in 1992, feminists heaved a deep sigh of relief. After twelve years of antifeminist politics from the White House, the siege was lifted, or so it seemed. As Wendy Kaminer has pointed out, despite impressive strides made in the recognition of such issues as sexual harassment and rape, the feminist movement that remained at the end of the Reagan-Bush years no longer resembled the strapping, prideful one that welcomed the eighties with the ERA campaign and a general quest for power in the workplace.[43]

The Anita Hill episode had lifted the veil on a commonplace dynamic between the sexes in the workplace, and not everyone was happy about it. Now Clinton's unabashed partnership with his feminist wife heralded the death knell for patriarchy as we'd known it, priming the public for a renewed attack on feminism. Clinton wasn't a year in office before feminists were blindsided by a cover line on a summer issue of *The New York Times Sunday Magazine* that shrieked: RAPE HYPE BETRAYS FEMINISM. Inside, the large, lavishly illustrated story was called "Date Rape's Other Victim"; a blurb announced: "In their claims of a date rape epidemic on campus, feminists subvert their own cause."[44] The author was Katie Roiphe, daughter of self-described feminist Anne Roiphe, a writer well known in New York literary circles. The article was an excerpt from her soon-to-be-published first book, *The Morning After: Sex, Fear, and Feminism on Campus.*

In her *Times Magazine* piece the younger Roiphe decried what she saw as sexual hysteria on college campuses, encouraged by feminist administrators and faculty in their presentation of date rape as a common campus occurrence. Women were being taught to view themselves as victims rather than agents of self-determination, Roiphe claimed. The classification of verbal coercion as rape infantilized women, she said, with the implication that they couldn't be expected to find the wherewithal to say no and walk away.[45]

Roiphe contended that what she called the "rape-crisis movement'' was rooted in sexual and class anxiety, not based on a widespread threat to college women. Challenging the results of the *Ms.* study with anecdotal material, she pooh-poohed the ''Take Back the Night'' rallies as much ado about nothing. Just assert your will, and all will be well, she seemed to be saying.

Although little of Roiphe's critique was new (much seemed derived from Paglia and libertarian feminists such as Ellen Willis and Wendy Kaminer), this was the first time these words were uttered by a woman who fit within the demographic profile of a likely date-rape target—in her twenties and living in an academic setting—so a media star was born. An unprecedented level of hype attended the publication of this slender volume by a first-time author. Much of the book was excerpted before it was published, and interviews with Roiphe appeared in nearly all the major women's magazines. It suddenly dawned that during the siege of the Reagan-Bush years, a new generation had sprung up that had no memory of the bad old days that had brought the feminist movement into being in the first place.

The reaction to Roiphe was swift and strong. By the time her polemic appeared in book form, the long knives were out for her. In the pages of *The New Yorker,* Katha Pollitt rebutted Roiphe in an angry piece that took the younger woman to task for her lack of life experience.[46] In *Newsday,* bell hooks attacked what she called ''Roiphe's brand of competitive feminism'' for ''turning the movement into a sport where privileged white girls are picked to be the ones who will call the shots.''[47] And despite the orgy of media attention that surrounded *The Morning After,* the book sold only modestly.

Some months later, another dilemma arose for feminists when Paula Corbin Jones, a former employee of the State of Arkansas, filed a sexual harassment suit against the President of the United States, whose alleged extramarital affair with a different woman had been an issue of some moment during his campaign for office. Though Jones's charges, advanced through the machinery of an anti-Clinton right-wing effort, seem spurious at best, feminists were left to field charges of hypocrisy for failing to rush to the side of the accuser, as they had in the case of Anita Hill.

By the time Roiphe's book hit the stands, it should have been apparent that something new was afoot with the sexual mores of young women. At the same moment that Roiphe complained that on campuses across the nation, young women rallied in public tear-fests to miscast bad sexual experiences as rape, a new sort of angry, in-your-face assertion of female sexuality was finding its way into the pop culture of Generation X.

Grunge had emerged to express, as we've heard *ad nauseam,* the alienation of suburban youth raised in dysfunctional families on Reaganistic Pablum. The women of grunge made their mark as "bad" girls who revel in the use of bad words and bad thoughts, sticking the male ethic in the male face. The very name of the band fronted by grunge's dowager queen, Courtney Love, attests to this fact; what does one make of an act named Hole?

In the pages of *Details,* the hippest of Condé Nast's offerings, Anka Radikovich engages the services of a male prostitute (in the interest of journalism, of course) and reports with powerful glee on the performance she demands from him.[48]

Singers Liz Phair and P. J. Harvey utter desires that were once unspeakable by women; a typical noisy Harvey anthem is called "Rub 'Til It Bleeds." While these women seem angry enough with men, they also appear to be taking on the taboos of what's come to be seen as the feminist dogma of egalitarian sex. In the eighties, some jokingly referred to Women Against Pornography as "Women Against Bad Things." Could this new crop of angry babes be constituted as "Women Who Want Bad Things"?

A recent issue of *Esquire* looked at this phenomenon and wishfully pronounced the rise of "Do-Me Feminism." Among the women profiled was Lisa Palac, editor until late of San Francisco's *Cybersex* magazine and the creator of a CD-ROM program for women called "Cyborgasm." When author Tad Friend suggested his squeamishness at the notion of doing anything to a woman that might be construed as degrading, she demanded: "Degrade me when I ask you to."[49]

If you think this all gives lie to Roiphe's contention that sexual correctness is ruining sex, in all its capricious glory, between postpubescents, consider the case of Antioch College, a bulwark of let-it-all-hang-out liberalism, where the students adopted a novel policy for sexual conduct designed to combat the miscommunication often inherent in date rape. Known colloquially as the Antioch Rules, students agreed to ask for consent before initiating each step of a sexual encounter, or face expulsion. (See Appendix C.) Constructed to subvert coercive tendencies, the policy was roundly denounced in the press with a fury that implied that some version of it would be passing through a House subcommittee any day now.

Pundits and editorial writers decried the death of sexual spontaneity that would ensue with the adoption of the measure. Potshots were taken at the unenforceability of the policy. And yet, one has to ask, why are all these people so concerned about the quality of sex had by the 650 students of a small, quirky college? Why has there never been this level of concern for the lack of spontaneity long experienced by women for fear of being hurt or stigmatized?

In the critique of Antioch's attempt to codify sexual behavior, little note has been made of the kinkiness inherent in a way of sex that involves so much speech, leading one to wonder if the attendant media hysteria that heralded the policy isn't more about our fear of articulating our desires than it is about free love. It's not as if the policy insists on the use of Latin terms for the sex acts or body parts under discussion. Lisa Palac's demand of degradation upon request is perfectly in keeping with the Antioch code, it seems, as long as she specifies the form of degradation she desires each step of the way.

Speech, in fact, seems to be where we're at with sex: It figures prominently in the debate over pornography, was the essence of Anita Hill's complaint against Clarence Thomas, and is what draws the line between the feminist and legal definitions of rape. A new generation is defining itself by its salty language, and news commentators have dispensed with polite euphemisms for sexual terms.

(Note the number of penis-sightings in the press in the wake of the Bobbitt case.)

Beyond the limits and possibilities of language lies our obsession with sex and what is fair within its context. Yet the law is limited by language, leaving a vast gray area of behavior beyond legal constraints.

In the *Newsweek* story on "sexual correctness" author Sarah Crichton, a former editor of *Seventeen* magazine, suggested a cultural lag between the way today's girls have been socialized (still to be passive and please men) and the world they enter as young adults, in which they are expected to express their desires without a thought given to offense. In other words, though the slogan of the anti-date-rape crusaders is "no means no," many girls never get to "no," and this leads to misunderstandings later construed as rape.[50]

If a conscious woman has sex with a man without protesting, and that man's behavior contained no threat of violence, can she fairly be said to have been raped? There are those who would say yes, that she was socialized in a way that would preclude any assertion of her will. But in making such allowances for her socialization, do we not encourage the continuance of her silence?

Though she needlessly ridiculed those coping with the very real problem of acquaintance rape, this is the point of Roiphe's worth consideration: agreeing to something you didn't really want is not the same thing as having it forced on you. And I speak as a somewhat embarrassed veteran of the sexual revolution who slept with too many men just because it was easier than saying no, effectively raping myself, as Mary Gaitskill might say.[51]

This position is not without its dangers, though. As I was writing, a Pennsylvania judge ruled that his state's rape laws apply only to victims who put up a physical struggle against their attackers. While I'm all for taking on the attacker, that is a judgment that must be left to the attacked. She has the right to survive by her wits, whatever form that takes.

Likewise, I've always been suspicious of efforts to give the state the power to reign in pornography, despite my belief that much of it does create an unhealthy environment for women. Though I don't support their ordinance, an incident from my recent past has given me a new appreciation of MacKinnon's and Dworkin's position on pornography.

I was sitting in a diner, at a table diagonally across the aisle from a booth occupied by two middle-aged men. The one within my eyeshot took note of me sitting alone and returned his gaze to a magazine spread open before him, then picked it up as if to show it to his companion, but given the visual trajectory, the display was purely for my edification. The exhibition was the centerfold of what is artfully termed in the smut business a "split beaver" magazine, one that specializes in photographs of wet, open vaginas. The curator caught my eye and leered; I sat stunned in the silence Dworkin contends porn forces on women. I thought about challenging him, ripping the magazine out of his hands, but decided it just wasn't worth it. And this was long after I'd taken to physically attacking men who grabbed me on the street.

Still, whatever the reasons, I believe my silence was my choice. Yet this is just one among many experienced by women that should explain why so many of us take issue with the popular notion that sexual correctness is overtaking the land, chilling the possibilities for liberational sex. For women who live in urban centers, a constant chorus of contempt—street harassment—provides the soundtrack for their travels through city streets, ranging from wolf-whistles and ass-grabbing to taunts both shouted and, most frighteningly, whispered.

We live these days on a tremorous landscape, one in which the sands seem to shift with every step. The old order, the old rules, have been declared null and void, but the new ones are still forming and the old ones still lived by in some arbitrary fashion. The daughter of Ronald Reagan, who railed against pornography, appears in her silicate altogether in the pages of *Playboy*. John Schlafly, son of Mrs. Family Values herself, announces to the world that he's gay. A Seventh-Day Adventist uses a feminist antiharassment statute to censor an art show. The pro-feminist President is sued for sexual harassment.

We have entered a brave new world in which all of us—but

especially women—are challenged to transcend our socialization every day. It may not be fair, but we must somehow rise to meet it. Feminism may be a movement, but it is also a state of mind, a way of thinking that, in order to be true to itself, must be invented and renewed by the practitioner on a daily basis.

As decisions come down from the courts and the sands continue to shift, it is hoped that the essays included in this collection, chosen from across generational and ideological divides, will set the current debate into context and provide some wisdom for the future.

NOTES

1. Nancy C. Stumhofer, "Goya's 'Naked Maja' and the Classroom Climate," *Teachers for a Democratic Culture,* Spring 1994.

2. Katie Roiphe, *The Morning After: Sex, Fear, and Feminism on Campus,* Little, Brown and Co., Boston, 1993, pp. 51–84.

3. Carole S. Vance, editor, *Pleasure and Danger: Exploring Female Sexuality,* Pandora Press, London, p. xvii (1992 edition).

4. John D'Emilio and Estelle B. Freedman, *Intimate Matters: A History of Sexuality in America,* Harper & Row, 1988, pp. 310–311 (Perenial Library edition, 1989).

5. Gloria Steinem, "A Bunny's Tale," *Show* magazine, 1963. Reprinted as "I Was a Playboy Bunny," in *Outrageous Acts and Everyday Rebellions* by Gloria Steinem; Holt Rinehart and Winston; New York, 1983.

6. Megan Boler, Robin Lake, and Bridget Wynne; "We Sisters Join Together . . . ," from *Take Back the Night: Women on Pornography,* Laura Lederer, editor; William Morrow and Co., Inc.; New York, 1980, p. 262.

7. Laura Lederer, "Women Have Seized the Offices of Grove Press Because . . ." in *Take Back the Night,* p. 267.

8. Ibid., p. 269.

9. Susan Brownmiller, *Against Our Will: Men, Women, and Rape,* Simon and Schuster, New York, 1975. Reference appears on p. 401, Fawcett Columbine edition, Ballantine Books, New York, 1993.

10. Ibid., p. 15, Fawcett Columbine edition, 1993.

11. Karen Lindsey, "Sexual Harassment on the Job and How to Stop It," *Ms.,* November 1977, p. 50.

12. Robin Morgan, "Theory and Practice: Pornography and Rape," from *Going too Far: The Personal Chronicle of a Feminist,* Random House, New York, 1977. Reprinted in *Take Back the Night,* reference appears on p. 136.

13. Ibid., reference appears on p. 139 of *Take Back the Night.*

14. John D'Emilio and Estelle B. Freedman, *Intimate Matters: A History of Sexuality in America.* (See note no. 3.) Also see Alison Assiter, *Pornography, Feminism and the Individual,* Pluto Press, London, 1989. Reference appears on p. 72, 1991 paperback edition.

15. Robin Morgan, ''Theory and Practice: Pornography and Rape'' from *Going too Far: The Personal Chronicle of a Feminist,* Random House, New York, 1977. Reprinted in *Take Back the Night,* reference appears on p. 138.

16. Laura Lederer, editor, *Take Back the Night,* p. 15. Also Andrea Dworkin, ''Pornography and Grief,'' *Letters from a War Zone,* Secker & Warburg, London, 1988. Article appears on p. 19 of 1993 edition by Laurence Hill Books, Brooklyn, New York.

17. Andrea Dworkin, ''The Lie,'' *Letters from a War Zone.* Article appears on p. 9 of the 1993 edition by Laurence Hill Books, Brooklyn, New York.

18. Carole S. Vance, editor, *Pleasure and Danger: Exploring Female Sexuality,* Pandora Press, London, 1992 edition, pp. xx–xvii, 434. (Originally published by Routledge & Kegan Paul, London, 1984, without material in first citation.)

19. Ibid, p. xxi.

20. Andrea Dworkin and Catharine A. MacKinnon, *Pornography and Civil Rights: A New Day for Women's Equality,* Organizing Against Pornography, Minneapolis, 1988, p. 33.

21. Ibid., p. 38.

22. Ibid., p. 55.

23. Mary Kay Blakely, ''Is One Woman's Sexuality Another Woman's Pornography?'' *Ms.,* April 1985, p. 44.

24. Ibid.

25. Catharine A. MacKinnon, *Only Words,* Harvard University Press, 1993, p. 23.

26. Conversation with Andrea Dworkin, September 24, 1994.

27. Conversation with Carol S. Vance, October 20, 1994.

28. Susan Brownmiller, *Against Our Will: Men, Women, and Rape,* p. 351, Fawcett Columbine 1993 edition.

29. Robin Warshaw, *I Never Called It Rape: The* Ms. *Report on Recognizing, Fighting and Surviving Date and Acquaintance Rape,* Harper & Row, New York, 1988.

30. ''Excerpts from Supreme Court Ruling on Sexual Harassment,'' *The New York Times,* November 10, 1993, Justice Sandra Day O'Connor writing for the Court, subhead ''Conflict Among Circuits.''

31. *Final Report of the Attorney General's Commission on Pornography,* United States Department of Justice, Government Printing Office, Washington, D.C., 1986, pp. 769–772.

32. Ibid., see witness list for Chicago hearing at back of the report.

33. Carole S. Vance, editor, *Pleasure and Danger: Exploring Female Sexuality,* pp. xxvii–xxxi. Also, John D'Emilio and Estelle B. Freedman, *Intimate Matters: A History of Sexuality in America,* pp. 350–352.

34. Andrea Dworkin, ''Pornography Is a Civil Rights Issue,'' *Letters from a*

War Zone, pp. 276, 289; 1993 edition, Laurence Hill Books, Brooklyn, New York. Also, Lindsy Van Gelder, "Pornography Goes to Washington," *Ms.,* June 1986. (Reprinted in this volume.)

35. "The NEA Four: Life After Symbolhood," *The New York Times,* Section 2, Sunday, June 5, 1994.

36. Carole S. Vance, editor, *Pleasure and Danger: Exploring Female Sexuality,* p. xxxii.

37. Ibid.

38. Paul Berman, editor, *Debating P.C.,* Dell Publishing, 1992, p. 22.

39. For thoughtful analyses of the legacy of slavery and racism in gender politics, see: Toni Morrison, "Introduction: Friday on the Potomac," *Race-ing Justice, En-gendering Power: Essays on Anita Hill, Clarence Thomas and the Construction of Social Reality,* Toni Morrison, editor, Pantheon Books, New York, 1992. Celia Morris, *Bearing Witness: Sexual Harassment and Beyond—Everywoman's Story;* Little, Brown and Co.; Boston, 1994, pp. 3–33. bell hooks, *Feminist Theory from Margin to Center,* South End Press, 1984, pp. 1–15.

40. E. J. Dionne, Jr., "As Variously Invoked, McCarthyism Seems to Have Lost Specific Meaning," *The Washington Post,* October 14, 1991, p. A21.

41. Naomi Wolf, *The Beauty Myth: How Images of Beauty Are Used Against Women,* William Morrow, New York, 1991. Reference appears on p. 167 of 1992 Anchor/Doubleday edition.

42. Camille Paglia, *Sex, Art and American Culture,* Vintage Books, 1992, p. 58.

43. Wendy Kaminer, "Feminism's Identity Crisis," *The Atlantic Monthly,* October 1993.

44. Katie Roiphe, "Date Rape's Other Victim," *The New York Times Sunday Magazine,* June 13, 1993.

45. Ibid., p. 30.

46. Katha Pollitt, "Not Just Bad Sex," *The New Yorker,* October 1993, p. 220.

47. bell hooks, "Color Roiphe Privileged," *New York Newsday,* October 27, 1993, Part 2, p. 57.

48. Anka Radikovich, *Details,* July 1993.

49. Tad Friend, "Yes." *Esquire,* February 1994, p. 48.

50. Sarah Crichton, "Sexual Correctness: Has It Gone too Far?" *Newsweek,* October 25, 1993, p. 56.

51. Mary Gaitskill, "On Not Being a Victim," *Harper's* magazine, March 1994. (Reprinted in this volume.)

PART ONE

Passionate Polemics

Sex Harassment

Letty Cottin Pogrebin

When this article appeared in 1976 as one of the author's regular columns for the *Ladies' Home Journal,* the magazine received an avalanche of mail from readers who at last had a name to give a problem from which many suffered in the workplace. Letty Cottin Pogrebin is a founding editor of *Ms.* and the author of many books, including *How to Make It in a Man's World, Family Politics,* and *Deborah, Golda and Me: Being Jewish and Female in America.* She edited *Stories for Free Children* and codeveloped, with Marlo Thomas, *Free to Be You and Me* and *Free to Be a Family.*

A restaurant owner grabs a waitress' rear whenever she passes the cash register. A police officer makes advances to the woman cop with whom he shares a patrol car. A politician bombards his female staff with vulgar remarks about their breasts. An executive offers his secretary to visiting buyers when he isn't chasing her around the desk himself.

These experiences are the stuff of cartoons and comedians' routines—but women aren't laughing anymore. Sexual harassment on the job isn't funny. The woman victimized by it can suffer great personal anguish, depression, and physical stress symptoms such as nausea, headaches, and severe body pain. If she's seen as a tool for sexual pleasure, she knows her work won't be taken seriously. She has no job security as long as she's used as a decorative office ornament or a prize to be bartered among clients and customers. If the attentions of a male co-worker become an embarrassment to the company, the double standard usually cools the scandal this way: He's reprimanded and she's fired. Sexual harassment, whoever perpetrates it, undermines a woman's job performance, poisons her work atmosphere, and carries the message "Put out or get out."

Why haven't we heard more about this problem? Susan Meyer and Karen Sauvigné, founders of the Working Woman United Institute (WWUI), offer this explanation: "We've been told over and over that 'boys will be boys,' this is not really serious, we should be good sports, or we should enjoy it. The truth is that women don't enjoy being subjected to unwanted sexual advances. It is humiliating and degrading. But because we've been wrongly taught to feel it is somehow our fault, we rarely even tell our friends, husbands, or family when it happens. We're afraid we'll be laughed at or blamed for it or even lose our jobs as a result."

In order to research and combat the problem, WWUI first had to define it: "Sexual harassment is any repeated and unwanted sexual comments, looks, suggestions, or physical contact that you find objectionable or offensive and that causes you discomfort on your job." Then WWUI surveyed 155 women in upstate New York and discovered that 70 percent of the sample group had experienced sexual harassment at least once. While most of the abuse was verbal, 56 percent of the cases also included physical harassment.

Teachers, factory workers, professionals, executives, waitresses, clerical workers, and domestics all reported incidents of sexual intimidation. One woman couldn't get into law school because an employer she had rebuffed refused to give her a recommendation. Other speakers reported leaving high-paid jobs to escape "pinchers" and "chasers."

All over the country women are beginning to break the silence and share their "war stories"—and some have exploded into the headlines. A Washington secretary told *The New York Times* that a Texas congressman had pressured her to have sexual relations with him and gave her a six-thousand-dollar-a-year raise without allowing her "any definite responsibility," despite the fact that she was exceptionally well versed in nuclear matters. An actress starring in a Boston play charged that she was fired for resisting the advances of the male lead. Last September a county district attorney in upstate New York was indicted for attempted sexual abuse of his twenty-year-old secretary. And a twenty-one-year-old woman became a *cause célèbre* in Washington, D.C., when she claimed that she was fired from her job at a VA hospital for refusing to "act right" for her boss.

Hundreds of cases that haven't made the newspapers *have* made waves at employment counseling services, human rights commissions, and in the courtrooms.

Helen Williams and Cathy Tombow of Cleveland Women Working have counseled several victims of sexual harassment.

"We usually get the less extreme complaints," says Williams. "Most women are still too ashamed to report anything more than touching, spoken vulgarities, or the forced kiss. Each woman assumes it's happening only to her—that she did something to cause it."

Tombow counsels women to share their experiences and resist as a unified group, but she finds a reluctance to confide in one another: Young women fear that older women will think the man's advance was provoked by the young woman, and older women don't confide because they think young women are too inexperienced to understand or help. Tombow contends that women who work alone in a one-man office are in the worst fix. "One secretary earning only four hundred dollars a month was fending off her boss single-handed," Tombow says. "No matter how often she told him she was happily married, he kept up the pressure. Since it was just the two of them in the office, there was no possibility of a women's coalition or a complaint to his superior. We advised her to quit. Fortunately her husband was earning enough to support her while she looked for another job, but a lot of women don't have that luxury."

Of course that's the crux of it. Sexual harassment is a virulent form of economic coercion practiced by men who have the power to hire or fire, promote or demote, give raises or deny them. A six-thousand-dollar sexual bribe from a congressman is the exception. Most often, small-time bosses take advantage of powerless and economically vulnerable women, who have to think twice before turning down a five-dollar-a-week raise or walking away from a regular paycheck. WWUI's survey found that low-wage women were more likely to encounter physical as well as verbal abuse. Age is no protection either. Teenagers and over fifties were afraid to resist their bosses because they felt themselves either too inexperienced, too young, or too old to get another job.

According to WWUI, victims of sexual harassment reported feeling "angry," "upset," "frightened," "guilty," "self-conscious," "trapped," "defeated," and physically ill.

These symptoms are not entirely unlike those reported by rape victims. Says an attorney for the Equal Employment Opportunity Commission (EEOC): "Sexual intimidation is like rape because women are afraid to file complaints—afraid of employer retaliation and social repercussions."

Both sexual harassment and rape are unwanted violations of a woman's sexuality, personal privacy, and human dignity. In rape a man overpowers a woman with brute strength or a weapon, and the ultimate threat is loss of life. In sexual harassment he overpowers her economically and threatens loss of livelihood. In both cases it's rare to find witnesses to the incident—and it's almost impossible for the woman to prove it happened. At best her word will be disregarded. At worst her entire moral and sexual history may be scrutinized; she'll be ridiculed, hassled, criticized, stigmatized, and/or dumped. The most expendable person is the woman who has never been anything more than a sex object in the eyes of management.

One would expect strong legal remedies to be available to victims of such an experience—and severe penalties to be imposed on harassing employers. Unfortunately, however, it's not even clear at the moment whether sexual harassment constitutes sex discrimination under Title VII of the Civil Rights Act. Five cases have reached the federal courts, and in three the judges have ruled that making sexual demands a condition of employment opportunity reflects the employer's "personal proclivity," not sex discrimination.

The U.S. Justice Department agrees. It has argued that since sexual harassment can be directed at women *or* men (homosexual bosses have "personal proclivities," too), it isn't sex discrimination. What's more, the Justice Department holds that because an employer acts out his sexual attraction toward one employee doesn't mean he is biased against all women (or men) as a gender class.

The EEOC disagrees. "Even if an employer doesn't harass all women," says a commission lawyer, "if he harasses one woman sexually, he does so *because* she is a woman. Likewise a homosexual boss who intimidates a male employee does so because of the male's gender. In both cases it's the employer's subjective bias and the employee's sex that counts—so the EEOC considers sexual harassment to be sex-based discrimination covered by Title VII. A woman can't always prove—and shouldn't have to—that other females were being similarly bullied. If it's happening to *her,* it's gender-based discrimination against *her.*"

The two courts that have found in favor of women complainants have done so on different reasoning from that of the EEOC. In *Garber v. Saxon Business Products,* the Fourth Circuit Court ruled that an employer who has a policy, or who acquiesces in a practice, of compelling female employees to submit to the sexual advances of male supervisors is in violation of Title VII. *Williams v. Saxbe,* a case involving a Department of Justice employee, was decided similarly. The court awarded Diane Williams sixteen thousand dollars back pay and required that all negative evaluations be expunged from her employment record. Though both *Garber* and *Williams* were favorable decisions (involving one private and one public employer), both cases were decided on grounds that suggest sexual harassment would *not* have been considered discrimination if both men and women were harassed.

This same reasoning seems to guide the decisions of the New York State Human Rights Commission. "Sex discrimination exists when the terms, conditions, and privileges of employment are different for a woman than for her male counterpart," explains Jeannine Dowling, director of public information for the commission. "We received sixty complaints of sexual harassment during the first nine months of 1976—ranging from sexist remarks about a woman's body, clothes, or contraceptive method to unnecessary touching, demanding sexual favors as a condition of employment, and firing a woman for resisting. I'd say those sixty are just the tip of a huge iceberg.''

One of the commission's conciliation agreements involved a hospital billing clerk whose superior had called her names, ''petted, rubbed, and bumped me'' and said she could make more money if she went out and peddled herself. The clerk was awarded three hundred dollars compensatory damages, the promise by the hospital of an improved work atmosphere, no retaliation for filing her complaint, and the guarantee of a letter of reference if and when she leaves her job.

In Wisconsin last March, State Assemblyman James Rutkowski introduced legislation that would subject a harassing employer to the Wisconsin Fair Employment Practices Law so that an employee can sue for back pay, damages, reinstatement, and an end to the objectionable behavior. Rutkowski's bill would also recognize sexual harassment as a valid reason for a woman to quit her job and qualify for unemployment insurance benefits—a crucial protection.

While several states are following this constructive route, many others refuse women's claims. In New York Carmita Wood, an administrative assistant at a university and sole support of two children, quit her job because her supervisor's frequent obscene gestures and lascivious looks had brought on tension cramps in her neck. Wood was denied unemployment benefits even though two witnesses testified in her behalf. The hearing officer didn't doubt that the harassment had occurred; he simply dismissed its importance. He said she left her job without ''good reason.''

Once again men's lechery is considered ''normal'' and women's complaints are trivialized. One unemployment compensation official put it bluntly: ''If we accepted sexual harassment as good reason for quitting, every woman would claim it.''

Maybe every woman should. Sexual harassment must be socially and legally condemned before women can resist it without fear of economic penalty.

You can try humor, charm, resistance, and threats. You can remind him that you have a husband or he has a wife; you can demand he respect you as a human being and as a worker; you can join other women who have been harassed; you can confront him or report him to his superiors. But when your voice is ignored and the "old-boy network" closes ranks against you, personal solutions count for nothing. You'll either surrender, as millions of women have before you, or you'll wage a public battle, take your case to your state's human rights commission, to the EEOC, or into the courts. While you're in combat, your opponents' heavy breathing, mauling, and X-rated reprisals may force you to quit to save your health. That's not surrender, as long as you apply for unemployment insurance and pursue your claim for all you're worth. Tell them we're not laughing anymore.

Date Rape:
The Story of an Epidemic

Ellen Sweet

While an editor on the *Ms.* staff in the 1980s, Ellen Sweet kept tabs on the data then emerging from the magazine's controversial study of acquaintance rape on college campuses. This article, which first appeared in *Ms.* in 1985, takes stock of the study's preliminary results. Ellen Sweet is the executive editor at the magazine *New Choices for Retirement Living* and served as the consulting editor on Robin Warshaw's 1988 book about the *Ms.* study *I Never Called It Rape.*

It was the beginning of spring break when I was a junior. I was in good spirits and had been out to dinner with an old friend. We returned to his college (dorm). There were some seniors on the ground floor, drinking beer, playing bridge. I'm an avid player, so we joined them, joked around a lot. One of them, John, wasn't playing, but he was interested in the game. I found him attractive. We talked, and it turned out we had a mutual friend, shared experiences. It was getting late, and my friend had gone up to bed, so John offered to see me safely home. We took our time, sat outside talking for a while. Then he said we could get inside one of the most beautiful campus buildings, which was usually locked at night. I went with him. Once we were inside, he kissed me. I didn't resist, I was excited. He kissed me again. But when he tried for more, I said no. He just grew completely silent. I couldn't get him to talk to me anymore. He pinned me down and ripped off my pants. *I couldn't believe it was happening to me.*

* * *

Let's call this Yale graduate Judy. Her experience and her disbelief, as she describes them, are not unique. Gretchen, another student victim of date rape (or acquaintance rape, as it is also called), had known for five years the man who invited her to an isolated vacation cabin and then raped her. "I considered him my best friend," she says on a Stanford University videotape used in discussions of the problem. "I couldn't believe it. *I couldn't believe it was actually happening to me.*"

Such denial, the inability to believe that someone they know could have raped them, is a common reaction of victims of date rape, say psychologists and counselors who have researched the topic and treated these women. In fact so much silence surrounds this kind of crime that many women are not even aware that they have been raped. In one study Mary P. Koss, a psychology professor at Kent State University, Ohio, asked female students if they had had sexual intercourse against their will through use of or threat of force (the minimal legal definition of rape). Of those who answered yes, only 57 percent went on to identify their experience as rape. Koss also identified the other group (43 percent) as those who hadn't even acknowledged the rape to themselves.

"I can't believe it's happening on our campus" is usually the initial response to reports such as Koss's. She also found that one in eight women students had been raped, and another one in four were victims of attempted rape. Since only 4 percent of all those reported the attack, Koss concluded that "at least ten times more rapes occur among college students than are reflected in official crime statistics." (Rape is recognized to be the most underreported of all crimes, and date rape is among the least reported, least believed, and most difficult to prosecute, second only to spouse rape.)

Working independently of Koss, researchers at Auburn University, Alabama, and more recently, University of South Dakota and St. Cloud State University, Minnesota, all have found that 1 in 5 women students were raped by men they knew.

Koss also found a core group of highly sexually aggressive men (4.3 percent) who use physical force to compel women to have intercourse but who are unlikely to see their act as rape. These "hidden rapists" have "oversubscribed" to traditional male roles, she says. They believe that aggression is normal and that women don't really mean it when they say no to sexual advances. Such men answer "True" to statements like "most women are sly and manipulating when they want to attract a man," "a woman will only respect a man who will lay down the law to her," and "a man's got to show the woman who's boss right from the start, or he'll end up hen-pecked."

In Koss's current study, one respondent who answered yes to a question about obtaining intercourse through physical force, wrote in the comment, "I didn't rape the chick, she was enjoying it and responding," and later, "I feel that sex is a very pleasant way to relieve stress. Especially when there are no strings attached."

"He acted like he had a right, like he *didn't believe me,*" says a coed from Auburn University on a videotaped dramatization of date-rape experiences. And several weeks later, when she confronts him, saying he forced her, he says no, she wanted it. "You raped me," she finally tells him. And the picture freezes on his look of incredulity.

Barry Burkhart, a professor of psychology at Auburn, who has also studied sexual aggression among college men, found that 10 percent had used physical force to have intercourse with a woman against her will, and a large majority admitted to various other kinds of aggression. "These are ordinary males operating in an ordinary social context," he says. "So what we conclude is that there's something wrong with that social context."

The something wrong is that our culture fosters a "rape-supportive belief system," according to social psychologist Martha Burt. She thinks that "there's a large category of 'real' rapes, and a much smaller category of what our culture is willing to call a 'real' rape. The question is, how does the culture manage to write off all those other rapes?" The way it's done, says Burt, currently director of the Social Services Research Center at the Urban Institute in Washington, D.C., is by believing in a series of myths about rape, including:

It didn't really happen (the woman was lying).

Women like rape (so there's no such thing as rape).

Yes, it happened, but no harm was done (she wasn't a virgin; she wasn't white).

Women provoke it (men can't control themselves).

Women deserve it anyway.

It's easy to write off date rapes with such myths, coupled with what Burt calls our culture's "adversarial sexual beliefs": the gamesmanship theory that everybody is out for what they can get and that all sexual relationships are basically exploitative and predatory. In fact most victims of date rape initially blame themselves for what happened, and almost none reports it to campus authorities. And most academic institutions prefer to keep it that way, judging from the lack of surveys on date rape—all of which makes one wonder if they don't actually blame the victim too.

As long as such attacks continue to be a "hidden" campus phenomenon, unreported and unacknowledged by many college administrators, law enforcement personnel, and students, the problem will persist. Of course the term has become much better known in the three years since *Ms.* reported on the prevalence of experiences such as Judy's and Gretchen's (see "Date Rape: A Campus Epidemic?" September 1982). It has been the subject of talk shows such as the *Donahue* show and TV dramas *(Cagney and Lacey)*. But for most people it remains a contradiction in terms. "Everybody has a stake in denying that it's happening so often," says Martha Burt. "For women, it's self-protective . . . if only bad girls get raped, then I'm personally safe. For men, it's the denial that 'nice' people like them do it."

The fault has not entirely been that of the institutions. "Ten years ago we were telling women to look over your shoulder when you go out at night and lock your doors," says Py Bateman, director of a nationally known rape education program in Seattle, Alternatives to Fear. The prevailing myth was that most rapes were committed by strangers in dark alleys.

"If you have to think that 60 to 80 percent of rape is by people you know—that's hard to deal with,'' says Sylvia Callaway, who directed the Austin, Texas, Rape Crisis Center for more than eight years before leaving last July. ''No rape center in a university community would be surprised that the university is not willing to deal with the problem.''

Statistics alone will not solve the problem of date rape, but they could help bring it out into the open. Which is why *Ms.* undertook the first nationwide survey on college campuses. The *Ms.* Magazine Campus Project on Sexual Assault, directed by Mary P. Koss at Kent State and funded by the National Center for the Prevention and Control of Rape, reached more than seven thousand students at a nationally representative sample of thirty-five schools, to find out how often, under what circumstances, and with what aftereffects a wide range of sexual assaults, including date rape, took place.

Preliminary results are now ready, and the information is no surprise. Participating schools were promised anonymity, but each will receive the results applying to its student body. Our hope is that the reaction of ''we can't believe it's happening on our campus'' will be followed by ''what can we do about it—now.''

Just how entrenched is denial of this problem today? One gauge might be the difficulty our own researchers had in persuading schools to let us on campus. For every college that approved our study, two others rejected it. Their reasons (in writing and in telephone conversations) were themselves instructive: ''We don't want to get involved,'' ''limited foreseeable benefit,'' ''too volatile a topic,'' ''have not had any problems in this area,'' ''worried about publicity,'' ''can't allow surveys in classroom,'' ''just can't invest the time now,'' ''would be overintrusive,'' ''don't want to be left holding the bag if something goes wrong.''

Several schools rejected the study on the basis that filling out the questionnaire might upset some students, and that we were not providing adequate follow-up counseling. (Researchers stayed on campus for at least a day after the distribution of the questionnaire, gave students listings of counselors or rape-crisis centers to consult if anything upset them, and offered to meet with school personnel to brief them.) But isn't it less upsetting for a student to recognize and admit that she has been the victim of an acquaintance rape than to have buried the trauma of that rape deep inside herself?

"It's a catch-22 situation. You want a survey to publicize a problem that has tremendous psychological implications. And the school says, 'Don't do it, because it will get people psychologically upset,' " admits John Jung, who heads the Human Subjects Review Committee at California State University–Long Beach (a school that declined our study).

One wonders just who are the "people" who will get most psychologically upset: the students, or their parents who pay for their educations, or the administrators who are concerned about the school's image. "There may have been an episode here," said John Hose, executive assistant to the president of Brandeis University, "but there is no *cause célèbre* surrounding the issue. In such cases the reaction of Student Affairs is to encourage the student to be in touch with her parents and to take legal action."

"Student Affairs" at Brandeis is headed by Rodger Crafts, who moved to this post about a year ago from the University of Rhode Island. "I don't think we have a significant problem here because we have a sophisticated and intelligent group of students," said Dean Crafts. As for the University of Rhode Island, more students there are "first-generation college attenders," as he put it, and therefore have "less respect" for other people. Vandalism and physical harm are more likely to occur with "lower educational levels." Respect for other people goes along with "intelligence level."

Back at the University of Rhode Island the counseling center is sponsoring a twelve-week support and therapy group this fall for male students who are coercive and abusive in their relationships with women. Even though Nancy Carlson, director of Counseling and Career Services, is enthusiastic about such programs and workshops, she notes, "The awareness about date rape has been a long time coming."

Another school where administrators were the last to confront the challenge to their school's self-image is Yale. Last year two student publications reported instances of date rape on campus that surprised students, faculty, and administration. "There are no full statistics available on rape between students at Yale anywhere. . . . There is no mention of rape in the 1983–1984 Undergraduate Regulations. There is no procedure for a victim to file a formal complaint of rape with the university. But there is rape between students at Yale,'' wrote Sarah Oates in the *Yale Daily News*. Partly in response to such charges, current Yale undergraduate regulations now list ''sexual harassment'' under ''offenses that are subject to disciplinary action''—but still no mention of rape.

Yale students brave enough to bring a charge of sexual harassment may go before the Yale College Executive Committee, a specially convened group of faculty, administrators, and students that can impose a series of penalties, graduated in severity, culminating in expulsion. All its hearings and decisions are kept secret (but can in theory be subpoenaed in a court of law). But Michael McBride, current chair of the committee, told me that cases of date rape have come up during the past year, leading in one instance to a student being asked to ''resign'' from the university, and in another the conclusion that there was not ''sufficient evidence.'' (In Judy's case, described at the beginning of this article, the senior she charged was penalized by being denied the privilege of graduating with his class. But she claims that after he demanded that the case be reconsidered, he was fully exonerated.) Said McBride, ''What surprised me the most was how complicated these cases are. It's only one person's word against another's. It's amazing how different their perceptions can be.''

Judy chose to take her case before the Executive Committee rather than report it to the local police, because she felt she would have complete confidentiality and quick action. Actually there were many delays. And then, because the man she accused hired a lawyer, she was forced to hire one too. As a result the meeting felt very much like a jury trial to her, complete with cross-examinations that challenged her truthfulness and raised excruciatingly embarrassing questions.

Judy's lawyer felt that such painful questions were necessary. But it seems as if the lesson feminists in the sixties and seventies worked so hard and successfully to make understood—not to blame the victim for stranger rape—is one that will have to be learned all over again in the case of acquaintance rape. Only this time the woman who reports the rape suffers a triple victimization. Not only is she attacked and then not believed, but she carries the added burden of losing faith in her own judgment and trust in other people.

In a recently published study of jurors in rape trials, University of Illinois sociologist Barbara Reskin found that jurors were less likely to convict a man if the victim knew him. "Consent is the preferred rape defense and gets the highest acquittal rates," Reskin observes. "In a date rape situation I would think the jury would assume that the woman had already accepted his invitation in a romantic sense. It would be a matter of how *much* did she consent to."

Personal characteristics also influence jurors, Reskin says. Those she studied couldn't imagine that certain men would commit a rape: if they were attractive, had access to sexual partners such as a girlfriend or a wife. More often than not, they'd say, "But he doesn't look like a rapist." Reskin imagines that this pattern would be "magnified in date rape, because these are men who could get a date, they're not complete losers."

It may turn out that solutions to the problem will turn up at places with a less genteel image to protect. Jan Strout, director of Montana State, Women's Resource Center, wonders if schools such as hers, which recognize that they are dealing with a more conservative student body and a "macho cowboy image," aren't more willing to take the first step toward acknowledging the problem. A group called Students Against Sexual Assault was formed there two and a half years ago after several students who were raped or resisted an attempted rape "went public." With men and women sharing leadership, this group is cosponsored by the Women's Resource Center and the student government.

Admitting to the problem isn't easy even when data are available, as doctoral student Genny Sandberg found at the University of South Dakota. Last spring she announced the results of a dating survey she coauthored with psychologists Tom Jackson and Patricia Petretic-Jackson. The most shocking statistic: 20 percent of the students (most from rural backgrounds and living in a rural campus setting) had been raped in a dating situation. The state board of regents couldn't believe it. "I just think that that's absolutely ridiculous," former regent Michael Rost said, according to the Brookings *Daily Register,* "I can't believe we would allow that to occur. If it is true, it's a very serious problem." Regent William Srstka agreed, "If this is true, it's absolutely intolerable."

Following testimony by one of the researchers, the board changed its tune. Members are now discussing how to begin a statewide education and prevention program.

An inspiring example of how an administration can be led to new levels of consciousness took place at the University of Michigan earlier this year. Spurred by an article in *Metropolitan Detroit* magazine, a group of students staged a sit-in at the office of a university vice president who had been quoted as saying that "Rape is a red-flag word. . . . [The university] wants to present an image that is receptive and palatable to the potential student cohort," and also that "Rape is an issue like Alzheimer's disease or mental retardation, [which] impacts on a small but sizable part of the population. . . . Perhaps it has to become a crisis that is commonly shared in order to get things done."

The students who spent the entire day in Vice President Henry Johnson's office claimed that rape had already become a crisis on their campus. They presented a list of twelve demands, ranging from a rape-crisis center on campus to better lighting and installation of outdoor emergency phones. By the end of the day Johnson had started to change his mind. Although he insisted that he had been misquoted and quoted out of context in the press, he told me that "I did not realize [before that] acquaintance rape was so much of a problem, that it was the most prevalent type of rape. There is a heightened awareness now on this campus. Whether we as a faculty and administration are as sensitive as we should be is another issue —and that will take some time."

In the meantime members of the Michigan Student Assembly Women's Issues Committee (one of the groups active in organizing the protest) took their demands before the school's board of regents.

The result: a $75,000 program for rape prevention and education on campus, directly reporting to Johnson's office. "We'll now be in a position to document the problem and to be proactive," says Johnson. Jennifer Faigel, an organizer of the protest, acknowledges a change in the administration's awareness but says the students themselves, disappointed in the amount of funding promised for the program, have already formed a group (Students Organized Against Rape) to develop programs in the dorms.

In just the three years since *Ms.* first reported on date rape, several new campus organizations have sprung up, and other ongoing programs have surfaced.

But the real measure of a school's commitment to dealing with this problem is the range of services it provides, says Mary Harvey, who did a nationwide study of exemplary rape programs for the National Center for the Prevention and Control of Rape. "It should have preventive services, crisis intervention, possibilities for long-term treatment, advocacy, and women's studies programs that educate about violence. The quality of a university's services to rape victims can be measured by the degree to which these other things are in place."

Minimally, rape counselors and educators feel, students need to be exposed to information about date rape as soon as they enter college. Studies show that the group most vulnerable to acquaintance rape are college freshmen, followed by high school seniors. In Koss's original survey, for example, the average age of the victim was eighteen.

"I'd like a program where no first-year students could finish their starting week at college without being informed about the problem of acquaintance rape," says Andrea Parrot, a lecturer in human service studies at Cornell University, who is developing a program to train students and dorm resident advisers as date-rape-awareness counselors. Parrot and others admit that this would be a bare minimum. Handing out a brochure to read, even conducting a workshop on the subject during the busy orientation week and counting on students voluntarily attending, needs to be followed up with sessions in dormitories or other living units. These are the most common settings for date rapes, according to a study by Parrot and Robin Lynk.

So how do we go about changing attitudes? And how do we do it without "setting student against student?" asks Gretchen Mieszkowski, chair of the Sexual Assault Prevention Committee at the University of Houston–Clear Lake. Chiefly a commuter campus, with a majority of married women students, Clear Lake nevertheless had seventeen acquaintance rapes reported to the local crisis hot line last year. "We had always focused on traditional solutions like lighting and escort services at night," Mieszkowski says. "But changing lighting in the parking lot is easy; it's only money."

Many who have studied the problem of rape education believe it has to begin with college-age women and men talking to each other more frankly about their beliefs and expectations about sex. Py Bateman of Alternatives to Fear thinks it has to start earlier, among teenagers, by developing rudimentary dating skills at the lower end of the sexual activity scale. "We need to learn more about holding hands than about sexual intercourse."

Bateman continues: "We've got to work on both sides. Boys don't know what they want any more than girls do. The way our sexual interaction is set up is that boys are supposed to push. Their peers tell them that scoring is what counts. They're as divorced from intimacy as girls."

Gail Abarbanel of the Rape Treatment Center at Santa Monica Hospital, agrees. Her center conducts educational programs for schools in Los Angeles County. In a recent survey of more than five thousand teenagers, she found a high degree of misconception and lack of information about rape: "Most boys say yes to the question 'If a girl goes back to a guy's house when she knows no one is home, is she consenting to sex?' And most boys believe that girls don't mean no when they say it."

Women clearly need to get more convincing, and men clearly need to believe them more. But until that ideal time, Montana State's Jan Strout warns, "Because men have been socialized to hear yes when women say no, we have to scream it."

Rape and the Modern Sex War

Camille Paglia

With the opening of the millennium's last decade, Camille Paglia burst into public view with her contentious opus *Sexual Personae: Art and Decadance from Nefertiti to Emily Dickinson.* A professor of humanities at the University of the Arts in Philadelphia, Paglia's most recent book is *Vamps and Tramps,* a collection of her essays and interviews. The essay printed here first appeared in *New York Newsday* on January 27, 1991, under the headline RAPE: A BIGGER DANGER THAN FEMINISTS KNOW.

Rape is an outrage that cannot be tolerated in civilized society. Yet feminism, which has waged a crusade for rape to be taken more seriously, has put young women in danger by hiding the truth about sex from them.

In dramatizing the pervasiveness of rape, feminists have told young women that before they have sex with a man, they must give consent as explicit as a legal contract's. In this way young women have been convinced that they have been the victims of rape. On elite campuses in the Northeast and on the West Coast, they have held consciousness-raising sessions, petitioned administrations, demanded inquests. At Brown University, outraged, panicky "victims" have scrawled the names of alleged attackers on the walls of women's rest rooms. What marital rape was to the seventies, "date rape" is to the nineties.

The incidence and seriousness of rape do not require this kind of exaggeration. Real acquaintance rape is nothing new. It has been a horrible problem for women for all of recorded history. Once, fathers and brothers protected women from rape. Once, the penalty for rape was death. I come from a fierce Italian tradition where, not so long ago in the motherland, a rapist would end up knifed, castrated, and hung out to dry.

But the old clans and small rural communities have broken down. In our cities, on our campuses far from home, young women are vulnerable and defenseless. Feminism has not prepared them for this. Feminism keeps saying the sexes are the same. It keeps telling women they can do anything, go anywhere, say anything, wear anything. No, they can't. Women will always be in sexual danger.

One of my male students recently slept overnight with a friend in a passageway of the Great Pyramid in Egypt. He described the moon and sand, the ancient silence and eerie echoes. I will never experience that. I am a woman. I am not stupid enough to believe I could ever be safe there. There is a world of solitary adventure I will never have. Women have always known these somber truths. But feminism, with its pie-in-the-sky fantasies about the perfect world, keeps young women from seeing life as it is.

We must remedy social injustice whenever we can. But there are some things we cannot change. There are sexual differences that are based in biology. Academic feminism is lost in a fog of social constructionism. It believes we are totally the product of our environment. This idea was invented by Rousseau. He was wrong. Emboldened by dumb French language theory, academic feminists repeat the same hollow slogans over and over to each other. Their view of sex is naive and prudish. Leaving sex to the feminists is like letting your dog vacation at the taxidermist's.

The sexes are at war. Men must struggle for identity against the overwhelming power of their mothers. Women have menstruation to tell them they are women. Men must do or risk something to be men. Men become masculine only when other men say they are. Having sex with a woman is one way a boy becomes a man.

College men are at their hormonal peak. They have just left their mothers and are questing for their male identity. In groups they are dangerous. A woman going to a fraternity party is walking into Testosterone Flats, full of prickly cacti and blazing guns. If she goes, she should be armed with resolute alertness. She should arrive with girlfriends and leave with them. A girl who lets herself get dead drunk at a fraternity party is a fool. A girl who goes upstairs alone with a brother at a fraternity party is an idiot. Feminists call this blaming the victim. I call it common sense.

For a decade feminists have drilled their disciples to say, "Rape is a crime of violence but not of sex." This sugar-coated Shirley Temple nonsense has exposed young women to disaster. Misled by feminism, they do not expect rape from the nice boys from good homes who sit next to them in class.

Aggression and eroticism are deeply intertwined. Hunt, pursuit, and capture are biologically programmed into male sexuality. Generation after generation, men must be educated, refined, and ethically persuaded away from their tendency toward anarchy and brutishness. Society is not the enemy, as feminism ignorantly claims. Society is woman's protection against rape. Feminism, with its solemn Carry Nation repressiveness, does not see what is for men the eroticism or fun element in rape, especially the wild, infectious delirium of gang rape. Women who do not understand rape cannot defend themselves against it.

The date-rape controversy shows feminism hitting the wall of its own broken promises. The women of my sixties generation were the first respectable girls in history to swear like sailors, get drunk, stay out all night—in short, to act like men. We sought total sexual freedom and equality. But as time passed, we woke up to cold reality. The old double standard protected women. When anything goes, it's women who lose.

Today's young women don't know what they want. They see that feminism has not brought sexual happiness. The theatrics of public rage over date rape are their way of restoring the old sexual rules that were shattered by my generation. Because nothing about the sexes has really changed. The comic film *Where the Boys Are* (1960), the ultimate expression of fifties man-chasing, still speaks directly to our time. It shows smart, lively women skillfully anticipating and fending off the dozens of strategies with which horny men try to get them into bed. The agonizing date-rape subplot and climax are brilliantly done. The victim, Yvette Mimieux, makes mistake after mistake, obvious to the other girls. She allows herself to be lured away from her girlfriends and into isolation with boys whose character and intentions she misreads. *Where the Boys Are* tells the truth. It shows courtship as a dangerous game in which the signals are not verbal but subliminal.

Neither militant feminism, which is obsessed with politically correct language, nor academic feminism, which believes that knowledge and experience are "constituted by" language, can understand preverbal or nonverbal communication. Feminism, focusing on sexual politics, cannot see that sex exists in and through the body. Sexual desire and arousal cannot be fully translated into verbal terms. This is why men and women misunderstand each other.

Trying to remake the future, feminism cut itself off from sexual history. It discarded and suppressed the sexual myths of literature, art, and religion. Those myths show us the turbulence, the mysteries, and the passions of sex. In mythology we see men's sexual anxiety, their fear of woman's dominance. Much sexual violence is rooted in men's sense of psychological weakness toward women. It takes many men to deal with one woman. Woman's voracity is a persistent motif. Clara Bow, it was rumored, took on the USC football team on weekends. Marilyn Monroe, singing "Diamonds Are a Girl's Best Friend," rules a conga line of men in tuxes. Half-clad Cher, in the video for "If I Could Turn Back Time," deranges a battleship of screaming sailors and straddles a pink-lit cannon. Feminism, coveting social power, is blind to woman's cosmic sexual power.

To understand rape, you must study the past. There never was and never will be sexual harmony. Every woman must take personal responsibility for her sexuality, which is nature's red flame. She must be prudent and cautious about where she goes and with whom. When she makes a mistake, she must accept the consequences and, through self-criticism, resolve never to make that mistake again. Running to Mommy and Daddy on the campus grievance committee is unworthy of strong women. Posting lists of guilty men in the toilet is cowardly, infantile stuff.

The Italian philosophy of life espouses high-energy confrontation. A male student makes a vulgar remark about your breasts? Don't slink off to whimper and simper with the campus shrinking violets. Deal with it. On the spot. Say, "Shut up, you jerk! And crawl back to the barnyard where you belong!" In general, women who project this take-charge attitude toward life get harassed less often. I see too many dopey, immature, self-pitying women walking around like melting sticks of butter. It's the Yvette Mimieux syndrome: Make me happy. And listen to me weep when I'm not.

The date-rape debate is already smothering in propaganda churned out by the expensive northeastern colleges and universities, with their overconcentration of boring, uptight academic feminists and spoiled, affluent students. Beware of the deep manipulativeness of rich students who were neglected by their parents. They love to turn the campus into hysterical psychodramas of sexual transgression, followed by assertions of parental authority and concern. And don't look for sexual enlightenment from academe, which spews out mountains of books but never looks at life directly.

As a fan of football and rock music, I see in the simple, swaggering masculinity of the jock and in the noisy posturing of the heavy-metal guitarist certain fundamental, unchanging truths about sex. Masculinity is aggressive, unstable, combustible. It is also the most creative cultural force in history. Women must reorient themselves toward the elemental powers of sex, which can strengthen or destroy.

The only solution to date rape is female self-awareness and self-control. A woman's number-one line of defense is herself. When a real rape occurs, she should report it to the police. Complaining to college committees because the courts "take too long" is ridiculous. College administrations are not a branch of the judiciary. They are not equipped or trained for legal inquiry. Colleges must alert incoming students to the problems and dangers of adulthood. Then colleges must stand back and get out of the sex game.

Pornography Is a Civil Rights Issue

Andrea Dworkin

Andrea Dworkin is one of the feminist movement's most indefatigable antipornography activists. Together with legal scholar Catharine A. MacKinnon, she authored the model antipornography civil rights law introduced in various forms in the cities of Minneapolis, Minnesota; Indianapolis, Indiana; and Cambridge, Massachusetts, in the mid 1980s. She is the author of eleven works of fiction, nonfiction, and poetry, including *Mercy, Pornography: Men Possessing Women,* and *Letters from a War Zone.* On January 22, 1986, Andrea Dworkin testified before the Attorney General's Commission on Pornography (commonly known as the Meese Commission) at a hearing that took place in New York City. Here is her testimony.

Andrea Dworkin called as a witness on behalf of the Attorney General's Commission on Pornography, testified as follows:*

MS. DWORKIN: Thank you very much. My name is Andrea Dworkin. I am a citizen of the United States, and in this country where I live, every year millions and millions of pictures are being made of women with our legs spread. We are called beaver, we are called pussy, our genitals are tied up, they are pasted, makeup is put on

* This text is based on the Justice Department's transcript, prepared by Ace-Federal Reporters, Inc., which was compared against tape recordings and revised for accuracy by the author. The author has also made slight editorial changes for clarity. The complete text of the author's testimony appears in *Letters from a War Zone* by Andrea Dworkin, Laurence Hill Books, Brooklyn, New York, 1993.

them to make them pop out of a page at a male viewer. Millions and millions of pictures are made of us in postures of submission and sexual access so that our vaginas are exposed for penetration, our anuses are exposed for penetration, our throats are used as if they are genitals for penetration. In this country where I live as a citizen, real rapes are on film and are being sold in the marketplace. And the major motif of pornography as a form of entertainment is that women are raped and violated and humiliated until we discover that we like it and at that point we ask for more.

In this country where I live as a citizen, women are penetrated by animals and objects for public entertainment, women are urinated on and defecated on, women and girls are used interchangeably so that grown women are made up to look like five- or six-year-old children surrounded by toys, presented in mainstream pornographic publications for anal penetration. There are magazines in which adult women are presented with their pubic areas shaved so that they resemble children.

In this country where I live, there is a trafficking in pornography that exploits mentally and physically disabled women, women who are maimed; there is amputee pornography, a trade in women who have been maimed in that way, as if that is a sexual fetish for men. In this country where I live, there is a trade in racism as a form of sexual pleasure, so that the plantation is presented as a form of sexual gratification for the black woman slave, who asks please to be abused, please to be raped, please to be hurt. Black skin is presented as if it is a female genital, and all the violence and the abuse and the humiliation that is in general directed against female genitals is directed against the black skin of women in pornography.

Asian women in this country where I live are tied from trees and hung from ceilings and hung from doorways as a form of public entertainment. There is a concentration-camp pornography in this country where I live, where the concentration camp and the atrocities that occurred there are presented as existing for the sexual pleasure of the victim, of the woman, who orgasms to the real abuses that occurred, not very long ago in history.

In the country where I live as a citizen, there is a pornography of the humiliation of women where every single way of humiliating a human being is taken to be a form of sexual pleasure for the viewer and for the victim; where women are covered in filth, including feces, including mud, including paint, including blood, including semen; where women are tortured for the sexual pleasure of those who watch and those who do the torture, where women are murdered for the sexual pleasure of murdering women, and this material exists because it is fun, because it is entertainment, because it is a form of pleasure, and there are those who say it is a form of freedom.

Certainly it is freedom for those who do it. Certainly it is freedom for those who use it as entertainment, but we are also asked to believe that it is freedom for those to whom it is done.

Then this entertainment is taken, and it is used on other women, women who aren't in the pornography, to force those women into prostitution, to make them imitate the acts in the pornography. The women in the pornography, 65 to 70 percent of them, we believe, are victims of incest or child sexual abuse. They are poor women; they are not women who have opportunities in this society. They are frequently runaways who are picked up by pimps and exploited. They are frequently raped, the rapes are filmed, they are kept in prostitution by blackmail. The pornography is used on prostitutes by johns who are expected to replicate the sexual acts in the pornography, no matter how damaging it is.

Pornography is used in rape—to plan it, to execute it, to choreograph it, to engender the excitement to commit the act. Pornography is used in gang rape against women. We see an increase since the release of *Deep Throat* in throat rape—where women show up in emergency rooms because men believe they can penetrate, deep-thrust, to the bottom of a woman's throat. We see increasing use of all elements of pornography in battery, which is the most commonly committed violent crime in this country, including the rape of women by animals, including maiming, including heavy bondage, including outright torture.

We have seen in the last eight years an increase in the use of cameras in rapes. And those rapes are filmed and then they are put on the marketplace and they are protected speech—they are real rapes.

We see a use of pornography in the harassment of women on jobs, especially in nontraditional jobs, in the harassment of women in education, to create terror and compliance in the home, which as you know is the most dangerous place for women in this society, where more violence is committed against women than anywhere else. We see pornography used to create harassment of women and children in neighborhoods that are saturated with pornography, where people come from other parts of the city and then prey on the populations of people who live in those neighborhoods, and that increases physical attack and verbal assault.

We see pornography having introduced a profit motive into rape. We see that filmed rapes are protected speech. We see the centrality of pornography in serial murders. There *are* snuff films. We see boys imitating pornography.

We see the average age of rapists going down. We are beginning to see gang rapes in elementary schools committed by elementary-school-age boys imitating pornography.

We see sexual assault after death where frequently the pornography is the motive for the murder because the man believes that he will get a particular kind of sexual pleasure having sex with a woman after she is dead.

We see a major trade in women, we see the torture of women as a form of entertainment, and we see women also suffering the injury of objectification—that is to say we are dehumanized. We are treated as if we are subhuman, and that is a precondition for violence against us.

I live in a country where if you film any act of humiliation or torture, and if the victim is a woman, the film is both entertainment and it is protected speech. Now, that tells me something about what it means to be a woman citizen in this country, and the meaning of being second class.

When your rape is entertainment, your worthlessness is absolute. You have reached the nadir of social worthlessness. The civil impact of pornography on women is staggering. It keeps us socially silent, it keeps us socially compliant, it keeps us afraid in neighborhoods; and it creates a vast hopelessness for women, a vast despair. One lives inside a nightmare of sexual abuse that is both actual and potential, and you have the great joy of knowing that your nightmare is someone else's freedom and someone else's fun.

Now, a great deal has happened in this country to legitimize pornography in the last ten to fifteen years. There are people who are responsible for the fact that pornography is now a legitimate form of public entertainment.

Number one, the lobby of lawyers who work for the pornographers; the fact that the pornographers pay lawyers big bucks to fight for them, not just in the courts but in public, in the public dialogue; the fact that lawyers interpret constitutional principles in light of the profit interest of the pornographers.

Number two, the collusion of the American Civil Liberties Union with the pornographers, which includes taking money from them. It includes using buildings that pornographers own and not paying rent; it includes using pornography in benefits to raise money. It includes not only defending them in court but also doing publicity for them, including organizing events for them, as the Hugh Hefner First Amendment Awards is organized by ACLU people for *Playboy*. It includes publishing in their magazines. It includes deriving great pride and economic benefit from working privately for the pornographers, while publicly pretending to be a disinterested advocate of civil liberties and free speech.

I want you to contrast the behavior of the ACLU in relation to the pornographers with their activities in relation to the Klan and the Nazis. The ACLU pretends to understand that they are all equally pernicious. But do ACLU people publish in the Klan newsletter? No. Do they go to Nazi social events? No. Do they go to cocktail parties at Nazi headquarters? No, they don't, at least not yet.

Finally, they have colluded in this sense, that they have convinced many of us that the standard for speech is what I would call a repulsion standard. That is to say we find the most repulsive person in the society and we defend him. I say we find the most powerless people in this society, and we defend *them*. That's the way we increase rights of speech in this society.

A third group that colludes to legitimize pornography are publishers and the so-called legitimate media. They pretend to believe that under this system of law there is a First Amendment that is indivisible and absolute, which it has never been.

As you know, the First Amendment protects speech that has already been expressed from state interference. That means it protects those who own media. There is no affirmative responsibility to open communications to those who are powerless in the society at large.

As a result, the owners of media, the newspapers, the TV networks, are comfortable with having women's bodies defined as the speech of pimps, because they are protecting their rights to profit as owners, and they think that that is what the First Amendment is for.

I am ashamed to say that people in my profession, writers, have also colluded with the pornographers. We provide their so-called socially redeeming value, and they wrap the tortured bodies of women in the work that we do.

Fourth, politicians have colluded with the pornographers in municipalities all over this country. They do it in these ways:

Zoning laws do not keep pornography out of cities. They are an official legal permission to traffic in pornography. And as a result politicians are able to denounce pornography moralistically while protecting it through zoning laws.

Zoning laws impose pornography on poor neighborhoods, on working-class neighborhoods, on neighborhoods where people of color live, and all of those people have to deal with the increase in crime, the terrible harassment, the degradation of the quality of life in their neighborhoods, and the politicians get to protect the property values of the rich. There is an equal protection issue here: why the state makes some people pay so other people can profit.

But that issue has never been raised. We have never been able to sue a city under the equal-protection theory, because lawyers are on the other side. Lawyers belong primarily to pornographers, and the people who live in these neighborhoods that are saturated with pornography are powerless people. They don't even have power in their own municipalities.

In addition, what pornographers do in municipalities is that they buy land that is targeted for development by cities. They hold that land hostage. They develop political power through negotiating around that land. They make huge profits, and they get influence in local city governments.

Five, not finally but next to the last, a great colluder with the pornographers was the last presidential Commission on Obscenity and Pornography. They were very effective in legitimizing pornography in this country. They appeared to be looking for a proverbial ax murderer who would watch pornography and within twenty-four or forty-eight hours go out and kill someone in a horrible and clear way. The country is saturated with pornography, and saturated with violence against women, and saturated with the interfacing of the two. And the commission didn't find it.

None of the scientific research that they relied on to come to their conclusions is worth anything today. It's all invalid. I ask you to take seriously the fact that society does not exist in a laboratory, that we are talking about real things that happen to real people, and that's what we are asking you to take some responsibility for.

Finally the ultimate colluders in the legitimizing of pornography of course are the consumers. In 1979 we had a four-billion-dollar-a-year industry in this country. By 1985 it was an eight-billion-dollar-a-year industry. Those consumers include men in all walks of life: lawyers, politicians, writers, professors, owners of media, police, doctors, maybe even commissioners on presidential commissions. No one really knows, do they?

And no matter where we look, we can't find the consumers. But what we learn is the meaning of first-class citizenship, and the meaning of first-class citizenship is that you can use your authority as men and as professionals to protect pornography, both by developing arguments to protect it and by using real social and economic power to protect it.

And as a result of all of this, the harm to women remains invisible; even though we have the bodies, the harm to women remains invisible. Underlying the invisibility of this harm is an assumption that what is done to women is natural, that even if a woman is forced to do something, somehow it falls within the sphere of her natural responsibilities as a woman. When the same things are done to boys, those things are perceived as an outrage. They are called unnatural.

But if you force a woman to do something that she was born to do, then the violence to her is not perceived as a real violation of her.

In addition, the harm of pornography to women is invisible because most sexual abuse still occurs in private, even though we have this photographic documentation of it, called the pornography industry.

Women are extremely isolated, women don't have credibility, women are not believed by people who make social policy.

In addition the harm of pornography remains invisible because women have been historically excluded from the protections of the Constitution; and as a result the violations of our human rights, when they don't occur the same way violations to men occur, have not been recognized or taken seriously, and we do not have remedies for them under law.

In addition pornography is invisible in its harm to women because women are poorer than men, and many of the women exploited in pornography are very poor, many of them are illiterate, and also because there is a great deal of female compliance with brutality, and the compliance is based on fear, it's based on powerlessness, and it is based on a reaction to the very real violence of the pornographers.

Finally, the harm is invisible because of the smile, because women are made to smile, women aren't just made to do the sex acts. We are made to smile while we do them.

So you will find in pornography women penetrating themselves with swords or daggers, and you will see the smile. You will see things that cannot be done to a human being and that are done to men only in political circumstances of torture, and you will see a woman forced to smile.

And this smile will be believed, and the injury to her as a human being, to her body and to her heart and to her soul, will not be believed.

Now, we have been told that we have an argument here about speech, not about women being hurt. And yet the emblem of that argument is a woman bound and gagged, and we are supposed to believe that that is speech. Who is that speech for? We have women being tortured and we are told that that is somebody's speech? Whose speech is it? It's the speech of a pimp, it is not the speech of a woman. The only words we hear in pornography from women are that women want to be hurt, ask to be hurt, like to be raped, get sexual pleasure from sexual violence; and even when a woman is covered in filth, we are supposed to believe that her speech is that she likes it and she wants more of it.

The reality for women in this society is that pornography creates silence for women. The pornographers silence women. Our bodies are their language. Their speech is made out of our exploitation, our subservience, our injury and our pain, and they can't say anything without hurting us, and when you protect them, you protect only their right to exploit and hurt us.

Pornography is a civil rights issue for women because pornography sexualizes inequality, because it turns women into subhuman creatures.

Pornography is a civil rights issue for women because it is the systematic exploitation of a group of people because of a condition of birth. Pornography creates bigotry and hostility and aggression toward all women, targets all women, without exception.

Pornography is the suppression of us through sexual exploitation and abuse, so that we have no real means to achieve civil equality; and the issue here is simple, it is not complex. People are being hurt, and you can help them or you can help those who are hurting them. We need civil rights legislation, legislation that recognizes pornography as a violation of the civil rights of women.

We need it because civil rights legislation recognizes the fact that the harm here is to human beings. We need that recognition. We need civil rights legislation because it puts the power to act in the hands of the people who have been forced into pornographized powerlessness, and that's a special kind of powerlessness, that's a powerlessness that is supposed to be a form of sexual pleasure.

We need civil rights legislation because only those to whom it has happened know what has happened. They are the people who are the experts. They have the knowledge. They know what has happened, how it's happened; only they can really articulate, from beginning to end, the reality of pornography as a human rights injury. We need civil rights legislation because it gives us something back after what the pornographers have taken from us.

The motivation to fight back keeps people alive. People need it for their dignity, for their ability to continue to exist as citizens in a country that needs their creativity and needs their presence and needs the existence that has been taken from them by the pornographers. We need civil rights legislation because, as social policy, it says to a population of people that they have human worth, they have human worth, that this society recognizes that they have human worth.

We need it because it's the only legislative remedy thus far that is drawn narrowly enough to confront the human rights issues for people who are being exploited and discriminated against, without becoming an instrument of police power to suppress real expression.

We need the civil rights legislation because the process of civil discovery is a very important one, and it will give us a great deal of information for potential criminal prosecutions, against organized crime, against pornographers, and I ask you to look at the example of the Southern Poverty Law Center and their Klanwatch Project, which has used civil suits to get criminal indictments against the Klan.

Finally, we need civil rights legislation because the only really dirty word in this society is the word *women,* and a civil rights approach says that this society repudiates the brutalization of women.

We are against obscenity laws. We don't want them. I want you to understand why, whether you end up agreeing or not.

Number one, the pornographers use obscenity laws as part of

their formula for making pornography. All they need to do is to provide some literary, artistic, political, or scientific value and they can hang women from the rafters. As long as they manage to meet that formula, it doesn't matter what they do to women.

And in the old days, when obscenity laws were still being enforced, in many places—for instance the most sadomasochistic pornography—the genitals were always covered because if the genitals were always covered, that wouldn't kick off a police prosecution.

Number two, the use of the prurient-interest standard—however that standard is construed in this new era, when the Supreme Court has taken two synonyms, *lasciviousness* and *lust,* and said that they mean different things, which is mind-boggling in and of itself. Whatever prurient interest is construed to mean, the reaction of jurors to material—whether they are supposed to be aroused or whether they are not allowed to be aroused, whatever the instructions of the court—has nothing to do with the objective reality of what is happening to women in pornography.

The third reason that obscenity laws cannot work for us is: what do community standards mean in a society when violence against women is pandemic, when according to the FBI a woman is battered every eighteen seconds and it's the most commonly committed violent crime in the country? What would community standards have meant in the segregated South? What would community standards have meant as we approached the atrocity of Nazi Germany? What are community standards in a society where women are persecuted for being women and pornography is a form of political persecution?

Obscenity laws are also woman-hating in their construction. Their basic presumption is that it's women's bodies that are dirty. The standards of obscenity law don't acknowledge the reality of the technology. They were drawn up in a society where obscenity was construed to be essentially writing and drawing; and now what we have is mass production in a way that real people are being hurt, and the consumption of real people by a real technology, and obscenity laws are not adequate to that reality.

Finally, obscenity laws, at the discretion of police and prosecutors, will keep obscenity out of the public view, but it remains available to men in private. It remains available to individual men, it remains available to all-male groups; and whenever it is used, it still creates bigotry, hostility, and aggression toward all women. It's still used in sexual abuse as part of sexual abuse. It's still made through coercion, through blackmail, and through exploitation.

I am going to ask you to do several things. The first thing I am going to ask you to do is listen to women who want to talk to you about what has happened to them. Please listen to them. They know, they know how this works. You are asking people to speculate; they know, it has happened to them.

I am going to ask you to make these recommendations. The first recommendation I would like you to make is to have the Justice Department instruct law-enforcement agencies to keep records of the use of pornography in violent crimes, especially in rape and battery, in incest and child abuse, in murder, including sexual assault after death, to take note of those murders that are committed for sexual reasons. They should keep track, for instance, of suicides of teenage boys, and the place of pornography in those suicides. They should keep track of both the use of pornography before and during the commission of a violent crime and the presence of pornography at a violent crime.

I want to say that a lot of the information that we have about this, what we are calling a correlation, doesn't come from law-enforcement officials; it comes from the testimony of sex offenders. That's how we know that pornography is meaningful in the commission of sexual offenses. Have the FBI report that information in the Uniform Crime Reports, so that we begin to get some real standard here.

Number two, get pornography out of all prisons. It's like sending dynamite to terrorists. Those people have committed violent crimes against women. They consume pornography. They come back out on the street. The recidivism rate is unbelievable, not to mention that prison is a rape-saturated society. What about the rights of those men who are being raped in prisons, and the relationship of pornography to the rapes of them?

No one should be sentenced to a life of hell being raped in a prison. You can do something about it by getting the pornography out of prisons.

Number three, enforce laws against pimping and pandering against pornographers. Pandering is paying for sex to make pornography of it. A panderer is any person who procures another person for the purposes of prostitution. This law has been enforced against pornographers in California. Prosecute the makers of pornography under pimping and pandering laws.

Number four, make it a Justice Department priority to enforce RICO [the Racketeer Influenced and Corrupt Organizations Act] against the pornography industry. Racketeering activity means, as you know, any act or even a threat involving murder, kidnapping, extortion, any trafficking in coerced women—which for reasons that are incomprehensible to me is still called white slaving, although the women are Asian, the women are black, all kinds of women are still being trafficked in in this way. This is how pornographers do their business, both in relation to women and in relation to distributing their product.

RICO, if it were enforced against the industry, could do a great deal toward breaking the industry up.

Number five, please recommend that federal civil rights legislation recognizing pornography as a virulent and vicious form of sex discrimination be passed, that it be a civil law. It can be a separate act or it can be amended as a separate title under the 1964 Civil Rights Act. We want the equal protection principle of the Fourteenth Amendment to apply to women. This is the way to do it. We want a definition of pornography that is based on the reality of pornography, which is that it is the act of sexual subordination of women. The causes of action need to include trafficking, coercion, forcing pornography on a person, and assault or physical injury due to a specific piece of pornography.

I also want to ask you to consider creating a criminal conspiracy provision under the civil rights law, such that conspiring to deprive a person of their civil rights by coercing them into pornography is a crime, and that conspiring to traffic in pornography is conspiring to deprive women of our civil rights.

Finally, I would like to ask you to think about pornography in the context of international law. We have claims to make. Women have claims to make under international law. Pornographers violate the rights of women under internationally recognized principles of law. The Universal Declaration of Human Rights says that everyone has the right to life, liberty, and security of person, that no one shall be subjected to torture or to cruel, inhuman or degrading treatment or punishment, that everyone has the right to recognition everywhere as a person before the law.

It also says that no one shall be held in slavery or servitude, that slavery and the slave trade shall be prohibited in all their forms, and in international law the trafficking in women has long been recognized as a form of slave trading.

President Carter signed, and I am asking you to recommend that Congress ratify, the United Nations Convention on the Elimination of All Forms of Discrimination Against Women, which includes the following article, Article 6: "State Parties shall take all appropriate measures, including legislation, to suppress all forms of traffic in women and exploitation and prostitution of women." That gives the United States government an affirmative obligation to act against the traffic in women. This is an international problem and it requires in part an international solution.

I am also asking you to acknowledge the international reality of this—this is a human rights issue—for a very personal reason, which is that my grandparents came here, Jews fleeing from Russia, Jews fleeing from Hungary. Those who did not come to this country were all killed, either in pogroms or by the Nazis. They came here for me. I live here, and I live in a country where women are tortured as a form of public entertainment and for profit, and that torture is upheld as a state-protected right. Now, that is unbearable.

I am here asking the simplest thing. I am saying hurt people need remedies, not platitudes, not laws that you know already don't work; people excluded from constitutional protections need equality. People silenced by exploitation and brutality need real speech, not to be told that when they are hung from meat hooks, that is their speech. Nobody in this country who has been working to do anything about pornography, no woman who has spoken out against it, is going to go backward, is going to forget what she has learned, is going to forget that she has rights that aren't being acknowledged in this country. And there are lots of people in this country, I am happy to say, who want to live in a kind world, not a cruel world, and they will not accept the hatred of women as good, wholesome, American fun; they won't accept the hatred of women and the rape of women as anybody's idea of freedom. They won't accept the torture of women as a civil liberty.

I am asking you to help the exploited, not the exploiters. You have a tremendous opportunity here. I am asking you as individuals to have the courage, because I think it's what you will need, to actually be willing yourselves to go and cut that woman down and untie her hands and take the gag out of her mouth, and to do something, to risk something, for her freedom.

Thank you very much for listening to me. I am going to submit into evidence a copy of Linda Marchiano's book *Ordeal,* which I understand you have not seen. She testified before you yesterday. I ask you, when you come to make your recommendations, think of her. The only thing atypical about Linda is that she has had the courage to make a public fight against what has happened to her.

And whatever you come up with, it has to help her or it's not going to help anyone. Thank you very much.

Feminism, Moralism and Pornography

Ellen Willis

For nearly two decades Ellen Willis was the feminist voice of the legendary radical weekly *The Village Voice,* to whose pages she has recently returned. One of the first within the women's movement to raise a red flag on antipornography feminism, Willis first published this essay in *The Voice* in October 1979. Her most recent book is *No More Nice Girls.*

For women, life is an ongoing good cop–bad cop routine. The good cops are marriage, motherhood, and that courtly old gentleman, chivalry. Just cooperate, they say (crossing their fingers), and we'll go easy on you. You'll never have to earn a living or open a door. We'll even get you some romantic love. But you'd better not get stubborn, or you'll have to deal with our friend rape, and he's a real terror; we just can't control him.

Pornography often functions as a bad cop. If rape warns that without the protection of one man we are fair game for all, the hard-core pornographic image suggests that the alternative to being a wife is being a whore. As women become more "criminal," the cops call for nastier reinforcements; the proliferation of lurid, violent porn (symbolic rape) is a form of backlash. But one can be a solid citizen and still be shocked (naively or hypocritically) by police brutality. However widely condoned, rape is illegal. However loudly people proclaim that porn is as wholesome as granola, the essence of its appeal is that emotionally it remains taboo. It is from their very contempt for the rules that bad cops derive their power to terrorize (and the covert approbation of solid citizens who would love to break the rules themselves). The line between bad cop and outlaw is tenuous. Both rape and pornography reflect a male outlaw mentality that rejects the conventions of romance and insists, bluntly, that women are cunts. The crucial difference between the conservative's moral indignation at rape, or at *Hustler,* and the feminist's political outrage is the latter's understanding that the problem is not bad cops or outlaws but cops and the law.

Unfortunately the current women's campaign against pornography seems determined to blur this difference. Feminist criticism of sexist and misogynist pornography is nothing new; porn is an obvious target insofar as it contributes to larger patterns of oppression— the reduction of the female body to a commodity (the paradigm being prostitution), the sexual intimidation that makes women regard the public streets as enemy territory (the paradigm being rape), sexist images, and propaganda in general. But what is happening now is different. By playing games with the English language, anti-porn activists are managing to rationalize as feminism a single-issue movement divorced from any larger political context and rooted in conservative moral assumptions that are all the more dangerous for being unacknowledged.

When I first heard there was a group called Women Against Pornography [WAP], I twitched. Could I define myself as Against Pornography? Not really. In itself pornography—which, my dictionary and I agree, means any image or description intended or used to arouse sexual desire—does not strike me as the proper object of a political crusade. As the most cursory observation suggests, there are many varieties of porn, some pernicious, some more or less benign. About the only generalization one can make is that pornography is the return of the repressed, of feelings and fantasies driven underground by a culture that atomizes sexuality, defining love as a noble affair of the heart and mind, lust as a base animal urge centered in unmentionable organs. Prurience—the state of mind I associate with pornography—implies a sense of sex as forbidden, secretive pleasure, isolated from any emotional or social context. I imagine that in utopia, porn would wither away along with the state, heroin, and Coca-Cola. At present, however, the sexual impulses that pornography appeals to are part of virtually everyone's psychology. For obvious political and cultural reasons nearly all porn is sexist in that it is the product of a male imagination and aimed at a male market; women are less likely to be consciously interested in pornography, or to indulge that interest, or to find porn that turns them on. But anyone who thinks women are simply indifferent to pornography has never watched a bunch of adolescent girls pass around a trashy novel. Over the years I've enjoyed various pieces of pornography—some of them of the sleazy Forty-second Street paperback sort—and so have most women I know. Fantasy, after all, is more flexible than reality, and women have learned, as a matter of survival, to be adept at shaping male fantasies to their own purposes. If feminists define pornography per se as the enemy, the result will be to make a lot of women ashamed of their sexual feelings and afraid to be honest about them. And the last thing women need is more sexual shame, guilt, and hypocrisy—this time served up as feminism.

So why ignore qualitative distinctions and in effect condemn all pornography as equally bad? WAP organizers answer—or finesse—this question by redefining pornography. They maintain that pornography is not really about sex but about violence against women. Or, in a more colorful formulation, "Pornography is the theory, rape is the practice." Part of the argument is that pornography causes violence; much is made of the fact that Charles Manson and David Berkowitz had porn collections. This is the sort of inverted logic that presumes marijuana to be dangerous because most heroin addicts started with it. It is men's hostility toward women—combined with their power to express that hostility and for the most part get away with it—that causes sexual violence. Pornography that gives sadistic fantasies concrete shape—and in today's atmosphere social legitimacy—may well encourage suggestible men to act them out. But if *Hustler* were to vanish from the shelves tomorrow, I doubt that rape or wife-beating statistics would decline.

Even more problematic is the idea that pornography depicts violence rather than sex. Since porn is by definition overtly sexual, while most of it is not overtly violent, this equation requires some fancy explaining. The conference WAP held in September was in part devoted to this task. Robin Morgan and Gloria Steinem addressed it by attempting to distinguish pornography from erotica. According to this argument erotica (whose etymological root is *eros,* or "sexual love") expresses an integrated sexuality based on mutual affection and desire between equals; pornography (which comes from another Greek root—*porne,* meaning "prostitute") reflects a dehumanized sexuality based on male domination and exploitation of women. The distinction sounds promising, but it doesn't hold up. The accepted meaning of erotica is literature or pictures with sexual themes; it may or may not serve the essentially utilitarian function of pornography. Because it is less specific, less suggestive of actual sexual activity, "erotica" is regularly used as a euphemism for "classy porn." Pornography expressed in literary language or expensive photography and consumed by the upper middle class is "erotica"; the cheap stuff, which can't pretend to any purpose but getting people off, is smut. The erotica-versus-porn approach evades the (embarrassing?) question of how porn is *used.* It endorses the portrayal of sex as we might like it to be and condemns the portrayal of sex as it too often is, whether in action or only in fantasy. But if pornography is to arouse, it must appeal to the feelings we have, not those that by some utopian standard we ought to have. Sex in this culture has been so deeply politicized that it is impossible to make clear-cut distinctions between "authentic" sexual impulses and those conditioned by patriarchy. Between, say, *Ulysses* at one end and *Snuff* at the other, erotica/pornography conveys all sorts of mixed messages that elicit complicated and private responses. In practice, attempts to sort out good erotica from bad porn inevitably come down to "What turns me on is erotic; what turns you on is pornographic."

It would be clearer and more logical simply to acknowledge that some sexual images are offensive and some are not. But logic and clarity are irrelevant—or rather, inimical—to the underlying aim of the antiporners, which is to vent the emotions traditionally associated with the word *pornography.* As I've suggested, there is a social and psychic link between pornography and rape. In terms of patriarchal morality both are expressions of male lust, which is presumed to be innately vicious, and offenses to the putative sexual innocence of "good" women. But feminists supposedly begin with different assumptions—that men's confusion of sexual desire with predatory aggression reflects a sexist system, not male biology; that there are no good (chaste) or bad (lustful) women, just women who are, like men, sexual beings. From this standpoint, to lump pornography with rape is dangerously simplistic. Rape is a violent physical assault. Pornography can be a psychic assault, both in its content and in its public intrusions on our attention, but for women as for men it can also be a source of erotic pleasure. A woman who is raped is a victim; a woman who enjoys pornography (even if that means enjoying a rape fantasy) is in a sense a rebel, insisting on an aspect of her sexuality that has been defined as a male preserve. Insofar as pornography glorifies male supremacy and sexual alienation, it is deeply reactionary. But in rejecting sexual repression and hypocrisy —which have inflicted even more damage on women than on men— it expresses a radical impulse.

That this impulse still needs defending, even among feminists, is evident from the sexual attitudes that have surfaced in the antiporn movement. In the movement's rhetoric pornography is a code word for vicious male lust. To the objection that some women get off on porn, the standard reply is that this only shows how thoroughly women have been brainwashed by male values—though a WAP leaflet goes so far as to suggest that women who claim to like pornography are lying to avoid male opprobrium. (Note the good-girl-versus-bad-girl theme, reappearing as healthy versus sick, or honest versus devious; for "brainwashed" read "seduced.") And the view of sex that most often emerges from talk about "erotica" is as sentimental and euphemistic as the word itself: Lovemaking should be beautiful, romantic, soft, nice, and devoid of messiness, vulgarity, impulses to power, or indeed aggression of any sort. Above all, the emphasis should be on *relationships,* not (yuck) *organs.* This goody-goody concept of eroticism is not feminist but feminine. It is precisely sex as an aggressive, unladylike activity, an expression of violent and unpretty emotion, an exercise of erotic power, and a specifically genital experience that has been taboo for women. Nor are we supposed to admit that we, too, have sadistic impulses, that our sexual fantasies may reflect forbidden urges to turn the tables and get revenge on men. (When a woman is aroused by a rape fantasy, is she perhaps identifying with the rapist as well as the victim?)

At the WAP conference lesbian separatists argued that pornography reflects patriarchal sexual relations; patriarchal sexual relations are based on male power backed by force; ergo pornography is violent. This dubious syllogism, which could as easily be applied to romantic novels, reduces the whole issue to hopeless mush. If all manifestations of patriarchal sexuality are violent, then opposition to violence cannot explain why pornography (rather than romantic novels) should be singled out as a target. Besides, such reductionism allows women no basis for distinguishing between consensual heterosexuality and rape. But this is precisely its point; as a number of women at the conference put it, "In a patriarchy, all sex with men is pornographic." Of course, to attack pornography, and at the same time equate it with heterosexual sex, is implicitly to condemn not only women who like pornography, but women who sleep with men. This is familiar ground. The argument that straight women collaborate with the enemy has often been, among other things, a relatively polite way of saying that they consort with the beast. At the conference I couldn't help feeling that proponents of the separatist line were talking like the modern equivalents of women who, in an era when straightforward prudery was socially acceptable, joined convents to escape men's rude sexual demands. It seemed to me that their revulsion against heterosexuality was serving as the thinnest of covers for disgust with sex itself. In any case, sanitized feminine sexuality, whether straight or gay, is as limited as the predatory masculine kind and as central to women's oppression; a major function of misogynist pornography is to scare us into embracing it. As a further incentive, the good cops stand ready to assure us that we are indeed morally superior to men, that in our sweetness and nonviolence (read passivity and powerlessness) is our strength.

Women are understandably tempted to believe this comforting

myth. Self-righteousness has always been a feminine weapon, a permissible way to make men feel bad. Ironically it is socially acceptable for women to display fierce aggression in their crusades against male vice, which serve as an outlet for female anger without threatening male power. The temperance movement, which made alcohol the symbol of male violence, did not improve the position of women; substituting porn for demon rum won't work either. One reason it won't is that it bolsters the good-girl/bad-girl split. Overtly or by implication it isolates women who like porn or "pornographic" sex or who work in the sex industry. WAP has refused to take a position on prostitution, yet its activities—particularly its support for cleaning up Times Square—will affect prostitutes' lives. Prostitution raises its own set of complicated questions. But it is clearly not in women's interest to pit "good" feminists against "bad" whores (or topless dancers, or models for skin magazines).

So far, the issue that has dominated public debate on the anti-porn campaign is its potential threat to free speech. Here, too, the movement's arguments have been full of contradictions. Susan Brownmiller and other WAP organizers claim not to advocate censorship and dismiss the civil liberties issue as a red herring dragged in by men who don't want to face the fact that pornography oppresses women. Yet at the same time, WAP endorses the Supreme Court's contention that obscenity is not protected speech, a doctrine I—and most civil libertarians—regard as a clear infringement of First Amendment rights. Brownmiller insists that the First Amendment was designed to protect political dissent, not expressions of woman-hating violence. But to make such a distinction is to defeat the amendment's purpose, since it implicitly cedes to the government the right to define "political." (Has there ever been a government willing to admit that its opponents are anything more than antisocial troublemakers?) Anyway it makes no sense to oppose pornography on the grounds that it's sexist propaganda, then turn around and argue that it's not political. Nor will libertarians be reassured by WAP's statement that "We want to change the definition of obscenity so that it focuses on violence, not sex." Whatever their focus, obscenity laws deny the right of free expression to those who transgress official standards of propriety—and personally I don't find WAP's standards significantly less oppressive than Warren Burger's. Not that it matters, since WAP's fantasies about influencing the definition of obscenity are appallingly naive. The basic purpose of obscenity laws is and always has been to reinforce cultural taboos on sexuality and suppress feminism, homosexuality, and other forms of sexual dissidence. No pornographer has ever been punished for being a woman-hater, but not too long ago information about female sexuality, contraception, and abortion was assumed to be obscene. In a male-supremacist society the only obscenity law that will not be used against women is no law at all.

As an alternative to an outright ban on pornography, Brownmiller and others have advocated restricting its display. There is a plausible case to be made for the idea that antiwoman images displayed so prominently that they are impossible to avoid are coercive, a form of active harassment that oversteps the bounds of free speech. But aside from the evasion involved in simply equating pornography with misogyny or sexual sadism, there are no legal or logical grounds for treating sexist material any differently from (for example) racist or anti-Semitic propaganda; an equitable law would have to prohibit any kind of public defamation. And the very thought of such a sweeping law has to make anyone with an imagination nervous. Could Catholics claim they were being harassed by nasty depictions of the pope? Could Russian refugees argue that the display of Communist literature was a form of psychological torture? Would pro-abortion material be taken off the shelves on the grounds that it defamed the unborn? I'd rather not find out.

At the moment the First Amendment issue remains hypothetical; the movement has concentrated on raising the issue of pornography through demonstrations and other public actions. This is certainly a legitimate strategy. Still, I find myself more and more disturbed by the tenor of antipornography actions and the sort of consciousness they promote; increasingly their focus has shifted from rational feminist criticism of specific targets to generalized, demagogic moral outrage. Picketing an antiwoman movie, defacing an exploitative billboard, or boycotting a record company to protest its misogynist album covers conveys one kind of message, mass marches Against Pornography quite another. Similarly there is a difference between telling the neighborhood news dealer why it pisses us off to have *Penthouse* shoved in our faces and choosing as a prime target every right-thinking politician's symbol of big-city sin, Times Square.

In contrast to the abortion-rights movement, which is struggling against a tidal wave of energy from the other direction, the antiporn campaign is respectable. It gets approving press and cooperation from the New York City government, which has its own stake (promoting tourism, making the Clinton area safe for gentrification) in cleaning up Times Square. It has begun to attract women whose perspective on other matters is in no way feminist ("I'm anti abortion," a participant in WAP's march on Times Square told a reporter, "but this is something I can get into"). Despite the insistence of WAP organizers that they support sexual freedom, their line appeals to the antisexual emotions that feed the backlash. Whether they know it or not, they are doing the good cops' dirty work.

Where Do We Stand on Pornography? A *Ms.* Roundtable

Marcia Ann Gillespie, Moderator
with
Gloria Jacobs, Marilyn French,
Ntozake Shange, Andrea Dworkin,
and Norma Ramos

Marcia Ann Gillespie is the editor-in-chief of *Ms.* magazine and the former editor of *Essence.* Gloria Jacobs is a senior editor at *Ms.* and the coauthor, with Barbara Ehrenreich and Elizabeth Hess, of *Re-making Love: the Feminization of Sex.* Marilyn French is the author of eight books, including *The Women's Room* and *The War Against Women.* Ntozake Shange is the author of the play *for colored girls who have considered suicide/when the rainbow is enuf* and the novel *Briliane.* Andrea Dworkin is the author of eleven books (see bio on "Pornography Is a Civil Rights Issue"). Norma Ramos is an attorney active in the antipornography and environmental movements.

Gillespie convened the roundtable in September of 1993; it appeared in the January–February 1994 issue of *Ms.*

The last time *Ms.* ran a cover story on pornography was in 1985. It focused on the antipornography ordinance drafted and conceived as a civil rights law by Andrea Dworkin and Catharine MacKinnon for the city of Minneapolis in 1983. The law did not pass there, but versions have been proposed in other areas of the country. And the questions raised in debates about the ordinance continue to challenge us. Is it censorship? Do we agree on the definition of pornography, its impact or its significance? Would the ordinance be a boon or a blow to women's rights? Passions run deep; the issue is wrenching. Trying to get people with opposing views to come together for a discussion on pornography is not easy. Fixed assumptions, ideological disagreements and battles, bitter words, and hurtful labels have strained friendships, severed alliances, and created rifts. Which is why *Ms.* is holding this discussion, to get feminists talking *to* instead of *at* each other—and listening; to get us thinking and sharing our thoughts and feelings and fears, our questions and concerns.

As a reality check the editors brought magazines—ranging from *Playboy* and *Hustler* to others that were not quite as slick but far more sexually explicit. We placed them on the table and asked the participants to spend a few moments thumbing through them before the discussion began.

Marcia Ann Gillespie: Let's talk about definitions. What is pornography? Andrea?

Andrea Dworkin: Catharine MacKinnon and I wrote a legal definition for the civil rights bill that we drafted in Minneapolis in 1983. The definition goes like this: Pornography is the graphic, sexually explicit subordination of women that includes one of a series of scenarios, from women being dehumanized—turned into objects and commodities—through women showing pleasure in being raped, through the dismemberment of women in a way that makes the dismemberment sexual. If men, children, or transsexuals are used in place of women, the material is still pornography.

A statutory definition has to be very concrete. But when we talk about what is pornographic in our culture, for most people that has many subjective dimensions to it.

Ntozake Shange: Pornography is the use of sex to intimidate and/or control women and children and anyone else who is subject to a situation like that. My definition would also pertain to movies of lynchings where people were having parties. It has to do with depicting something that is violent and possibly life-threatening for entertainment.

Norma Ramos: I haven't seen anything define pornography in clearer terms than the ordinance does. Outside of the legal setting I look at pornography as a system and practice of prostitution, as evidence of women's second-class status. It is a central feature of patriarchal society, an essential tool in terms of how men keep power over women.

Marilyn French: I don't have a definition of pornography and I would be very hard put to distinguish between erotic art and pornography.

There was a time when it was very clear to me that pornography involved both the use of the body—usually a female body—and power, so that what you had in essence was sadism. Now, I am not sure what human sexuality is. I am not sure to what degree normal human sexuality contains elements of power, an element of sadism.

Ramos: So many of the movements for social change in this country are very focused on creating social justice, but they tiptoe around the pornographers; they never understand violence against women. They talk about crime in gender-neutral terms, but all around us is this major sexual exploitation of women.

I began to look at that because I could no longer look away from it. And I became very sure that I would dedicate the rest of my life to ending sexual exploitation, which is exactly what pornography—in all of its forms—is to me. Some may want to defend it and call it erotica, or liberty of sexual expression, but I'm working to eliminate sexual exploitation at its core—I'm working to end prostitution.

Shange: There are two dilemmas that I've been grappling with for years. One is that part of the exploitation of people of color—especially women—has been to rob us of any inner life, to rob us of our own sexuality and our own sensuality. So I spend a great deal of my time trying to think about how I can write about intense, wonderful, creative sex among people of color without exploiting anybody and without exploiting myself. It's very hard. I hesitate to strip us of a concrete and vital language for sexual activities and desires and fantasies, because I don't think we can afford to lose too much more.

The second is that I have a great deal of difficulty understanding what people think exploitation is when I'm involved. I know it when I see other women being exploited, but I'm stunned when people think I am. A case in point that's very heavy on my heart: I was on the cover of *Poets & Writers* and I wore a pretty lace top. In the next two issues, there were letters asking if *Poets & Writers* is now a flesh magazine—why was I appearing in my underwear? Bare shoulders are exploitation now? You know, there are other things to talk about.

We have to remember that we can get people railroading each other into being very, very rigid. I'm sure that every feminist I know believes that when *we* are defining the worlds that we live in, they become richer and not poorer.

Dworkin: It's very hard to look at a picture of a woman's body and not see it with the perception that her body is being exploited, because so much happens that way in this culture. It's very difficult to draw a line between sensitivity and hypersensitivity.

What strikes me about dealing with sexual exploitation and the whole system of pornography is that it requires such a deep process of decolonialization: Women must be freed from the domination of the male system. People are frightened because they think that they're in quicksand. A lot of these questions have never been raised, especially with concrete commitments to social change. They haven't been raised with an international movement of women saying, "This is going to stop. Our question is how do we stop it?"

What you just described, that response to your photograph, Ntozake, happens in part because of the fear other women have that something bad has happened to you. Sometimes that seems almost hostile. But it comes out of a question: How do we know what this picture means?

French: We don't know, and that is exactly my point. The only pornography movies I ever saw were *Deep Throat* and *The Devil and Miss Jones*. When I see what goes on in these films, I just want to leave. But there was a scene in *Deep Throat* in which a very large and very erect penis came up to the vulva. The coloring of the shot was extremely beautiful. It threw me completely. Now why shouldn't it be beautiful? Why shouldn't we all see it as beautiful? Why is it not beautiful even though that was not a beautiful movie?

Dworkin: No, it wasn't. Part of the question is, why did a woman have to be brutalized to make that film?

Ramos: I see the sexuality that's presented in pornography as extremely limiting. Andrea, you coined the phrase *eroticized bigotry*.

The folks that defend pornography as free expression are actually defending some of the narrowest thinking I can imagine. When people consider the misery that it takes to make this stuff, the lives that have to be exploited and shattered to produce these images. . . . It isn't just about what you see, it's what it took for a human being to be in that position—it takes a whole lot of abuse. It takes women who have been sexually abused in childhood, who have been robbed of their self-esteem, and who are vulnerable to this exploitative sexuality.

French: I've been working for ten years on a history of women. It starts in prehistory and deals with the rise of the state everywhere. In every single culture that I mention, they passed the same laws against women. They established a double standard very early on.

We are talking about five thousand years of culture. What does this mean? There may be some of us in this room who would defend the First Amendment rather than see these magazines end—I'm one of them. But the problem is never, never going to be solved unless we start thinking about what this stuff means to men. What is prostitution about?

Censorship exists in this country. You cannot make a movie or write a book that defends the practices of the Holocaust or that exalts black slavery. But you can make a movie, any movie you like, you can write a book, any book you like, that shows any kind of torture, enslavement, or murder of women. How come?

Shange: You're right, Marilyn. We don't buy these things, and we don't go see these movies. But since I don't buy pornography, it's not going to change anything if I don't use it.

So, if I come at it another way, if we unionized or organized women who work in pornography like COYOTE organizes prostitutes. . . . But then they'd get reformed and they wouldn't want to practice anymore. So it's like a revolving door. Once women learn that they can *learn* enough not to do this anymore, they stop doing it.

Ramos: I'd never subscribe to a movement whose goal was reforming slavery. You work to abolish it.

One of the most difficult things for me is exactly what you just did, Marilyn, the way you posed this notion that some of us in this room would defend the First Amendment and would be against censorship—as if there were people here who would *advocate* censorship. This movement has never advocated censorship. It advocates the elimination of sexual exploitation in all of its forms.

There are people in this room who would fight to ensure that laws against sexual harassment exist. I don't know of a sexual-harassment situation that does not involve speech. It's most often done through words: "Sleep with me or you're fired." It's the same with racial discrimination: "The apartment has been rented already." Does that make you against the First Amendment? Does that make you for censorship? But because pornography is packaged as sexual entertainment for men, we'll tiptoe around the pornographers, we'll canonize it and call it speech. Any woman who dissents will be called a person who's against the First Amendment—which I am not.

French: That's why I say this formulation of the argument goes nowhere. Nevertheless Andrea and Catharine's ordinance is a form of censorship. To say that it's not is also tiptoeing around something.

Dworkin: The movies that you said are *not* being made, Marilyn, *are* made—by pornographers. There is racist pornography in which the African American slave has an orgasm every time the master rapes her. Pornography sexualizes racism. There is anti-Semitic pornography in which the concentration camps are the site of sexual pleasure and the Jewish woman begs the Nazi to do medical experiments on her that were actually done to women in the camps. Pornographers are scavengers, parasites on history.

I just have to deal with the censorship thing you brought up. In the United States, *censorship* seems to have an ever-expanding meaning depending on who's using the word and how they're using it. In legal terms *censorship* has always meant "prior restraint": you pass a law that stops something from being made or being done.

The notion that the ordinance does that is wrong. It is a civil law that allows somebody to bring a lawsuit after they've been injured on very specific grounds. But if the ordinance and all the political activism that women do against the pornography industry were to work, it is true that these magazines would not exist in the way that they currently exist. And many people seem to feel that if these magazines are threatened in their ability to publish, that is proof that it's censorship. But when you look at an institution of sexual exploitation, and what you want is to destroy it, you're not really talking about censorship.

The Constitution protects the magazines. It's not the speech of the women that's being protected. It's a way of making women into chattel. Whom do they belong to? The pimps and the consumers of the magazines and the movies.

Ramos: We have to expand our definitions and vision of civil rights. As a woman of color who's spent a lot of time fighting to end racism, I realize that the men of color whom I've struggled with on all these issues are ignoring women's issues. Women are being raped at higher and higher rates. Women are battered at rates that are just mind-boggling. Why doesn't the civil rights movement understand *that* in terms of civil rights?

Gillespie: We almost automatically speak of pornographers and consumers of pornography as "he," but there's material made by and for women.

Shange: I went to a panel in Philadelphia, and there were two women who produced pornography for women. This is supposed to be our erotica. So I looked at it, and all I could figure out is that there was more of a story line and he was a little gentler with her, but I didn't get excited. If they're trying to make it for us, they haven't succeeded yet.

Ramos: The pornographers see a new market in women and so they take women who are still a part of the industry and call them makers of "erotica." When you look at what's being done and you look at the context, there's no difference. The conditions that produce pornography—and we have upward of a ten-billion-dollar-a-year industry in this country—are hostile to the production of real erotica. In the terms that we're talking about, you need equality for women to produce life-affirming sexuality.

French: There are pictures in these men's magazines in which women are making love to women; they're not hurting each other. This is a situation of equality. It's upsetting because of what has been done and the way they're holding their bodies.

Dworkin: But they're *not* making love to each other. There's a social relationship between the photograph and the consumer. So-called lesbian layouts in heterosexual male pornography provide two women for the male consumer. What you see are the orifices of their bodies turned for his sexual pleasure.

French: I know that, but how can you say, "You can't do this?"

Dworkin: I'm not saying that.

French: In the ordinance you say "demeans, degrades." There's nothing in those films or pictures that's sadistic. How do you describe it? How do you stop it?

Dworkin: In this law, part of the definition of pornography is that it turns women into commodities, puts women in postures of sexual submission to be dominated by men. You have two wires that have to be tripped under this law. One, the material has to fall under the definition, and two, something has to have happened so that, for instance, the woman is forced to make pictures even if there is no violence in the pictures. You didn't see any in *Deep Throat,* but an enormous amount of violence was used to make the picture.

The pornographers make a product. And the way that the product is made depends on women being vulnerable enough—by being hurt as children, by being poor, by being homeless—to be brought into prostitution and to be involved in pornography.

The mind-set has to change. It's not a question of looking at a magazine and censoring the content. It's a matter of looking at the social reality, the subordination of women necessary to create the magazine, and the way that the magazine is then used in the world against women.

But now we're dealing with a technological change too. Because of film and photography, the pornography industry requires the use of real people, endless new batches of young women. And that's the future that we're leaving for our children, in the name of freedom of speech, or in the name of sexual liberation.

Gillespie: Norma, you said there can be no erotica, as long as patriarchy exists. Am I clear?

Ramos: I'm saying the social conditions that are favorable to the production of pornography are hostile to the production of erotica. You need equality for women and you need a vision of human sexuality that is life-affirming. Those conditions do not exist. That doesn't mean that some mind, somewhere, could not create something that would be erotic.

Gillespie: I'm still intrigued about the images that women are making, for example, lesbian pornography.

Shange: I've gotten letters from people who say that my work is profane and abusive to black people and to women. I'm sure the reason they say that is because I'm taking words that men have used to make us dirty. I'm taking them to make us able to use them any way we choose, or showing how, when we use them the way men do, we hurt ourselves. There is a piece that I do called "Crack Annie" where the woman gets all involved with her boyfriend to supply her habit, and he won't give her any drugs unless she gives him her little girl, so she does. And she refers to herself and her little girl as either his pussy or her pussy to be given away and taken, like you're going to get a piece of gum or something. That was done to show the disassociation and lack of value—not realizing one's own vulnerability, not knowing when we hurt.

I can get myself in a big bind and never be able to write anything that is honest if I can't somehow uproot words or images that have been malignant and make them constructive for me.

French: The entire discourse about sex has been created by men. There's nothing we can do about it. Either we use their words or we avoid them. It's like anything we do in feminism—what we face is a long wall of closed doors. And all we can do is bang on them and open them a little bit.

Dworkin: I see my writing as a series of assaults on male culture, and as a way of destabilizing male control over women. On your question about the lesbian pornography, Marcia, from my point of view, they are reifying the status quo. I think that there's a difference between trying to explode the discourse, trying to bring new light to it, versus simply imitating it. And I think lesbian pornography is extremely male-identified.

French: But do we have a female model? Do we have an image of ourselves? I don't think we do.

Ramos: Well, that's one of the tasks that we have before us. But there's no distinction between what lesbian pornographers are doing and what these women who are fronting for the pornography industry are doing. It is not anything that is going to advance us as women.

They may package it as art, or say that they are introducing a new vision. But it is sexual exploitation. The pornographers have a lot to gain by fusing the two, by saying, "It's in the eyes of the beholder."

French: I have to say that I have really learned something from you today. In the male world things stand on pedestals and are sacrosanct —art, mathematics, government. And these things may not be questioned and are worth any sacrifice. What the three of you are saying in your different ways is that no, nothing's on a pedestal. There's art and there's government and there's mathematics and there's feeding children and there's housing the homeless, and all of these things are equally important. No one of them is sacrosanct. And they are all subordinate to the one important thing: the well-being of the human race.

Gillespie: But where does female sexual pleasure and female sexual fantasy play out here?

Shange: I write about it. I write fantasies and dreams constantly.

Gillespie: You are exploring erotica.

Shange: Oh, absolutely, I hope so. I do it because I don't like things being kept from me as a woman. That's why I started writing: I didn't like anything kept from little brown girls. Our lives are kept from us and our dreams are kept from us. No one ever told me anything like this and I know I'm not the first colored woman who had dreams.

When I read my work in public places, I get rapt attention from the women, but the men giggle or stare at me like they wish I'd disappear. I don't know—is it because the pleasure isn't from what her partner is doing but from the sensations her body is actually experiencing? We don't have novels that tell us how my body felt when so and so made love to me. We need to do that, so that eventually we'll have a multiple kind of vocabulary just like we have multiple orgasms.

Dworkin: One of the disgraceful things that the pornography industry does is that it takes the word *fantasy* and robs it of its meaning. For instance, if a man uses a prostitute, he calls it a fantasy. The society is willing to let him do that, but something has actually happened, a transaction has taken place, somebody has done something to someone. That's not a fantasy, that's a social relationship that has to do with power and presumably with someone's pleasure, usually his.

I spent a lot of years out on the streets, prostituting at different times, a lot of times homeless. I don't come to this subject from a middle-class abstraction about these words. While there's been a great deal of sexual pleasure in my life, I also became aware, very early, that sex is a medium to convey hostility and antagonism and ownership and control and outright hatred.

So when people insist that women talk about sexuality in terms of pleasure, it's almost a demand that constricts the discussion. We're always supposed to prove that we're for or against sex. Male writers have a tremendous range of ambivalence about sexual experience. They express a lot of antagonism, a lot of hostility, a lot of anger—all kinds of deep, complex emotions. But women are supposed to say yes or no. And we're being judged according to whether our answer is the right one.

Ramos: Men are getting sexual pleasure from our subordination. What if racism had been turned into sexual pleasure the way the oppression of women has been? When you struggle against that oppression, the opposition stands up and says, "No, you are fighting against my pleasure.'' A very big piece of that is learned behavior, and in our society it's socialized by the pornography. Even if you're not directly consuming the pornography, you're getting those images through advertising and movies.

French: I used to teach creative writing, and one time a young woman in the class read two paragraphs she had written. By the time she finished, the class was gasping with erotic delight. They were filled with desire. You didn't realize until the very end that she was talking about peeling an orange. It had nothing to do with the body —it was peeling, smelling, tasting, juice, it just went on like that. Now, I call that women's erotica. So there's a possibility for it, but there's just so much fruit in the world.

Gillespie: There does seem to be an assumption here that female sexuality is inherently kinder, gentler.

Dworkin: That critique has been coming from a certain part of a certain women's subculture—the notion that dangerous, hard, cruel sex is real sex. And those of us who have different experiences and notions of eroticism and sensuality are quite simply dismissed. The pejorative word having been, for a while, *vanilla,* which is, ironically, one of the most sensual aromas.

We have been treated with such contempt for valuing a wider eroticism, for not having a fetishized and alienated view of sexual function, for not having a brutality-based view, for not honoring power differentials. We're treated as if it's some kind of reassertion of Victorian values and has something to do with a view of women as frail.

Gloria Jacobs: But what about the possibility that some women are saying: ''We enjoy certain kinds of sex that have power differentials, but it's not sadistic, and we don't want to be attacked for it. We don't want to have our sexuality negated because we probably can't change how we feel about sex in our lifetime.''

Dworkin: If that is the kind of sexual experience you want in this world, you're going to get it. If what you want is something different, you're living in a world that you've got to find a way to change. The way that argument has always come at me has been that if I'm going to make the people that you're talking about happy, I have to stop writing. They're saying, ''What you write makes us so unhappy about what we're doing that we can't coexist. So you shut up.''

Ramos: Sexuality is socialized. They did not get their pleasure principles by accident. I understand what you're saying: They're in this place. But if people are in a place that is about taking sexual pleasure from scenarios that involve abuse. . . . Pedophiles don't want to stop doing what they're doing either.

Jacobs: I'm not talking about abuse. There's a middle ground that isn't about peeling oranges but is not about abuse. . . .

Ramos: But what I'm saying is that women are socialized into actually getting sexual pleasure through their powerlessness. And it's very hard to opt out of this socialization. So I understand your question speaks to this reality. It's a struggle that a lot of us wage personally. Here I am in this place and I'm getting sexual pleasure from this, so what do I do about this? You work to change that. You have to challenge it. Do you want to stay in that place, or do you want to open up the possibility that maybe human sexuality doesn't have to be this limited, this brutal?

French: I seriously doubt that anybody can change their sexuality.

Dworkin: Oh, people can.

French: I never denied that a person can change their sexual behavior. But I think you can't change your sexual fantasies.

Dworkin: But they do change. As your life changes, your fantasies change.

I've experienced it, other people have experienced it. I'm not telling people what they have to think or what they have to feel, but I am saying that change is a part of life in the sexual realm as it is in every other realm.

Gillespie: Both Norma and Andrea see this as a civil rights issue. Do you agree, Ntozake?

Shange: I think that it's a dilemma we've been confronting with men of color all through the twentieth century, which is, regardless of how oppressed they are, they still get some goodies for being a male. And until they're ready to move away from that for our sake, if not for their own unconscious desires to be full human beings, then we're not going to be able to do anything with them. And we have to proceed as if it's not going to happen, because otherwise we get stalled too.

Gillespie: What about the ordinance?

Shange: I would love to see the ordinance passed in Philadelphia, where I live. People are going to say this is for the cities. It's not just for the cities. It's for the malls and the residential neighborhoods and the truck stops and tourist places. But I think there should also be a retraining and reeducation package for sex-industry workers who need to be directed into other careers.

French: I guess I'd like to see the ordinance tried. But I don't trust the government. Censorship has to be backed by the government—the same government that showed sadistic, pornographic movies to the pilots who were going to bomb Iraq the next day. This government is going to uphold our freedom?

Maybe the ordinance—which is after the fact rather than before, and therefore not censorship, as you say, and would be in the hands of local authorities—might work. Not that I trust local authorities either.

Dworkin: It would be in the hands of women. Somebody would have to bring a lawsuit. There's no police enforcement of any kind. It will go into the courts; that's where the government becomes a part of it. But in terms of enforcement, a person initiates it because her civil status has been hurt.

It places women in a different place inside the legal system. If it were used, it would have a tremendous impact on the way the legal system sees and treats rape victims, the way the legal system sees and treats women and prostitution. It's the first thing that says, "If these things have been done to you, that doesn't make you nobody. You get to be somebody under this law. Your life matters. We're going to try to give you back some part of it."

Ramos: I've heard that before: "I don't trust the government, so we'd better not do anything on pornography." Well, we don't trust the government, but we have other civil rights laws.

French: The government is not going to use a sexual-harassment law to keep me from publishing a novel, but it could use an anti-pornography law.

Dworkin: The obscenity laws can already be used against you. I think they should be repealed.

Ramos: I think censorship helps pornography flourish; the laws should be repealed. Let's have some power in the hands of women, and then we'll have some real political discussion about censorship and sexual exploitation.

PART TWO

Flashpoints: The Meese Commission, Tailhook, Hill-Thomas, and the Antioch Sex Code

Pornography
Goes to Washington

Lindsy Van Gelder

As a contributing editor to *Ms.*, Lindsy Van Gelder reported on topics ranging from technology to lesbian politics for the magazine throughout the 1980s. She is now the staff writer for *Allure*. Here is her account of the January 1986 hearing before the Attorney General's Commission on Pornography, at which Andrea Dworkin testified. This piece first appeared in the June 1986 issue of *Ms.*

In late June, Attorney General Edwin Meese's Commission on Pornography is expected to release a report on what President Ronald Reagan calls "one of the nation's most significant domestic issues." There are rumors that its recommendations will include such Draconian measures as a ban on vibrators and on videos portraying oral and anal sex. Whether or not the rumors are true, it's a safe bet that the commission will take a far tougher line than the 1970 presidential commission on the same subject—which decided that pornography has no ill effects on consumers, and might even provide a safety valve.

The question for feminists is whether the new recommendations will speak to feminist concerns—by which I mean *either* the Andrea Dworkin–Women Against Pornography position, which views much available porn as an assault on women's civil rights (and which has been extremely critical of the 1970 report), *or* the opposing Feminist Anti-Censorship Taskforce (FACT) position, which views the free speech accorded to pornographers as a necessary bedfellow to free speech for feminists and to the creation of our own erotica.

For the past year the Meese Commission has been holding public hearings all over the country; hearing topics have included "child pornography," "pornography and law enforcement issues," "production and distribution," "social science issues and other scientific findings relating to pornography," and "organized crime and pornography." The astute reader will notice right off that no hearings were scheduled on, say, "pornography and domestic violence," "pornography and the status of women," or "pornography and female sexual freedom." I attended several days of hearings in New York in January, and I came away from them with the overwhelming sense that I've been living for some time in a feminist cocoon—that the antiporn and anticensorship arguments that have raged among my friends (and in my own mind) for years occupy only a small, quirky corner of the Big Debate. Although some feminists (and nonfeminist women) did get a chance to testify, the structure of the hearings easily turned them into cheerleaders in a game between the male pornographers and the male smut-busters.

At the moment the smut-busters seem to be winning. In fact the commission has been widely criticized (especially by civil libertarians) as a group that didn't need to hold hearings at all, since it had decided its conclusions before it started. The chair of the panel, Henry Hudson, is a hard-nosed prosecutor who has successfully chased most of the "adult" bookstores out of his home county in Virginia. The other seven men and the four women on the panel include a few moderates, but the group's overall drift is perceptibly toward the right; among others it includes a former Nixon speechwriter and a president of a national "profamily" organization. Antiporn witnesses outnumbered anticensorship witnesses at the New York hearings by more than two to one. (On the other hand the commission's admittedly less-than-dazzling $500,000 budget has been criticized as inadequate by the extreme right, which is worried that its pornography agenda won't get any farther than its school prayer and abortion agendas.)

The New York hearings officially dealt with the relationship between pornography and organized crime. Most of the first day's and part of the second day's testimony were taken up by law enforcement officials who used maps, flow charts, tapes, and whatnot to "link" various pornography distributors to organized-crime "families." Why these links were important to chart (since the porn in question was largely legal) wasn't immediately apparent. Several witnesses charged that the mob makes money from the distribution of pornography, which it then reinvests in narcotics and other illegal businesses; other witnesses complained that pornography was the means by which racketeers made enough money to go into *legitimate* businesses. (Former pornographers, retired FBI agent William Kelly charged, were involved, for example, in the distribution of the Hollywood film *The Texas Chainsaw Massacre.* "And that's not obscene," he added, apparently outraged that porno profits could serve as seed money for respectable art. That some people might find massacre movies more obscene than skin flicks didn't seem to occur to him.) Much was made of the fact that porn is "clustered" with other bad industries—a charge that could be lodged against Times Square junk-food stands. It all seemed wildly beside the point.

Well, it turned out that the point was (brace yourself) whether Real Men Don't Bust Pornographers. The *click!* that made the Mafia-porn connection clear—at least to me—came toward the end of the first day, when the commission heard testimony from Carl Shoffler of the District of Columbia police department, who prepared a report for law enforcement personnel on racketeering and porn. Shoffler pointed out that many witnesses had already testified that (except for kiddie-porn statutes) most obscenity that could be prosecuted isn't. Some witnesses had even charged "reluctance" on the part of their superiors to accept porn as a serious priority. The reason, Shoffler suggested, was that most law enforcement types were "macho" guys themselves, guys who couldn't understand why anyone had it in for *Playboy* and *Penthouse.* (Kelly had earlier complained that some of his colleagues thought he was "weird" for never having watched stag films for pleasure himself.) Shoffler added, "The people who are involved [in fighting pornography] are often ostracized by their own peers. . . . There's a feeling about these cases, that they're unmanly or something . . . if I had to investigate porn with the current situation, I'd feel the intimidation." The reason that he had put together his study, he told the commission, was so that some would-be porn-smasher could "go in [to his superior] and say, 'This isn't just this little dirty bookstore, it's part of a big crime empire' "—and thereby not lose machismo points.

But there was also sometimes an eerie sense of abstraction about pornography—as if no "real" people ever bought it. Pornography was a Force, like some Old Testament plague; Mormon spokeswoman Ardeth G. Kapp called it "psychological warfare against the mind of man," which Americans should unite to fight, with God's help. (She compared our sluggish preparations against "the enemy" thus far to our failure to anticipate Pearl Harbor.) Retired FBI agent Homer E. Young went so far as to suggest that the way to nip the problem in the bud was to explain to the fellows in the truck drivers' union "the harms these materials may do" and encourage them not to carry it. A trio of law enforcement officials from North Carolina repeatedly described porn as a huge, lucrative business, saturating their state, whose population nonetheless consisted of "wholesome" folks, more than 80 percent of them church-goers. Finally, a commission member directly asked one of them who was buying the porn. "In any church," U.S. Attorney Sam Currin replied, "of course its membership *is* composed of sinners."

Not surprisingly, the religious right was well represented. The most bizarre of this group was June Griffin of the Cumberland Missionary Society, who led the assembly in impromptu prayer, ranted against gay men with AIDS, "Ms. Androgyny, strapped into your blue jeans," Gloria Steinem, and other predictable right-wing targets, as well as a few that were news to me—like John Wayne and Bob Hope, who, she thought, provided poor role models for Christian married men. (Wayne was one of Hollywood's "unattached male types" who cause homosexuality, and Hope, she later said, because he uses scantily clad women for overseas troop shows. Really.) Griffin also railed against those who let themselves be corrupted by the fleshpots of the world—New York, Paris, London . . . and Switzerland. (What? Obscene cuckoo clocks?)

The commission members sat politely through all comers. There were also witnesses like FBI-man Young, who publicly thanked God that he had never become addicted to porn himself and wondered aloud why some people in America are more concerned about clean air and clean rivers than clean minds. Another witness, Patrick F. Fagan, executive vice president of the Free Congress Research and Education Foundation, declared, "That sex which I think is good for society is that sex which is good for marriage." A slide show presented by Fayetteville, North Carolina, police captain Bill Johnson revealed that "there are sixty different areas of deviant behavior." (At this point the screen showed a pulp novel entitled *Women Who Love Women.*) Johnson also disclosed that at porn shops in his state people can actually buy "dildos, ointments, and edible panties."

Interestingly, *none* of these people engendered the audience hostility that greeted Andrea Dworkin (coauthor of the controversial civil rights and antiporn bill introduced in various versions in Minneapolis, Indianapolis, and elsewhere). FACT did not testify in New York (the anticensorship stance in this particular session being defended by the American Civil Liberties Union, *Penthouse,* and representatives of professional groups of librarians, writers, and other artists); nor did a number of other feminist groups in both camps. Consequently Dworkin was by default *the* official feminist presence at the hearings in the media capital of the world. When word spread that Dworkin was about to come to the witness stand, I happened to be sitting in front of a group at least some of whom I recognized as *Penthouse* employees. One woman turned to her male companion, rolled her eyes, and sneered, "I wonder if she's wearing her *coveralls!*" These and numerous other people in the audience (including feminists and civil libertarians) groaned and jeered throughout Dworkin's presentation. During her testimony she was even heckled by a female voice shouting, "You don't speak for all women!"

I'm sure some of Dworkin's anticensorship detractors don't like her legal approach, and I have some serious reservations about it myself—but after feeling all the palpable contempt in that room, I can't believe that's *all* it is. Because Dworkin comes out of both the left and the early feminist movement, I suspect she's seen by the anticensorship side as not just an adversary but a turncoat. She and they speak a common political language; her arguments against pornography thus have an intellectual basis that challenges the left in a way that the laughable antismut types simply don't (and from the left point of view, Dworkin ought to know better). The bottom line is that Dworkin is seen as threatening in a way that the far more powerful true-believing vice cops and religious nuts aren't. By the same token, one of Dworkin's colleagues assailed me for even interviewing FACT members for *Ms.*—since, she said, they couldn't possibly be feminists. It all reminded me of the old joke about how to form a liberal firing squad. (Get in a circle.)

Nor was Dworkin's message—that porn categorically victimizes women—received with totally open arms by the commission and the rest of the antiporn side. Though Fagan, of the Free Congress, said he agreed with what she said, he chastised her for concentrating on the victimization of women rather than on ''the whole area of [male] homosexual porn''; commissioner Park Dietz asked her ''what about porn depicting men?''; she was also asked why she had concentrated on women and not children in her remarks.

Although Dworkin has been criticized by the left for making alliances with the right wing on this issue, I think that what the commissioners were responding to in this instance was her refusal to play the game—that is, by approaching pornography in terms of its impact on ''family'' or ''marriage'' or some other approved institution. Two female witnesses who did try to play the game were former *Deep Throat* porno star Linda (Lovelace) Marchiano and former *Penthouse* ''Pet'' centerfold (and current *Penthouse* executive) Dottie Meyer. Marchiano, who has written a book describing how she was forced into the filming at gunpoint, spoke as ''a victim of pornography''; Meyer's message was that she was ''here today to tell you that I am *not* a victim of so-called pornography.'' Although they represented opposite sides, the two were curiously alike—soft-spoken, well dressed, middle-class women who both presented their experiences in the context of marriage-centered womanhood.

Marchiano was a touching and almost childlike witness—a "good girl" who tried to answer all questions conscientiously. (When she testified that she had been forced to have sex with a dog, she modestly spelled out "d-o-g" rather than say it.) Pornography, she told the commission, had grossly compromised her relationship with her children and her ability to teach them good values. "There are times when I'm with my children and having a wonderful afternoon," she added, "and I'll flash back on something that happened to me and I'll just cry." Meyer in turn presented *her* experiences in the context of someone who had "a traditional upbringing" before she was a Pet and had since had a happy marriage for seventeen years. "I'm a typical suburbanite," Meyer testified. "I cook and I clean my own home and I even take out the garbage." More than anything else, these two presentations told me how the issue is defined outside the feminist cocoon—and the issue is not whether pornography destroys or exalts the souls of women, but whether or not it interferes with the carrying out of traditional female roles.

Not that it really helped. The commissioners, most of whom normally asked easy, open-ended questions of witnesses (for instance their *opinions* about the link between porn and crime), suddenly turned prosecutory. Marchiano was cross-examined about whether she knew the difference between a revolver and an automatic, but (possibly because she was on the "right" side) was merely patronized. It was Meyer's testimony that provided one of the most dramatic sequences of the hearings.

Meyer appeared with Alan Dershowitz, a Harvard Law School professor and ACLU activist who writes a column for *Penthouse*. Dershowitz was the brains of the duo—an obnoxious but brilliant legal whiz who tauntingly challenged the commission members to have the "guts" to acknowledge that whatever controversy exists about violent porn, there's "no scientifically valid evidence that nonviolent, nonsexist adult 'pornography'—pure explicit erotica—contributes in any manner to violent crime." (At one point the proceedings nearly ground to a halt as Dershowitz and Commissioner

Frederick Schauer, professor of law at the University of Michigan, engaged in an arcane verbal duel about whether obscenity laws could rightly or wrongly be compared with the laws governing contaminated cans of tuna fish.) Dressed all in pink with plastic and pink leather high heels, Meyer was the stereotypical beauty, soothing the feathers that Dershowitz ruffled and busy explaining that *pet* is actually "a term of endearment."

Then commission chair Hudson pressed them for information about the release forms signed by *Penthouse* models. He specifically had questions about a photo layout allegedly showing Asian women bound and tied up in trees. When the two witnesses hemmed and hawed a bit about whether they could recollect the spread, Hudson jumped in like Perry Mason. "Let me refresh your recollection," he said—and suddenly the lights went down and the (totally ghastly) photo spread went up on a movie screen. The audience gasped.

But Hudson wasn't through. With what was obviously a copy of Meyer's centerfold on his desk, he began to fire questions at her. Earlier Meyer had testified that the text accompanying the centerfold was factual—just like any other personality profile. Why, then, was she identified in the text as Dominique Mauré? (It was, she explained, a stage name.) Why did it say that she was "French-born"? (Meyer replied that she was Canadian and therefore of French heritage. She had earlier testified that she grew up not in Quebec but Saskatchewan.) Commissioner Dietz joined in the questions: Was it true that she liked to be dominated in bed? Was it true that she was attracted to men who were "rough and tough"? Was it true that "I want a man who takes charge of my life and tells me what to do"? With as much dignity as she could muster, Meyer replied that those were indeed her "own personal preferences."

It was at this point that quite a few feminists in the audience, regardless of their politics, nearly lost their lunch. Was Hudson about to flash the centerfold on the giant screen? As it happens, he didn't. As it happens, he was also well within his rights in terms of questioning the witness. My personal reaction, I confess, was a morass of contradictory emotions, most of them nothing to be proud of —utter contempt for Meyer for getting herself (and by extension all of us) into this, identification with her, pity, admiration for Hudson's showmanship, the desire to strangle him, and a voyeuristic curiosity about what would happen next. It was a sleazy moment. Some would say pornographic.

Ann Snitow of FACT predicts that feminists of all stripes "could be horrified at what comes out of this [commission]. I think maybe they'll cynically pretend to a concern for women, but it's important to see this commission in the context of what the Reagan administration *hasn't* done to protect women—like giving us pay equity, affirmative action, day care, and legal and social services. There won't be any help here to beef up laws against violence against women—instead we'll just have a hit list with masturbation and sodomy on it."

Catharine A. MacKinnon, the attorney who coauthored the civil rights approach with Dworkin, said that she has "doubts" that the commission's report will reflect her ideas. "We have our own agenda," she commented. "We are a political movement. We're doing something, and we will continue. We have no alliances, and whoever wants to work with us on our terms is welcome to." She added, "Conservatives have never taken pornography seriously—they've just deplored it in public while ensuring access to it in private, as opposed to the left, which publicly defends it."

Stay tuned.

Going Wild

Susan Faludi

In 1991 the Tailhook Association of Navy Pilots held its annual convention at a Los Angeles Hilton. Afterward dozens of women, led by Lieutenant Paula Coughlin, told of a weekend in which a systematic form of sexual assault was conducted against the women in attendance by many of the men. Here Susan Faludi, author of *Backlash*, assesses the navy's prosecution of the men accused in the scandal. This essay first appeared on the op-ed page of *The New York Times* on February 16, 1994.

"You know what really stinks?" the young navy officer asked me. He pushed aside his third Scotch and leaned across the table in a chain restaurant near the naval air station in Norfolk, Virginia, where the Tailhook prosecutions have crept along for more than a year and where he was one of the dozens accused of "conduct unbecoming."

"What about all the *female* officers who were going wild at Tailhook? How come they haven't been prosecuted?"

Going wild?

"You know, wearing sexy clothes, dancing like a bunch of party girls, getting their legs shaved in the suites." He lowered his voice. Some, he continued darkly, even had sex with other officers. "How come they aren't being prosecuted for *that*? This whole thing stinks of a double standard."

The "double standard" lament comes up repeatedly with Tailhookers. How come the female officers got to "go wild" and not the guys?

At first look, this seems a ludicrous argument. Assault, not partying, was the offense that prompted protest from the female officers who attended the annual convention of naval aviators in Las

Vegas in 1991. Lieutenant Paula Coughlin, a helicopter pilot, blew the whistle on Tailhook because a crowd of men formed a gantlet down a hallway and tore at her clothes, grabbed her breasts and seized her buttocks with such force, she was hoisted airborne.

The dozens of other women attacked in the hallway said their fellow officers hurled them to the floor, yanked off their underwear, and molested them. This was not fun and games; many women who fought back only met with fiercer assaults and epithets, such as "whore" and "bitch."

Perpetuating the confusion between assault and mere bad taste may be the only lasting achievement of the Tailhook affair. The prosecution stumbled to a close last week with the dismissal of the three final cases that were pending court-martial and the resignation of Lieutenant Coughlin. In the end she's the only junior officer who is out of a job.

Sure, the investigation embarrassed the top brass and cut short some careers. Yesterday Admiral Frank Kelso, the navy's top officer, requested early retirement so the navy could close "this difficult chapter." Last week a military judge found that, contrary to his denials, Admiral Kelso had witnessed misconduct at the convention and failed to stop it.

But the twenty-eight junior officers actually disciplined were censured for these charges only: "indecent exposure," "conduct unbecoming an officer," and making "false official statements." In other words they were reprimanded for making half-naked buffoons of themselves and lying about it later.

None of the twenty-eight—and none of the original forty-three men who faced administrative action—was charged with assaulting or molesting women. They got in trouble for such sins as streaking and dropping their pants. By focusing on the officers' adolescent antics, the navy not only missed the point, it reinforced the same false message that has become increasingly prevalent in recent years: Advocates of the rights of women are really just prudes, antisex. Feminism, we hear once again, is just a euphemism for puritanism.

Ironically the prudes waggling their fingers at the male

Tailhook exhibitionists weren't female officers or feminists; they were men from the military establishment. It was the military that granted immunity to ringleaders of the gantlet so that they could testify against a bunch of streakers.

Tellingly, in his 111-page ruling last week dismissing the final three Tailhook cases, the navy judge, Captain William T. Vest, Jr., focused not on the violence against women but on Tailhook's "reputation for wild partying, heavy drinking and lewd behavior." When he suggested that sex, not assault, was on trial here, the young accused officer I talked to had a point.

If there's anything to gain from the hash made of the Tailhook investigation, perhaps it's the (slim) possibility that the bawdy officers who were disciplined might feel more empathy for women—who, after all, have always faced censure for exhibitions of lustiness. The men might remember that if there is a "double standard" at play here, that shoe is generally on the other, feminine foot. If they don't like how the shoe feels, maybe they won't insist that women wear it.

It's a Case of the Powerless Versus the Powerful

Susan Estrich

In October 1991 the nation sat riveted as law professor Anita Hill made allegations of sexual harassment against then–Supreme Court nominee Clarence Thomas in a nationally televised hearing that took place before the Senate Judiciary Committee. Susan Estrich, who ran Michael Dukakis's presidential campaign, is a professor of law at the University of Southern California and the author of *Real Rape*. Here she argues Anita Hill's case in an essay that first appeared on the op-ed page of the *Los Angeles Times* on October 13, 1991.

In forcing the Senate to delay its vote on Clarence Thomas's nomination to the Supreme Court, women exercised power in American politics in a way that has never happened before.

For all the talk of women's votes and women's issues and the gender gap, until last week it was difficult for politicians to harness the potential of women as a political power. As a Democrat I wish it were my party that had tapped the energy and anger of women; I wish it had been the Democratic leaders who had recognized immediately the seriousness of sexual harassment and demanded a delay. But the sexual-harassment issue—like those of congressional pay, money in politics, the savings-and-loan mess, the Los Angeles police-brutality incident, and most of the issues that resonate most deeply with the public—cuts across party lines. The divide is not between Republicans and Democrats, but between the powerful and the powerless.

Anita F. Hill's story of sexual harassment was just too unfamiliar to many senators, and just too familiar to many Americans. Studies of federal employees, in 1981 and 1987, found that 40 percent of the women had been sexually harassed on the job, and scholars estimate that as many as 85 percent of America's working women face sexual harassment in the workplace at some point in their careers.

Like Hill, most never report the incident; many continue to work for the men; some continue to have cordial relationships with them. Hill never complained, she says, because she was afraid to burn her bridges. She was a vulnerable young woman at the beginning of her career. She moved from one post to another with Thomas because she hoped for the best, thought it might stop, and needed her job.

The reaction of women to sexual harassment may be difficult for senators to understand. Sexual harassment is abuse of power. You can't hang up on your boss when he asks you out, because he has the power to fire you. You stay at the job because you need it, not because you find conditions tolerable. You maintain a cordial relationship because the man may be called as a reference, because you don't want to be known as a troublemaker.

That's not how U.S. senators would react if they were harassed by someone. Senators are used to complaining if they've been wronged. They take action—make a speech, fire the consultant, get even, not mad. But then senators don't have bosses. They have power.

Federal judges are equally removed from realities of workplace harassment, and how people without power respond to it. They don't have bosses either.

Since the mid 1970s, when the federal courts first recognized that Title VII of the 1964 Civil Rights Act prohibits sexual harassment, federal judges have been in the business of deciding whether women who complain of sexual harassment are telling the truth, and whether the conditions are bad enough to justify relief. In doing so they have too often imposed tests of credibility that even legitimate victims cannot meet, and tests of strength and endurance that no victim should be required to meet.

The tests are familiar, borrowed almost wholesale from the law of rape—as if decades of criticism had never taken place. Doctrines of consent, corroboration, fresh complaint, and provocation have long been used in the law of rape to shift the focus from the wrongs of the defendant to those of the victim. In rape law it has been all too common to ask what she did to invite the attack; why she didn't fight back; why she didn't complain immediately; why there are no witnesses. In rape cases too many courts have applied standards of objective reasonableness that expect women to stand up against stronger men and to fight back when attacked—to behave, in short, like reasonable men.

The worst of rape litigation stands, in many federal courts, more as an example followed in sexual harassment suits than as one rejected. That is painful proof not only of the endurance of sexism in the law but also of the vast divide between the powerful and the powerless.

The absence of a prompt complaint, the absence of corroboration, and the continuation of a relationship are not irrelevant to a woman's credibility in a sexual-harassment case—but they do not prove nearly as much as most judges believe. "Unwelcomeness" is a required element of any sexual-harassment suit. But to decide, as some courts have, that a "pleasant" rejection is not enough to meet this test is to apply the discredited notion of "no means yes" to women who may lose their jobs if they say no too clearly.

No one has suggested that every workplace slight amounts to a federal case—harassment must be "pervasive," and pervasiveness must be judged by the standard of the reasonable person. For many judges, however, in sexual harassment as in rape cases, the standard of reasonableness is an invitation to substitute their levels of tolerance and sensitivity for the victim's. Those who complain too much find themselves punished for their "hypersensitivity," and those who don't complain ("How bad could it be if she didn't complain?") for their strength.

I believe the American people understand sexual harassment far better than judges and senators. Ask any defense lawyer and he will say he'd rather try such a case before a judge than a jury—with good reason.

What has been striking about so much of the public debate in the case of Thomas and Hill is that it has focused not on whether the allegations are serious but on whether they are true. One is hard pressed to hear citizens making the arguments that lawyers have made so often, and successfully, in federal court: that a boss should be able to ask his assistant out—a few times anyway; or that pornography is funny—women shouldn't be so thin-skinned, even if the boss is someone who should know better; or that the charges should automatically be discredited because of the passage of time and the failure to complain. The Senate seemed content to leave the charges unresolved. It was the American people who forced them to be addressed.

Even as Hill assumed the witness chair on Friday morning, the White House continued to insist that Thomas had been smeared. One day after George Bush gave a speech about pornography, the President and his team seemed unable to believe this woman could even possibly be telling the truth. Indeed, even after her testimony, Senator Orrin Hatch (R-Utah) still could not understand how Hill could have continued to work for Thomas. In a fundamental way they made clear that they still do not get it.

Much has been made of the gender gap between men and women in their attitudes toward sexual harassment. Certainly men often regard as welcome advances that women find hostile and threatening. Women are socialized not to complain—to internalize, to bite your lip and blame yourself and hope he will still like you. But as important as gender may be, it is not the only factor at work.

In the last analysis the larger gap may be based on power. Last week people without power—women, and some men too—sent a message to the powerful. The Senate and the law will never be quite the same. And in coming together to send that message, the people demonstrated to their leaders where the real power ultimately lies.

Taking Sides Against Ourselves

Rosemary L. Bray

For African American women the Hill-Thomas hearings formed a particularly vexing moment, one that called the question on the often conflicting loyalties to race and gender. Rosemary L. Bray, then an editor of *The New York Times Book Review* and a former member of the *Ms.* editorial staff, was one of the first to address this issue in the essay that follows. It appeared in *The New York Times Sunday Magazine* on November 17, 1991. She is the author of a political memoir, *Unafraid of the Dark* (to be published by Random House in 1995), and the author of a children's biography of Martin Luther King to be published by Greenwillow Books.

The Anita Hill–Clarence Thomas hearings are over; Judge Thomas is Justice Thomas now. Yet the memories linger on and on. Like witnesses to a bad accident, many of us who watched the three days of Senate hearings continue to replay the especially horrible moments. We compare our memories of cool accusation and heated denial; we weigh again in our minds the hours of testimony, vacuous and vindictive by turn. In the end even those of us who thought we were beyond surprise had underestimated the trauma.

"I have not been so wrenched since Dr. King was shot," says Jewell Jackson McCabe, the founder of the National Coalition of 100 Black Women, an advocacy group with chapters in twenty-one states and the District of Columbia. "I cannot begin to tell you; this thing has been unbelievable."

The near-mythic proportions that the event has already assumed in the minds of Americans are due in part to the twin wounds of race and gender that the hearings exposed. If gender is a troubling problem in American life and race is still a national crisis, the synergy of the two embodied in the life and trials of Anita Hill left most of America dumbstruck. Even black people who did not support Clarence Thomas's politics felt that Hill's charges, made public at the eleventh hour, smacked of treachery. Feminist leaders embraced with enthusiasm a woman whose conservative political consciousness might have given them chills only a month earlier.

Even before the hearings began, the nomination of Clarence Thomas had taken on, for me, the quality of a nightmare. The particular dread I felt was one of betrayal—not a betrayal by President Bush, from whom I expected nothing—but by Thomas himself, who not only was no Thurgood Marshall but also gradually revealed himself to be a man who rejoiced in burning the bridges that brought him over.

I felt the kind of heartbreak that comes only to those of us still willing to call ourselves race women and race men in the old and honorable sense, people who feel that African Americans should live and work and succeed not only for ourselves but also for our people.

The heated debates about gender and race in America have occurred, for the most part, in separate spheres; the separation makes for neater infighting.

But black women can never skirt these questions; we are their living expression. The parallel pursuits of equality for African Americans and for women have trapped black women between often conflicting agendas for more than a century. We are asked in a thousand ways, large and small, to take sides against ourselves, postponing a confrontation in one arena to address an equally urgent task in another. Black men and white women have often made claims to our loyalty and our solidarity in the service of their respective struggles for recognition and autonomy, understanding only dimly that what may seem like liberty to each is for us only a kind of parole. Despite the bind, more often than not we choose loyalty to the race rather than the uncertain allegiance of gender.

Ours is the complicity of guilty survivors. A black man's presence is often feared; a black woman's presence is at least tolerated. Because until recently so much of the work that black women were paid to do was work that white men and women would not do—

cleaning, serving, tending, teaching, nursing, maintaining, caring—
we seem forever linked to the needs of human life that are at once
minor and urgent.

As difficult as the lives of black women often are, we know we
are mobile in ways black men are not—and black men know that we
know. They know that we are nearly as angered as they about their
inability to protect us in the traditional and patriarchal way, even as
many of us have moved beyond the need for such protection. And
some black men know ways to use our anger, our sorrow, our guilt,
against us.

In our efforts to make a place for ourselves and our families in
America, we have created a paradigm of sacrifice. And in living out
such lives, we have convinced even ourselves that no sacrifice is too
great to ensure what we view in a larger sense as the survival of the
race.

That sacrifice has been an unspoken promise to our people; it
has made us partners with black men in a way white women and
men cannot know. Yet not all of us view this partnership with respect. There are those who would use black women's commitment
to the race as a way to control black women. There are those who
believe the price of solidarity is silence. It was that commitment that
trapped Anita Hill. And it is a commitment we may come to rue.

As I watched Hill being questioned that Friday by white men,
by turn either timid or incredulous, I grieved for her. The anguish in
her eyes was recognizable to me. Not only did she dare to speak
about events more than one woman would regard as unspeakable,
she did so publicly. Not only did she make public accusations best
investigated in private, she made them against a man who was black
and conservative, as she was—a man who in other ways had earned
her respect.

"Here is a woman who went to Sunday school and took it
seriously," says Cornel West, director of the African American
Studies department at Princeton University and a social critic who
felt mesmerized by what he called "the travesty and tragedy" of the
hearings. "She clearly is a product of the social conservatism of a
rural black Baptist community." For black women historically, such

probity, hard-won and tenaciously held, was social salvation. For white onlookers it suggested an eerie primness out of sync with contemporary culture.

In the quiet and resolute spirit she might very well have learned from Sunday school, Hill confronted and ultimately breached a series of taboos in the black community that have survived both slavery and the postsegregation life she and Clarence Thomas share. Anita Hill put her private business in the street, and she downgraded a black man to a room filled with white men who might alter his fate —surely a large enough betrayal for her to be read out of the race.

By Sunday evening Anita Hill's testimony lay buried under an avalanche of insinuation and innuendo. Before the eyes of a nation a tenured law professor beloved by her students was transformed into an evil, opportunistic harpy; a deeply religious Baptist was turned into a sick and delusional woman possessed by Satan and in need of exorcism; this youngest of thirteen children from a loving family became a frustrated spinster longing for the attentions of her fast-track superior, bent on exacting a cruel revenge for his rejection.

These skillful transformations of Anita Hill's character by some members of the Senate were effective because they were familiar, manageable images of African American womanhood. What undergirds these images is the common terror of black women out of control. We are the grasping and materialistic Sapphire in an "Amos 'n' Andy" episode; the embodiment of a shadowy, insane sexuality; the raging, furious, rejected woman. In their extremity these are images far more accessible and understandable than the polished and gracious dignity, the cool intelligence that Anita Hill displayed in the lion's den of the Senate chamber. However she found herself reconstituted, the result was the same. She was, on all levels, simply unbelievable.

Anita Hill fell on the double-edged sword of African American womanhood. Her privacy, her reputation, her integrity—all were casualties of an ignorance that left her unseen by and unknown to most of those who meant either to champion or abuse her. As credible, as inspiring, as impressive as she was, most people who saw her had no context in which to judge her. The signs and symbols that might have helped to place Hill were long ago appropriated by officials of authentic (male) blackness, or by representatives of authentic (white) womanhood. Quite simply, a woman like Anita Hill couldn't possibly exist. And in that sense she is in fine historical company.

More than a century earlier, black women routinely found themselves beyond belief, and thus beyond help, solace, and protection. In 1861 the most famous of the few slave narratives written by a black woman, *Incidents in the Life of a Slave Girl,* was published. (The book was regarded as fiction for more than one hundred years, until in 1987 Jean Fagin Yellin of Pace University completed six years of painstaking research substantiating the existence of its author, Harriet Jacobs, and her harrowing story.) Writing under the pseudonym "Linda Brent," Jacobs outlined for the genteel white woman of the nineteenth century the horrors, both sexual and otherwise, that awaited the female slave. Jacobs spent close to seven years hiding from her master ensconced in a garret, with food smuggled in by her recently freed grandmother.

In the story of Harriet Jacobs the powerful man she fears is white. In the story of Anita Hill the powerful man she fears is black. But the vulnerability of each woman is a palpable presence in the stories they tell. Jacobs's tale is enlivened by the dramatic structure of the nineteenth-century sentimental novel; Hill's accounts are magnified through the image of her presence on television. Indeed Jacobs's first lines are a plea to her audience to be taken seriously: "Reader, be assured this narrative is no fiction. I am aware that some of my adventures may seem incredible; but they are, nevertheless, strictly true."

Later she recounts the beginning of her owner's pursuit of her, the year she turned fifteen: "My master began to whisper foul words in my ear. Young as I was, I could not remain ignorant of their import. I tried to treat them with indifference or contempt. . . . The other slaves . . . knew too well the guilty practices under that roof; and they were aware that to speak of them was an offense that never went unpunished. . . . I longed for someone to confide in. I would have given the world to have laid my head on my grandmother's faithful bosom, and told her all my troubles. . . . I dreaded the consequences of a violent outbreak; and both pride and fear kept me silent.''

Harriet Jacobs had good reason to fear; even free African American women of the nineteenth century possessed no rights that anyone was bound to respect. Regarded as immoral and loose, black women spent an inordinate amount of time in the years after slavery in attempts to establish themselves as virtuous women, as a rebuke to the rash of hypersexual images that flooded contemporary consciousness in those days, images that rationalized the routine sexual abuse of black women—both slave and free—by white men.

It was a stereotype that had consequences for black men as well: "Historically, the stereotype of the sexually potent black male was largely based on that of the promiscuous black female," explained Paula Giddings, in *When and Where I Enter,* her history of black women in America. "He would have to be potent, the thinking went, to satisfy such hot-natured women."

Such myths of sexual potency and promiscuity, written and disseminated by trained nineteenth-century historians, fueled the widespread fears of black men as rapists of white women—and provided the engine for a campaign of terrorism against newly freed black people that included a rash of lynchings. Thus, it was especially troubling that Clarence Thomas should refer to the second round of hearings as "a high-tech lynching."

Thomas evoked one of the most emotional images in African American consciousness, flinging himself across history like Little Eva clinging to an ice floe and at the same time blaming a black woman for his troubles. A century earlier it was the courageous and single-minded investigative reporting of a black female journalist, Ida B. Wells, that finally galvanized a recalcitrant United States into taking lynching seriously.

Incidents in the Life of a Slave Girl would have made far more instructive reading for the Senate Judiciary Committee than *The Exorcist.* It was, after all, the Senate's appalling lack of familiarity with what it feels like to be powerless, vulnerable, and afraid that rendered Anita Hill and her behavior incomprehensible to most of them. In her preface Jacobs writes that she has "concealed the names of places and given persons fictitious names. I had no motive for secrecy on my own account, but I deemed it kind and considerate toward others to pursue this course.'' It is likely that she is more fearful than she lets on.

But it is just as likely that Jacobs evokes a way of seeing the world that transcends nineteenth-century female gentility, that Jacobs is acting out of Christian charity to those who have persecuted her. And it is just as likely that she held on to her fragile dreams of connection, however slight, to home and friends, however frightening the context in which she enjoyed them.

Studying this connected way of seeing the world has been the work of Carol Gilligan's professional life. The author of *In a Different Voice: Psychological Theory and Women's Development,* she has written extensively on women's psychological development and the issues of justice and care that characterize the relationships of many women, both personal and professional. Thus she did not find it implausible that Anita Hill might have experienced the events she described, yet continued to work with Judge Thomas.

''It amazed me that no one understood the underlying logic of what she did,'' Gilligan says. ''Her basic assumption was that you live in connection with others, in relationship with others. Now her experience of that relationship was one of violation; it was offensive to her. But she was making the attempt to work it through in the relationship; trying to resolve conflict without breaking connection.'' The possibility that such an ethic might have motivated Anita Hill in her choices is rarely voiced in discussions about her.

It may be that this low-key approach does not fit the image of the black woman who stands ready to challenge and confront offensive behavior. The surly black wife with a frying pan in her hand is the flip side of the nurturing mammy, and it is abundantly clear to millions by now that Anita Hill is neither.

Thus her profound self-possession, particularly in the face of the behavior she ascribed to Thomas, seemed impossible to observers—in large part because her response was not the conditioned one for black women. Hill showed no signs of the Harriet Tubman syndrome, the fierce insistence on freedom or death that made Tubman an abolitionist legend. Anita Hill grabbed no blunt objects with which to threaten her superior, she did not thunder into his office in righteous anger or invoke the power to bring suit. She was not funny, or feisty, or furious in response to the behavior she described. She was disgusted, embarrassed, and ambivalent. Therefore it must have been a dream.

"It was quite fitting that the bulk of the hearings took place on the weekend that Redd Foxx died," says Stanley Crouch, a cultural critic and author of *Notes of a Hanging Judge: Essays and Reviews 1979–1989*. "A bunch of the material sounded like stuff from a Redd Foxx–Richard Pryor–Eddie Murphy routine."

But few people were laughing. That week in October my phone rang nonstop. Friends called to talk about their stories of sexual harassment, their memories of vengeful, jealous women who lie, their theories of self-loathing black men who act out their hostility toward black women while lusting after white women. My sister, Linda, called from Chicago the night before the vote, then used her conference-call feature to add her good friend to the line, with whom she had been arguing for an hour already. "I already know you believe her," Linda announced to me. "I just want to hear you tell me why."

The buses and trains and elevators were filled with debates and theories of conspiracy: Hill set up Thomas to bring a black man down. Thomas was a man; what man didn't talk about his prowess? In a Harlem restaurant where I sat with a cup of tea and the papers that Saturday, the entire kitchen staff was in an uproar. The cook, an African woman, wanted to know why Hill waited ten years to bring it up. The waitress, an African American woman, said she couldn't tell what to think.

A young black man in his twenties announced he had a theory. "Clarence got jungle fever, and she got mad," he said with a laugh. *Jungle fever* is the code term, taken from the Spike Lee film of the same name, for a black man's desire to sleep with a white woman. Clarence Thomas's second wife is white, therefore Anita Hill was overcome with jealous rage and hungry for revenge.

"We all know that the animosity of black women toward black

men who marry white women is on the level of the recent fire in Oakland,'' Stanley Crouch said. ''That's a major fact. They might be as racist about that as white people used to be.''

Then again some black women might not care at all—a reasonable assumption, given the statistics indicating that interracial relationships between black women and white men have more than tripled in the last twenty years.

Some black women may feel rejected or betrayed by black men lured by a white standard of beauty few of them could emulate. Some may just hate white women. But there is no real evidence to suggest that any of these scenarios apply to Anita Hill and her galvanizing testimony. Most people with an opinion about why she stepped forward regard it as a matter of ideology, not, as some people still want to think, romance.

Yet the issues of race and sex illuminated by the hearings remain. So, too, do the myriad ways in which race and gender combine to confuse us. But for the first time in decades the country has been turned, for a time, into a mobile social laboratory. A level of discussion between previously unaligned groups may have begun with new vigor and candor.

Segments of the feminist movement have been under attack for their selective wooing of black women. Yet many of these same women rallied to Hill with impressive speed. Some black women who had never before considered sexism as an issue serious enough to merit collective concern have begun to organize, including a group of black female academics known as African-American Women in Defense of Ourselves. And even in brusque New York, people on opposite sides of this issue, still traumatized by the televised spectacle, seem eager to listen, to be civil, to talk things over.

''I am so pleased people are starting to ask questions, not only about race and gender but about the America that has frustrated and disappointed them,'' says Jewell Jackson McCabe. ''People who had become cynical, people who have not talked about issues in their lives, are talking now. I think the experience was so bad, it was so raw. I don't know a woman who watched those hearings whose life hasn't been changed.''

"It was an international drama," says Michael Eric Dyson, assistant professor of ethics, philosophy, and cultural criticism at Chicago Theological Seminary. "Anita Hill has put these issues on the American social agenda. She has allowed black men and women to talk freely for the first time about a pain that has been at the heart of our relationships since slavery. Black wives are beginning to tell their husbands about the kind of sexism they have faced not at the hands of white men, but black men."

What was most striking about the hearings, in the end, was the sense of destiny that surrounded them. There was something rewarding about seeing what began as a humiliating event become gradually transformed only in its aftermath. Two African Americans took center stage in what became a national referendum on many of our most cherished values. In the midst of their shattering appearances, Anita Hill and Clarence Thomas each made us ask questions that most of us had lost the heart to ask.

They are exactly the kinds of questions that could lead us out of the morass of cynicism and anger in which we've all been stuck. That is an immensely satisfying measurement of the Hill-Thomas hearings. It would not be the first time that African Americans have used tragedy and contradiction as catalysts to make America remember its rightful legacy.

Sex Amidst Semicolons

George F. Will

In the fall of 1993 the students of Antioch College adopted a policy for on-campus sexual behavior that caused an uproar in the media. Here George F. Will, ABC News commentator, syndicated columnist, and author of *Men at Work,* argues against the policy in an essay that first appeared in the October 4, 1993, issue of *Newsweek.*

The social air is heavily scented with sex. It saturates commerce and amusement—advertising, entertainment, recreation. Eros is rampant everywhere. Make that almost everywhere. In Yellow Springs, Ohio, home of Antioch College, the god of love has a migraine, the result of reading that institution's rules regulating "interactions" of a sexual sort.

Declaring the frequency of "sexual violence" on campuses "alarming," Antioch displays nice evenhandedness regarding eligibility for the coveted status of victim. Antioch notes that most victims are female but "there also are female perpetrators and male victims." Furthermore, "there also are many students who have already experienced sexual violence before arriving at Antioch; healing from that experience may be an integral part of their personal, social and academic lives while they are here." Having postulated a vast supply of unhealed victims and probable new ones, Antioch lays down the law:

"*All sexual contact and conduct* between any two people *must be consensual;* consent must be obtained *verbally* before there is any sexual contact or conduct; if the level of sexual intimacy increases during an interaction (i.e., if two people move from kissing while fully clothed—which is one level—to undressing for direct physical contact, which is another level), the people involved need to express their clear verbal consent before moving to that new level; if one person wants to *initiate* moving to a higher level of sexual intimacy in an interaction, *that person is responsible for getting the verbal consent of the other person(s) involved before moving to that level;* if you have had a particular level of sexual intimacy before with someone, you must still ask each and every time. . . . Asking 'Do you want to have sex with me?' is not enough. The request for consent must be specific to each act.''

Antioch meticulously defines terms ('' 'Sexual contact' includes the touching of thighs, genitals, buttocks, the pubic region, or the breast/chest area''), although some terms seem somewhat spacious. For example, ''insistent and/or persistent sexual harassment'' includes, ''but is not limited to, unwelcome and irrelevant comments, references, gestures or other forms of personal attention which are inappropriate and which may be perceived as persistent sexual overtones or denigration.'' Imagine being charged with making a ''gesture'' that was ''irrelevant'' or ''perceived'' as denigrating.

Campuses, being concentrations of young people, are awash with hormones, which are powerful. However, hormonal heat may be chilled by Antioch's grim seasoning of sex with semicolons. This is what happens when sexual emancipation comes to a litigious society. Antioch's many dense pages setting forth procedures for prosecuting and reforming offenders will keep batteries of lawyers busy debating whether a particular request for consent was sufficiently specific. (''May I touch that?'' ''Is a caress more than a touch?'' ''May I unbutton that?'' ''Have you consented regarding all the buttons?'') Imagine the litigation that can arise from questions about what constitutes movement from one ''level'' to another. (Is the movement of a hand from this body part to that one necessarily a movement to a new level? If only John Marshall were alive to help us cope.) And what is the significance of the *(s)* attached to the word *person* two paragraphs above? Sexual freedom sure seems to require an elaborate regulatory apparatus.

Our nation opted for the moral deregulation of sex a decade before deregulating airlines. About twenty years ago colleges, like a lot of parents, stopped acting *in loco parentis* regarding sexual matters. Official indifference about what students do with their bodies includes all organs except the lungs: about smoking, colleges are as stern as they once were about copulating. (Health care may be paid for partly with a "sin tax" on cigarettes. A million abortions a year is a mere matter of "choice"—an achievement of the "pro-choice" movement—but choosing to smoke is a sin. Interesting.) Today students can do anything their physiognomies will permit regarding sex, but they must observe due process.

Rules like Antioch's are both causes and effects of an odd "crisis" on campuses. Such rules are written in response to supposed "sexual violence" that supposedly is so frequent that "many students" arriving at Antioch already are victims in need of "healing." By punctiliously codifying due process regarding "levels" of consensual "interactions" with "other person(s)," the rules multiply the opportunities for, and increase the probability of, sexual offenses. All this serves the interests of two classes that have much in common.

The rules, and the assumption of "crisis" that they reflect, give the "caring professions," as they like to be called, lots of victims to care for. These professionals include counselors, "gender equity" bureaucrats, sensitivity "facilitators" who conduct "safe-sex workshops," and others. And the rules, by postulating a culture of female victimization and by creating many permutations of sexual offenses, delight those feminists who consider America a predatory "rape culture." The title of Antioch's Sexual Offense Prevention and Survivors' Advocacy Program encourages a sense of intense peril, of life lived precariously in a sexual jungle. People who experience, say, "irrelevant comments" are *survivors*.

One function of the "caring professions" is to heighten the sensitivity of persons who might not "perceive" sexual harassment where they should. Professionals can help young people be as offended and frightened as they should be in phallocentric America. A really caring professional can get a young woman to see that if she has no memory of being a victim of sexual violence, that may prove either how awful the memory is that she has "repressed" or how inadequate her definition of "sexual violence" is.

At Antioch, as young people go from level to level in their interactions, they are taught that there is one cardinal value: consent. The rules say, "Do not take silence as consent; it isn't. Consent must be clear and verbal (i.e., saying: yes, I want you to kiss me now)."

Actually, not now, dear. I have a headache.

Playing by the Antioch Rules

Eric Fassin

Amid the chorus of derision that greeted the Antioch sex rules, a few lonely voices argued in favor of the policy. Eric Fassin, assistant director of New York University's Institute of French Studies, made his case in this essay, which appeared on the op-ed page of *The New York Times* on December 26, 1993.

A good consensus is hard to find—especially on sexual politics. But the infamous rules instituted last year by Antioch College, which require students to obtain explicit verbal consent before so much as a kiss is exchanged, have created just that. They have provoked indignation (this is a serious threat to individual freedom!) as well as ridicule (can this be serious?). Sexual correctness thus proves a worthy successor to political correctness as a target in public debate.

Yet this consensus against the rules reveals shared assumptions among liberals, conservatives, and even radicals about the nature of sex in our culture.

The new definition of consent at Antioch is based on a "liberal" premise: It assumes that sexual partners are free agents and that they mean what they say—yes means yes, and no means no. But the initiator must now obtain prior consent, step by step, which in practice shifts the burden of clarification from the woman to the man. The question is no longer "Did she say no?" but "Did she say yes?" Silence does not indicate consent, and it becomes his responsibility to dispel any ambiguity.

The novelty of the rules, however, is not as great as it seems. Antioch will not exert more control over its students; there are no sexual police. In practice you still do what you want—as long as your partner does not complain . . . the morning after. If this is censorship, it intervenes *ex post facto,* not *a priori.*

In fact the "threat" to individual freedom for most critics is not the invasion of privacy through the imposition of sexual codes but the very existence of rules. Hence the success of polemicists like Katie Roiphe or Camille Paglia, who argue that feminism in recent years has betrayed its origins by embracing old-style regulations, paradoxically choosing the rigid 1950s over the liberating 1960s. Their advice is simply to let women manage on their own, and individuals devise their own rules. This individualist critique of feminism finds resonance with liberals, but also, strangely, with conservatives, who belatedly discover the perils of regulating sexuality.

But sexual laissez-faire, with its own implicit set of rules, does not seem to have worked very well recently. Since the collapse of established social codes, people play the same game with different rules. If more women are complaining of sexual violence, while more men are worrying that their words and actions might be misconstrued, who benefits from the absence of regulation?

A laissez-faire philosophy toward relationships assumes that sexuality is a game that can (and must) be played without rules, or rather that the invention of rules should be left to individual spontaneity and creativity, despite rising evidence that a rule of one's own often leads to misunderstandings. When acted out, individual fantasy always plays within preordained social rules. These rules conflict with the assumption in this culture that sex is subject to the reign of nature, not artifice, that it is the province of the individual, not of society.

Those who believe that society's constraints should have nothing to do with sex also agree that sex should not be bound by the social conventions of language. Indeed this rebellion against the idea of social constraints probably accounts for the controversy over explicit verbal consent—from George Will, deriding "Sex Amidst Semicolons," to Camille Paglia railing "As if sex occurs in the verbal realm." As if sexuality were incompatible with words. As if the only language of sex were silence. For *The New Yorker,* "the [Antioch] rules don't get rid of the problem of unwanted sex at all;

they just shift the advantage from the muscle-bound frat boy to the honey-tongued French major."

This is not very different from the radical-feminist position, which holds that verbal persuasion is no better than physical coercion. In this view sexuality cannot be entrusted to rhetoric. The seduction of words is inherently violent, and seduction itself is an object of suspicion. (If this is true, Marvell's invitation "To His Coy Mistress" is indeed a form of sexual harassment, as some campus feminists have claimed.)

What the consensus against the Antioch rules betrays is a common vision of sexuality that crosses the lines dividing conservatives, liberals, and radicals. So many of the arguments start from a conventional situation, perceived and presented as natural: a heterosexual encounter with the man as the initiator, and the woman as gatekeeper—hence the focus on consent.

The outcry largely results from the fact that the rules undermine this traditional erotic model. Not so much by proscribing (legally), but by prescribing (socially). The new model, in which language becomes a normal form of erotic communication, underlines the conventional nature of the old one.

By encouraging women out of their "natural" reserve, these rules point to a new definition of sexual roles. "Yes" could be more than a way to make explicit the absence of a "no"; "yes" can also be a cry of desire. Women may express demands, and not only grant favors. If the legal "yes" opened the ground for an erotic "yes," if the contract gave way to desire and if consent led to demand, we would indeed enter a brave new erotic world.

New rules are like new shoes: they hurt a little at first, but they may fit tomorrow. The only question about the Antioch rules is not really whether we like them, but whether they improve the situation between men and women. All rules are artificial, but, in the absence of generally agreed-upon social conventions, any new prescription must feel artificial. And isn't regulation needed precisely when there is an absence of cultural consensus?

Whether we support or oppose the Antioch rules, at least they force us to acknowledge that the choice is not between regulation and freedom, but between different sets of rules, implicit or explicit. They help dispel the illusion that sexuality is a state of nature individuals must experience outside the social contract, and that eroticism cannot exist within the conventions of language. As Antioch reminds us, there is more in eroticism and sexuality than is dreamt of in this culture.

PART THREE

Rights and Wrongs in the Intimate Arena

The First Amendment Under Fire from the Left

A Conversation with Floyd Abrams and Catharine A. MacKinnon
Anthony Lewis, Moderator

Antipornography activists are often depicted as members of a demolition squad whose target is the First Amendment to the Constitution, which guarantees the right to free speech and freedom of the press, along with separation of church and state. Anthony Lewis, a columnist for *The New York Times,* called the question when he sat down with Catharine A. MacKinnon and Floyd Abrams in the newspaper's offices early in 1994 for this discussion. MacKinnon is the coauthor, with Andrea Dworkin, of the model antipornography civil rights ordinance that was introduced in 1983 in Minneapolis. She is a professor of law at the University of Michigan; her most recent book is *Only Words.* Floyd Abrams is a prominent First Amendment lawyer. This discussion first appeared on March 13, 1994, in *The New York Times Sunday Magazine.*

"Congress shall make no law . . . abridging the freedom of speech, or of the press." The late Justice Hugo L. Black wrote memorably about that proposition: "First in the catalogue of human liberties essential to the life and growth of a government of, for and by the people are those liberties written into the First Amendment to our Constitution."

Are those guarantees in trouble? That is the question put by *The New York Times Magazine* to two quite different authorities: Floyd Abrams, the prominent First Amendment lawyer, and Professor

Catharine A. MacKinnon, the author of *Only Words* and an advocate of legal measures to curb pornography. They met at *The New York Times* for the discussion excerpted here. Anthony Lewis, a columnist for *The New York Times,* was the moderator.

Anthony Lewis: Repression in this country, repression of speech, has historically come from the right. It was so with the Sedition Act of 1798; it was so when Attorney General A. Mitchell Palmer arrested thousands of supposed radicals in 1920; it was so when Senator Joseph McCarthy tyrannized the nation. Now I think there is a significant movement for repression from the political left. There have been calls, especially on campus, to repress certain kinds of expression—speech demeaning to minorities and disadvantaged groups, pornography. Mr. Abrams, could you comment on this phenomenon?

Floyd Abrams: Well, I think there is a significant effort to restrict First Amendment values, if not legally defined First Amendment rights, which comes from the liberal community or the left-liberal community. Why is that so? It is human nature. People don't like to permit speech of which they thoroughly disapprove, and liberals are no more able to disassociate themselves from trying to impose into law what they wish people would say than conservatives are. It's true that most of the efforts, historically speaking, that have posed direct threats to the First Amendment have come from the right. Now we see on campuses around the country in a wide range of circumstances things being done, limitations on speech being imposed, that if they came from the right we would call them McCarthyism. And so they are.

Lewis: Professor MacKinnon, has anything been said so far that you take exception to?

Catharine MacKinnon: I agree that First Amendment values are in trouble on the ground. But the trouble I see is different from what Professor Abrams sees. It seems to me that the lack of access to speech by those with dissident views—views not allowed to be expressed in the media, by a publishing world that excludes these, as well as by systematic forms of exclusion like lousy educational systems that promote illiteracy—are all forms of trouble for the First

Amendment. But there are other distortions of the First Amendment, where it protects direct harm: I refer to the pornography industry, as well as cross-burning, an act of terrorism that's defended as an act of speech. As for limitations on speech on campus, I'm not sure what Mr. Abrams was referring to. There have been grievance procedures on campuses to restrict sexual harassment for over a decade. Is that what you mean by limits on speech on campus? Are you saying that when a teacher says to a student, "Sleep with me and I will give you an A?" that is protected speech so long as it is done on a campus? Procedures to allow students to bring complaints about that kind of activity have been recognized as necessary for equal access to the benefits of an education for some time. That's just one example of an abuse that can hide behind freedom of speech when in fact it is an act of inequality.

Lewis: Let me test your proposition by citing one much-advertised example of campus speech problems—the seizure of student newspapers at the University of Pennsylvania. It's happened elsewhere; it happened at Brandeis when a student newspaper carried a paid ad from one of those Holocaust revisionist outfits, and students who didn't like the ad trashed the newspaper.

MacKinnon: That is, they engaged in a demonstration.

Lewis: Well, that's my question. Is it your notion that nothing should be done about that? Is it permissible to trash newspapers if you don't like something that's in them?

MacKinnon: There is expressive value in what the students did, and there is also expressive value in letting the paper publish.

Abrams: I am prepared to make a somewhat stronger value judgment than that. I think that the students who seized and destroyed newspapers at Penn, at Brandeis, and elsewhere were doing something profoundly antithetical to First Amendment values, and I think they are the product of bad teaching. They justify what they have done either because they think it's right politically or because they think they are engaging in expressive conduct, and therefore "anything goes." But anything can be said to fall within the rubric of expressive conduct, including murder and rape. It seems to me that burning newspapers is something that should be beyond the pale in our society—that there should be far more agreement around this table that it is wrong to do and contrary to First Amendment values to do.

MacKinnon: What I think about it would depend on the position I was in or in whose shoes I was acting. It would seem to me to have been preferable for the people who ran the ad to have decided not to run it—for reasons of not promoting lies or not endangering or targeting specific groups for abuse.

Lewis: In 1919 Justice Holmes wrote an opinion in which he said that the First Amendment envisaged freedom for ideas "that we loathe and believe to be fraught with death." You can't get any stronger or more poetic language than that. I take it that you don't agree with it.

MacKinnon: I do agree with that, but one thing freedom of speech gives editors is the right to make decisions not to run lies. If it's false, you don't have to run it just because you disagree with it, to respect Holmes.

Abrams: But even someone living on a university campus, it seems to me, should know that newspapers may not be destroyed. That seems to me self-evident.

MacKinnon: But what about the idea that newspapers should not publish lies, including lies that target groups of people for abuse and aggression in that community?

Abrams: Newspapers are permitted—as you just said—to publish what they choose. It is an editorial decision, as you just said, whether to publish an advertisement like this. Once the student newspaper has decided to publish it, it is unacceptable for other students to respond by seizing the papers and taking that topic out of the realm of public debate.

MacKinnon: But is it acceptable to you that the newspaper chose to publish it?

Abrams: Yes, I think that it's important that there be public debate even about statements that I think are lies and in some cases that I am sure are lies.

MacKinnon: If you had been in a position to have a discussion with those students, would you have urged them to publish such material or not to publish it?

Abrams: I have had that discussion with some college newspapers, and I have urged them to publish it and to run editorials denouncing it. And that is the way I think the First Amendment should work on campus.

Lewis: Another area: speech codes. One speech code—it was at the University of Connecticut—prohibited inappropriately directed laughter. That's perhaps an extreme example; but a good many of them go very far in prohibiting bad manners. How do you two feel about speech codes, university speech codes in particular?

MacKinnon: I found that sexual-harassment prohibitions or policies that allow students to complain about acts of harassment that are actionable under federal law have been included under the rubric of speech code. So I don't frankly know what you are talking about. Title VI of the Civil Rights Act promotes equal access to the benefits of an education on the basis of race; it's a federally guaranteed right. So one could say that if you have epithets, invective, harassment, and abuse on the basis of race or religion or sexual orientation, you have an environment in which the equal ability of students to learn is obstructed. These grievance procedures arise under federal equality guarantees.

Abrams: In my view they threaten the values and sometimes the text of the First Amendment itself.

MacKinnon: I'm not defending every one of these codes in each of their particulars. I want to make clear that many of them include procedures that make it possible to bring complaints about sexual harassment in education. The litigation that has attacked these codes on First Amendment grounds has also attacked these complaint procedures, although the results on that are inconclusive.

Abrams: I think it's important to distinguish between different forms of speech. First, I agree with Professor MacKinnon that a professor who says, "Sleep with me and I'll give you an A," not only violates the law but should be fired. There was too much of that and too little was done about it for too long. I think that is very different from the situation of a professor now challenging sanctions imposed upon him by the University of New Hampshire, Prof. J. Donald Silva, who during a lecture to his students made some references to sex. He was brought up on charges, suspended for a year, and directed to get counseling to cure him of what the university thus far has found to be sexual harassment. I think that example—and there are a number of others—is one in which what is wrong is not the procedure. Professor MacKinnon is quite right in my view that there have to be procedures to implement our abhorrence of sexual harassment. But on more than one campus, charges have been made by students about words not proposing sexual conduct or suggesting any harm to a student but words used in a lecture and other statements made that have been accused of constituting sexual harassment. There at least First Amendment values are implicated, and I think it's very important for the university community to look very, very hard before they find violations of sexual-harassment codes or law in such situations.

MacKinnon: I certainly agree with the hard look, but I do have a question about what you said. Is it possible for sexual harassment to occur in a setting in which a teacher uses words in a classroom to a group of students?

Abrams: Yes, I suppose, but it would have to be very direct. It would have to be something that simply leaps off the page as constituting harassment and not just a reference to sex. There are people who are offended, for reasons I understand full well, but who are offended at sexual references. It's very important that we not engage in a sort of puritanical cleansing effort on campus to strike such references from the vocabulary of faculty and students.

MacKinnon: I agree with that. There's no problem between us on that. Nothing I have been involved in has had anything to do with being offended, with clean language, or with restricting ideas I don't like, for that matter.

Lewis: Sometime not so long ago, if I remember it correctly, a professor at a major law school quoted an opinion of Justice Robert Jackson's. Jackson in turn quoted Byron's Julia, a character in his poem "Don Juan" who—I think I have this right—"whispering 'I will ne'er consent,' consented." I've forgotten what the context was, but charges were pressed quite vigorously against the professor. What do you think of that rather marginal sexual reference passing through two learned authors, Byron and Justice Jackson? Does it bother you? Should it be ground for a complaint?

MacKinnon: I guess what is being raised there is a positive-outcome rape scenario.

Lewis: What do you mean by that? I'm sorry, I don't understand.

MacKinnon: A positive-outcome rape scenario—it's one of the most common in pornography—is one in which the woman is shown being subjected to sexual aggression. She resists; she's further aggressed against. She further resists; the more she's aggressed against, the more she begins to get into it. Finally she is shown to be ecstatically consenting and having a wonderful time—in other words, it could be described as "whispering that she would ne'er consent, consented." Not consenting is itself the turn-on, saying no is part of meaning yes.

Lewis: What do you think about professors who have made sexually oriented comments in class that students have found offensive or even to constitute harassment? Is it your view that professors ought be free to do that?

MacKinnon: The campus is different from the workplace, but in both we have equality guarantees, and an analogy between work and school has been a helpful starting place. Students are guaranteed equal access to the benefits of an education without discrimination on the basis of race or sex. So the question is Does what you are asking about interfere with this, together with rights to academic freedom and freedom of speech? In the workplace, harassment has to be sufficiently severe or pervasive to change the conditions of work. Just as a beginning, think by analogy of a hostile learning environment—one in which sexualized, demeaning, denigrating comments, subordinating comments or materials were sufficiently pervasive or severe as to alter the learning environment so it was discriminatory. I don't think professors should be free to do that.

Abrams: I start not with federal statutes as my model, but with the proposition that a university is fundamentally a place of free expression, that professors ought to be free to have their say and to teach their courses as they see fit, and that students ought to be free to talk to each other openly, candidly and sometimes very roughly. The price tag will inevitably be some discomfort—sometimes a lot of discomfort. That doesn't begin to lead me to the proposition that the students who feel bad about what has been said should have the power to prevent, to bar, or to sanction the speech involved. It's true that at some point comments can get to a point where the learning experience is not only altered but nonexistent. But I am more concerned at this point about the pall of orthodoxy that I believe has descended upon our campuses, where professors are afraid to talk about certain topics. Rape is not being taught in a lot of law schools now because it's just not worth the hassle. Anthropology students are not being taught about race because it isn't worth the risk to professors involved. I know professors who have found themselves in a situation where the choice they have made is to teach other things. And I think that this is the result of an explosion not only of criticism but of threats, made against faculty members by students who have come to believe that if they are troubled by the terms in which they are taught, the remedy is to stifle their professors.

MacKinnon: But one of the things they are doing is speaking. In fact there is now an explosion of speech from previously silenced quarters, including those who have been targeted by the subjects you mentioned. If teachers are now afraid to teach rape because it's not worth the hassle or the risk, the question is What is the risk? It includes that their students will *speak* to them and say things that formerly they had not said. There are a great many more women in law schools than before. They are speaking out in opposition to the way rape has always been taught, which frankly has often been from the standpoint of the perpetrator. Much of the rape law is written from that standpoint, and it has implicitly been taught largely as a defendant's rights issue. A lot of women and some men are *dissenting* from that. They won't sit quietly and take it anymore, because it affects the conditions of their lives. There's been a challenge to the power of professors to control discussions from the point of view from which they've always controlled it. Instead of taking the chance to become educated, some professors take their marbles and go home.

Abrams: I think dissent in class is a marvelous thing.

MacKinnon: Well, a lot of professors don't.

Abrams: I understand that, but what concerns me is that what is going on is less dissent than students basically making charges, formal charges; charges of sexual harassment, charges of racial insensitivity, where what is involved—at worst—is a difference of opinion about how best to teach a course.

MacKinnon: Ultimately that is also a challenge to what has been the absolute power of teachers to control the terms of discourse. You're sensitive to how professors feel about dissent. But what you're characterizing as a pall of orthodoxy I think is a breath of freedom. It's a challenge to the absolute authority of dominant groups to control the discussion from the standpoint of white male and upper-class privilege and power. It isn't cheap anymore to denigrate people's human dignity in class. It isn't free anymore. Teachers have to pay a price in terms of being challenged now in ways that they didn't before. The question is Is there *ever* a legal bottom line that gives students something they can use? Do they *ever* have legal rights in this area?

Abrams: But the price that is being paid is not always for denigration. Sometimes, indeed often, there is genuine disagreement about how to teach and what to teach. There is far too much censure in a formal, juridical sense, far too much use of procedures with a capital *P* to punish professors who don't view things the way you do.

Lewis: You have talked repeatedly, Professor MacKinnon, about what you call equality rights. I'd like to know precisely what you mean by this term. Analyze for us how a judge or a sensible citizen should weigh the equality concern as against free speech or freedom of the press.

MacKinnon: Well, the concern of my book *Only Words* has been that discussions like this one have been conducted as if the only ground rule were free expression, and if someone feels bad about what's been said, those are the breaks. Feeling good is not an equality right. Equal access to an education that you don't have to absorb years of abuse to get *is*.

Abrams: Can I add a word about equality rights? It ought to be said that there's no inherent conflict between First Amendment principles and equality principles and indeed in most circumstances they flow together. More speech has been the savior in a good part of minorities in this country; the ability of minorities to speak out, to have their say, to be heard, not to be punished for what they think is at the core of this country at its best. To put in conflict equality rights and free-expression rights is to put in conflict principles that are not in conflict at all.

Lewis: In *Only Words* you suggest, if I read that book correctly, that equality can trump First Amendment values. In this regard I'd like to offer a quote from the Canadian lawyer Kathleen Mahoney, who argued and won a landmark pornography case in which the Supreme Court of Canada adopted Professor MacKinnon's broad view of what should be suppressed as pornography: "The law has not treated women and other minority groups fairly. If we truly believe in democracy in the fullest sense of the word, then everyone should be able to participate. That means some sort of cutting back of individual rights as we've always known them." Is that your view?

MacKinnon: Well, freedom of expression and equality are both individual rights. The traditional model of civil liberties has been more generous to those rights that the people who set up the system wanted to keep for themselves. And equality wasn't something they guaranteed because they didn't need it. So equality—as much as it has always been an important systemic value, an important formal value in the legal system—as a substantive value it's only been recently recognized. It wasn't in the Constitution in the first place; it took a long time and a lot of blood and grief to get it in there at all. Guarantees of equality in social life have been even more recent. Equality guarantees conflict with individual rights that powerful groups already had—or thought they had. It is their power, but they take it for their freedom and their rights. If you look at the First Amendment properly, you may not ultimately have this conflict. But because the First Amendment has not been seen properly, we've got a conflict between equality guarantees and views of individual rights that preexist serious equality guarantees. That's what Kathleen Mahoney is referring to.

Lewis: In your book you suggest that the First Amendment has been of use primarily to those who hold power. But isn't it true that since the 1920s, when the First Amendment began to be seriously enforced in this country, it has been primarily of use in protecting the free speech and press rights of the dissident—the Seventh-Day Adventists, the Communists, the Ku Klux Klan, the civil rights movement? Not the powerful. The First Amendment is of use to the nonpowerful. Is that wrong?

MacKinnon: It's partly wrong and it's partly right. It's not that there haven't been dissidents who have found that the First Amendment is helpful. It's that the First Amendment only protects that speech that can manage to get itself expressed, and often that is the speech of power. Only that speech that can be expressed is speech that the government can attempt to silence; in the name of dissent one can then attempt to use the First Amendment to defend that speech. But what about those layers of society that have been deeply silenced, among them sexually violated women, including prostituted women, including groups who are kept illiterate and thus not given access to speech from slavery times through the present. Those groups the First Amendment doesn't help. They need equality to get access to speech—to get to the point where the First Amendment could help them by keeping the government from interfering with their speech. We have barely heard from those groups.

Lewis: Why aren't *you* a representative of the women you say have been voiceless? It seems to me that in terms of First Amendment expression, the women's movement is one of the most successful and admirable reform movements in American history.

MacKinnon: Yes, and one of our jobs is to keep talking to you about all the women you're not listening to, all the women who can't speak, instead of getting bought off by some illusion of preeminence. We are here to talk not only about all the things that haven't been said, but also about all the women who haven't been heard and are still unheard. . . . I am no substitute for them.

Abrams: I agree with Professor MacKinnon in so far as what she's saying is that our society rewards power and to a large extent rewards wealth. People who have money have a lot more say about how our society is run than people who don't. People who are powerful by definition have a lot more say about what happens in our society than people of the underclass. There are ways to try to deal with that if one chooses to. One way is to speak about it. Another way is to legislate about it. But one way that I would oppose trying to deal with it is to suppress speech with which we disagree.

MacKinnon: What about the film, *Deep Throat,* which Linda "Lovelace" was coerced into making? Is that what you call the expression of ideas I disagree with?

Abrams: Well, I think first of all it is the expression of ideas—

MacKinnon: So is the rape of women.

Abrams: The rape of women is handled by rape laws.

MacKinnon: And *Deep Throat*—how should that be handled?

Abrams: Judged by obscenity laws.

MacKinnon: It's been judged obscene in some places and not in others. You think Linda "Lovelace" should have no equality rights in relation to that film? How does that film give rise to a speech interest you want to protect?

Abrams: I don't even know what you mean in this case about equality rights. She has a perfect right not to be raped.

MacKinnon: I mean that, as a woman, Linda was sexually subordinated to make it and that—as she puts it—"every time someone watches that film they are watching me be raped." She has an equality right not to have that done. And to stop the film that is doing it, and whose profit is an incentive to keep doing it.

Lewis: Am I right in thinking that coercion as you would define it in the law you drafted with Andrea Dworkin—that is, graphic, sexually explicit materials that subordinate women through pictures and words—disallows voluntarily engaging in a pornographic film since it says that a written consent shall not be proof that there was no coercion?

MacKinnon: No, you're not. If you can force a woman to have sex with a dog, you can force her to sign a contract. The mere fact of a contract being signed doesn't in itself negate a finding of coercion. The coercion itself would have to be proven under our ordinance.

Abrams: Look, your statute provides in part that graphic, sexually explicit subordination of women in which women are presented as sexual objects for domination, conquest, violation, exploitation, possession or use, etc., can give rise to a private cause of action. The court of appeals in holding the statute unconstitutional—a decision affirmed by the Supreme Court—indicated that books like Joyce's *Ulysses,* Homer's *Iliad,* poems by Yeats, novels by D. H. Lawrence, and the like could all be subject to a finding of violation of the statute that you have drafted.

MacKinnon: And that's just simply false.

Abrams: Well, I don't think it *is* false.

MacKinnon: Those materials are not even sexually explicit. They don't even get in the door.

Lewis: Why don't you just repeat your definition of pornography?

MacKinnon: Professor Abrams just quoted the definition. Andrea Dworkin's and my approach to pornography is to define it in terms of what it does, not in terms of what it says, not by its ideas, not by whether someone is offended by it, not by whether somebody doesn't like it. None of that has anything to do with our definition. Our definition, and our legal causes of action, all have to do with what it *does* to the women in it, to the children in it, and to other people who can *prove* that as a direct result of these materials they were assaulted or made second-class citizens on the basis of sex.

Abrams: You mean because people will think less of women on account of how they're portrayed?

MacKinnon: No, because people will *do* things to them like not hiring them, like sexualizing them and not taking them seriously as students, the entire array of violent and nonviolent civil subordination, when they can prove it comes from pornography.

Abrams: That is why your legislation is so frontal an attack on the First Amendment. When the court of appeals said that the impact of your statute is such that it could apply to everything from hard-core films to the collected works of James Joyce, D. H. Lawrence, and John Cleland, it was entirely correct. It is correct because what you have drafted as a definition of actionable pornography is "graphic sexual explicit subordination of women, in which women are presented as sexual objects for domination." Lots of great art as well as cheap and vile productions have depicted women in just that way— *The Rape of the Sabine Women,* for example. And my point is not that your definition is vague, but that it is clear. It includes any art, whether it is good or bad, art or nonart, that you have concluded may do harm. That's an unacceptable basis and it should be.

MacKinnon: Okay, there are several things wrong with this. Number one, those materials are not sexually explicit. The court was told exactly what *sexually explicit* means in law and in ordinary use, and it should have known better. Number two, these materials have never yet been shown in any study to have produced any of the effects that pornography produces. So no one could prove that women are subordinated as a result of them. This statute does not cover those materials, period. It is false as a matter of statutory construction. The statute could potentially cover something like a film in which somebody was actually killed but claims are made that it has artistic value—an artistic snuff film—or in which someone is raped but the film has interesting camera angles. That does raise a conflict between existing law and our statute. The examples you cite do not.

Lewis: Professor MacKinnon, we do have a concrete example of what your view of the law might result in. The Canadian Supreme Court adopted your view. Since then there has been an intensification of gay and lesbian books being intercepted at the border. That seems to be the result of a country actually adopting your standard.

MacKinnon: That's disinformation. Canada customs has singled out those materials for years, and customs law was not involved in the case I was part of in Canada. What happened was, the Supreme Court of Canada rejected its morality-based standard for obscenity and held that when pornography hurts equality, it can be stopped. Customs has not reviewed its standards since. I think that if Canada customs is still stopping materials because they are gay or lesbian, on a moral ground not on a harm ground, they have lost their constitutional authority to do it under this ruling. If the materials hurt women or men or their equality, they can still stop them. But Andrea

Dworkin and I do not favor addressing pornography through criminal law, especially obscenity law, so in that way Canada has not adopted our approach.

Lewis: Professor MacKinnon, there's an assumption explicitly stated in your book that pornography as you define it results in antisocial, abusive activity by the customers.

MacKinnon: There's overwhelming documentation of it.

Lewis: But it is a fact that in countries in which pornography is lawful and there are no legal restraints whatever on sexually explicit materials, the incidence of sexual crimes is much lower than in this country.

MacKinnon: Actually that isn't true. It's urban legend.

Lewis: In Denmark, in Germany, in Japan—

MacKinnon: In Denmark data on reported rape after liberalization are inconclusive. It did not drop, though. Also, the definitions and categories of sexual offenses were changed at the same time that pornography was decriminalized. Also, reporting may well have dropped. If your government supports pornography, reporting sexual abuse seems totally pointless to women. So, too, Germany and Sweden. Once pornography is legitimized throughout society, you get an explosion in sexual abuse, but women don't report it anymore because they know that nothing will be done about it. Feminists and sex educators in Denmark are beginning to say that selling twelve-year-old children on street corners is not what they mean by sexual liberation. What's happened in Japan and other places is that much of sexual abuse is just part of the way women are normally treated. If you're still essentially chattel, what is it to rape you? In Sweden there aren't any rape-crisis centers. All there are is battered-women's shelters. So the battered-women's movement has been pushing the government to look at the reality of rape there, which is massive.

Abrams: But those countries that are harshest on what you would call pornography are also harshest on women. In China promulgation of pornography leads to capital punishment. In Iran it leads to the harshest and most outrageous physical torture. These are not good countries for women to live in. If you look at countries like

Sweden and Japan and Holland and Germany, which have allowed more rather than less free expression in this area of sexually explicit speech, you'll find that these are the countries in which sexual abuse of women is not particularly prevalent. It's one thing for you to advocate a statute such as you have proposed in Sweden, but I dare-say it has not been seriously suggested that Swedish women as a group have been victimized by their free press and free-speech laws.

MacKinnon: Swedish women have seriously supported our law against the legalized victimization of pornography. But it's hard to know what the reality is. It's wrong to base how much rape there is on reported rape. It's also very hard to know how much pornography is actually available. You could look at the United States laws and get the impression that pornography was being taken seriously as a problem in this country.

Abrams: But when you cite, for example, the Balkans as a place where there's been a vast amount of rape and infer that it has some-thing to do with the existence of sexually explicit materials, you don't tell us that in 1913 there was an orgy of rapes at a time when such material didn't exist at all. It puts into question the validity of the whole thesis.

MacKinnon: It is not an exclusive thesis. There are lots of ways of sexualizing subordination—religion, veiling, clitoridectomies. Por-nography is one way, and some of the abuses it is connected to we can do something about. In countries where women have recently got more voice, like the United States and Sweden, women are be-coming more able to identify the sources of our subordination. The United States is a mass culture, media-saturated and capitalistic. In asking how women are subordinated in the United States, it would be wrong to eliminate the capitalistic mass media of the pornogra-phy industry. At other times and places the ways in which women are subordinated are different. But now the United States is export-ing this form of subordination to the rest of the world.

Abrams: Didn't you say you were going to give us a few minutes to summarize?

Lewis: Yes, we'd better do it.

MacKinnon: In looking at areas in which women are most distinctively kept unequal, surely those areas include the workplace and school. But they also include the home and the street and the public order. That's why, in Andrea Dworkin's and my approach to freedom of speech, we don't limit ourselves to the traditional equality areas. Women haven't been permitted to address the ways in which we are distinctively subordinated. And the equality interests at stake for women, for people of color, for all people who are subjected to inequality on the basis of sex or race or sexual orientation in particular—those are interests that the First Amendment as it has been interpreted has not taken into account. It has not been a real legal concern. That doesn't mean that it couldn't be. These rights can be accommodated. A First Amendment properly understood would give everyone greater access to speech. It would also recognize that to violate someone, to subordinate someone, to abuse someone, to rape someone are not First Amendment–protected activities. They aren't what the freedom of speech is about. Trafficking in sexual slavery is not a discourse in ideas any more than an auction block is a discourse in ideas or burning a cross is a discourse in ideas. They are activities that subordinate people. They are of course expressive. Rape is expressive. Murder is expressive. My punching someone in the face to express my contempt for that person's ideas is expressive. That doesn't make it protected expression. The fact that abuse is well organized and highly profitable and produces a product that produces more abuse does not make it protected speech, just because that product is pictures and words. The pornographic industry does not promote speech; it silences women. It contributes to creating a context, an objectified and sexualized and denigrated context, for the deprivation of women's human rights on a mass scale.

Abrams: The First Amendment in my view is not at odds with, not at war with, not even in conflict with principles of equality. It is one of the great forces by which equality comes to occur in our society. We don't need a First Amendment for a lot of speech in our society. I don't think I've ever said anything that required any First Amendment protection, because no one would ever put me in jail for what I had to say or for what I suspect Professor MacKinnon or Mr. Lewis has to say. We need a First Amendment most of all to protect people who say very unpopular things, unpopular with government, unpopular with the public at large. We do not permit and should not permit the First Amendment to be overcome on the basis of some sort of continuous balancing, where we simply look at the supposed harm caused by speech as against the supposed value of what is said. I might conclude that what Professor MacKinnon had to say today is harmful; maybe she'll persuade some people and in the course of persuading some people do some real harm to the First Amendment as I perceive it and to freedom of expression as I hope we will continue to have it in this country. I don't think we can engage in any such balancing process. She's allowed to say what she has to say; I'm allowed to say what I have to say; Mr. Lewis is allowed to say what he has to say. In only the rarest case do we even start down the road of saying, well, this speech is so likely to cause harm of such extraordinary, provable, damaging nature that we won't allow it. I don't believe we ought to do that in almost any case on a university campus. There more than anywhere freedom ought to be the rule and almost the invariable rule. I don't believe we should do it in the area of sexually oriented speech beyond the law of obscenity as we now have that law. That body of law looks to whether a speech has serious artistic value. If it does, by the definition of our law, it can't be obscene. It can be outrageous, it can be pornographic in the sense that Professor MacKinnon defines it, but we protect it because we think that ideas—even disagreeable ideas—matter so much that we are unwilling to pay the price of suppression of speech. I think that at the end of the day what animates me most in this area—and what I don't think Professor MacKinnon takes sufficient account of —are the risks of suppression of speech. There's a lot of speech that isn't very helpful or useful or societally beneficial—and even some speech that may well do some harm—that I'm not at all willing to suppress or to allow lawsuits to punish. That's because I think our First Amendment is right in reflecting a profound distrust of the government telling us what we can say, what we can think, how we can express our views; and I think that to start down the road of suppressing more speech, limiting the speech that we are free to express as a people, would be to strip us of what makes us so unique: a commitment to free expression that makes us one of the wonders of the world. I think we should be proud of that, and I think we should leave it the way it is.

MacKinnon: I don't think our pornography industry is one of the wonders of the world, nor is our rape rate. I've got a question . . . a rude question. You haven't ever represented a pornographer, have you?

Abrams: I've got to think of everyone you might consider a pornographer.

MacKinnon: Start where the industry starts, with *Playboy* or *Penthouse* or *Hustler*.

Abrams: No.

MacKinnon: I didn't think you had.

Thomas versus Clinton

Anita F. Hill

In 1991 Anita Hill's life took a dramatic turn when she testified before the Senate Judiciary Committee on the Supreme Court nomination of Judge Clarence Thomas, whom she said sexually harassed her during the period she worked for him at the Equal Employment Opportunity Commission. By the time the hearings concluded, her name had become known in virtually every household in the land. Here the law professor of the University of Oklahoma compares her charges against Clarence Thomas to those lodged against President Clinton by Paula Corbin Jones. This essay appeared on the op-ed page of *The New York Times* on May 29, 1994. Anita Hill is now at work on her memoirs.

Over the past few weeks, a wide range of commentators have drawn parallels between the claims raised during the hearings on Judge Clarence Thomas's nomination to the Supreme Court and the recent charges of sexual harassment against President Clinton. Comparisons can be useful if they illuminate the obscure or help resolve a problem. But simply likening the events of 1991 and the events of 1994 ignores the complexities of sexual harassment. As the Supreme Court noted just last year, sexual harassment that creates a hostile environment defies "a mathematically precise test," and calls for examining "all the circumstances" of a case.

In fact, the differences in the Clinton and Thomas situations teach us more about sexual harassment than do the similarities.

Perhaps the most striking difference is that the Thomas hearing was held in a political arena, the Senate Judiciary Committee, while Paula Corbin Jones's complaint will be heard in a Federal District Court. Members of the federal judiciary have the legal procedures and precedent to ensure that the complaint, and Mr. Clinton's defense, will get a fair hearing. The court will allow time for discovery of evidence and the opportunity to hear experts on sexual harassment. So far, there is no sign that it will show disregard for her claim, or any predisposition about whether she is telling the truth. We are encouraged to expect an orderly proceeding, befitting the dignity of the tribunal and the parties involved.

The record of the Senate hearings is in striking contrast.

No one on the court has threatened Ms. Jones with "real harassment." No one on the court has suggested that Ms. Jones will be destroyed in the process of the hearing. No one on the court has "looked into the eyes" of one principal witness and decided the veracity of the other. And, one hopes, no member of the judicial tribunal will take on the dual role of fact-finder and prosecutor.

Members of the Judiciary Committee engaged in this kind of prejudgment before and during the 1991 hearing, even regarding testimony that they had not yet heard. There was no time to gather evidence, and no expert testimony about sexual harassment, which would have been essential to the committee's and the public's understanding.

There are vast differences between what we knew in 1991 about sexual harassment and what we know today. Awareness of that gulf illuminates other important differences between these two high-profile cases.

In 1991 the issue and the surrounding circumstances caught society by surprise. The general public was unaware of sexual harassment as a legal question, and no one viewed it as a political issue —even though it was a reality in the workplace. The hearings touched deep feelings about power, race and sex—complex, volatile emotions that came together on television as a real-life story. For many, the impact was astonishing.

Among women, the reactions were quick, almost instinctive. Women had not often spoken publicly about sexual harassment until then, but by doing so during and after the hearing, they educated society. By talking about their own painful experiences they showed how pervasive the problem is, while explaining why they have been reluctant to raise claims. Since 1991 women in record numbers have filed sexual harassment complaints. The Senate's perceived lack of fairness toward one woman's claim came to stand for society's lack of fairness toward all women's claims.

In the political reaction that followed the hearing, women and men rallied behind eleven female candidates for the Senate and helped elect four of them, including the first African American woman. For many voters, including Republican and independent women who crossed party lines to vote for him, Bill Clinton's election represented a chance to have sex-related issues addressed more sympathetically.

Because the times and the circumstances are different, the Jones complaint raises different challenges, which are also marked by hesitancy on the part of some women to get involved in the case. Why are they reluctant?

First, many longtime leaders in the fight against sexual harassment are skeptical about the commitment of recent converts to the cause—especially those who have disparaged that cause until now.

Many women may feel some uneasiness that Mr. Clinton, who represented a chance for more enlightened federal policies on these issues, is himself charged with sexual harassment. Others may not see the issue in the stark, either-or terms in which it has been presented. In 1991, women simply asked that claims of sexual harassment be taken seriously, without the prejudicial stereotypes, unfounded assertions and political hyperbole that threatened to prevail. After nearly three years, that danger has diminished, thanks to the collective effort of women committed to eliminating sexual harassment. We should take the opportunity to advance it even further.

The law of sexual harassment is evolving, with the number of complaints finally falling closer into line with experience on the job. We are learning to talk about harassment in more informed terms. Few people assert that women invite harassment by the way they look or dress. We are also reacting more intelligently to claims of sexual harassment. We no longer assume, for example, that women claim harassment prompted by work-related or romantic disappointment. Yet we fail to confront many unresolved problems in our public discussion, legislative agendas and workplace relations.

For example, society must see sexual harassment for what it is: sex discrimination that is prohibited by the civil rights laws. It is not purely personal behavior, nor simply natural attraction gone awry. To discuss it in these terms trivializes the illegality and undermines efforts to eliminate it.

Second, according to recent testimony before the House Armed Services Committee harassment in the military continues, and complaints are still ignored—even after the Tailhook scandal and the subsequent early retirement of Adm. Frank B. Kelso 2d. Congress should establish complaint procedures in the military similar to those governing the civilian work force and make the leadership accountable when the procedures are not followed.

The 1991 Civil Rights Act was important in the fight against sexual harassment, but it failed to provide adequate damages for those who filed claims when the legislation was pending and it placed a cap on damages in sex discrimination cases. Congress should address the retroactivity question and remove the cap.

Finally, employers should continue to establish and enforce policies against harassment. This ought to include educational programs that send a clear message about management's seriousness and the consequences of violating the rules.

Every day I hear from people who need help in identifying whether their treatment on the job is illegal; who fear retaliation from individuals or institutions for which they work, and who are personally and professionally abused because they speak out. And I hear from men and women who wonder whether we can ever eliminate what appears to be an intractable social malady.

The solutions will require still more legal, personal, social and legislative effort. And once again we will have to look beyond short-term political struggles like those of 1991 and 1994 to achieve them.

Dirt and Democracy

Alan Wolfe

Alan Wolfe teaches sociology at Queens College in New York City
and is author of *Whose Keeper: Social Science and Moral Obligation.* He takes on the politics of porn in this essay, which first
appeared in *The New Republic* on February 19, 1990.

Pornography exists where sex and politics meet. Since few other
activities are as fascinating as these two pleasures, it is no wonder
that questions involving pornography have been with us so long.

Sex is, or at least is supposed to be, intimate, caring, invisible
to others: the very definition of private. Politics is, or is supposed to
be, open, debatable, a spectacle: the essence of public. A world in
which sex and its representations were of no concern to others could
not, by force of definition, contain pornography. A world in which
politics regulated all sexual activities and their representation could
not, by force of police, contain pornography either. To discuss pornography is always to discuss a matter of balance.

Our politics—the way we balance public and private things—
are those of liberal democracy. As Richard Randall stresses in his
Freedom and Taboo: Pornography and the Politics of a Self Divided,
a comprehensive treatment of the subject, both liberalism and democracy are intimately linked to the pornographic inclination, even
if that link is troubling and contradictory. Liberalism respects a
private sphere within which government—that is, other people—
ought not to find itself. Although the founders of liberalism might be
unable to imagine their arguments for freedom of expression used in
defense of the prurient, pornography could not exist without the two
most fundamental props of the liberal world order: a market that

efficiently responds to supply and demand, with little concern for the morality of what is traded; and a legal system that places a premium on individual rights.

Yet if liberalism is inclined to protect the pornographic, democracy is inclined to forbid it. Randall is correct to emphasize that it is the elite that seeks to defend the right of pornographic expression and the majority that seeks to curtail it. Politicians never run for office in favor of pornography. Unmoved by appeals to artistic expression, little concerned for constitutional subtleties, worried about the vulnerability of their children, Americans would gladly give up this one liberal right if they could be guaranteed that in return they would be rid of unwanted ugliness. Legislatures and city councils, responsive to democratic demands, regularly try to control pornography; courts, undemocratic in principle and liberal in practice, try to stop them.

In the past twenty years liberalism and democracy have both expanded in scope. Pornographers have shared, surely disproportionately, in the expansion of liberal rights that has defined American judicial practice since the Warren Court. The rise of the Moral Majority and other censorial movements, on the other hand, is one of the by-products of increasingly plebiscitary democratic urges. The result of these simultaneous developments is what Donald Downs calls a "new politics of pornography," in which few of the older images, alliances, positions, and judicial standards make sense. Three developments since around 1970 have set the stage for the new politics of pornography.

First, the form of pornography has changed beyond recognition. Any images men may have in their heads about stag films—any leftover memories of fraternity bashes of the 1950s—have nothing to do with what pornography represents now. The sex is far more explicit; today's hard core is tomorrow's R-rated movie, or, to put it another way, yesterday's illegality is today's television commercial. In addition, the "quality" has improved. As Linda Williams points out in *Hard Core: Power, Pleasure and the "Frenzy of the Visible,"* plots have been added, full-length feature status is now the norm, and efforts at credibility have been introduced. The symbol of these changes of course is video; most people now watch pornography at home in living color, not in grungy inner-city arcades. And high-definition television, once the Japanese get around to supplying it, is next.

Second, nearly all legal efforts used by local communities to control pornography in recent years have failed. The Supreme Court's 1957 decision in *Roth* v. *United States*—despite its famous language banning material that "appeals to the prurient interest—" effectively opened the door to previously forbidden sexual expression: thirty-one obscenity convictions were reversed between 1967 and 1973. The ability of pornographers to use courts and the First Amendment to their advantage (Downs notes that in Minneapolis the MCLU offices were in a building owned by its leading pornographic client, presumably rent-free) led local police to give up even trying to win convictions. Even a town as conservative as Indianapolis was able to initiate only two obscenity cases between 1979 and 1985. During the 1970s and early 1980s, in short, pornography grew increasingly worse as the ability to regulate it declined proportionately.

Third, our awareness that pornography involves violence against women has increased. Of the three developments this is the most controversial, because there is no absolute proof—nor will there ever be—that pornography *definitely* results in harm to women. (Based on the Danish experience with legalization, the opposite case is equally as plausible: Pornography may also be an excuse for men to masturbate and be done, and thus protect women.) Still, the images contained in pornography, brutal toward all, are most brutal toward women. Pornography is to some degree a feminist issue. How much it is a feminist issue is the most passionately debated question in the current writing on the subject.

If questions involving pornography always involve matters of balance, the rise of a new politics of pornography has placed in doubt what ought to be balanced with what. Under the rules of the "old" politics of pornography, the right to free expression stood on one side and the ability of a community to protect itself from untoward sexuality stood on the other. Under the new politics of pornography, violence against women is defined as what we need protection against, whereas what pornography might stand for is not completely clear.

The new politics of pornography crested with the report of the Meese Commission in 1986, which concluded that pornography (including the violent kind) had increased to the point of being out of control. What was most striking about the Meese Commission was not its conclusions, but the way it reached them. For the commission focused specifically on the insult and injury to women involved in pornography, even to the extent of quoting, without attribution, Robin Morgan's fighting words: "Pornography is the theory, and rape the practice." The feminist critique of pornography had arrived.

That critique was the product of the meeting of two minds: legal theorist Catharine A. MacKinnon and essayist Andrea Dworkin. Dworkin expounded her ideas in *Pornography: Men Possessing Women,* recently republished with a new introduction. In Dworkin's view sex is power, nothing else; and all the power belongs to the man. Every man is a beast, every women an innocent and (remarkably, for a feminist) passive victim. Pornography, like heterosexual sex in general, is merely an extreme form by which men exercise power over women.

The philosophy in Dworkin's bedroom is the philosophy of Hobbes. She tells me, for example, that I have refrained from raping my son not because I love him but because of the fear that when he grows up, he might rape me back. Dworkin, in that sense, is really not all that interested in pornography as such; the chapter of that name in her book is four pages long, whereas the one called "Force" is seventy. (Brutal treatments of gay men or animals would not, presumably, bother her.) Let Dworkin herself speak:

In the male system, women are sex; sex is the whore. The whore is porné, the lowest whore, the whore who belongs to *all* male citizens: the slut, the cunt. Buying her is buying pornography. Having her is having pornography. Seeing her is seeing pornography. Seeing her sex, especially her genitals, is seeing pornography. Seeing her in sex is seeing the whore in sex. Using her is using pornography. Wanting her means wanting pornography. Being her means being pornography.

Dworkin believes that what men do to women in pornography is *worse* than what Nazis did to Jews in concentration camps: "The Jews didn't do it to themselves and they didn't orgasm. . . . No one, not even Goebbels, said that the Jews liked it." Dworkin does Robin Morgan one better: Sex is the theory and extermination the practice. Women, though, unlike Jews in the camps, are fighting back. (Totally passive, they suddenly found a voice.) Her advice to them is: "Know the bastard on top of you." Men are scared. The women they have treated pornographically all their lives are massed to castrate them, and Dworkin is wielding the biggest knife.

This kind of analysis would hardly seem the stuff of local ordinances—especially in the American Midwest. But, as Donald Downs recounts in *The New Politics of Pornography,* his illuminating history of these events, one of Dworkin's readers was Catharine MacKinnon, by all accounts a brilliant political strategist. In 1983 MacKinnon invited Dworkin to teach a class with her at the University of Minnesota School of Law. Two essential conclusions were quickly reached in the seminar: first, that pornography is not a question of free speech, because women cannot speak; and second, that pornography, because it harms women, does not extend civil liberties, it violates civil rights.

The resulting Minneapolis ordinance, which was killed by the mayor's veto, would have been a first in American law. Pornography —not, as in most judicial decisions since *Roth,* the narrower notion of obscenity—was defined as discrimination against women. Finding herself depicted in what she believed to be pornographic fashion by any image—nine definitions of such depictions were given in the ordinance—any woman could lodge a complaint with the local Civil Rights Commission and, after a series of steps were followed, could win the right to a hearing. An Indianapolis version of the ordinance was eventually declared unconstitutional in 1985. Still, we may hear more from the feminist antipornographers. Given a censorial mood on campus, which makes it against university policy to say anything derogatory against women, minorities, gays, Native Americans, and the handicapped, we may soon see efforts to ban pornographic films from campus facilities or pornographers from rostrums. There is no way around it. Since the threat of an antidiscrimination suit is designed to stop the practice of depicting women pornographically *before* it occurs, the issue raised by Dworkin and MacKinnon is censorship. Is the harm to women represented in pornography so great that we are justified in using our democratic powers to stop it?

The first reaction to the rise of a feminist movement for censorship was to argue on empirical grounds that the harm done to women by pornography is not as great as feared. It has been said that pornography has targets other than women; that women make and enjoy pornography themselves; that no harm against women from pornography can be proved. Although in a narrow and technical sense these arguments are accurate, they miss the point. When a political position has as much popularity as the desire to control pornography, we ought to give those who hold it credit for their views, not dismiss them as know-nothings, anti-intellectual Philistines, or (as Randall unfortunately does) people repressing the pornographic within. When the rage of women is eloquent and dramatic, we ought not let Dworkin's absurd rhetoric deny an important point. Pornography is demeaning, women are its primary targets, and even if we cannot prove that it causes violence, it certainly offends the sensibility of some very engaged citizens.

At this point a second line of defense against censorship enters: Even though pornography demeans women, it serves positive goals that are more important. Whether or not pornography has value, one form of this argument runs, liberty clearly does. Hence pornography can be bad, but what it symbolizes—free speech—is good. Pornography therefore has redeeming value in spite of itself. A similar response to the Dworkin-MacKinnon position has arisen among feminists who, objecting strenuously to their depiction of the passivity of women, argue that free sex has as much value as free speech. Did it ever occur to Dworkin and others like her, these thinkers have asked, that women like sex? It was hardly the intent of the feminist movement, after all, to turn all women into Puritans. (For similar reasons, gays objected vehemently to the Minneapolis ordinance.) Revisionist feminists—if they may be called that—also find indirect value in pornography. We have libidos. They need outlets. Free speech and free sex both make a certain toleration of pornography necessary.

Both of these arguments are trying to balance the way that the new politics of pornography defines harm with the way that the old politics of pornography defined freedom. It is not easy to do. Harm is concrete, sensate, unambiguous. Rights are abstract and intellectualized, at least one remove away from immediate experience. Weigh the two, and the argument against harm will win, at least with the popular majorities that decide such things. Similarly the argument for sexual freedom is unhelpful in this debate. Its images of sex correspond exactly to ACLU images of rights: Free speech and free sex are private matters, not the business of anyone else. The age of AIDS should teach us otherwise: so long as tax monies are used to save lives, there *is* a public interest in private sex. The state may not be the best regulator, the regulation itself can often misfire, but a community cannot take a position of moral neutrality toward the libido. Most people recognize, in short, that your sexuality is at least partly my concern. Some sexual freedom is clearly necessary to discover the self. Some regulation is clearly necessary to protect the society, without which there can be no selves.

Pornography has little redeeming social value. By artistic criteria it is close to worthless. Heroic attempts to defend the pornographic imagination by Angela Carter and Simone de Beauvoir (in the case of Sade) or Susan Sontag (in the case of Georges Bataille and Pauline Réage) treat a rarefied aspect of the genre that has little to do with the predictability and the sheer mediocrity of much of the pornographic expression. By criteria of psychological development, moreover, pornography fails again. It infantilizes people, mostly men, locking them into a stage in which limits do not exist, all desires can be satisfied, and every complexity avoided. By the Kantian criterion of respect for persons, furthermore, pornography fails a third time, treating women as things available for the whimsical pleasures of men; pornography in that sense is also without redeeming moral value.

By civic criteria, finally, pornography flunks most severely. Although free speech gives much to pornography, pornography gives almost nothing to free speech. It does not enhance our capacity to act as citizens. It does not cause us to reflect on rights and responsibilities. It does not encourage participation in the life of the community. Pornographers are free riders on the liberties of everyone else. If a human activity with so little value is balanced against even a slight possibility that it may cause rape and mayhem, the feminist case for censorship would seem to win.

Still, for all that, the bad taste that censorship leaves in the mouth cannot be easily washed away. The question of pornography raises a host of complex moral and symbolic issues that cannot be resolved by banishing the problem's manifestations. On moral grounds, for example, the case for censorship and the case for unrestricted rights to pornography are quite similar—and similarly without nuance. Feminists like Dworkin, who would regulate all the fine details of private life, believe that there is no morality to speak of when discussing pornography; everything is power. Civil libertarians, on the other hand, ruling private behavior beyond the pale of public scrutiny, also believe that there is no morality at issue; everything is principle. The moral neutrality of both positions can hardly win a hearing among most people, who believe that pornography, which is obviously about sex, is also about morality.

Pornography raises issues about the nature of the self, moreover, that cannot be addressed either by banning pornography or by celebrating it. One of the unanticipated benefits of the feminist case for censorship has been to sharpen the sense of what we are in danger of losing if the urge to censor gets out of hand. It is not individual freedom to do or say anything one wants with little regard for the sensitivity of the community. The loss would be deeper, for pornography symbolizes fundamental human needs without which we would not be fully human. Two of them are the need to be aware of the dark side of sexuality and the need to make sense out of multiple realities. If we have learned anything about texts at all in

this century, it is that the more readers, the more interpretations—
that reality, in short, is never simply one unambiguous thing.

Those who would censor pornography have complete epistemo-
logical confidence that they know exactly what it is. Reflecting on
the experience in Minneapolis, Dworkin writes, "For women who
are hurt by pornography, this law simply describes reality; it is a
map of the real world." None of the contingencies and ambiguities
of language, representation, and meaning that one finds in thinkers
like Derrida or Rorty has made it into the consciousness of feminist
censors. For example, Joan Hoff, who frequently cites Foucault on
the social contingency of knowledge, argues that we know what
pornography is, even though no history of it is available to us. When
that history is written, she already knows what it will say. What is at
stake is not whether her unwritten history is correct but that such
certainty about historical development is the exact opposite of what
Foucault teaches us about genealogies. In Hoff's view—and in the
view of many of the contributors to *For Adult Users Only: The
Dilemma of Violent Pornography,* the book that she edited with Susan Gubar—there is only one representation in any pornographic
work, the one that brutalizes women.

Linda Williams's book *Hard Core* is a brilliant demolition of
the position that pornography represents one thing only. Arguing
against the feminist case for censorship, Williams urges that we take
pornography seriously, which does not mean that we like it or that
we believe it is art. Remarkably nonevaluative in her description of
pornographic films since the invention of moving pictures (she offers a negative assessment only once, on the quality of the music in
Deep Throat), Williams wants us to learn the rules of the pornographic genre.

All forms of representation have genre rules, and Williams
turns to musical comedies to help understand pornography; like
hard-core porno films, they regularly break narrative to introduce
numbers. (She might also have looked at operas. They, too, have
numbers, and one of the greatest works of art written in any genre at
any time is about a man who lusts uncontrollably, indeed
pornographically, after women. *Don Giovanni* would surely have

been actionable under the Dworkin-MacKinnon ordinance.) The rules of the pornographic genre are defined by a fundamental contradiction: If a man enjoys pleasure inside a woman, generally viewed by men as the most satisfying way to experience sexual pleasure, the physical evidence of his pleasure is invisible. The conventions of pornography follow from efforts to capture what the trade calls a "money shot": proving visibly that the man has satisfied himself.

Pornography cannot mean one thing, and one thing only, because genre conventions, instead of confining all reality within preestablished frames, enable multiple interpretations of reality to exist simultaneously. That is why pornography is not, as Dworkin claims, *only* about men brutalizing women. It may equally be the case that what men want to see in pornographic movies is not the naked woman, since most men, in the course of their lives, get to see that with some frequency, but the image of another man enjoying himself visibly, which most men never get to see. We do not know of course whether this interpretation is correct. But Williams's subtle and fascinating explications suggest that, in not knowing, we are best off allowing pornographic representations to exist. Despite what Hoff says, the history, or at least a history, of pornography has been written, and it does not show what she thought it would.

If the feminist censor's conviction that pornography reflects an unambiguous map of reality is naive, so is her conviction that, knowing the single-minded evil it represents, we can abolish it by force of law. Randall makes a convincing case that such an optimistic view of the powers of law is not justified. It is, in his view, the dark side of pornography that makes it important. Humans are the "pornographic" animal, fascinated and appalled by their sexuality. The pornography that we see out there is a reflection of the pornographic deep within ourselves. Since pornography is part of what we are, we harm only ourselves by regulating it too severely. At the same time, however, since "complete sexual freedom is a contradiction of the human condition," we will need to control our sexual impulses in some way. Neither censors nor civil libertarians, Randall argues, understand "the paradoxical, mutually supportive relationship between pornography and censorship." We will have to live with various efforts to reconcile sexuality and its control, none of which will ever solve the problem.

The recognition that pornography speaks to needs within the self—its need to interpret as well as its need to express itself sexually—is a much firmer guide for sorting out the new politics of pornography than the purely libertarian notion of individual freedom. For one thing the issue is not the abstract right of shady businessmen to sell dirty pictures, or the equally abstract right of sexual pleasure seekers to purchase them—rights that in both cases apply to minorities. Pornography is important, rather, because in speaking to the self, it is speaking to a universal: We all have an interest in the many ways in which fundamental human conflicts are represented in print and in film.

In addition, both the free-speech and the free-sex argument, reflecting the optimism of liberal rationality, claim that our thoughts and our libidos, if left free to roam, will, like prices in an equally anarchic market, be guided by invisible hands into public benefits. Liberals, adherents to an all-too-optimistic faith, do not want to peek too closely into private spaces. They fear what they will find there.

Imperfect creatures growing to adulthood with sexual conflicts unresolved, many of us (surprisingly many, by most sociological accounts) need outlets for our imaginations, relying on our power to give meaning to representations of fantasies buried deep within the self, even if the pictorial representations of those fantasies involve, on the surface, harm to others. A case against censorship ought to argue not that we can discover some redeeming virtue in pornographic expression, but that we cannot.

Considering how rapidly the terrain has shifted in the debate over pornography, we are a long way from developing legal standards that will help us keep in balance the needs pornography obviously serves with the offensiveness it obviously entails. Until such a standard is developed, the debate over pornography will be social, not legal, and its participants will be intellectuals and academics, not lawyers. What we have a right to expect in the debate is honesty. Such an objective is not helped by politicizing pornography as exclusively a women's issue, as if women should compete with other oppressed groups in demonstrating how submissive they really are. The category of woman is both too broad and too narrow to make much sense in this debate.

Two political scientists among the authors reviewed here, Donald Downs and Richard Randall, ought to be commended for trying to develop standards, even though neither is successful. Randall argues that we should make offensiveness, not harm, the crucial offense, a position that would restrict expression far more than any current standard—given how offensive people like Dworkin find loving and intimate sex, let alone what most people mean by pornography. Downs has a better proposal. He would extend the definition of obscenity to include violence, an attempt he recognizes as largely symbolic but still important in responding to concerns about abuse of women. Downs is essentially arguing that the best course is to have laws on the books against certain representations but not to enforce them. Such an approach makes sense to the degree that it is sensitive to all the contradictions of pornography, but it also is a recipe for disaster in fueling paranoia.

It is no wonder that none of the standards we have established for balancing the concerns involved in pornographic expression—including those tried, valiantly, by the Supreme Court—seems any longer to work. In concerning themselves with freedom on the one hand and community standards on the other, they are balancing the wrong things. We need a standard for pornography capable of putting into balance what we know about the self and what we know about potential harm to others. The feminist case against pornography is powerful and eloquent. But it establishes a border for the public debate, it does not resolve it. Moral philosophers long ago demonstrated convincingly that harm, though a tragedy, does not settle the question of what is morally permissible.

The Privacy Problem

Wendy Kaminer

Wendy Kaminer is a lawyer and the author of *I'm Dysfunctional, You're Dysfunctional* (a critique of the Twelve-Step movement) and *A Fearful Freedom: Women's Flight From Equality*. "The Privacy Problem" first appeared in the April 1994 issue of *Mirabella*.

"There no longer exists an unpolitical sphere of life." It sounds like a line from a feminist sampler, but it was uttered by a German court in 1937. Long before "the personal is political" became a feminist slogan, the Nazis attacked the boundaries between the private and the public, the personal and the political spheres.

With their all-inclusive definition of political life, the Nazis sought complete control over private thoughts in addition to private relations, as totalitarian regimes do. They defined sexual assaults broadly to include thought crimes and metaphorical assaults, such as uninvited glances—eerily prefiguring some feminist protests against pornography and harassment.

Consider these cases reported by Ingo Müller in his book *Hitler's Justice:* In 1939, a Jewish man was sentenced to prison for one month for looking at an Aryan girl. His look constituted an assault, the court ruled. It "had a clearly erotic basis and could only have had the purpose of effecting an approach to the girl who interested him. This approach failed to occur only because the witness refused to cooperate and summoned the police to her aid." In another case a Jewish man was sentenced to two years in prison for allegedly being "excited" by a massage, despite the masseuse's insistence that the defendant did not appear to have been aroused. Based on a "confession" to the Gestapo, which he later recanted, the man was convicted of having "attained sexual gratification," thereby dishonoring the Aryan race. The court held that the defendant had obtained a massage for "lascivious purposes and to abuse women as objects of his sexual lust, regardless of whether or not they were aware of it."

Like the slogan There is no "unpolitical sphere of life," neither of these cases would be terribly out of place, rhetorically or ideologically, in some hard-line feminist tract. The Nazi view of Jewish male sexuality, like the white-supremacist view of black-male sexuality, has an unsettling resemblance to the demonization of generic male sexuality that is particularly clear in the antipornography movement. The more extreme feminist protests against harassment, as well as virtually all demands to censor pornography, assume, as did the Nazis, that the state should punish private, "lascivious" thoughts and glances. Women are encouraged to confuse actual and metaphorical assaults: we're said to be violated or assaulted by a leer, just as we're said to be abused or subordinated by a man's reading or viewing of pornography. If merely enjoying pornography, in a room all by yourself, is a crime or a tort, it can only be a thought crime. Catharine MacKinnon suggests that men who use pornography are engaging in actual sex discrimination, which is a little like saying that Jimmy Carter engaged in actual adultery when he harbored lust in his heart.

I point all this out at the considerable risk of inadvertently implying that Rush Limbaugh may have reason to call us feminazis. Apart from its democratic history, feminism is too complicated and diverse a movement to be characterized by invective (or encomium). Nor is this quick review of the Nazi campaign to politicize the personal offered as a reproach to feminists who fought for more equitable regulation of the private sphere. It's not as if a democratic state has no interest in family life or procreative behavior and no history of regulating them—through domestic-relations laws, for example. For much of our history these laws were grossly discriminatory and sometimes dangerous for women. In the 1970s feminists declared that the personal was political partly so that men would stop beating their wives, not so that kids would inform on their parents.

Privacy has been a mitigated good for women, given its role in shielding marital rape and other forms of family violence. Privacy had pitfalls for women even when it was invoked in their favor. In 1973, in *Roe* v. *Wade,* the Supreme Court grounded abortion rights in the right to privacy, which made it easier for the government to deny Medicaid funding for abortions. Privacy rights arguably impose no obligation on government to provide abortions for women who cannot afford them. As many feminists have pointed out, the Court could have based abortion rights in equality rights: Abortion prohibitions are fundamental bars to full equality because they impose unique restrictions on women. Had the Supreme Court recognized this in 1973, the government would have had a clearer responsibility to ensure equal access to abortion services.

But if privacy rights do not imply rights to social services, they do include fundamental civil liberties. The Nazis' utter obliteration of the private sphere is a reminder that in a free society the personal is not simply political—which should be obvious. Do we want the government tapping our phones or reading our letters and diaries? Do we want the states enforcing archaic laws against adultery, oral sex, or contraception? In 1986 the Supreme Court devalued the privacy rights of homosexuals when it upheld the sodomy conviction of a homosexual man in Georgia who was apprehended by police in his own home while engaged in consensual sex with another adult. This was a highly controversial decision; had it involved heterosexuals, it would have been universally condemned.

Feminists deplore the persecution of homosexuals, in practice, but feminist theorizing about sexuality is sometimes as dogmatic and authoritarian as conservative religious campaigns against gay rights. Consider the preachings of Sally Cline, a British feminist whose book *Women, Passion, and Celibacy,* presents celibacy as the correct feminist choice for virtually all women. Ms. Cline endorses the familiar critique of heterosexual activity as generally oppressive to women: it "rarely" offers equal pleasure and passion; focused on satisfying "masculine needs and desires" it requires the passivity and masochism of women, she argues. For Sally Cline, and many American antiporn feminists, it seems, sex is only an instrument of power for men, never a way of expressing affection.

How does Sally Cline know what all men and women experience in bed? Why must she dictate female celibacy with the same fervor with which antifeminists dictate female submissiveness? Fundamentalist feminists tend to share the unthinking belief that the personal is political, absolutely. If all relations are suffused with power plays, then a personal predilection, like celibacy, becomes a political imperative. And, simplistically equating the personal and political sphere not only allows you to tell other people how to conduct their lives, it also transforms your problems and preferences into important public issues. (So, Sally Cline can girlishly list her favorite "passions" in the belief that she's engaging in political debate.)

A similar confusion of the personal and political is a hallmark of popular therapeutic culture, as well as feminist theory. People in recovery groups and on talk shows routinely assume that their problems are matters of public interest. But the vilification of male sexuality evident in the antiporn movement and in calls for female celibacy, coupled with the denunciation of sexual privacy, is not exactly mainstream (even for feminists).

Many people agree that consensual relations between adults should be private, but they disagree about what constitutes consent and how it should be monitored. Do we want the state or any other official body, such as a college administration, deciding what men and women should say to each other in private? Is it possible or desirable to regulate private relations so that no one is ever hurt, deceived, manipulated, or merely misunderstood? Some attempts to dictate dating and mating rituals or to police private conversations between men and women reflect the childish belief that there is a political solution, and a public policy, for every interpersonal problem.

That is the kind of thinking that leads people into court. Last year Northwestern University law professor Jane Larson created a small stir with a law-review article proposing a new civil action for sexual fraud—"an act of intentional, harmful misrepresentation made for the purpose of gaining another's consent to sexual relations." This might make sense if applied to cases involving knowing transmission of disease, when the harmfulness of the misrepresentation is clear and sometimes deadly. But some of these cases are already being successfully pursued without Professor Larson's proposed cause of action, which is intended to provide a remedy for intangible, emotional harm as well. Questions about emotional damage in workplace sexual-harassment cases have been plaguing the courts for several years, and the effort to control "offensive" sexual behavior (particularly when only speech is involved) has been quite controversial. How do we formulate a fair, relatively objective standard for offensiveness, while maintaining respect for free speech? In employment cases the effort to monitor harassment is worth the trouble: The public interest in eradicating sexism from the workplace is clear, unlike the interest in eradicating sexism from the bedroom. Attempts at regulating sexism in private, nonviolent relations could at best be only marginally successful—and would involve substantial sacrifices of sexual privacy. If heterosexual relations in a sexist society are inherently abusive, as some feminists say, the prospects for regulating sexism in the bedroom take your breath away. We'd have an orgy of litigation.

Private lives have long been played out in court, especially in divorce cases, but at least the litigants had the grace to be embarrassed by the dramas; today they're supposed to feel empowered. And if their trials aren't televised by Court TV, they can take their indiscretions to Geraldo. Feminism's denigration of privacy has been greatly exacerbated by talk shows and personal-development experts who warn that privacy is "toxic." Indiscriminate sharing of intimacies is considered therapeutic.

There is also a kind of incipient totalitarianism in the insistence that public revelation is the route to private redemption. It's reminiscent of political prisoners recanting their beliefs and denouncing false consciousness. Privacy is one of the first casualties of totalitarian states, which aim to control thinking, sexual and reproductive behavior, and religion—the passions in which we seek freedom from politics. Imagine a world with no personal sphere and you imagine a world with no refuge.

Public Policy, Private Ritual

William Broyles, Jr.

William Broyles, Jr., is the former editor-in-chief of *Newsweek*. He now works in television and was cocreator of the prime-time show *China Beach*. This essay appeared on *The New York Times* op-ed page on October 16, 1991, in the wake of the Hill-Thomas hearings.

At a birthday party in my office the celebrant was feted with a cake in the shape of male genitals. The cake was devoured with great gusto, to the mirth and entertainment of many of those present and the intense discomfort of others. The cake was presented to a woman by the other women in the office. Those most uncomfortable were men.

If men had sponsored the party, it could have been considered as an example of insensitivity and the abuse of male power. Since women did it, the party was all camaraderie and good fun, and any man who was offended simply kept it to himself.

Sex arrived in the workplace when women did, and, ever since, men have been unsure just what women believe its boundaries are. Over the past twenty years I have seen a steady increase in frank language and sexual innuendo, much of it coming from the women, no matter whether they were my boss or the lowest subordinate. The tougher the job and the greater the pressure, the franker the language and the more intense the sexual atmosphere.

Wherever I have worked, sexual relationships among co-workers have been a fact of life—from hasty couplings in closets, to serious affairs, to love and marriage. The law can't eliminate sex at work; it can only try to keep it within reasonable boundaries.

During the Senate Judiciary Committee hearings [on the nomination of Clarence Thomas to the Supreme Court], the senators fell over themselves to express their horror at the language Judge Thomas allegedly used in asking Anita Hill out—language unfortunately not that different from the average hit record, movie or television show, where jokes about male anatomy, suggestive language, double entendres, and frank sexuality have become commonplace. This pervasiveness of sex in our public life makes determining standards of acceptable behavior much more difficult.

If a man asks a co-worker out, discusses personal matters with her, and in other ways tries to advance the relationship, he can, through the same actions, be responsible for consequences ranging from sexual harassment to beginning a lifetime relationship. What is offensive to one woman may be obnoxious, amusing, or even endearing to another.

Where men and women are together, there is misunderstanding and mystery. I have seen highly professional, otherwise respectable men commit sexual harassment, just as I have seen highly professional, otherwise capable women imagine relationships that did not exist (this happened in fact to me) and contrive harassment charges to revenge other slights or to advance themselves.

It's crucial to legally define sexual harassment as clearly as possible so that the true victims of sexual abuse and discrimination don't have their suffering trivialized. Otherwise we will be treated in our courts to interchanges every bit as bizarre as Senator Joseph Biden and John Doggett [a witness for Clarence Thomas] arguing over how to ask a woman out. This is not and should never be a matter of law or public policy.

One troubling aspect of the Thomas hearings was that they put on public display the private rituals by which men and women come together. The man usually initiates relationships and therefore subjects himself to embarrassment, rejection, and misunderstanding, particularly since these matters are not always conducted in straightforward, businesslike ways.

Men don't get it. That's what the professional feminists tell us. And they are right, we don't. We may get some of it, but not all—not even many of us who have promoted and encouraged our woman subordinates and oppose any form of sexual discrimination or harassment.

And that's because the rules of sexual harassment are not objective but determined by the reactions of the woman involved. Each woman makes her own law. Women want to be treated equally but don't want to be considered sexless. They want to be sexually attractive but only to the right man and only with the proper approach. That leaves considerable possibility for error. The man must read the woman's signals; the woman must make those signals clear.

Women today enrich the workplace at all levels and in all jobs. They are police officers and firefighters. They make a strong case for being qualified to carry arms into combat. If women are tough enough for that, to kill and risk being killed, they are tough enough to handle a dirty joke or a clumsy flirtation without rushing to join the women who are truly victims.

Women want to be respected, capable workers without losing their sexual identities, and they should be able to have it both ways. But if a man wants to ask a co-worker out, he shouldn't have to bring his lawyer along.

PART FOUR

Ways of Seeing (Viewer Discretion Advised)

Date Rape's Other Victim

Katie Roiphe

In 1993 at the age of twenty-four, Princeton doctoral candidate Katie Roiphe roiled the feminist world with the publication of her first book, *The Morning After: Sex, Fear, and Feminism on Campus.* The excerpt reprinted here first appeared as a cover story in *The New York Times Sunday Magazine* on June 13, 1993, announced by the cover line RAPE HYPE BETRAYS FEMINISM.

One in four college women has been the victim of rape or attempted rape. One in four. I remember standing outside the dining hall in college looking at a purple poster with this statistic written in bold letters. It didn't seem right. If sexual assault was really so pervasive, it seemed strange that the intricate gossip networks hadn't picked up more than one or two shadowy instances of rape. If I was really standing in the middle of an "epidemic," a "crisis"—if 25 percent of my women friends were really being raped—wouldn't I know it?

These posters were not presenting facts. They were advertising a mood. Preoccupied with issues like date rape and sexual harassment, campus feminists produce endless images of women as victims—women offended by a professor's dirty joke, women pressured into sex by peers, women trying to say no but not managing to get it across.

This portrait of the delicate female bears a striking resemblance to that fifties ideal my mother and other women of her generation fought so hard to leave behind. They didn't like her passivity, her wide-eyed innocence. They didn't like the fact that she was perpetually offended by sexual innuendo. They didn't like her excessive need for protection. She represented personal, social, and intellectual possibilities collapsed, and they worked and marched, shouted and wrote to make her irrelevant for their daughters. But here she is again, with her pure intentions and her wide eyes. Only this time it is the feminists themselves who are breathing new life into her.

Is there a rape crisis on campus? Measuring rape is not as straightforward as it might seem. Neil Gilbert, a professor of social welfare at the University of California at Berkeley, questions the validity of the one-in-four statistic. Gilbert points out that in a 1985 survey undertaken by *Ms.* magazine and financed by the National Institute of Mental Health, 73 percent of the women categorized as rape victims did not initially define their experience as rape; it was Mary Koss, the psychologist conducting the study, who did.

One of the questions used to define rape was "Have you had sexual intercourse when you didn't want to because a man gave you alcohol or drugs?" The phrasing raises the issue of agency. Why aren't college women responsible for their own intake of alcohol or drugs? A man may give her drugs, but she herself decides to take them. If we assume that women are not all helpless and naive, then they should be held responsible for their choice to drink or take drugs. If a woman's "judgment is impaired" and she has sex, it isn't necessarily always the man's fault; it isn't necessarily always rape.

As Gilbert delves farther into the numbers, he does not necessarily disprove the one-in-four statistic, but he does clarify what it means—the so-called rape epidemic on campuses is more a way of interpreting, a way of seeing, than a physical phenomenon. It is more about a change in sexual politics than a change in sexual behavior. Whether or not one in four college women has been raped, then, is a matter of opinion, not a matter of mathematical fact.

That rape is a fact in some women's lives is not in question. It's hard to watch the solemn faces of young Bosnian girls, their words haltingly translated, as they tell of brutal rapes; or to read accounts of a suburban teenager raped and beaten while walking home from a shopping mall. We all agree that rape is a terrible thing, but we no longer agree on what rape is. Today's definition has stretched beyond bruises and knives, threats of death or violence, to include emotional pressure and the influence of alcohol. The lines between rape and sex begin to blur. The one-in-four statistic on those purple posters is measuring something elusive. It is measuring her word against his in a realm where words barely exist. There is a gray area in which one person's rape may be another's bad night. Definitions become entangled in passionate ideological battles. There hasn't been a remarkable change in the number of women being raped; just a change in how receptive the political climate is to those numbers.

The next question, then, is who is identifying this epidemic and why. Somebody is "finding" this rape crisis, and finding it for a reason. Asserting the prevalence of rape lends urgency, authority to a broader critique of culture.

In a dramatic description of the rape crisis, Naomi Wolf writes in *The Beauty Myth* that "cultural representation of glamorized degradation has created a situation among the young in which boys rape and girls get raped *as a normal course of events.*"

The italics are hers. Whether or not Wolf really believes rape is part of the "normal course of events" these days, she is making a larger point. Wolf's rhetorical excess serves her larger polemic about sexual politics. Her dramatic prose is a call to arms. She is trying to rally the feminist troops. Wolf uses rape as a red flag, an undeniable sign that things are falling apart.

From Susan Brownmiller—who brought the politics of rape into the mainstream with her 1975 best seller *Against Our Will: Men, Women and Rape*—to Naomi Wolf, feminist prophets of the rape crisis are talking about something more than forced penetration. They are talking about what they define as a "rape culture." Rape is a natural trump card for feminism. Arguments about rape can be used to sequester feminism in the teary province of trauma and crisis. By blocking analysis with its claims to unique pandemic suffering, the rape crisis becomes a powerful source of authority.

Dead serious, eyes wide with concern, a college senior tells me that she believes one in four is too conservative an estimate. This is not the first time I've heard this. She tells me the right statistic is closer to one in two. That means one in two women are raped. It's amazing, she says, amazing that so many of us are sexually assaulted every day.

What is amazing is that this student actually believes that 50 percent of women are raped. This is the true crisis. Some substantial number of young women are walking around with this alarming belief: a hyperbole containing within it a state of perpetual fear.

Acquaintance Rape: Is Dating Dangerous? is a pamphlet commonly found at counseling centers. The cover title rises from the shards of a shattered photograph of a boy and girl dancing. Inside, the pamphlet offers a sample date-rape scenario. She thinks:

"He was really good-looking and he had a great smile. . . . We talked and found we had a lot in common. I really liked him. When he asked me over to his place for a drink, I thought it would be okay. He was such a good listener and I wanted him to ask me out again."

She's just looking for a sensitive boy, a good listener with a nice smile, but unfortunately his intentions are not as pure as hers. Beneath that nice smile, he thinks:

"She looked really hot, wearing a sexy dress that showed off her great body. We started talking right away. I knew that she liked me by the way she kept smiling and touching my arm while she was speaking. She seemed pretty relaxed so I asked her back to my place for a drink. . . . When she said yes, I knew that I was going to be lucky!"

These cardboard stereotypes don't just educate freshmen about rape. They also educate them about "dates" and about sexual desire. With titles like *Friends Raping Friends: Could It Happen to You?* date-rape pamphlets call into question all relationships between men and women. Beyond warning students about rape, the rape-crisis movement produces its own images of sexual behavior, in which men exert pressure and women resist. By defining the dangerous date in these terms—with this type of male and this type of female, and their different expectations—these pamphlets promote their own perspective on how men and women feel about sex: Men are lascivious, women are innocent.

The sleek images of pressure and resistance projected in rape-education movies, videotapes, pamphlets, and speeches create a model of acceptable sexual behavior. The don'ts imply their own set of dos. The movement against rape, then, not only dictates the way sex *shouldn't be* but also the way it *should be.* Sex should be gentle, it should not be aggressive; it should be absolutely equal, it should not involve domination and submission; it should be tender, not ambivalent; it should communicate respect, it shouldn't communicate consuming desire.

In *Real Rape,* Susan Estrich, a professor of law at the University of Southern California Law Center, slips her ideas about the nature of sexual encounters into her legal analysis of the problem of rape. She writes: "Many feminists would argue that so long as women are powerless relative to men, viewing a 'yes' as a sign of true consent is misguided. . . . Many women who say yes to men they know, whether on dates or on the job, would say no if they could. . . . Women's silence sometimes is the product not of passion and desire but of pressure and fear."

Like Estrich, most rape-crisis feminists claim they are not talking about sex; they're talking about violence. But, like Estrich, they are also talking about sex. With their advice, their scenarios, their sample aggressive male, the message projects a clear comment on the nature of sexuality: women are often unwilling participants. They say yes because they feel they have to, because they are intimidated by male power.

The idea of "consent" has been redefined beyond the simple assertion that "no means no." Politically correct sex involves a yes, and a specific yes at that. According to the premise of "active consent," we can no longer afford ambiguity. We can no longer afford the dangers of unspoken consent. A former director of Columbia's date-rape education program told *New York* magazine, "Stone silence throughout an entire physical encounter with someone is not explicit consent."

This apparently practical, apparently clinical proscription cloaks retrograde assumptions about the way men and women experience sex. The idea that only an explicit yes means yes proposes that, like children, women have trouble communicating what they want. Beyond its dubious premise about the limits of female communication, the idea of active consent bolsters stereotypes of men just out to "get some" and women who don't really want any.

Rape-crisis feminists express nostalgia for the days of greater social control, when the university acted *in loco parentis* and women were protected from the insatiable force of male desire. The rhetoric of feminists and conservatives blurs and overlaps in this desire to keep our youth safe and pure.

By viewing rape as encompassing more than the use or threat of physical violence to coerce someone into sex, rape-crisis feminists reinforce traditional views about the fragility of the female body and will. According to common definitions of date rape, even "verbal coercion" or "manipulation" constitute rape. Verbal coercion is defined as "a woman's consenting to unwanted sexual activity because of a man's verbal arguments not including verbal threats of force." The belief that "verbal coercion" is rape pervades workshops, counseling sessions, and student opinion pieces. The suggestion lurking beneath this definition of rape is that men are not just physically but also intellectually and emotionally more powerful than women.

Imagine men sitting around in a circle talking about how she called him impotent and how she manipulated him into sex, how violated and dirty he felt afterward, how coercive she was, how she got him drunk first, how he hated his body and he couldn't eat for three weeks afterward. Imagine him calling this rape. Everyone feels the weight of emotional pressure at one time or another. The question is not whether people pressure each other but how our minds and our culture transform that pressure into full-blown assault. There would never be a rule or a law or even a pamphlet or peer counseling group for men who claimed to have been emotionally raped or verbally pressured into sex. And for the same reasons— assumption of basic competence, free will, and strength of character —there should be no such rules or groups or pamphlets about women.

In discussing rape, campus feminists often slip into an outdated sexist vocabulary. But we have to be careful about using rape as metaphor. The sheer physical fact of rape has always been loaded with cultural meaning. Throughout history women's bodies have been seen as property, as chaste objects, as virtuous vessels to be "dishonored," "ruined," "defiled." Their purity or lack of purity has been a measure of value for the men to whom they belonged.

"Politically I call it rape whenever a woman has sex and feels violated," writes Catharine MacKinnon, a law professor and feminist legal scholar best known for her crusade against pornography. The language of virtue and violation reinforces retrograde stereotypes. It backs women into old corners. Younger feminists share MacKinnon's vocabulary and the accompanying assumptions about women's bodies. In one student's account of date rape in the *Rag,* a feminist magazine at Harvard, she talks about the anguish of being "defiled." Another writes, "I long to be innocent again." With such anachronistic constructions of the female body, with all their assumptions about female purity, these young women frame their experience of rape in archaic, sexist terms. Of course sophisticated modern-day feminists don't use words like *honor* or *virtue* anymore. They know better than to say date-rape victims have been "defiled." Instead they call it post-traumatic stress syndrome. They tell the victim she should not feel "shame," she should feel "traumatized." Within their overtly political psychology, forced penetration takes on a level of metaphysical significance: date rape resonates through a woman's entire life.

Combating myths about rape is one of the central missions of the rape-crisis movement. They spend money and energy trying to break down myths like "She asked for it." But with all their noise about rape myths, rape-crisis feminists are generating their own. The plays, the poems, the pamphlets, the Take Back the Night speakouts, are propelled by the myth of innocence lost.

All the talk about empowering the voiceless dissolves into the image of the naive girl child who trusts the rakish man. This plot reaches back centuries. It propels Samuel Richardson's eighteenth-century epistolary novel, *Clarissa:* after hundreds of pages chronicling the minute details of her plight, her seduction and resistance, her break from her family, Clarissa is raped by the duplicitous Robert Lovelace. Afterward she refuses to eat and fades toward a very virtuous, very religious death. Over a thousand pages are devoted to the story of her fall from innocence, a weighty event by eighteenth-century standards. But did these twentieth-century girls, raised on Madonna videos and the six-o'clock news, really trust that people were good until they themselves were raped? Maybe. Were these girls, raised on horror movies and glossy Hollywood sex scenes, really as innocent as all that? Maybe. But maybe the myth of lost innocence is a trope—convenient, appealing, politically effective.

As long as we're taking back the night, we might as well take back our own purity. Sure, we were all kind of innocent, playing in the sandbox with bright red shovels—boys too. We can all look back through the tumultuous tunnel of adolescence on a honey-glazed childhood, with simple rules and early bedtimes. We don't have to look at parents fighting, at sibling struggles, at casting out one best friend for another in the Darwinian playground. This is not the innocence lost; this is the innocence we never had.

The idea of a fall from childhood grace, pinned on one particular moment, a moment over which we had no control, much lamented, gives our lives a compelling narrative structure. It's easy to see why the seventeen-year-old likes it; it's easy to see why the rape-crisis feminist likes it. It's a natural human impulse put to political purpose. But in generating and perpetuating such myths, we should keep in mind that myths about innocence have been used to keep women inside and behind veils. They have been used to keep them out of work and in labor.

It's not hard to imagine Clarissa, in jeans and a sweatshirt, transported into the twentieth century, at a Take Back the Night march. She would speak for a long time about her deception and rape, about verbal coercion and anorexia, about her ensuing post-traumatic stress syndrome. Latter-day Clarissas may worry more about their "self-esteem" than their virtue, but they are still attaching the same quasi-religious value to the physical act.

Calling It Rape, a play by Sonya Rasminsky, a recent Harvard graduate, is based on interviews with date-rape victims. The play, which has been performed at Harvard and may be taken into Boston-area high schools, begins with "To His Coy Mistress," by the seventeenth-century poet Andrew Marvell. Although generations of high school and college students have read this as a romantic poem, a poem about desire and the struggle against mortality, Rasminsky has reinterpreted it as a poem about rape. "Had we but world enough, and time, this coyness, lady, were no crime." But what Andrew Marvell didn't know then, and we know now, is that the real crime is not her coyness but his verbal coercion.

Farther along, the actors recount a rape that hinges on misunderstanding. A boy and girl are watching videos and he starts to come on to her. She does not want to have sex. As the situation progresses, she says, in an oblique effort to communicate her lack of enthusiasm, "If you're going to [expletive] me, use a condom." He interprets that as a yes, but it's really a no. And, according to this play, what happens next, condom or no condom, is rape.

This is a central idea of the rape-crisis movement: that sex has become our Tower of Babel. He doesn't know what she wants (not to have sex) and she doesn't know what he wants (to have sex)—until it's too late. He speaks boyspeak and she speaks girlspeak, and what comes out of all this verbal chaos is a lot of rapes. The theory of mixed signals and crossed stars has to do with more than gender politics. It comes in part from the much-discussed diversity that has so radically shifted the social composition of the college class since the fifties.

Take my own Harvard dorm: the Adams House dining hall is large, with high ceilings and dark paneling. It hasn't changed much for generations. As soon as the students start milling around gathering salads, ice cream, and coffee onto green trays, there are signs of change. There are students in jeans, flannel shirts, short skirts, girls in jackets, boys in bracelets, two pierced noses, and lots of secondhand clothes.

Not so many years ago this room was filled with boys in jackets and ties. Most of them were white, Christian, and what we now call privileged. Students came from the same social milieu with the same social rules, and it was assumed that everyone knew more or less how they were expected to behave with everyone else. Diversity and multiculturalism were unheard of, and if they had been, they would have been dirty words. With the shift in college environments, with the introduction of black kids, Asian kids, Jewish kids, kids from the wrong side of the tracks of nearly every railroad in the country, there was an accompanying anxiety about how people behave. When ivory tower meets melting pot, it causes tension, some confusion, some need for readjustment. In explaining the need for intensive "orientation" programs, including workshops on date rape, Columbia's assistant dean for freshmen stated in an interview in *The New York Times,* "You can't bring all these people together and say, 'Now be one big happy community,' without some sort of training. You can't just throw together somebody from a small town in Texas and someone from New York City and someone from a conservative fundamentalist home in the Midwest and say, 'Now without any sort of conversation, be best friends and get along and respect one another.' "

Catharine Stimpson, a university professor at Rutgers and longtime advocate of women's-studies programs, once pointed out that it's sometimes easier for people to talk about gender than to talk about class. *Miscommunication* is in some sense a word for the friction between the way we were and the way we are. Just as the idea that we speak different languages is connected to gender —the arrival of women in classrooms, in dorms, and in offices— it is also connected to class.

When the southern heiress goes out with the plumber's son from the Bronx, when the kid from rural Arkansas goes out with a boy from Exeter, the anxiety is that they have different expectations. The dangerous "miscommunication" that recurs through the literature on date rape is a code word for difference in background. The rhetoric surrounding date rape and sexual harassment is in part a response to cultural mixing. The idea that men don't know what women mean when women say no stems from something deeper and more complicated than feminist concerns with rape.

People have asked me if I have ever been date-raped. And thinking back on complicated nights, on too many glasses of wine, on strange and familiar beds, I would have to say yes. With such a sweeping definition of rape, I wonder how many people there are, male or female, who haven't been date-raped at one point or another. People pressure and manipulate and cajole each other into all sorts of things all of the time. As Susan Sontag wrote, "Since Christianity upped the ante and concentrated on sexual behavior as the root of virtue, everything pertaining to sex has been a 'special case' in our culture, evoking peculiarly inconsistent attitudes." No human interactions are free from pressure, and the idea that sex is, or can be, makes it what Sontag calls a "special case," vulnerable to the inconsistent expectations of double standard.

With their expansive version of rape, rape-crisis feminists are inventing a kinder, gentler sexuality. Beneath the broad definition of rape, these feminists are endorsing their own utopian vision of sexual relations: sex without struggle, sex without power, sex without persuasion, sex without pursuit. If verbal coercion constitutes rape, then the word *rape* itself expands to include any kind of sex a woman experiences as negative.

When Martin Amis spoke at Princeton, he included a controversial joke: "As far as I'm concerned, you can change your mind before, even during, but just not after sex." The reason this joke is funny, and the reason it's also too serious to be funny, is that in the current atmosphere you *can* change your mind afterward. Regret can signify rape. A night that was a blur, a night you wish hadn't happened, can be rape. Since "verbal coercion" and "manipulation" are ambiguous, it's easy to decide afterward that he manipulated you. You can realize it weeks or even years later. This is a movement that deals in retrospective trauma.

Rape has become a catchall expression, a word used to define everything that is unpleasant and disturbing about relations between the sexes. Students say things like "I realize that sexual harassment is a kind of rape." If we refer to a whole range of behavior from emotional pressure to sexual harassment as "rape," then the idea itself gets diluted. It ceases to be powerful as either description or accusation.

Some feminists actually collapse the distinction between rape and sex. Catharine MacKinnon writes, "Compare victims' reports of rape with women's reports of sex. They look a lot alike. . . . In this light, the major distinction between intercourse (normal) and rape (abnormal) is that the normal happens so often that one cannot get anyone to see anything wrong with it.''

There are a few feminists involved in rape education who object to the current expanding definitions of sexual assault. Gillian Greensite, founder of the rape-prevention-education program at the University of California at Santa Cruz, writes that the seriousness of the crime ''is being undermined by the growing tendency of some feminists to label all heterosexual miscommunication and insensitivity as acquaintance rape.'' From within the rape-crisis movement, Greensite's dissent makes an important point. If we are going to maintain an *idea* of rape, then we need to reserve it for instances of physical violence, or the threat of physical violence.

But some people want the melodrama. They want the absolute value placed on experience by absolute words. Words like *rape* and *verbal coercion* channel the confusing flow of experience into something easy to understand. The idea of date rape comes at us fast and coherent. It comes at us when we've just left home and haven't yet figured out where to put our new futons or how to organize our new social lives. The rhetoric about date rape defines the terms, gives names to nameless confusions, and sorts through mixed feelings with a sort of insistent consistency. In the first rush of sexual experience the fear of date rape offers a tangible framework to locate fears that are essentially abstract.

When my fifty-five-year-old mother was young, navigating her way through dates, there was a definite social compass. There were places not to let him put his hands. There were invisible lines. The pill wasn't available. Abortion wasn't legal. And sex was just wrong. Her mother gave her ''mad money'' to take out on dates in case her date got drunk and she needed to escape. She had to go far enough to hold his interest and not far enough to endanger her reputation.

Now the rape-crisis feminists are offering new rules. They are giving a new political weight to the same old no. My mother's mother told her to drink sloe gin fizzes so she wouldn't drink too much and get too drunk and go too far. Now the date-rape pamphlets tell us, "Avoid excessive use of alcohol and drugs. Alcohol and drugs interfere with clear thinking and effective communication." My mother's mother told her to stay away from empty rooms and dimly lighted streets. In *I Never Called It Rape,* Robin Warshaw writes, "Especially with recent acquaintances, women should insist on going only to public places such as restaurants and movie theaters."

There is a danger in these new rules. We shouldn't need to be reminded that the rigidly conformist fifties were not the heyday of women's power. Barbara Ehrenreich writes of "re-making love," but there is a danger in remaking love in its old image. The terms may have changed, but attitudes about sex and women's bodies have not. Rape-crisis feminists threaten the progress that's been made. They are chasing the same stereotypes our mothers spent so much energy escaping.

One day I was looking through my mother's bookshelves and I found her old battered copy of Germaine Greer's feminist classic *The Female Eunuch.* The pages were dog-eared and whole passages marked with penciled notes. It was 1971 when Germaine Greer fanned the fires with *The Female Eunuch,* and it was 1971 when my mother read it, brand new, explosive, a tough and sexy terrorism for the early stirrings of the feminist movement.

Today's rape-crisis feminists threaten to create their own version of the desexualized woman Greer complained of twenty years ago. Her comments need to be recycled for present-day feminism. "It is often falsely assumed," Greer writes, "even by feminists, that sexuality is the enemy of the female who really wants to develop these aspects of her personality. . . . It was not the insistence upon her sex that weakened the American woman student's desire to make something of her education, but the insistence upon a *passive* sexual *role* [Greer's italics]. In fact, the chief instrument in the deflection and perversion of female energy is the denial of female sexuality for the substitution of femininity or sexlessness."

It is the passive sexual role that threatens us still, and it is the denial of female sexual agency that threatens to propel us backward.

Not Just Bad Sex

Katha Pollitt

Katha Pollitt is a critically acclaimed poet who is on the staff of
The Nation, where she is known for her editorial writing. She also
writes for *The New Yorker,* in which this refutation of Katie
Roiphe's thesis appeared in October 1993. She is the author of
the collection *Reasonable Creatures.*

"Stick to straight liquor," my father advised me when I left for
college, in the fall of 1967. "That way, you'll always know how
drunk you are." I thought he was telling me that real grown-ups
didn't drink brandy Alexanders, but of course what he was talking
about was sex. College boys could get totally plastered, and the
worst that would happen to them would be hangovers and missed
morning classes. But if I didn't carefully monitor my alcohol intake
one of those boys might, as they used to say, take advantage of me.
Or, as they say now, date-rape me.

Veiled parental warnings like the one my father gave me—
don't go alone to a boy's room, always carry "mad money" on a
date, just in case—have gone the way of single-sex dorms, parietal
hours, female-only curfews, and the three-feet-on-the-floor rule,
swept away like so much Victorian bric-a-brac by the sexual revolution, the student movement, and the women's movement. The kids
won; the duennas and fussbudgets lost. Or did they? In *The Morning
After: Sex, Fear, and Feminism on Campus,* Katie Roiphe, a twenty-
five-year-old Harvard alumna and graduate student of English at
Princeton, argues that women's sexual freedom is being curtailed by
a new set of hand-wringing fuddy-duddies: feminists. Antirape activists, she contends, have manipulated statistics to frighten college

women with a nonexistent "epidemic" of rape, date rape, and sexual harassment, and have encouraged them to view "everyday experience"—sexist jokes, professorial leers, men's straying hands and other body parts—as intolerable insults and assaults. "Stranger rape" (the intruder with a knife) is rare; true date rape (the frat boy with a fist) is even rarer. As Roiphe sees it, most students who say they have been date raped are reinterpreting in the cold gray light of dawn the "bad sex" they were too passive to refuse and too enamored of victimhood to acknowledge as their own responsibility. Camille Paglia, move over.

These explosive charges have already made Roiphe a celebrity. The *New York Times Magazine* ran an excerpt from her book as a cover story: "Rape Hype Betrays Feminism." Four women's glossies ran respectful prepublication interviews; in *Mirabella* she was giddily questioned by her own mother, the writer Anne Roiphe. Clearly, Katie Roiphe's message is one that many people want to hear: Sexual violence is anomalous, not endemic to American society, and appearances to the contrary can be explained away as a kind of mass hysteria, fomented by man-hating fanatics.

How well does Roiphe support her case? *The Morning After* offers itself as personal testimony, with Roiphe—to use her own analogy—as a spunky, commonsensical Alice at the mad women's-studies-and-deconstructionism tea party familiar from the pages of Paglia and Dinesh D'Souza. As such, it's hard to challenge. Maybe Roiphe's classmates really are as she portrays them—waiflike anorexics, male-feminist wimps, the kind of leftist groupthinkers who ostracize anyone who says Alice Walker is a bad writer. Maybe Roiphe was, as she claims, "date raped" many times and none the worse for it. The general tone of her observations is unpleasantly smug, but in her depiction of a tiny subculture on a few Ivy League campuses, she may well be onto something. The trouble is that *The Morning After,* although Roiphe denies this, goes beyond her own privileged experience to make general claims about rape and feminism on American campuses, and it is also, although she denies this, too, a "political polemic." In both respects, it is a careless and irresponsible performance, poorly argued and full of misrepresentations, slapdash research, and gossip. She may be, as she implies, the rare grad student who has actually read *Clarissa,* but when it comes to rape and harassment, she has not done her homework.

Have radical feminists inundated the nation's campuses with absurd and unfounded charges against men? Roiphe cites a few well-publicized incidents: At Princeton, for example, a student told a Take Back the Night rally that she had been date raped by a young man she eventually admitted she had never met. But Roiphe's claim that such dubious charges represent a new norm rests on hearsay and a few quotations from the wilder shores of feminist theory. "Recently," she writes, "at the University of Michigan, a female teaching assistant almost brought a male student up on charges of sexual harassment," because of some mildly sexist humor in a paper. When is "recently"? In what department of the vast University of Michigan did this incident occur? How does Roiphe know about it—after all, it only "almost" happened—and know that she got it right? Roiphe ridicules classmates for crediting and magnifying every rumor of petty sexism, but she does the same: Hysterical accusations are always being made at "a prominent university." Don't they teach the students at Harvard and Princeton anything about research anymore?

Where I was able to follow up on Roiphe's sources, I found some fairly misleading use of data. Roiphe accuses the legal scholar Susan Estrich of slipping "her ideas about the nature of sexual encounters into her legal analysis" in *Real Rape,* her study of acquaintance rape and the law—one such idea being that women are so powerless that even *yes* does not necessarily constitute consent to sex. In fact in the cited passage Estrich explicitly lays that view aside to pursue her own subject, which is the legal system's victimization of women who say no. Nowhere does Roiphe acknowledge that—whatever may happen in the uncritical, emotional atmosphere of a Take Back the Night rally or a support-group meeting for rape survivors (a term she mocks)—in the real world women who have been raped face enormous obstacles in obtaining justice in the courts or sympathy from their friends and families. Nor does she seem to realize that it is the humiliation and stigmatization and disbelief reported by many rape victims, and documented in many studies, that have helped to produce the campus climate of fear and credulity she deplores. Indeed the only time Roiphe discusses an actual court case, it is to argue that the law veers too far to the victim's side:

> In 1992 New Jersey's Supreme Court upheld its far-reaching rape laws. Ruling against a teenager charged with raping his date, the court concluded that signs of force or the threat of force is [*sic*] not necessary to prove the crime of rape—no force, that is, beyond that required for the physical act of penetration. Both the plaintiff and the defendant admitted that they were sexually involved, but the two sides differed on whether what happened that night was rape. It's hard to define anything that happens in that strange, libidinous province of adolescence, but this court upheld the judgment that the girl was raped. If the defendant had been an adult, he could have gone to jail for up to ten years. Susan Herman, deputy public defender in the case, remarked, "You not only have to bring a condom on a date, you have to bring a consent form as well."

Roiphe should know better than to rely on a short item in the Trenton *Times* for an accurate account of a complicated court case, and she misrepresents even the sketchy information the article contains: The girl was not the boy's "date," and they did not both "admit" they were "sexually involved." The two indeed disagreed about the central facts of the case. The article does mention something Roiphe chose to omit: The girl was fifteen years old. The Supreme Court opinion further distinguishes this case from Roiphe's general portrait of date-rape cases: the hypersensitive female charging an innocently blundering male with a terrible crime for doing what came naturally and doing it without a peep from her. The offender, it turns out, was dating another girl living in the house where the rape took place, and not the victim, who, far from passively enduring his assault, did what Roiphe implies she did not: She slapped him, demanded that he withdraw, and, in the morning, told her mother, whereupon they went immediately to the police. It is absurd to use this fifteen-year-old victim—who had surely never heard of Catharine MacKinnon or Take Back the Night—as an example of campus feminism gone mad. And it is equally absurd to suggest that the highly regarded New Jersey Supreme Court, which consists of one woman and six middle-aged men, issued a unanimous decision in the victim's favor because it had been corrupted by radical feminism.

The court did affirm that "signs of force or the threat of force" —wounds, torn clothes, the presence of a weapon—were not necessary to prove rape. This affirmation accords with the real-life fact that the amount of force necessary to achieve penetration is not much. But it is not true that the court opened the door to rape convictions in the kinds of cases Roiphe takes for the date-rape norm: sex in which the woman says yes but means no, or says yes, means yes, but regrets it later. The court said that consent, which need not be verbal, must be obtained for intercourse. It's easy to parody this view, as the defense counsel did with her joke about a "consent form"—but all that it really means is that a man cannot penetrate a woman without some kind of go-ahead. Roiphe ridicules this notion as "politically correct" and objects to educational materials that remind men that "hearing a clear sober 'yes' to the question 'Do you want to make love?' is very different from thinking, 'Well, she didn't say no.' " But is that such terrible advice? Roiphe herself says she wants women to be more vocal about sex, yet here she is dismissive of the suggestion that men ought to listen to them.

Roiphe's attempt to debunk statistics on the frequency of rape is similarly ill informed. A substantial body of research, by no means all of it conducted by feminists, or even by women, supports the contention that there is a staggering amount of rape and attempted rape in the United States and that most incidents are not reported to the police—especially when, as is usually the case, victim and offender know each other. For example the National Women's Study, conducted by the Crime Victims Research and Treatment Center at the Medical University of South Carolina, working under a grant from the National Institute of Drug Abuse, which released its results last year, found that 13 percent of adult American women—one in eight—have been raped at least once; 75 percent by someone they knew. (The study used the conservative legal definition of rape which Roiphe favors: "an event that occurred without the woman's consent, involved the use of force or threat of force, and involved sexual penetration of the victim's vagina, mouth or rectum.") Other researchers come up with similar numbers or even higher ones, and are supported by studies querying men about their own behavior: in one such study, 15 percent of the college men interviewed said they had used force at least once to obtain intercourse.

Roiphe does not even acknowledge the existence of this sizable body of work—and it seems she hasn't spent much time studying the scholarly journals in which it appears. Instead she concentrates on a single 1985 article in *Ms.* magazine, which presented a preliminary journalistic account of an acquaintance-rape study conducted by Dr. Mary Koss, a clinical psychologist now at the University of Arizona. Relying on opinion pieces by Neil Gilbert, a professor of social welfare at Berkeley, Roiphe accuses Koss of inflating her findings—one in eight students raped, one in four the victims of rape or attempted rape—by including as victims women who did not describe their experience as rape, although it met a widely accepted legal definition. It is unclear what Roiphe's point is—that women don't mind being physically forced to have sex as long as no one tells them it's rape? Surely she would not argue that the victims of other injustices—fraud, malpractice, job discrimination—have suffered no wrong as long as they are unaware of the law. Roiphe also accuses Koss of upping her numbers by asking respondents if they had ever had sex when they didn't want to because a man gave them alcohol or drugs. "Why aren't college women responsible for their own intake of alcohol or drugs?" Roiphe asks, and it may be fair to say that the alcohol question in the study is ambiguously worded. But it's worth noting that the question doesn't come out of feminist fantasyland. It's keyed to a legal definition of rape that in many states includes sex obtained by intentional incapacitation of the victim with intoxicants—the scenario envisioned by my father. Be that as it may, what happens to Koss's figures if the alcohol question is dropped? The number of college women who have been victims of rape or attempted rape drops from one in four to one in five.

One in five, one in eight—what if it's "only" one in ten or twelve? Social science isn't physics. Exact numbers are important, and elusive, but surely what is significant here is that lots of different studies, with different agendas, sample populations, and methods, tend in the same direction. Rather than grapple with these inconvenient data, Roiphe retreats to her own impressions: "If I was really standing in the middle of an epidemic, a crisis, if 25 percent of my female friends were really being raped, wouldn't I know about it?" (Roiphe forgets that the one-in-four figure includes attempts, but let that pass.) As an experiment, I applied Roiphe's anecdotal method myself, and wrote down what I knew about my own circle of acquaintance: eight rapes by strangers (including one on a college campus); two sexual assaults (one Central Park, one Prospect Park); one abduction (woman walking down street forced into car full of men); one date rape involving a Mickey Finn, which resulted in pregnancy and abortion; and two stalkings (one ex-lover, one deranged fan); plus one brutal beating by a boyfriend, three incidents of childhood incest (none involving therapist-aided "recovered memories"), and one bizarre incident in which a friend went to a man's apartment after meeting him at a party and was forced by him to spend the night under the shower, naked, while he debated whether to kill her, rape her, or let her go. The most interesting thing about this tally, however, is that when I mentioned it to a friend, he was astonished—he himself knew of only one rape victim in his circle, he said—but he knows several of the women on my list.

It may be that Roiphe's friends have nothing to tell her. Or it may be that they have nothing to tell *her*. With her adolescent certainty that bad things don't happen, or that they happen only to weaklings, she is not likely to be on the receiving end of many painful, intimate confessions. The one time a fellow student tells her about being raped (at knifepoint, so it counts), Roiphe cringes like a high school vegetarian dissecting her first frog: "I was startled. . . . I felt terrible for her. I felt like there was nothing I could say."

Confronted with someone whose testimony she can't dismiss or satirize, Roiphe goes blank.

Roiphe is right to point out that cultural attitudes toward rape, harassment, coercion, and consent are slowly shifting. It is certainly true that many women today, most of whom would not describe themselves as feminists, feel outraged by male behavior that previous generations—or even those women themselves not so long ago—quietly accepted as "everyday experience." Roiphe may even be right to argue that it muddies the waters when women colloquially speak of "rape" in referring to sex that is caddish or is obtained through verbal or emotional pressure or manipulation, or when they label as "harassment" the occasional leer or off-color comment. But if we lay these terms aside, we still have to account for the phenomenon they point to: that women in great numbers—by no means all on elite campuses, by no means all young—feel angry at and exploited by behavior that many men assume is within bounds and no big deal. Like many of those men, Roiphe would like to short-circuit this larger discussion, as if everything that doesn't meet the legal definition of crime were trivial, and any objection to it mere paranoia. For her, sex is basically a boys' game, with boys' rules, like football, and if a girl wants to make the team—whether by "embracing experience" in bed or by attending a formerly all-male college—she has to play along and risk taking some knocks. But why can't women change the game and add a few rules of their own? What's so "utopian" about expecting men to act as though there are two people in bed and two sexes in the classroom and in the workplace?

Roiphe gives no consistent answer to this question. Sometimes she dismisses the problems as inconsequential: Coerced intercourse is bad sex, widespread sexual violence a myth. Sometimes she suggests that the problem is real but is women's fault: They should be more feisty and vociferous, be more like her and her friends, one of whom she praises for dumping a glass of milk on a boy who grabbed her breast. (Here, in a typical muddle, Roiphe's endorsement of assertive behavior echoes the advice of the antirape educational materials she excoriates.) Sometimes she argues that the women's movement has been so successful in moving women into the professions that today's feminists are whining about nothing. And sometimes she argues that men, if seriously challenged to change their ways and habits, will respond with a backlash, keeping women students at arm's length out of a fear of lawsuits, retreating into anxious nerdhood, like her male-feminist classmates, or even, like the male protagonist of David Mamet's *Oleanna,* becoming violent: "Feminists, Mamet warns, will conjure up the sexist beast if they push far enough."

Coming from a self-proclaimed bad girl and sexual rebel, this last bit of counsel is particularly fainthearted: now who's warning women about the dangers of provoking the savage male? When Roiphe posits a split between her mother's generation of feminists— women eager to enter the world and seize sexual freedom—and those of today, who emphasize the difficulties of doing either, she has it wrong, and not just historically. (Sexual violence was a major theme of seventies feminism, in whose consciousness-raising sessions women first realized that rape was something many of them had in common.) The point she misses is that it was not the theories of academics or of would-be Victorian maidens masquerading as Madonna fans that made sexual violence and harassment an issue. It was the movement of women into male-dominated venues—universities, professions, blue-collar trades—in sufficiently great numbers to demand real accommodation from men both at work and in private life. If Roiphe's contention that focusing on "victimhood" reduces women to passivity were right, the experience of Anita Hill would have sent feminists off weeping, en masse, to a separatist commune. Instead it sparked a wave of activism that revitalized street-level feminism and swept unprecedented numbers of women into Congress.

Roiphe is so intent on demonizing the antirape movement that she misses an opportunity to address a real deficiency of much contemporary feminism. The problem isn't that acknowledging women's frequent victimization saps their get-up-and-go and allows them to be frail flowers; it's that the discourse about sexuality says so little about female pleasure. Unfortunately Roiphe, too, is silent on this subject. We hear a lot about heavy drinking, late nights, parties, waking up in strange beds, but we don't hear what made those experiences worth having, except as acts of rebellion. In a revealing anecdote, she cites with approval a friend who tells off obscene phone callers by informing them that she was her high school's "blow-job queen." Not to detract from that achievement, but one wonders at the unexamined equation of sexual service and sexual selfhood. Do campus bad girls still define their prowess by male orgasms rather than their own?

It's sad for Roiphe and her classmates that they are coming of age sexually at a time when sex seems more fraught with danger and anxiety than ever. Indeed AIDS is the uneasily acknowledged specter hovering over *The Morning After*—the condom, not the imaginary consent form, is what really put a damper on the campus sex scene. Certainly AIDS gives new urgency to the feminist campaign for female sexual self-determination and has probably done a lot, at both conscious and unconscious levels, to frame that quest in negative rather than positive terms. But that's just the way we live now—and not only on campus. Rape, coercion, harassment, the man who edits his sexual history and thinks safe sex kills passion, the obscene phone call that is no longer amusing because you're not in the dorm anymore but living by yourself in a not-so-safe neighborhood and it's three in the morning. It's not very hard to understand why women sometimes sound rather grim about relations between the sexes.

It would be wonderful to hear more from women who are nonetheless "embracing experience," retaining the vital spark of sexual adventure. Roiphe prefers to stick to the oldest put-down of all: Problems? What problems? It's all in your head.

Under His Thumb

Amy Taubin

Amy Taubin is a regular contributor to *The Village Voice*, where this essay first appeared on March 15, 1994.

"Does he fuck you like this?" my therapist inquired, banging his right fist into his left palm fast and hard enough to make the effect clear. "No," I muttered, irritably, and then wondered if I wished he did. Because it would be proof that the he in question had some feeling for me, even if it were only anger. "Do you get a kick out of fucking like that?" I countered. "Or just from the demonstration?"

A discussion of my rapidly disintegrating love affair was thus transformed into a conversation about "hate fucking," as my unorthodox but profoundly useful therapist termed it, and where it fit on the sex-power continuum. All rape is hate fucking, but not all hate fucking is rape. A fuck gone bad can turn into a rape—although the parties involved wouldn't necessarily agree about when, or even if, it happened. Pragmatically, when a woman feels she has been raped, then she's been raped. But some guys fuck, some or all of the time, as if they're raping. Some know what they're doing. Some don't.

If, in the accepted definition, sexual pleasure encompasses the widest possible range of feeling, then anger, hate, fear, coldness are as much part of the experience as tenderness, generosity, love, whatever. When sex becomes the proof of male power—when the prick is used as a weapon to put a woman in her place—it turns into hate fucking or rape. There's no mutuality in hate fucking, which is what differentiates it from consensual rough sex or S&M. Hate fucking is what the Ethan Hawke character in *Reality Bites* probably does off-screen to his one-night stands. He might even hate-fuck the Winona

Ryder character once or twice when their relationship goes sour, as it inevitably will, after the final fade. Then they'll probably stop having sex entirely.

As opposed to rape, which Hollywood uses to jack up its thrill quotient, hate fucking is severely underrepresented in the movies. Kept offscreen, it's also off-the-record in the current feminist discourse. Which is why Mike Leigh's *Naked,* a film that works the boundary between hate fucking and rape, left confusion in its wake. For me the film's unromanticized depiction of rape and hate fucking was closer to my own experience than is either the MacKinnon or the Roiphe side of the current feminist debate or the various wild cards (Paglia, Brownmiller) in between.

I've experienced one rape and one attempted rape. The rape was clear-cut in that both the rapist and I agreed about what had gone down. I woke up to find him burglarizing my apartment; for him rape was inherent in the structure of the event. When I pointed out, mid-copulation, how silly it was, he stopped. Although I knew it was rape, it was less disturbing than any number of consensual sexual experiences I've had.

The attempted rape terrified me, partly because the man, who was extremely violent and in a murderous rage toward women (directed at me just because I happened to be there), kept denying that this was rape even as he punched me out and tore off my clothes. He was the then-superintendent of my building, and although I'd never said more than two words to him, he seemed under the delusion that I'd invited him into my apartment. I fought back, but he was a foot taller and a hundred pounds heavier. Because the building was deserted (it was a holiday weekend), there didn't seem to be any purpose in calling for help. At some point, however, I became hysterical and starting screaming. Whereupon he fled. I called the cops; they arrested him a few hours later, coming home with a bag of groceries. He was amazed that I had turned him in. He claimed in his plea bargain that women always said no when they meant yes, and that he'd had a relationship with another woman in the building whom he treated just like he'd treated me, so why was I so upset?

Although there's a major class difference between them, this guy was a lot like *Naked*'s secondary male character, the sadistic yuppie landlord who enjoys terrorizing women, causing them pain during sex, and then pretending that the experience has been mutually satisfactory. He hangs around, savoring his power, enjoying the fact that Sophie, the punkette, can't call the cops because she's afraid of being thrown out on the street. In the case of the landlord Sophie knows she's been raped. But she's confused about what happens between her and Johnny, the film's hate-fucking protagonist, who charms with his wit and then uses his prick to violate not only women's bodies but their expectations of pleasure; to punish them for *his* desire, for luring him from the straight and narrow. When Johnny assaults her with his cock, we see her expression change from desire to pain and fear. Afterward she tries to rationalize what's happened: She and Johnny are two of a kind, he can reveal himself to her, she loves him.

Johnny does violence to every woman who feels sympathy for him or believes he has access to special knowledge and gives him an opening. The violence is always sexual, although it doesn't always involve a sex act. If anything, Johnny is more damaging to the women he can't bring himself to fuck: his long-term girlfriend and the drunken older woman who reminds him of his mother. Johnny's attractive because his experience of the world, as an outsider, has taught him that it's seriously bent out of shape. He's a misogynist, not because he blames women for the mess but because he takes out his anger on them for their inability to set it right. His misogyny is omnipresent—it can't be controlled or legislated away by Antioch rules. On the other hand the film doesn't naturalize him; his actions are not a function of male biology or animal nature. Infinitely sad, *Naked* shows that in the world that is, sexual matters cannot be easily settled.

How to Avoid Date Rape

Nelson W. Aldrich, Jr.

Nelson W. Aldrich, Jr., is the author of *Old Money: The Mythology of America's Upper Class*. His essay on date rape first appeared in the spring 1994 issue of *The Wilson Quarterly*.

Date rape, whirlpooling, *kultur*-rape in Bosnia, the Spur Posse in southern California, the Manassas penis cutter—sexual horror stories shuddered through the media last year, each paroxysm more horrible than the last.

The erotic mayhem got so bad, it even sustained an intelligent conversation for a few months. That's my subject—the talk, especially the talk about date rape and what to do about it. It has fascinated me. One reason, alas, is personal. Legally it may be true that rape is rape, and that "date" is a needless qualifier of a simple, brutal crime. Trouble is, it may qualify me. The topic reminds me of squalid scuffles in dimly lit rooms, of desperate moves in the back-seats of cars. Legal rape is for the poor, the crazy, the unlucky. Date rape, I have to say, may, at least in its broader connotations, be for me.

The other reason for my fascination may have more general implications. Talk of date rape is appallingly destructive for everyone, even for those who merely talk about it. Anyone peering into the thick cloud of charges and denials can see the corpses. Hope and love died on that date, some sort of hope, anyway—and some sort of love. The truth was another casualty. With charges of date rape, often, one doesn't even have the consolation of knowing that "someone here is lying." Maybe neither of them has been lying.

That's the worst of the destruction, isn't it? To language, to our faith that an apparently common language can create common understandings. Join an argument about date rape, and within minutes we are spinning around in a maelstrom of multiple perspectives. Round and round we go, down and down, until at last we all go gurgling out into Humpty-Dumpty land:

> "When I use a word," Humpty-Dumpty said in a rather scornful tone, "it means just what I choose it to mean, neither more nor less."
>
> "The question is," said Alice, "whether you *can* make words mean so many different things."
>
> "The question is," said Humpty-Dumpty, "which is to be Master—that's all."

Humpty-Dumpty land is where events like date rape may happen, or not happen, simply because someone's word, or spin on a word, masters all competing words, or spins. This land is our land. It's where we come out after our multiple perspectives are so thoroughly separated—each from others, each from itself over time—that all reality is suddenly up for cognitive grabs. In Humpty-Dumpty land every fourth word looks like it's suspended between sarcastic quotation marks. The simple *was*ness of things is lost in a dustup of desperately performative utterances. "Let there have been date rape!" says you; "Let there have been some good clean sex!" says I. And in the end (if there ever is an end), since no one in Humpty-Dumpty land really is Master, all conflicts are settled by force—physical force, or, as we say, the forces of law and order.

Humpty-Dumpty land has been on the map since long before Lewis Carroll. Pick your own Fall—with Heraclitus, Montaigne, Locke, whenever. And one can get fetched up in that country in the course of almost any sort of conversation. Political journalists, for example, spend most of their days there, dizzied and dizzying, as they put competitive spins on the spins of spin masters. This is dismaying enough: A pall of mistrust falls between ourselves and our democracy, our self-government. But imagine what it must be like to get into a word fight over . . . well, let's call it an "intercourse event." Such fights can have consequences for the body. A raped body feels different from a body that has enjoyed a truly erotic moment. A rapist's body (or a "date rapist's") feels different in jail than it does at large.

That was the sort of fight, and the stakes, that were at issue last fall, for example, when two undergraduates submitted their contest for mastery over an intercourse event to the arbitration of a court. The trial happened to be in London, but it might have been anywhere in the English-speaking world. She said she'd been raped. He said he'd been seduced and was now the victim of the woman's "self-repugnance after the fact." His word was declared Master, it turned out, but as always in the woozy world of Humpty-Dumpty, it had been a near thing.

Nor was the contest over. Isabel Hilton, a columnist for London's *Independent,* confidently opined after the trial that wild bids for mastery such as this woman's are "an abuse of the power that many generations of feminists fought for—the power to *make* their word count and to be taken seriously" (italics mine). But Hilton is naive. Do courts have the final word on other words? Can anyone but God, by saying the word, *make* it so?

But this is the horror: that meaning for the body should ever be contingent on the uses and abuses of *power,* yours, mine, and the next guy's, all mixing it up in a battle for mastery. Yet so it seems.

Many people find the prospect of endless semantic warfare extremely disagreeable. I know I do, which is why I am sympathetic to the largest and loudest group in the date-rape debate, the people who say they can't understand what all the fuss is about. I can tell one of them by the first words out of his or her mouth. "When I was dating . . . ," they begin, and invariably go on to claim that they always knew how to get what they desired (or to avoid what they did not) without feeling bad about it, or being thought bad, or being punished as bad, or actually being bad.

The women I've heard on this topic say they knew how to behave on dates because someone taught them: say, how to drink without getting (too) drunk. Their mothers told them what sort of boys to avoid. Their girlfriends explained how to put off the really heavy breathers without enraging them. One would think, listening to these women, that they'd grown up in the oral traditions of a tribe.

The men knew how to date because . . . well, they just knew. As a friend of mine put it, "I was always easily discouraged, is all."

Gnostics of the dating game are Romantics, direct descendants of the divine Jean-Jacques, nostalgists (as he was) of the unconscious conscience. They may also be romantic, lovers of romance, though this is uncertain. But they are certainly naive, like Isabel Hilton. Their tone is usually complacent at first, even bored. But as soon as they find themselves gurgling into Humpty-Dumpty land, they become petulant, frightened, furious. Accusations follow, notably against the people who set off the date-rape alarm. Romantics insist that these people are lying, twisting words for political, specifically feminist effect. A buzzword here is *problematize,* as in, "Why are these women problematizing romance?"

But of course the Romantics want to be Master, too, though they seem scarcely aware of it. They want to be masters of the debate, to stop the spinning. It threatens something valuable to them, some broad understanding of "life," the common language that underwrites a pleasing, morale-sustaining arrangement of (moral) relationships and possibilities. Nietzsche called such an arrangement a "horizon," declaring that everyone must either draw one around himself, or "restrict [his] vision to the limits of a horizon drawn by another." We like to call such things a "culture."

Culture is a key concept in this debate. Romantics want one that exerts more or less preemptive control over our words and deeds. You can tell, listening to them, that what they have in mind is what we used to call a second nature, a sort of quasi-reflex that mediates between our primal nature, where all our lusts and terrors and rages roil around, and the dry, repressive artifacts of society, where our rewards and punishments come from. In a culture like that, laid down deep, knowledge of how to behave on dates, and elsewhere, appears to those who have it as simple realism, basic common sense.

Romantics believe they have it, or, more accurately, that they are had by it. The Romantic notion of culture almost always betrays a longing for that prelapsarian state where moral choices (if choices they are) seem somehow to have merely *happened,* to have come about without the slightest sense of personal agency. Thus, in the Romantic view, dating is always being anthropologized ("a ritual"), or aestheticized ("a dance"), or otherwise jollied into some morally reassuring condition ("a game") in which everyone knows the "moves," the "signals," the "score."

Who can't sympathize with that? I can. What is supremely annoying about the date-rape debate is that it's making everyone horribly mistrustful and self-conscious about something that ought to proceed easily and naturally. "How absurd!" we say, about the dating rules in force at Antioch College. "You can't legislate court-ing behavior!" Rules for the management of sexual desire ought to be, as it were, *inherited.* They should do their thing as a trust fund does its thing, releasing their instructions directly into the nerves and fibers of the body, like dividends into the bank account, without the distressing necessity, as one might say, of "working at it."

I speak as a man, but there are Romantic women who are quite as annoyed by the date-rape alarmists as the men are. "What's the problem?" they ask. "Why can't they *handle* these guys?" One heard this refrain often during the Hill-Thomas hearings, when southern women, black and white, were reported to be scorning their beleaguered "sister." "What *is* the matter with that woman," they'd say, "to let a man treat her so bad?" Camille Paglia, catching the refrain, has made a media career out of sneering at abuse-sensi-tive feminists. To Paglia they are a bunch of complainers who can't seem to seize the full possibilities of their liberation: that they, too, as *naturally* as any man, can yearn for an intercourse event.

The notion of deep culture serves Romantics well. Too well, say the feminists, the second-loudest participants in the date-rape debate. To them it seems obvious that the culture that these latter-day Romantics want to defend is "patriarchy." Cut through the persiflage, feminists say, and what you find is the very source of date rape, men's domination of women. Date rape occurs because the deep-cultural structures of patriarchy—a "second nature" if there ever was one, founded on the "natural" physical power of men—cannot accommodate the right of women to say no.

Forgive me if I seem Clintonesque here, not to say wimpish, but I find that I am as sympathetic to the feminist drive to destroy patriarchy as I am to the Romantic desire to restore "ritual." I am a liberal, that is to say, a grateful beneficiary of liberal revolutions, the American Revolution in particular. And what happened in that revolution, among other things, was a semantic struggle over "the King" in which we liberals gained the mastery. "The King," once a deep-cultural instruction of obligation and deference, was henceforth to be understood as a tyrannical claim on our deference and obedience. This justified the overthrow of the institution behind the word. American men today live on the spoils of that glorious triumph, and it seems to me that feminists want only to push it to its logical conclusion. As they see it, patriarchy lay at the bottom of the King, the Church, the Great Chain of Being, and God the Father. Patriarchy is the root system of a once-vast tree. The tree has been felled, by the American and other revolutions, but the roots still send up noxious shoots (such as rape) to pollute the good clean air of freedom and equality. This is feminism's self-appointed task: to whack away at these last extrusions of a deep, underlying culture—to cover it in darkness, so that it will die.

Romantics of the dating game can't be expected to applaud this task, but they can hardly protest it, either, having profited so handsomely from its first cuts. The only thing they can do is ask the feminists the same question that was always asked of their predecessors in the liberal revolution: What happens when you've won? And if patriarchy is the last, deepest culture of them all, what on earth will take its place as a deep, preemptive control on our desires, as our new moral habit? And if nothing should take its place, how shall we ever be *good*?

Feminists seem not overly responsive to these questions. They appear much too busy with the more joyful part of their task, the liberating whacking part. Beyond that they are usually content with the immemorial reply of previous liberal warriors. Deep-dead cultures will simply have to be replaced by education. In the date-rape instance this means presumably the marvelous educative powers of principle—No Fornication Without Representation! Failing that, feminists will demand contracts, like Antioch's. Failing those, they will call, as exasperated liberals always do, for lashings of laws and punishments.

Somehow the liberal response doesn't seem to satisfy anymore, not as it used to. It especially doesn't satisfy those, such as Charles Taylor, Robert Bellah, and others, who are often called communitarians. Communitarians have a strong voice in the date-rape debate, and in some of them, the softer ones, it throbs equally with Romance and alarm. Like the feminists, if far less enthusiastically, the communitarians acknowledge that daters should treat each other as equals, lest there be no self-respect and mutual respect on dates. For, without those, dating will always be prone to corruption, unhappiness, and lousy sex.

Like Romantics, however, communitarians believe that it will take more than freedom and equality, more even than education, Antioch-like contracts, and the police to assure smooth dating. Like Romantics, they believe it will take a culture. Daters need a culture to preserve the romance of dating of course, but even more urgently they need one to save civil society from increasing violence. Or rather, to save us from two great evils that lead to violence.

One evil was flagged first by Jean-Jacques himself: the hypocrisy, the falsity, that comes with studied behavior. To that one might add the gaucherie: If "education" is all that stands between us and moral chaos, then good behavior is all a matter of study. It doesn't matter what sort of study, whether one gets it in school, or from how-to books, or at the feet of preachers, gurus, or fee-for-service therapists, or from any of the thousands of moral curricula that modern society has generated to help us control our desires. It might even come from the always-handy "discipline of the marketplace." As soon as we depend on "study" or "work," we find ourselves on the slippery slope from frustration to rage, thence to the divine afflatus of fury that lifts us high, high, high above all conflict, mistrust, restraint, and lets us scream out at last the most blissful obscenity of rejection.

And that evil leads straight to the other: a society that has to whip itself into obedience with laws, rules, and regulations, all backed up by the police, the courts, and the prisons. The pendulum of American violence swings like that—back and forth between antinomian ecstasy and Arminian wrath.

No surprise there, say the communitarians. America, more than any other modern society, has neglected its communities. It is only "community," they say, that can provide us with both a Romantic's notion of culture and a feminist's notion of equality. More accurately, a strong, pervasive, and, yes, mildly repressive *sense* of community is what is needed. It takes a whole village, goes a favorite communitarian proverb, to raise a child. Cultures do not insinuate themselves, by themselves, into the mainsprings of people's behavior, as many Romantics seem to believe. They are cultivated, and constantly reinforced, by the example, the pressure, the approval, and if need be the condemnation, of members of a community. To imagine that "culture" could be an agent of self-government without community, as Romantics often do, is to imagine that Ralph Lauren breeds ladies and gentlemen. This is not just romantic; it is hopelessly romantic.

Against the feminist-liberals, on the other hand, communitarians take a decidedly skeptical view of freedom. Liberation is okay apparently: freeing us from the oppression of inequality. Liberty is more dubious. But "community" subdues liberty, almost without our knowing it. It does this by replacing liberty with the great human goods that liberation has uprooted: a sense of place, of belonging, of the givenness of things; continuity between the generations; and, derived from these goods, a common, dependable language of speech and gesture, and a "horizon" to embrace and contain a renewed order of self-government.

As it happens, I have some personal experience of these benefits of "community." I grew up in as realistic a copy of a village culture as you'll find in America. Not among the Amish or the Hassidim; nor in an assimilation-resistant ghetto, immigrant or drug infested. These places are arguably not in America, or not yet. I was raised in patrician Boston, with its bleak virtues of thriftiness, trustworthiness, grim fortitude, and moral candor; its *cursus honorum* of boarding school, outdoor discipline, and Harvard; and its endless, manifold repressions—sexual repression not least among them. This culture was laid down deep in me, or was supposed to have been, and to a quite specific purpose—the breeding of an all-'round boy, who would become a prudent, gentlemanly, civic-minded man, a sort of Renaissance trustee.

But the culture, deep as it was, was not deep enough. It did not take. Nor did it take with my childhood friends. It couldn't have: The Fall had occurred. Even in Boston there is no inherited culture; it must be chosen, worked for, studied.

This was the great flaw in Katie Roiphe's famous *New York Times Magazine* article of last summer, which brought the date-rape debate home to her parents' generation. Roiphe is an apostle of a rather Pagliesque sort of Romanticism in dating. "No problem" is her view of date rape: How can it be rape if I'm loving it? (No, I am unfair. Her view is more like, "I may not be loving it, but it's not rape either.") Still, she does try to account for the date rapes—in her view, the very few date rapes—that do happen. And her answer is: cross-cultural dating on today's multicultural campuses. In my terms this translates as: If I'd only stuck to ladylike Bostonians in my dating career, I could never even imagine, as I can now imagine all too well, that I had ever committed date rape.

But Roiphe has made a truly nasty problem for herself here, and it's a problem I don't see communitarians finessing either. For if it's true that our erotic mayhem, such as it may be, is a consequence of crossed cultural signals, then all we have to do to fix matters is a little cultural cleansing. Schools, singles bars, neighborhoods, municipal swimming pools, cruise ships, wherever people meet to date and mate (and possibly to rape) need only be segregated by village culture, that is, by the variety of second-nature nurture they received at birth, merely because of their birth, and all will be well.

This is dangerous rubbish. Cultural cleansing may cut down rape within cultures, assuming there is such a thing, but at the cost of increasing it along their (always expanding, always violent) frontiers. Moreover Nazis, fascists, and Greater Serbians have all tried this sort of hygiene, and none has managed to remain clean for long.

Beyond the rubbish, though, I want to ask Roiphe what cultures she has in mind, in this New World, that are so determinative of male dating behavior that the word *no* actually gets translated as *yes*.

To me the Romantic-communitarian theory of cultured behavior is just another twitch of tribal nostalgia. "Culture" serves these people, as does the chauvinism of a typically mixed-ethnic American who, of all the leaves in his genetic salad, chooses to claim the one called "German." Such ploys are just some of the desperate ways we have of coping with, by somehow delimiting, the single greatest constitutive achievement of modern societies, certainly of American society—our democratization of the franchise of desire. Anybody has the right to want anything, even to *be* anything.

It's easy to forget that not long ago a full range of desires was possible only for the privileged, by birth or traditional office. Everyone else was embedded in ignorance and poverty, surviving on fatalism, faith, and the remissive powers of alcohol. Today everyone, including our children, especially our children, is promised the freedom, the opportunity, the *possibility* of wanting almost everything there is to want—and the possibility of getting what he or she wants. (Not wanting, in fact, is a form of invisibility, a kind of death.) This achievement is the glorious reward of our long, bloody struggle for freedom and equality against kings, nobles, priests, and (soon now) patriarchs. It's as if all those old oligopolists had been dispossessed of their estates, with the privileges auctioned off to the richest bidders (richest in talents, luck, and money), and their hopes and dreams given freely to everyone else. In America, where the franchise of desire has spread wider and gone deeper than anywhere else in the world, this magnificent process is called the pursuit of happiness.

But no culture, not even Boston's, can possibly withstand the temptations of democratized desire. First, the franchise sends everything spinning. It may be an accident that the "Rashomon effect," everybody's favorite denominator of the vertigo of multiple perspectives, refers to a movie about a rape. But a drama of desire it had to be, of one kind or another. Desire is what pumps Humpty-Dumpty up.

Second, the free-market system combines with the franchise to abstract cultures and communities from their settings—to commodify, package, and send them to market. (Watch: In a generation or so, someone is sure to be selling us on the beauties of the Patriarchal lifestyle.) All the so-called cultures available in the modern world—the "culture" (which is also the "community," mind you) of your business, your favorite sport, your neighborhood, your social class, your region, your neurosis, your religion, your taste in food and drink, your therapy, your profession, and on and on—all the desire-control devices manufactured by a desire-driven polity are all simply elective curricula, more or less costly, more or less exchangeable, more or less thorough. But all, lest desire be hedged about, perfectly shallow.

Therefore, *pace* Katie Roiphe, it is not communities of common culture that intradate and make love, or interdate and rape, on campuses these days; it is individual closets of cultures. They may be a bit jumbled, these closets, Ralph Lauren suits on the hangers, grunge outfits on the floor. But the kids can't be expected to have their own personal style right off the dime, can they? Not any more than adults can be expected to keep a lifestyle for the length of a life. The modern principle applies to young and old: Mix and match your own cultures! Be your own Humpty-Dumpty! Select, don't settle.

Finally, to finish off any lingering fantasy we may have about cultivating deep cultures, there's the only common, truly pervasive culture we have, the consumer culture. Its Idol, as Auden called it, is possibility. The cultural horizons of communitarian nostalgia exerted desire-control by letting poverty, fatalism, religion edit (out, for the most part) possibility. There were some things you just did not want or do; they were utterly unimaginable. Humpty-Dumpty sat on his wall. Moreover, these pre- and proscriptions did seem inherited, "natural" as egg and sperm and "blood" are natural. However, as an added assurance of good behavior, the moral culture was passed along with an equally "natural" inherited status—as Slave, say, or Father, or First-Born Son, or Woman. Without a hereditary-status hierarchy, in fact, no community culture of the sort longed for by communitarians has ever existed. Nor, thanks to our democratic access to the sense of possibility, will it ever exist again.

Thus, in the actual world, it is impossibility that is unimaginable—for everyone. With the glory of liberation now hard-wired to the universality of the consumer "culture," the most compelling instruction of modern life, and of the whole worldwide economy built upon it, is that there is not now, nor ought there *ever* to be, any controls on our possibilities, our desires, at all.

Some communitarians seem to recognize the hopelessness of their cause. Like Charles Taylor, they pray that we may somehow see, and choose, the wisdom of embedding ourselves in some sort of community, of restricting ourselves within some Nietzschean horizon of the possible. But to judge by the activities of some of their agents—for example the American Association for Rights and Responsibilities—the only way many communitarians can think of to accomplish this feat is to help "communities" lash the miscreants in their midst with new laws, more police, and harsher punishments. Any old liberal could have thought of that. But thought, too, that it will never do the trick.

No wonder date rape managed to get a good conversation going. The date is the perfect synecdoche for our modern predicament. We are always out on dates of some sort or other, petting and being petted, breathing heavily, tumescent, possessed by the passion to possess—something. Even objects of desire (subject to fear) have this experience. But at the same time, in the shadow of this heady arousal, the thought occurs that we can't get all we want all the time. There are too few resources, too many desires, too many objects of desire, too many ways of getting what we desire. Not to mention too many other desirers, each with multiple needs, wants, yearnings of their own, and multiple perspectives to go with them. It's enough to drive one mad.

Whereupon we sense the melancholy summons to self-government. The thing is melancholy in just about every way. It means choosing, which eliminates possibilities and reminds us that no one is chosen, that nothing is given. It means taking responsibility, thereby inhibiting desire and inviting blame. It means calculation, plans, cost-benefit analyses, all of which promote self-consciousness, prepare for embarrassment, and stifle romance. Above all, self-government is terribly difficult, and not just because of the possibilities and temptations of desire. For the fact is that all the King's horses of "community," and all the King's men of "culture," cannot disguise the fact that we govern ourselves alone, and that we have to choose our own stars to guide us. It's only when we fail to do so that we find we have company—the police, for example.

Other help is available. Self-government is depressing, but not impossible. As Philip Rieff reminded us thirty years ago in *The Triumph of the Therapeutic,* all the while that "cultures" were being rendered elective, and their "communities" with them, portable culture substitutes were being prepared in the consulting rooms of psychotherapists. Of course it's a highly contentious question in Humpty-Dumpty land how helpful fee-for-service therapy may be to self-government. Many Romantics loathe it as another plague of self-consciousness, another blight on romance. Many communitarians complain that without family, neighborhood, and peer group to reinforce the therapized behavior, the help will come to naught. And many feminists consider most schools of therapy just so many shoots of the old patriarchal root system, to be slashed and buried. No one claims that it will do anything for the loneliness of the task.

But even here help may be on the way. People have been "problematizing" the franchise of desire and the worship of possibility for a very long time. And again and again they've concluded that what's needed is to reverse the whole economic ethos that underwrites the franchise and the idolatry. This means turning upside down some of our most cherished values—"economic growth," "mobility" (always upward of course), the whole ideological apparatus that Plato condemned as "pleonexia," more-more-ism, the fatal disease of democracy.

The question is, how? There's been a surprising unanimity about this. Generation after generation of worriers about behavior have hit upon the same old counterethos—asceticism. It has been propounded in many forms, Christian mostly, but also classical.

Among my sort of Bostonians, for example, the secret appetite suppressant (and capital preservative) was Stoicism. Today it seems to me that there are more asceticisms on the morality market than ever before: Buddhism, New Ageisms, especially varieties based on Native American practices, radical environmentalism, and so on. More to the point of date rape, a vast network of quasi-communities, ad hoc villages, has grown up around the possibility of impossibility and the folly of insatiable desire. This is the Twelve-Step movement set in motion by Alcoholics Anonymous, but now established among "communities" of incontinents of every conceivable description—including the lustful, the panicky, and the enraged.

But of course none of these curricula will make much headway against pleonexia so long as the marketplace keeps up its relentless arousal of desire. James Madison knew this in the 1790s, as did William James in the 1890s. Jimmy Carter knew it, too, when he echoed James's call for the moral equivalent of war to ground a new asceticism for the 1970s. Poor Carter. But now the rage for more, more, more is bumping up against a tiny but fully mobilized political opposition, as well as some brutal denials of desire in the environment. If it weren't for injustice, the sickening (and widening) gap between the desire possibilities of the rich and the poor, one might even suggest that the ascetic curriculum looks like a good long-term investment. There are no grounds for optimism, as Christopher Lasch pointed out recently, but we can always hope.

Meanwhile, as we await the future of asceticism, two things will change. The conversation about date rape will move on to other frightful subjects, and fewer and fewer intercourse events will be performatively declared "date rapes" by feminist-alarmist Humpty-Dumpties. The reason is not that these events will become universally consensual, still less that we'll all wrap ourselves in horizons of factitious culture communities and date only within them. The reason is that, long before society becomes just or we become ascetics, the feminist revolution will succeed and patriarchy will die.

After that it seems likely that the worst fears of the Romantics will come true. Mistrust and self-mistrust should become even more commonplace than they have been, spreading deeper and deeper into all social relations and all activities—schooling, politics, art, therapies. With this, love should become even less "natural," even more of a studied achievement, than it already is. Perhaps then we will finally accept what we hear so often but don't want to believe: that love is "hard work."

Self-government, meanwhile, will be as hard as it always was, even with a proliferation of rules and contracts. And its failures, like rape, will be what they've always been in liberal regimes—ever more harshly, ever more ineffectually punished crimes. If you have seen Antioch, you have seen the future of America. And (up to a point) it works.

If this sounds disagreeable, as it surely does already to many millions of people, something can be done about it without waiting for the doubtful triumph of asceticism. There are any number of groups dedicated to the promulgation of a stable, inerrant language, and to a "natural," unequivocal moral law. These groups differ in the warrant they believe they've found for these certainties: the Bible, the Koran, the Roman Catholic doctrine of natural law, the tribe, the "original intent" of the Founders of the Republic, God's Word, your genes, and so on. They vary, too, in their attitude toward the free market and its indefatigable spirit of consumerism. But they do not vary in their hostility to liberty, to possibility, to democratic desire, and to individual self-government.

This is a high price to pay, it seems to a conversationalist like me, merely for a little semantic security. Moreover it seems extremely unlikely that merely by subjecting himself to one Humpty-Dumpty, enclosing himself within the wall of his horizon, that anyone can put him back together again. And even if one could, what of the H-Ds on the other side? What of the H-Ds inside one's own head? We know now that the fat boys are here, there, everywhere. And as we'll never be able to forget it, we will never be together again either.

Looking at Pictures

Celia Barbour

The pornography debate has reached a new generation, as demonstrated in this essay by Celia Barbour, an associate editor at *Martha Stewart Living,* which first appeared on the op-ed page of *The New York Times* on April 23, 1994.

Most women I know had a brief, intense affair with pornographic magazines when they were young. It happened around age twelve or thirteen and was marked by the same avid fascination as a boy's early forays into *Playboy.*

Many girls secretly plundered the libraries of fathers or brothers. I relied on the houses where I baby-sat, discovering endless, astonishing photos of air-brushed flesh. Nancy Clausen of the National Coalition Against Pornography admits she explored forbidden closets herself. "My dad had a collection," she says, "and I was, you know, curious."

We were all curious. But the infatuation didn't last. Before long, we realized that an interest in naked women wasn't exactly appropriate for a teenage girl. So we taught ourselves not to feel anything but discomfort when we saw a picture of a naked body. By the time I got up the nerve (and the allowance money) to buy *Playgirl,* it was too late: I had already forbidden myself to enjoy it. In college I found myself agreeing with the pervasive notion that women simply aren't turned on by pictures.

But why wouldn't we be, when we are as moved as men by every other kind of image? What blocks the passageway between our eyes and libidos? Whatever it is, it almost certainly was placed there by culture rather than by biology. In Japan pornographic art used to be enjoyed by men and women: it was traditionally given as wedding gifts. Only in recent years has their pornography come to resemble ours, catering almost exclusively to men.

The feminist lawyer and antipornography activist Catharine MacKinnon would like to protect girls from male sexual arousal by doing away with pornography altogether. In *Only Words,* her most recent polemic against pornography, she conveys the same message as the material she hates: Sex is created by dirty-minded men and imposed on innocent women.

Women deserve to create their own sexuality. But the way to do that just might be to give women a pornography of their own, available to them when their curiosity begins to develop. Not watered-down erotica or Harlequin romances. Not *Playgirl*'s polite hunks, and certainly not *Playboy*'s passive centerfolds. Adolescent girls need sexy magazines that are passed along by their sisters and given as gift subscriptions by maiden aunts, with nudges and winks all around. Magazines that encourage them to look without shame at dirty pictures. Some feminists would like to dictate women's sexual tastes, but such tastes are rich and varied and they aren't always politically correct. A man can buy pornography that caters to every fantasy under the sun. Women deserve the same.

In the absence of pornography made for them, adolescent girls grow up with no choice but to define their sexuality in response to what the boys and men around them want. Their early exposure to *Playboy* or *Penthouse* leaves them with a vivid impression of what that is: a thirteen-year-old learns that sex is something that will happen to her, not for her, and then only if she is built like a pinup.

For a flat-chested seventh-grader, that's going to take a lot of work. The mirror becomes her centerfold, and the hormonal storm inside her is channeled into an obsession with her body. Everyone knows what girls put themselves through to be lovely—from eating disorders and plastic surgery, to hours spent with depilatories and blow dryers.

In *Only Words,* Ms. MacKinnon argues that pornography has more in common with discriminatory speech prosecuted under the Fourteenth Amendment than with the artistic expression protected by the First Amendment, because pornography harms women. Though compelling, her argument goes too far, attacking pornography's very power to arouse, as if the mere fact that men have physiological reactions to lifeless images is pernicious. She idealizes a world in which "sex between people and things, human beings and pieces of paper . . . will be a turnoff."

Yet in pornography's power to arouse lies its potential for good as well as harm. It allows adolescents to explore the unsettling feelings occasioned by the opposite sex (or the same sex, if that's their pleasure) in the safety of their own bedrooms.

It is easy for women to resent men their easy access to sexual arousal since our own is often wrapped in thick layers of guilt and insecurity. Banished from the world inhabited by men and their magazines (or their CD-ROM playmates), most women declare they never wanted any part of it anyway. But depriving men of their pleasures is an act of spite, not sanity. More good pornography for women would be a healthier way to even the score.

Beauty and the Beast

Robin Morgan

Robin Morgan has been at the forefront of the modern feminist movement since its inception in the 1960s. Activist, poet, and former *Ms.* editor-in-chief, she is also the author of several books of feminist theory, including *Going Too Far: The Personal Chronicle of a Feminist,* and the editor of the anthologies *Sisterhood Is Powerful* and *Sisterhood Is Global.* Reprinted here is an excerpt from her book *The Anatomy of Freedom: Feminism in Four Dimensions,* published in 1982.

Is it because sexual intelligence is an expression not only of desire, curiosity, and freedom, but of *energy,* that something so simple can be seen as so fearful? Blake also wrote, "Energy is eternal delight." But energy is never predictable; it cannot with certainty be controlled; it *is* movement and change by definition. How do you codify it, focus it, channel it, make it "serve" you? Well, one (illusory) way might be to separate yourself from it, pretend that you yourself are not a miraculous assemblage of particles of energy. Distance yourself literally from it (a task that, although not possible, has preoccupied many fine minds who should have known better). See it "through a glass, darkly." Tell yourself, and others, that the volatility of energy makes it untrustable, potentially destructive (truth, but not the whole truth), and then go farther: make energy a simile for and ultimately a synonym of *violence.*

Now we begin to recognize modern sexuality, frighteningly described by Michel Foucault as

an especially dense transfer point for relations of power: between men and women, young people and old people, parents and offspring, teachers and students, priests and laity, and administration and a population. . . . [It is] endowed with the greatest instrumentality: useful for the greatest number of maneuvers and capable of serving as a point of support, as a linchpin, for the most varied strategies.*

But we can break this power politics of sexuality down into still finer components—into the way Man has made men approach the subject, and the way in which Woman has made women approach it. A metaphor for the former would be the fable of Beauty and the Beast; for the latter, the myth of Psyche and Eros.

Beauty and the Beast, you will remember, is the story of how Beauty comes to live with a rich, powerful, and magical Beast, as hostage-payment for her father's offense of having poached a rose from the Beast's garden. Fearing the Beast at first, she comes to feel a strange affection for him, since he does try to please her with little courtesies, intellectual games (he's not a *stupid* Beast), lavish gowns, gourmet foods, a great palace—everything material she could wish for. Yet he is nonetheless a Beast, and she persists in refusing his repeated offers of marriage, persists in refusing his plea that she tell him she loves him. She comes to feel guilty for this—but she persists. And he persists in being a Beast. Indeed the desperation of his "cruelly unrequited" love almost drives him to rape her —but, not being a stupid Beast, he knows it is her love he needs even more than his own lust, and he retreats. When she discovers him feeding on the carcass of a slain deer, Beauty is at last overcome with revulsion and returns home to her family, no matter what the consequences. The Beast even lets her go. Yet her sisters' bitchy enviousness ("Who in hell cares if he's a Beast? *Look* at that pearl necklace you're wearing!") drives her to revulsion for humans (especially, notice, other women). In a magical mirror, she sees that the Beast, back at the palace, is dying for want of her presence. In contrast to her sisters, he looks good now, so Beauty returns to him.

* Michel Foucault, *The History of Sexuality,* Vol. 1 (Paris: Editions Gallimard, 1976; New York: Random House, 1978).

When she thinks him (safely?) dying in her arms, she tells him that she loves him, and would have wed him had he lived. Instantly a handsome prince springs forth from the Beast's remains, the spell long ago cast upon him (as punishment for his pride) now broken by her love. That love having, so to speak, "civilized" him, they now can live happily ever after.

Keep this fairy tale in mind while we look at some real-life facts about sexual violence as the cultural synonym for sexual energy. We need focus on only two examples out of many blatant ones, such as rape, battery, forced incest, war itself. It might be more useful to pick as one of our examples an issue still, in the 1980s, considered controversial (meaning, "Well, they've come up with the statistics on the other issues, but these crazy broads still have to prove it to us all over again on this one"): pornography. As a second example we can choose an issue hardly broached yet at all: sports rituals.

I don't intend here to reexplain the feminist positions on pornography, since a number of excellent books are now available on that subject, and since I can especially recommend three of these to the reader: *Take Back the Night: Women on Pornography,* a comprehensive anthology edited by Laura Lederer; *Pornography: Men Possessing Women,* a factual exposé and theoretical analysis by Andrea Dworkin; and *Ordeal: An Autobiography,* by Linda "Lovelace" Marchiano, with Mike McGrady, a story of a woman's courageous escape from the real-life world of being a "porn star"—a world of imprisonment, beatings, rape, and forced prostitution. No thoughtful reader can come away from these three books without a thorough understanding of the complicated, *pro*-free-speech, painfully-arrived-at unity among feminists on this issue, the depth of research and analysis, *and* the diversity of tactical approaches being suggested. This permits me, then, to concentrate on two aspects of the pornography issue: the Causality Defense, and what I've termed the New Pornocracy.

Elsewhere I've written in detail about why I feel that pornography as sexual-violence propaganda is in effect the "theory," while rape, battery, molestation, and other increasing crimes of sexual violence against women are, not so coincidentally, the "practice." But causality has never been proved, the pornographers and their fellow travelers smirk. Neither has it been *disproved,* and there is evidence that the 1970 Presidential Commission on Obscenity and Pornography suppressed information on such casual connections. Both the Hill-Link Minority Report and Dr. Victor Cline's testimony before the commission analyzing its methodology discuss suppression of findings. We may well ask, was this alleged manipulation of facts because of the porn industry's political and economic power (a four-billion-dollar-a-year business regularly written up in the *Wall Street Journal*)? Or because only two of the eighteen commissioners were women? Or because researchers are hardly immune from cultural biases, including the possibility that they are sexual fundamentalists?

Recently a reevaluation of the "porn as a harmless outlet" theory seems to have begun. Press and police investigators noted the quantities of pornography both in David Berkowitz's apartment (Berkowitz is the convicted "Son of Sam" killer of New York "lovers' lane" couples, including five women, during 1977), and in the harem commune of convicted murderer Charles Manson. Psychologists and sociologists (among them Dr. Natalie Shainess of New York and Dr. Frank Osanka of Illinois) record a growing resistance to therapy among convicted rapists, who no longer view their acts as socially aberrant, given the greater acceptability of pornography in mainstream films and magazines during the 1960s and 1970s.

Two experiments that gained attention at the 1980 convention of the American Psychological Association were even more revealing. In one experiment Dr. Edward Donnerstein (University of Wisconsin at Madison) measured induced aggressiveness in terms of the number of electric shocks the subject gave to a male or female confederate. The findings showed that men who had watched sexual violence were likely to administer more electric shocks to their partners than those who had watched nonviolent sexual films—and that they were even more aggressive against females than against male partners. In the other experiment doctors Neil M. Malamuth and James V. Check (University of Manitoba at Winnipeg), assessed the effects of pornographic violence via responses to a long question-naire; the findings indicated that heightened aggressiveness toward women persists for at least a week after exposure to pornographic materials.

Perhaps a few social scientists seriously are trying to free them-selves from their sexual fundamentalism, trying to practice a genu-ine scientific method of objective research. This is certainly a heart-ening development, although it's tempting to point out that such research has begun only after a decade or more of intensifying pro-test by women. Still, it is interesting that such proof of causality is demanded at all. Isn't it time to admit that on some level we've always recognized the connections—between anti-Semitic tracts and the pogrom, between Klan pamphlets and the lynching? Would con-temporary morality (or even taste) tolerate entire bookstores and cinemas specializing in the defamation of an ethnic group? Wouldn't we protest "entertainment" glamorizing the systematic torture of animals? How long must women alone prove the cause-and-effect reality we experience daily as an adrenaline surge not only of emotional outrage but of bodily terror?* How long must the Women Against Pornography and Women Against Violence in Por-nography and media groups across the United States and in other countries stage Take Back the Night marches? How long before the new Brutality Chic—evinced not only in hard-core porn but in *Play-boy* and *Penthouse,* in art-film houses, in department-store window displays, in magazine and television advertising—is comprehended as propagandistic reinforcement of the soul-deadening myth that men who are Real Men must act like beasts and that women who are Real Women must be understanding, may resist (up to a point), and must capitulate in the end? Worse, how long will it be before society acknowledges that women do *not* "want it," do not secretly long to

* "When the Nazis took over the government of Poland, they flooded the Polish bookstalls with pornography—on the theory that to make the individual con-scious only of the need for personal sensation would make the chances of unifying people in rebellion more difficult."—Irene Diamond, "Pornography and Repression," quoting Pamela Hansford Johnson in a paper delivered at the annual meeting of the Western Social Science Association, Denver, April 1978.

be raped, battered, brutalized? How long until we all realize that women—and surely, somehow, somewhere, under the Beast's fur and claws and snout, men—long for *energy* in sexuality, but have been forced to settle for *violence* instead?

The length of time may well depend on our exposing the depth and breadth of the New Pornocracy—the porn aristocracy. Because pornography no longer consists (if it ever did) of seedy entrepreneurs slobbering along society's lunatic fringe. Like the Mob (usually in business partnership with gangster empires), pornographers have gone "legit," complete "with all the characteristics of conventional industries—a large workforce, high-salaried executives, brisk competition, trade publications, board meetings, and sales conventions." The New Pornocracy obviously encompasses that exploitative standby, "gay porn," as well as the more recent atrocity, "kiddie porn," rock-music lyrics, distinguished statesmen and politicians and beloved culture heroes (Atlanta mayor and former U.N. ambassador Reverend Andrew Young, former president Jimmy Carter, New York Mayor Ed Koch, and John Lennon all consented to be interviewed in *Playboy,* cheek-by-jowl with the centerfold).

The New Pornocrats (like the Beast) are not stupid. Their virulent sexual fundamentalism more and more emerges in tones peculiarly resembling civil-libertarian, revolutionary, and even feminist rhetoric. They degrade the First Amendment by claiming that any objective research done on pornography's harmful effects is book burning. They stand on their platforms of "sexual liberation" and deliberately try to confuse *sexual revolution* with *feminist revolution* —a circumnavigation that preserves and expands their power even if it does seem, logically, rather like putting the cart before the horse; they insist on putting the coarse before the heart. They push forward *their* "token women," like Christine ("Christie") Hefner, who calls herself a feminist and defends her father's *Playboy* empire with all the zeal of an heiress. They are shrewd corporation executives with no concern for how they manipulate emotional or political values of genuine worth. As a legitimizing publicity event in 1980 the Manhattan Playboy Club sponsored a Valentine's Day group wedding for sixteen couples, offering a free wedding ceremony, reception, and three-day honeymoon at the Playboy Resort in New Jersey; it was all of course done "for love." Playboy "Bunnies" were the brides' attendants, and Justice Ralph Sherman of the State Supreme Court in Queens, New York, performed the mass ceremony from a swinging platform above them—a platform built to hold a disco dancer in a G-string. Some of the brides *were* said to have been embarrassed by the surroundings, but, as the grooms pointed out, it was *free* (how that word does get abused!), and besides, have you no sense of humor?

Perhaps the most stunning example of the business acumen wielded by the New Pornocrats is also the most alarmingly clear example of the way that *all sexual fundamentalists, at some level, bond together.* The TAB Report (The Adult Business Report) was begun in 1978 as an information and rallying point for the pornography industry, complete with promotional aids, business guides, and eight separate newsletter reports, a wholesale and trade catalog, an extensive mailing list of adult business (including movie theaters, massage parlors, publishers, distributors, product manufacturers, etc.), as well as swing clubs, gay bars, escort services, sex boutiques, videodisc producers, specialty lawyers, advisers, and investors. The following is quoted from an editorial/letter aimed at gaining new subscribers, and was signed by Dennis Sobin, president of TAB Report, in a 1981 mailing:

> It is now more imperative than ever that you keep informed of the events that shape the industry today. The rise of the Moral Majority will have a far-reaching impact that may be as strong as the Sex Revolution of the 60's. With an increasing number of fundamentalist born-again Christians being elected to serve in legislatures on the national, state, and local levels, we can expect tighter controls on present laws concerning the adult industry. And yet, this *religious conservatism will prove to be an advantage,* too—*wherever sex becomes forbidden fruit it increases in value.* . . . Erotica and the sale of sex flourished in Victorian England. . . . Ours is an industry that has traveled a long and enduring road to survival and success. *The*

> *Moral Majority will, like all great conservative institutions, provide new audiences and wider avenues for the adult industry* [italics mine].

Never has the lie been so exposed—the lie that pornography is revolutionary, progressive, and an adversary of reactionary politics. All that stuff about the First Amendment may be useful to pull the bedsheets over liberals' eyes in liberal times, but when politically fascistic tendencies begin to be felt in the land, then sexually fascistic tendencies can admit that what was really necessary all along for this so-called "sexual freedom" was *repression*. Rarely has the difference between freedom and license been so revoltingly blatant. Feminists, to be sure, have been saying for years that patriarchal thinking, whether of the right or the left, spanned not a spectrum but looped into a circle, taking turns at power, profiting from one another, promulgating the same message in different dialects. Time and time again we have been forced to tolerate political "revolutionaries" or "sexual liberationists" or avant-garde "artists": ranks of pretentious male supremacists who carry their moral laziness over into a torpor of technique while remaining conveniently alienated from the human suffering that surrounds their aleatory violations of politics, sexual passion, or art. Just as frequently we have been forced to endure "the proscribers": men whose comstockery is merely the denial of their own lechery—and sometimes women, unable to name a justifiable revulsion at being so used (as constituency), so abused (as sexual object), and so trivialized (as artist), women who consequently mistranslate their own unrecognized feminist rage into campaigns for "virtuous standards." (Can we, after all, blame the victim for being unable to tell the rapist from the rape?) But it *is* tiresome to keep encountering such troglodytic choices: "radical" terrorism or establishment totalitarianism, sexual license or sexual repression, self-indulgent sexist "aesthetics" or self-righteous censorship. *As if they were not always two sides of the same coin of the same realm.* This time, thanks to Mr. Sobin, the pornocrats actually have come right out and said it themselves. *Now* will women be believed?

But even some women will not believe women. Given the power of the image of Woman, there always have been women willing to pledge their lives and sacred honor as the price of admission into Man's presence. Their tragedy of course is that they are forced to realize only after it's too late that the antechamber is as far as they get; they never make it into the inner sanctum of real power. (Did Phyllis Schlafly win a cabinet appointment in recompense for her labor to elect Reagan, after all?) Whether such women seek acceptance in the cabinet meetings and boardrooms of the right or in the central-committee catacombs of the left, two things remain constant: the price (selling out other women) and the reward (an approximation of authority instead of real power, indulgence instead of freedom). For the women who are *being* sold out, the hardest thing is to realize and then admit that it actually is a few other women who are doing the selling. (So must Central and West African peoples have felt when their African neighbors raided their villages—and then turned the captured villagers over to European slavers.) The incredulity is deep, because one *knows* that others of one's "own kind" experience the same oppression as one does oneself; therefore how can they do this? The denial is just as deep, because a despair about changing the situation waits just the other side of acknowledgment that this really has happened. So it is that a sexual-fundamentalist tendency, small but given expectably high visibility and respect by the power establishment, has emerged *within* the women's movement in the past few years almost unchallenged.

As usual it is a strange-bedfellow alliance that sexual fundamentalists make. In this case the bonding includes a few women calling themselves militant lesbian feminists, others defining themselves as socialist feminists, and one or two self-styled radical feminists who happen to have well-known public positions of unsubtle homophobia. This eclectic group includes a woman named Pat Califia, who at odd moments calls herself a feminist in between writing an S&M-"rights" sex column in the gay male newspaper *The Advocate;* such heterosexual and lesbian "so-cialist feminist" women as Diedre English, Amber Hollibaugh, and Gayle Rubin, who together conducted a rather sophomoric round-table analysis of why pornography is defensible, for the pages of the *Socialist Review;* and Ellen Willis, a heterosexual writer who has on various occasions championed pornography and has implied that feminists are brownshirts, Puritans, frigid neurotics, or fools for daring to criticize this fun-loving industry. Perhaps this is all expectable. What *is* a source of repeated shock to feminists, however, is that such women as Willis et al. call themselves feminists. Their tactics range from a rather cloddish approach (''It feels good, and I like it —so *there*!'') delivered in a toe-scuffed combat-booted pouting style, to a far more sophisticated attack on feminists as being antisex because we are antisexist. Some defend child molestation as ''boy love,'' most defend sadomasochistic practice as ''liberating, kinky sex.'' Some (the lesbian women, in this case) defend their pro-porn and/or pro-S&M position by saying that among same-sex partners it's a ''gesture of trust,'' it's different, more equal—and therefore reading about, viewing, or practicing power games regarding sex doesn't pack the same clout. Others (the heterosexual women in this case), hypothesize that power games must just be a natural part of sex, that they or their men can't imagine this ever changing, and that since they don't wish to give up their men, they will affirm whatever goes with them.

This bizarre phenomenon has a peculiar effect on feminists (and on millions of other women who, whether calling themselves feminists or not, have had the common sense to loathe pornography even before it became a women's-movement cause). It can tend to make us feel as if the mirror we trusted to give back an honest reflection of the truth in our souls had become a fun-house mirror, so distorting our features that we lose our balance when we try to take a step. Everything gets reversed: the pro-porn and pro-S&M women claim that they are the revolutionary voices of a free sexuality, that they must fight against being stifled by fuddy-duddy feminist sexual mores. ''But,'' respond thoughtful feminists, ''pain *hurts*. Suffering is *not* 'trust,' just as war isn't peace, and freedom isn't slavery. Dominance and submission, violence, power games, humiliation—what do these have to do with real trust, real sexual joy, real sensual freedom?'' But Sade's new Juliettes refuse to see the very rearguard sexuality they are defending for what it is, persisting instead in claiming that this regression is avant-garde.

Yet the truth is that pain does hurt—as women know all too bitterly. And the truth also is that games of torture are hideous travesties of the actual torture that is practiced officially and unofficially all around the world today.

It took an inexcusably long time to understand that whites wearing blackface, no matter what jolly denials accompanied that act, carried a political message: mockery of black people. It took a comparably long while to understand that men wearing "drag," no matter how sexually revolutionist they purported this act to be, really carried a political message: mockery of women. It seems intolerable that we must wait as long to understand that "bondage," "discipline," props of whips and chains and leather thongs, and allegedly "loving games" between "trusting lovers" carry a political message too: a ghastly mockery of the human beings who suffered under Iran's SAVAK torturers, of the human beings who were electroded by Idi Amin's henchmen, of the human beings who scream in real and agonized pain in the interrogation chambers of South Africa or Chile or East Germany or the Philippines at this very moment. Surely even women so damaged by our androcentric and fundamentalist culture as those who defend pornography and S&M can realize that when you find titillating the same attitudes or acts around which Auschwitz and Belsen and Treblinka revolved, something is wrong. And surely such women can realize that what they, in their piteously twisted sexuality, are upholding has nothing, nothing to do with the feminist vision of freedom.

I'd like to suggest another reaction, however, one that feminists might take beyond the vertigo caused by pseudofeminist sexual fundamentalists, beyond the pain, beyond even the attempt to ignore such women or pity them, beyond anger and certainly beyond taking them seriously. It might be simply to realize that women taking such stands have given up all hope of connecting with real sexual energy and thrown in utterly with its offered substitute of violence. That they defend the violence *as* sex is their confusion—and we know where that comes from; it's all around us. That they mistake the present (and past) as the inevitable future is reminiscent of people who saw the earth around them as flat and so insisted that it must continue to be so beyond their perception.

Galileo was forced by the Catholic Church to recant his "heretical" position that the earth moved about the sun, but this recantation ultimately meant not one prune pit to the earth or the sun. Galileo of course knew this—as we must. Rising from his kneeling pose before the Church fathers after his recantation, he was heard to mutter to himself, smiling slightly, "Nevertheless it moves."

PART FIVE

Sex War in the Media

The Peeping Tube:
America Is Shocked. Shocked!

Walter Goodman

Walter Goodman is *The New York Times*'s television critic. His analysis of the TV coverage of the William Kennedy Smith date-rape trial and the Hill-Thomas hearings first appeared in the "Arts and Leisure" section of the *Times*'s Sunday edition on December 22, 1991.

The age of X-rated educational television has arrived, with flourishes. The William Kennedy Smith rape trial and the Senate committee hearings on Anita F. Hill's charges against Judge Clarence Thomas may have owed their popularity to the spicy nature of the encounters. But viewers who managed to keep their calm while all around them were being titillated by uncommonly explicit discussions of common doings could glimpse matters that are usually treated in drier fashion. There was much to be noted about the interplay of money, class, race, and gender in America today.

Alert viewers could see how Kennedy money and power play to a nation of outsiders looking in, through the tube. They could see class differences being used to influence a society that often deludes itself into thinking it is classless. They could see expectations of black failure, based on long experience and ingrained assumptions, upset by displays of education and success. And they could be even more confused than usual by the mixed messages about sexual relations that have for some time been sent forth by television. And so unlike the packaged goods that fill television, most of these events came through unedited, unpolished, raw. They made the *MacNeil/Lehrer NewsHour* seem like junior high school.

All right, millions did not tune in day after day for incidental insights into the confusions of race and class in America. They were drawn there, as George Bush would surely put it, by the woman-man thing and were rewarded with some curious disquisitions on sexual behavior.

In their vociferous championings of Judge Thomas, Senator Orrin G. Hatch and Senator Alan K. Simpson rested their case on the impossibility that a man like the judge would say the things that Ms. Hill said he said because such things could only be said to a woman by a certified pervert, in Utah and Wyoming anyhow. And in her questioning of William K. ("Who's Michael?") Smith and her summation, the prosecutor, Moira K. Lasch, waxed sarcastic at the possibility that this young man and young woman (perhaps any man and woman) could meet in a bar one Friday night and have intercourse an hour or so later, even in Florida during Easter break.

When the stakes are high and protagonists are playing to a camera or a jury, it often becomes difficult to take them seriously or to know how seriously they take themselves, but you can tell what they think will work on the audience. The Hatch-Simpson line was more successful than Ms. Lasch's, but both were cast into a general unease, evident on television, about what the right relations are these days between men and women.

The tube is more awash than ever with sex in many forms; everybody is doing it with everybody. That's show biz. But under pressure to exhibit social responsibility along with the flesh, news and entertainment divisions have picked up fast on the evils of sexual harassment, date rape, AIDS, pornography, and various pathologies celebrated on talk shows. Sex is dangerous.

Here is the piety of the panderer. Television is like a brothel with rooms set aside for lectures on why visitors should stay out of brothels. The virtuous voyeur can add the satisfaction of judgment to the kick of peeping: Shame on him! On her! On them! On television! (The criticism of CNN and Court Television for lowering the level of television by carrying the Smith trial wins the year's Emmy for high-minded mindlessness.)

Senator Hatch and Senator Simpson played into widespread disgust for the dirty stuff all over the tube and distaste for the urban sophisticates who create and defend it and probably practice it when the Senate is not watching. Imagine what the senators would have made of the Palm Beach scene.

Ms. Hill's supporters and, to some extent, supporters of Mr. Smith's accuser, also known as the Alleged Victim (but don't call her Cathy), resorted to a vision of sex promulgated by some feminists as an age-old imposition upon women: to accuse a man of rape is a tautology, to acquit him is in effect lynching his accuser. Meanwhile Mr. Smith's supporters were swinging along with the sex-comes-naturally crowd, who seem bent on emulating television's beautiful people. Palm Beachers will have to dance fast to keep up the reputation lately shed on them by the tube.

Watching the Smith defense team batter the prosecution was like taking a course in the power of cash. You knew that Roy E. Black and the two other men who took turns presenting their case, and the lone woman at the defense table, who never said a word but was probably mistressminding the whole campaign, and the lesser lawyers off camera, and the rent-by-the-hour experts who delivered objective conclusions that benefited the defendant, and the anonymous researchers and investigators, and all the travel and hotels, and who knows what else did not come cheap. Jurors heard it cost one million dollars, and they might have been forgiven a chuckle when Mr. Smith said he could not afford to fly first-class from Washington to Palm Beach.

And it was not just money, it was Kennedy money. Ms. Lasch did not fail to call attention to the defense's resources, the family's history of sex and booze and its proven ability to manipulate the press and television, but it didn't take. The popularity of shows like *Falcon Crest* and concoctions like *A Current Affair* indicate that people like to watch the rich living it up and acting down. Despite a strain of populism that seems to have reawakened in this difficult period, most Americans do not spend much time hating the very rich. The nobs seem to exist not to exploit the plebes but for their vicarious enjoyment. Marx got it wrong again.

In his counterattack Mr. Black touched on the affectionate fascination with the Kennedys, kept alive by movies and television since John F. Kennedy's assassination. The clan being the closest thing this country has ever had to a royal family, we can cluck over a night of hopping from bar to Au Bar, but the royals are ours just as the Windsors belong even to British Socialists.

Mr. Black made sure the jurors and viewers were reminded in the testimony of Senator Edward M. Kennedy, Jean Kennedy Smith, and the defendant himself that the family's many sacrifices and its record of public service and good works add up to much more than Chappaquiddick, the albatross that immobilized Senator Kennedy during the Thomas hearings. After the trial Mr. Black said he saw tears in jurors' eyes during Ms. Lasch's direct examination of the senator, and there must have been a little mist in front of television sets too.

Mr. Black put on a class act. It may have been just fortuitous that the main corroborating witness for the prosecution, Anne Mercer, turned out to have sold her story to a junk television show and that the friend whom the accuser did not at first remember visiting on the big night turned out to be a bartender named Anthony Liott, whom Mr. Black made sure to display on the stand. The lawyer knew as well as any soap-opera director how to set such types against the clean-cut young assistant district attorneys who were Kennedy houseguests that Easter weekend. Look at the people the accuser associates with, Mr. Black was saying without saying it, and then look at the nice young folks who sit around playing parlor games at the Kennedy compound.

Class differences showed up in the Thomas hearings too. Remember the woman, a character witness for Judge Thomas, who presented herself as just your ordinary middle American, by way of putting down the big-name women who were supporting Ms. Hill, not to mention Ms. Hill herself? What made the criticisms of Ms.

Hill for not being one of the girls striking of course was that she is black. Is it possible, a viewer might fairly ask, that even people who are by no means racist may find a black woman as self-possessed as Ms. Hill was in her committee appearance a little off-putting? Is it possible that even some black women may feel that way? You could imagine that Ms. Hill, the Yale Law School graduate, might find it easier to get along with, say, Jean Kennedy Smith than with some of her co-workers in the Washington lower bureaucracy.

The main revelation of the Thomas hearings was the appearance, like a line of sparkling cars of tomorrow being unshrouded for the cameras, of an array of successful black professionals. People who rely on local news must have been astonished: Where have they been hiding?

Not only were they not in show business or sports or jail, they were not all liberals. They actually disagreed, but on matters like affirmative action that are articles of faith among black personages who are confirmed as leaders by their frequent appearances on talk shows. You might not care to spend a lot of time with the woman who seemed to be rigid with dislike of Ms. Hill or with the self-infatuated man who thrust his ego at the audience, but their peculiarities did not fit any racial stereotype.

It's all so complicated for the tube. But to get back to sex, which is where most viewers doubtless wanted to be in the first place, one thing is simple and sure: Television can be counted on to respond to whatever is in the wind. After the Thomas hearings sexual harassment in the workplace was decried on all channels. The Smith trial brought new exhortations against date rape. Now, with the acquittal [of William Kennedy Smith], watch for the latest prescription for young men on the prowl: For really safe sex, wear a good lawyer.

Are You a Bad Girl?

Naomi Wolf

Naomi Wolf is the author of 1991's best-seller, *The Beauty Myth: How Images of Beauty Are Used Against Women,* and more recently *Fire With Fire: The New Female Power and How It Will Change the Twenty-first Century.* She is a sought-after lecturer on college campuses throughout the country. Her essay here on the media treatment received by the woman who accused William Kennedy Smith of rape first appeared in the November 1991 issue of *Glamour.*

I have a terrible confession to make: As a result of months of intensive media coverage of several rape and sexual-abuse cases, I have realized the awful truth about myself, and I want to thank *Newsweek, USA Today, Esquire* and *The New York Times* for showing me the error of my ways: I am a bad girl.

It's true. Wild, cheap, and probably beyond redemption. In looking back over my twenty-eight years, I have to confess to having committed almost all the acts that would put virtually any woman who may have been sexually assaulted or abused beyond the pale of respectability—at least in the eyes of the press, the courts and those who buy into their sexual double standards.

Like the alleged victim in the St. John's University case—who was, she says, sodomized against her will by members of the lacrosse team—*I have talked to boys.* The defense attorneys tried to cast doubt on her lack of consent by producing a witness who testified he observed her speaking flirtatiously to a member of the team, engaging in sexual banter and using intimate body language. *I, too, have bantered.* Her word was suspect because she had had several vodka-and-orange drinks. On more than one occasion as an under-graduate, *I, too, had too much to drink.*

The more I think about it, the more depressed I get. Not only am I a bad girl, but nearly every girl I know is just as bad. One of my best friends, for instance, is a twenty-eight-year-old college profes-sor, highly respected in her field. But so what? She wears tight spandex outfits and plans to have a baby, with or without a husband. This friend's sexual activity began when she was in her mid teens; it was followed by fast driving, hard partying, and numerous lovers. My other best friend teaches at an equally prestigious university and has a book coming out. But she wears dangling earrings, began her sex life at sixteen, went to parties and has also had a few lovers: guilty, too.

And me, of course, my own résumé is mere whitewash on a checkered past. Sexually active in my teens, I went to late-night parties, had several nonmarital relationships, and spent an adoles-cence that some of my acquaintances, if pressed by *The New York Times* reporter who profiled the alleged Palm Beach rape victim, might well characterize as "wild." Did the alleged victim in Florida have, as the paper triumphantly uncovered, outstanding traffic viola-tions? Me, I've owed books to my college library since 1984. We are clearly, my friends and I, depraved.

Or are we? In fact we're just details in a generational group portrait. Far from being part of some marginal slut minority, we are as boringly representative of our time and generation as bobby-sox-ers were of the 1940s. According to a 1988 survey of women's sexual behavior by the Alan Guttmacher Institute, more than half of teenage girls are sexually active. Of single women twenty to twenty-nine years old, 80 percent have had sex. College women are the most experienced of all: According to one study, almost 90 percent of them have had sexual intercourse. These percentages indicate what statisticians like to call a gross majority.

Nonetheless in each of these recent cases the woman is posi-tioned, by lawyers or journalists, against an imagined, Doris Day-like norm of stainless chastity. The only problem with doing so is that, demographically, this cherished virgin coed just doesn't exist.

In 1991 eight out of ten young American women outside convent walls are sexually experienced. As we go to press, the Smith case has not yet been tried; all the facts are not in. But in the coverage of the facts already known, one thing is clear: It is Bad to have a sexual history by your mid-twenties. If that judgment is allowed to stand, if that transforms you, once you take the stand in a rape or sexual-abuse trial, into a whore or a provocative, deserving victim—then let's face it: There are no good girls. By that standard, precious few American women can expect respect or fair play, or simple justice.

Jennifer Levin, the victim in the so-called "preppie murder case," recorded sexual events in a highly publicized journal. My perfectly respectable sister-in-law kept such a journal when she was a teenager; so have many other nice young women of my acquaintance. Like Levin, many of us have even had sex outdoors. Like the alleged victim in the William Kennedy Smith case—she is a mother —the number of young women who choose to have a child outside marriage grows yearly. If the "promiscuity" attributed to the alleged victims means they deserve censure, then so do most of us. *The New York Times* implied that the mother of William Smith's alleged victim was a cynical gold digger because she married a divorced man who earned a higher income than she. If that was fair, you'd be hard-pressed to find many American women who by those standards do not equally deserve the name.

Young women are no longer expected to go straight from their fathers' protection to their husbands', their virginity intact. *Griswold* v. *Connecticut* signaled society's willingness to make contraception widely available; *Roe* v. *Wade,* as long as it stands, signals our acceptance of women's right to reproductive freedom, within and without the marital bond. Universities have gone coed and abandoned the double standard for curfew. Current fashion makes it obvious that the 1950s sartorial distinction between respectable girls and "tramps" no longer holds.

Clearly it has become both normative and acceptable for young women to be sexually active and physically independent—everywhere but in the courtroom and the press. Who's getting it wrong?

Us? No. The fault lies with the press and the judicial system, both of which seem determined to scrutinize alleged victims of sex crimes with a moral lens thirty years out of focus.

We have come a long way in telling our daughters that they have many of the sexual freedoms and rights their brothers enjoy. Why, then, when a young woman who acts on those rights says she's been raped or sexually abused, is it suddenly 1954? How can we ask her what she was wearing, and what has become of her virtue, her chaperone and her shame?

We've seen before how preposterous outdated moral posturing in the press can be. When Douglas Ginsburg was nominated to the U.S. Supreme Court, such a furor surrounded his admission that he had smoked marijuana that he requested his name be withdrawn.

In the few years that separate Douglas Ginsburg from current nominee Clarence Thomas, who also admits to having tried marijuana, lawmakers and journalists have belatedly realized that if you're going to discredit every potential justice or legislator who has ever gotten high, you might as well disband the Supreme Court and send Congress home. Using pot smoking as a criterion for legitimacy would throw into question the merit and credibility of an entire generation, as does using a sexual past to evaluate the victims of alleged sex crimes. The same sensible conclusion—that the criterion is obsolete—is long overdue.

What trips up the press is its confusion at best—and at worst its double dealing—over the issues of consent and blame. Let's get it straight: Consenting to sex with one or more men in the past does not indicate consent for all future time to anyone who demands it.

"On our campuses far from home," Camille Paglia lamented recently in *Newsday,* "young women are vulnerable and defenseless. . . . The old double standard protected women. When anything goes, it's women who lose." Paglia, exemplifying in her stance the moral cowardice that she tries to pin on other women, has, backhandedly, got it half right. The old double standard of shotgun weddings and sexual surveillance "protected" some women—but only as the sexual property of individual men.

That system has, thankfully, broken down. But because we as a nation are too weakly committed to the feminist ideal, young women are now caught in the open in unsafe territory. The romanticized militias of "fathers and brothers" that people Paglia's dangerous nostalgic vision are gone; the authentic defense by the courts and the press of women's right to bodily integrity has yet to be established beyond lip service.

In the biblical era it took several male witnesses to corroborate the word of a female rape victim. We have not come very far. Three more women have come forward to allege that Smith raped or tried to rape them; one of the victims, a doctor, said she hoped that her good reputation would give the charges credibility. But as soon as those charges were made public, the press was suddenly on the alert about whether Smith could get a fair trial. Notice that it takes the word of four women—at least one of whom is aware of how high are the standards for victims' respectability—to offset the lack of credibility created by a couple of midnight drinks at Au Bar. Given the way the press has stacked the cards, is there any way the alleged victim would have had a fair trial had these charges *not* come out?

The sexual revolution was supposed to abolish the double standard that separated the bad girls from the good. Should the press continue to decide that the revolution can be suspended—only insofar as the woman is concerned—when her word clashes uncomfortably with his? Did we as a nation support sexual freedom only to eventually define it as young men's freedom to rape their acquaintances, and young women's freedom to be raped?

I am a sexual person with a history, dreams and desires, and the right to act on them. So is your daughter, your sister, and every woman that William Kennedy Smith has ever known. Whether we choose proudly to disclose that—or whether the press discloses it for us—never means that we have bartered away our legal right to protection from forced sex. We should speak up in solidarity with our anonymous heroines—the woman in the Smith case and her three courageous supporters; the woman in the St. John's case, who endured a public ordeal only to see three of her alleged attackers acquitted—and remove the stigma isolating them by saying, "Me too." We are all bad girls, all of us, America's daughters.

Maybe that alone can force an end to this ritual undressing by the press of the victims of alleged sex crimes. Like these women, we are not saints or virgins, nor do we want to be. We are merely human: lively, adventurous, brave and scared; as independent as we were raised to be. But when we are forced to put our trust in the courts and the Fourth Estate, we are all too vulnerable still.

Women of the Year?

Barbara Lippert

Through her unique lens as a columnist for the industry magazine *Adweek*, Barbara Lippert examined the impact of advertising and pop culture on the gender battles of 1991 in a piece that appeared in the magazine's December 16 issue.

It was a season of trial, denial, and major gender fury, all covered microscopically on TV. More bizarre than *L.A. Law,* more graphic than *Geraldo,* these were news events of the murkiest, most upsetting kind. But because we've become used to receiving similar tidbits on talk shows and soap operas, even the most crackpot vulgarity seemed to have a familiar television ring: There's a giant in my washer, a dove in my kitchen, a pubic hair in my Coke.

The most obvious difference between the hearing/trial subjects and the typical talk-show guests of Sally Jessy Raphael, or even Oprah, was that these people had all of their teeth and could speak somewhat grammatically.

Clarence Thomas took center stage in the outrage department. His peculiar genius was in the way he lightened his inflammatory language ("this is a high-tech lynching for uppity blacks") with just the right amount of Joe Consumer brand names ("I don't need this. I can still see my kid and have a Big Mac"). Have it your way: It's the perfect diversionary tactic.

Overall it was a threatening and conflicted and confrontational time in gender city. While there seemed to be some progress in acknowledging the issues of sexual harassment and rape, in doing so we got a simultaneous—and chilling—display of the workings of the old power game: attack, deny, evade, and blame the victim. Indeed both Anita Hill and the "alleged victim" in the William Kennedy Smith trial were the most unlikely feminist icons. But from the reaction to *Thelma and Louise* through the success of the book *Backlash,* there was an electricity and a new, unembarrassed candor in the air. Even for people who automatically recoil from the F-word, it seemed as if there was a new willingness to confront the roadblocks between men and women and to see them as human issues, and not "feminist" ones.

What follows is a brief analysis of some of the touchstones for women in the year of He Said/She Said:

That's Our Blob, or Mr. Smith Goes to Palm Beach

Even during the pretrial media show, lawyers for William Kennedy Smith seemed to be hatching the Victoria's Secret Defense. That's based on the fact that the "alleged victim" was wearing a new, sheer brassiere from the store that made Frederick's of Hollywood safe for yuppies. In bringing up the bra, Smith's lawyers seemed to be taking a page from the old Maidenform campaign that featured men talking about women's underwear. "When a woman wears beautiful lingerie," actor Michael York told us in one such spot, "it shows how she feels . . . playful, romantic, mysterious." And surely a sexy black bra shows that the "alleged victim" was asking to do the nasty, using every weapon in her underwire arsenal. (As the sexist Maidenform ads showed, we're conflicted about this underwear idea: It's the stuff of male fantasy, yet mother always told us that "good girls" wear nice new underwear.)

And isn't it odd and dehumanizing that we got to inspect this woman's bra and pantyhose but we couldn't see her face? The Big Blue Blob has got to go; this case made clear that the tradition of omitting the rape victim's name and blocking her face to protect her no longer works in the age of television. It brought a mantle of shame to her testimony, suggesting everything from the Elephant Man to a science fiction parody on *Saturday Night Live.* On the other hand we got to see on the stand the full range of Willie Smith's emotions, from A to B.

Backlash

Something's up: Susan Faludi's book about antifeminism in the 1980s is inching up best-seller lists, and paperback rights have been auctioned for a fortune.

An encyclopedic look at the counterassault against women's rights in the past decade, the book is enlightening, upsetting, and sometimes downright funny. Any little dip is worth taking, from the reporting on the surprisingly sexist agenda of the writer-producers of *thirtysomething* (now you know why you hated Hope) to the hilarious account of how radio's Dr. Toni Grant raked in millions while asking listeners to "surrender into womanhood."

Anita Hill: She's Got Them Female Delusions and the Boogie-Woogie Blues

Branded a witch, a bitch, or a psycho straight out of *Fatal Attraction,* Anita Hill was a walking Rorschach test of backlash culture. Polls showed that she was not believed by a majority of Americans.

The panel of women who testified on behalf of their boss, Supreme Court nominee Clarence Thomas, suggested that at the very least Hill had a little crush on the judge and she was too uppity. A conservative Ivy League academic, Hill's biggest problem might have been not using brand names in her testimony. For many observers that made her difficult to place.

Never mind the sex thing; Hill also became a lightning rod for the equally thorny and divisive issues of race, class, and status. Many women who had been the victims of sexual harassment themselves offered no sympathy: "Deal with it! Get over it!" they said. But just as the backlash effect has been subtle and cumulative, so, too, will the results of Hill's testimony start to hit home. Stroh's Swedish Bikini Team will be the first to go.

Finally: Why Diamonds Are Forever, or Never Underestimate the Power of Kathie Lee

Far, far away from real-life hearings and the trials and anguish over power and violence, there's an entirely different kind of female icon on American television: Ms. Kathie Lee Gifford. No woman is an island, of course, but the perky cohost of *Live with Regis and Kathie Lee* does her best. At a time of confusion and ambivalence for women, she's not a bit conflicted in her devotion to home, family, more and better TV gigs and more and better endorsement deals.

"Host chat," the opening portion of *Live,* is when Reege and Kathie Lee sit and talk, unscripted, about their lives. At a time of stringent family values, it's the perfect forum for Kathie to flaunt her wifely devotion (her husband is older-man/ex-sports-hero Frank Gifford) and motherly concern (Cody seems to be the hardest-working baby in show business; he's already appeared on countless magazine covers with his mother and in several ads). But her genius is in interweaving plugs and brand names in her family capers. The best was the story of Cody's conception on a Carnival Cruise Line, which she happens to plug.

Last September Regis and Kathie Lee cohosted the Miss America Pageant. And while Anita Hill's strict Baptist upbringing made her seem a bit out of sync with the Washington culture, conversely, as a born-again cabaret singer/TV host, Kathie Lee seemed exactly in tune with all the contestants. Those beauty queens who weren't studying broadcast journalism seemed to be getting their doctorates in liturgy.

It's exactly that combination of evangelical zest and beauty-contest competitiveness that seems to spark Kathie Lee. But the secret of her success is in never underestimating the value of family —and brand names.

Entertainment for Men

Hendrik Hertzberg

Hendrik Hertzberg, the executive editor of *The New Yorker,* who formerly held that post at *The New Republic,* compared the treatment by two different soft-core men's magazines of two consorts of fallen evangelical preachers, in this essay, which first appeared in the July 4, 1988, issue of *TNR.*

I'd appreciate it if the following recommendation is greeted with a minimum of whistles, elbow digs, and Groucho Marx eyebrow flaps. Thank you. Now: check out *Penthouse* this month. It's interesting—and, in a reversal of the usual alibi for buying magazines of this genre, more for the pictures than for the articles. Guccione's boys have had the astute if obvious idea of engaging the services of Debra Murphree, the New Orleans prostitute whose trysts with Jimmy Swaggart got that aptly named evangelist in a world of trouble. In exchange for, presumably, some multiple of her usual twenty-dollar fee, Murphree has told all to *Penthouse*'s team of crack reporters, who have spread the results over seven full pages of dense print. Their revelations leave unchanged the broad outlines of what has already been reported in thousands of family newspapers. But the highly specific details do flesh out a tale of degradation, hypocrisy, greed, furtive lust, revenge, and pathos so stern in its relentless trajectory to destruction that no novelist would dare invent it (except that Sinclair Lewis already did). More to the point, Debra Murphree has also posed for a series of photographs in which she reproduces the pornographic (*Penthouse*'s word, and it is exact) poses it was Swaggart's custom to ask her to assume. These are published in a sixteen-page section that is sealed shut by a perforated strip, thus forcing the casual drugstore peruser to lay out $4.50 if he (or she) wishes to gratify his (or her) curiosity—a clever innovation in magazine marketing, one that no doubt will be widely imitated.

The pictures show what Swaggart paid, first cheaply and then dearly, to see. Their chief interest, however, is not in what they have to say about Swaggart but in what they have to say about *Penthouse*. They are a devastating critique of the magazine in which they appear. The critique is clearest in the contrast between the pictures of Debra Murphree and the pictures of other naked women elsewhere in the magazine. The positions assumed by Murphree and by (for example) the "Pet of the Month" are identical. But while the pictures of the Pet are shot in lush color and she is bathed in soft, warm light, the pictures of Murphree are shot in harsh black and white in a brutal style reminiscent of the work of Diane Arbus. The Pet luxuriates on pastel satin sheets amid backgrounds of flowers and gilded antiques. Murphree lies on the coarse linen of a crummy motel bed in the light of an unshaded bulb hanging from the pasteboard ceiling. The Pet's skin is perfect and her makeup glistens. The pictures of Murphree deliberately emphasize her body hair, the pimples on her backside, the crude "Debbie" tattoo on her arm. The relation between the two sets of pictures is made explicit in a quote, supposedly a remark made by Swaggart to Murphree, that introduces the sealed section: "Pull your panties up your crack like a magazine I've seen. . . ." The basic business purpose of magazines like *Penthouse*—which was also Murphree's business purpose, at least with her most famous client—is the provision of an aid to male masturbation in exchange for cash. What is unusual is that this should be so forthrightly acknowledged by one of the two leading "respectable" skin magazines, and that the acknowledgment should be in a context that so strongly stresses the sordid, degrading, and exploitative aspect of the transaction.

Playboy, the other of the Big Two stroke books, also publishes a series of black-and-white photographs this month. These pictures, too, are of a naked woman. But the aim of the *Playboy* pictures, taken by Herb Ritts, a well-known fashion photographer—of Cindy Crawford, a beautiful *Vogue* model—is the opposite of that of the

Penthouse ones. Where *Penthouse* uses black and white because it makes the pictures raw, ugly, and "realistic," *Playboy* uses black and white because it makes the pictures refined, pretty, and "artistic." *Playboy* has been trying for some years now to distance itself from the masturbatory nexus that called it and its competitors (notably *Penthouse)* into being. Hugh Hefner, the founder, is in semiretirement in California, and the now-diminished empire is run out of the Playboy Building in Chicago by his daughter, Christie, an intelligent woman of proclaimed feminist sympathies. Presumably as a result, *Playboy* has dropped the gassy blather about "philosophy," the ratings of porn videos, and the photos of Hef with pipe and bathrobe surrounded by off-duty Bunnies. *Playboy*'s pictures draw the line a bit closer than *Penthouse*'s, and the copy accompanying them is chockablock with girl-next-door banalities. (This month's Playmate likes rainy days, hates cruelty to animals.) *Playboy* tries to show its new attitude by publishing admiring articles about serious, accomplished women. All this is commendable enough in its tiny way. The problem is that because the magazine is no longer so stupid as to believe in itself and its mission, it has no spirit. Its smile is fixed, its eyes glassy, its cheeriness forced.

The big Swaggart-Murphree takeout was *Penthouse*'s revenge against *Playboy* for cornering the market, some months ago, on Jessica Hahn, the "church secretary" who defenestrated Jim Bakker. The synergistic parallels between the Bakker-Swaggart and *Playboy-Penthouse* rivalries are of course delicious, but the two magazines displayed their trophies in very different ways. *Playboy* chose to show Hahn in the Playmate style: wholesome outdoor backgrounds, frilly half-open dresses, flattering poses, airbrushed Kodachrome skin. Hahn is now installed in the Playboy Mansion West, reportedly recuperating from cosmetic surgery in preparation for another photo session. *Playboy*'s pictures of Hahn implicitly played to Bakker's fantasies, while *Penthouse*'s pictures of Murphree implicitly condemned Swaggart's (even as the rest of the magazine exemplified them). *Playboy* turned Hahn into a Stepford wife, a replicant who by now surely does love rainy days and hates cruelty to animals. *Penthouse* gave Murphree a check but left her in the gutter. *Playboy*'s hypocrisy was timorous and subtle; *Penthouse*'s is heedless and blatant. It's hard to know which approach is "preferable." As Gary Hart once said, let the people decide.

Behind the
Paula Jones Story

Mortimer Zuckerman

Mortimer Zuckerman is the editor-in-chief of *U.S. News and World Report* and the publisher of the New York *Daily News.* He is frequently seen as a television commentator on NBC's *The McLaughlin Group.* This essay, on the charges of sexual harassment against President Clinton, first appeared as an editorial in the May 23, 1994, issue of *U.S. News.*

Every time you think politics and the media cannot get sleazier, there's a nasty surprise around the corner. The escalation of the depressing and disgusting charge of sexual harassment leveled at President Clinton epitomizes how much downscale tabloid values now pervade American discourse. No doubt the alleged scene will soon be on Court TV in some form with a motion picture to follow. The bandwagon everybody wants to jump onto is a garbage truck.

It does not pass the smell test. Paula Corbin Jones, then a state employee, says that when Bill Clinton was governor of Arkansas, he used a state trooper to invite her to a hotel room in Little Rock during a state-sponsored conference and put pressure on her to engage in a sexual act. Why didn't she yell foul the next day? Why did she fail to make the charge during the six months required under law for such charges? Why did she keep silent during the presidential campaign, when Clinton's relations with women were a hot issue? Why now? What we have is the moral and legal equivalent of a late hit in football.

The odor intensifies with the information about attempts to

profit from the alleged incident. According to an affidavit signed by a Little Rock businessman, one of Jones's lawyers tried to send word to Clinton that he should reach a settlement with Jones or be publicly embarrassed and that "it would help if President Clinton would get Paula a job out in California," where the president has Hollywood friends. (The lawyer claims he was misunderstood.) Only when Clinton refused was the suit filed.

Can anybody doubt that this suit would not have been filed if Paula Jones was not counting on the press being right outside the door, salivating to cover the case and offer her money? The down-and-dirty tabloids and that new affliction, tabloid TV, have no qualms about such a story. Digging up dirt, or manufacturing it, is their business. That is not new. What is new is the alacrity with which the mainstream press and television seem to feel obliged to regurgitate the bile.

Cliff Jackson, the perennial Clinton hater, understood this well. He saw how Clinton's enemies could seize the suit as a political weapon. He recognized that this is a feminist era: The general presumption is that a woman would not claim sexual harassment unless it were true. Otherwise why would she expose herself to the publicity? Wendy Kaminer has analyzed it in the *Atlantic Monthly*. "Sexual violence," she writes, "is a unifying focal point for women. . . . It is heresy, in general, to question the testimony of self-proclaimed victims of date rape or harassment. . . . All claims of suffering are sacred and presumed to be absolutely true."

That sexual harassment exists is unquestionable, but that many minor acts of sexual misconduct are overdramatized is also true. To avoid trivializing those who suffer the real thing, we must reject the idea that any unwanted advance or remark constitutes harassment. There is a difference between an unwanted encounter, which may upset a woman, and pressure applied—such as threatening a woman's job security—or ongoing demeaning treatment. Those wrongly accused have their own kind of ordeal trying to prove a negative.

The sad fact is that the news cycle works in such a way that allegations alone, without proof, burst into the headlines. It is all very well to say the accused later went free without a stain on his character. The reality was more accurately portrayed by Anthony Trollope in his account of Phineas Finn, who was acquitted but could never go into the House of Commons without being made to feel guilty: "He had been so hacked and hewed about, so exposed to the gaze of the vulgar, so mauled by the public, that he could never more be anything but the wretched being who had been tried for the murder of his enemy. He could never more enjoy that freedom from self-consciousness, that inner tranquillity of spirit which [is] essential to public utility."

That is the cost to the public in the degradation of standards we are witnessing today. We can do more than regret this. We can take a public stance against the abuse of the courts for political and personal purposes. Let us oblige the plaintiffs to pay all or part of the legal costs of both sides if their claims are found wanting. And it is high time the media forbore to give such claimants a victory in the court of public opinion before they are heard in a court of law.

PART SIX

When the Personal Becomes Political

Seduced by
Violence No More

bell hooks

bell hooks is a writer, feminist theorist, and cultural critic. She is also the author of six books published by South End Press—the most recent being *Black Looks: Race and Representation*. She is currently completing a new work, *Sisters of the Yam: Black Women and Self-Recovery*.

We live in a culture that condones and celebrates rape. Within a phallocentric patriarchal state the rape of women by men is a ritual that daily perpetuates and maintains sexist oppression and exploitation. We cannot hope to transform "rape culture" without committing ourselves fully to resisting and eradicating patriarchy. In his recent essay "Black America: Multicultural Democracy in the Age of Clarence Thomas and David Duke," Manning Marable writes: "Rape, spouse abuse, sexual harassment on the job, are all essential to the perpetuation of a sexist society. For the sexist, violence is the necessary and logical part of the unequal, exploitative relationship. To dominate and control, sexism requires violence. Rape and sexual harassment are therefore not accidental to the structure of gender relations within a sexist order." This is no new revelation. In all our work as thinkers and activists, committed feminist women have consistently made this same point. However, it is important to acknowledge that our movement to transform rape culture can only progress as men come to feminist thinking and actively challenge sexism and male violence against women. And it is even more significant that

Manning speaks against a sexist order from his position as an African American social critic.

Black males, who are utterly disenfranchised in most every arena of life in the United States, often find that the assertion of sexist domination is their only expressive access to that "patriarchal power" they are told all men should possess as their gendered birthright. Hence, it should not surprise or shock that many black men support and celebrate "rape culture." That celebration has found its most powerful contemporary voice in misogynist rap music. Significantly, there are powerful alternative voices. Mass media pays little attention to those black men who are opposing phallocentrism, misogyny, and sexism, who "rap" against rape, against patriarchy. The "It's a dick thing" version of masculinity that black male pop icons like Spike Lee and Eddie Murphy promote is a call for "real" black men to be sexist and proud of it, to rape and assault black women and brag about it. Alternative progressive black male voices in rap or cinema receive little attention, but they exist. There are even black males who do "rap against rape" (their slogan), but their voices are not celebrated in patriarchal culture.

Overall cultural celebration of black male phallocentrism takes the form of commodifying these expressions of "cool" in ways that glamorize and seduce. Hence, those heterosexual black males that the culture deems most desirable as mates and/or erotic partners tend to be pushing a "dick thing" masculinity. They can talk tough and get rough. They can brag about disciplinin' their woman, about making sure the "bitch" respects them.

Many black men have a profound investment in the perpetuation and maintenance of rape culture. So much of their sense of value and self-esteem is hooked into the patriarchal "macho" image; these brothers are not about to surrender their "dick thing" masculinity. This was most apparent during the case against Mike Tyson. Brothers all over the place were arguing that the black female plaintiff should not have gone to Tyson's hotel room in the wee hours of the morning if she had no intention of doing the wild thing. As one young brother told me last week, "I mean if a sister came to my room that late, I would think she got one thing on her mind."

When I suggested to him and his partners that maybe a woman could visit the room of a man she likes in the wee hours of the night because she might like to talk, they shook their head, saying "no way." Theirs is a deeply engrained sexism, a profoundly serious commitment to rape culture.

Like many black men, they are enraged by any feminist call to rethink masculinity and oppose patriarchy. And the courageous brothers who do, who rethink masculinity, who reject patriarchy and "rape culture," often find that they cannot get any play—that the very same women who may critique macho male nonsense contradict themselves by making it clear that they find the "unconscious brothers" more appealing.

On college campuses all over the United States, I talk with these black males and hear their frustrations. They are trying to oppose patriarchy and yet are rejected by black females for not being masculine enough. This makes them feel like losers, like their lives are not enhanced when they make progressive changes, when they affirm the feminist movement. Their black female peers confirm that they do indeed hold contradictory desires. They desire men not to be "sexist," even as they say "but I want him to be masculine." When pushed to define masculine, they fall back on sexist representations. I was surprised by the number of young black women who repudiated the notion of male domination but who would then go on to insist that they could not desire a brother who could not take charge, take care of business, be in control.

Their responses suggest that one major obstacle preventing us from transforming "rape culture" is that heterosexual women have not unlearned a heterosexist-based "eroticism" that constructs desire in such a way that many of us can only respond erotically to male behavior that has already been coded as masculine within the sexist framework. Let me give an example of what I mean. For most of my heterosexual erotic life I have been involved with black males who are into a "dick thing" masculinity. I was in a nonmonogamous relationship of more than ten years with a black man committed to nonsexist behavior in most every aspect of daily life, the major exception being the bedroom. I accepted my partner's insistence that his sexual desires be met in any circumstance where I had made sexual overtures (kissing, caressing, etc.). Hence ours was not a relationship where I felt free to initiate sexual play without going forward and engaging in coitus. Often I felt compelled to engage in sexual intercourse when I did not want to.

In my fantasies I dreamed of being with a male who would fully respect my body rights, my right to say no, my freedom to not proceed in any sexual activity that I did not desire even if I initially felt that I wanted to be sexual. When I left this relationship, I was determined to choose male partners who would respect my body rights. For me this meant males who did not think that the most important expression of female love was satisfying male sexual desire. It meant males who could respect a woman's right to say no irrespective of the circumstance.

Years passed before I found a partner who respected those rights in a feminist manner, with whom I made a mutual covenant that neither of us would ever engage in any sexual act that we did not desire to participate in. I was elated. With this partner I felt free and safe. I felt that I could choose not to have sex without worrying that this choice would alienate or anger my partner. Braggin' about him to girlfriends and acquaintances, I was often told, "Girl, you betta be careful. Dude might be gay." Though most women were impressed that I had found such a partner, they doubted that this could be a chosen commitment to female freedom on any man's part and raised suspicious questions. I also began to feel doubts. Nothing about the way this dude behaved was familiar. His was not the usual "dick thing" masculinity that had aroused feelings of pleasure and danger in me for most of my erotic life. While I liked his alternative behavior I felt a loss of control—the kind that we experience when we are no longer acting within the socialized framework of both acceptable and familiar heterosexual behavior. I worried that he did not find me really desirable. Then I asked myself, would aggressive emphasis on his desire, on his need for "the pussy," have reassured me? It seemed to me then that I needed to rethink the nature of female heterosexual eroticism, particularly in relation to black culture.

Critically interrogating my responses, I confronted the reality that despite all my years of opposing patriarchy, I had not fully questioned or transformed the structure of my desire. By allowing my erotic desire to still be determined to *any extent* by conventional sexist constructions, I was acting in complicity with patriarchal thinking. Resisting patriarchy ultimately meant that I had to reconstruct myself as a heterosexual desiring subject in a manner that would make it possible for me to be fully aroused by male behavior that was not phallocentric. In basic terms, I had to learn how to be sexual with a man in a context where his pleasure and/or his hard-on is decentered and mutual pleasure is centered. That meant learning how to enjoy being with a male partner who could be sexual without viewing coitus as the ultimate expression of desire.

Talking with women of varying ages and ethnicities about this issue, I am more than ever convinced that women who engage in sexual acts with male partners must not only interrogate the nature of the masculinity we desire, we must actively construct radically new ways to think and feel as desiring subjects. By shaping our eroticism in ways that repudiate phallocentrism, we oppose rape culture. Whether this alters sexist male behavior is not the point. A woman who wants to engage in erotic acts with a man without re-inscribing sexism will be much more likely to avoid or reject situations where she might be victimized. By refusing to function within the heterosexist framework, which condones male erotic domination of women, females would be actively disempowering patriarchy.

Without a doubt, our collective conscious refusal to act in any way that would make us complicit in the perpetuation of rape culture within the sphere of sexual relations would undermine the structure. Concurrently, when heterosexual women are no longer attracted to ''macho'' men, the message sent to men would at least be consistent and clear. That would be a major intervention in the overall effort to transform rape culture.

How Dirty Pictures Changed My Life

Lisa Palac

Lisa Palac is the former editor of San Francisco's *Cybersex* magazine and the creator of the CD-ROM program *Cyborgasm*. This
piece first appeared in *Next,* the 1994 anthology of writers in their
twenties.

"Burn it," I said. The words clinked together like ice cubes. "Burn
every last bit of it. Or it's over."

I pointed at the stockpile of hard-core porn that had just slid out
of the closet like an avalanche. If looks could kill, my boyfriend
would have dropped dead. How could he, Mr. Sensitive Guy, enjoy
looking at such disgusting trash? Oh, I was livid. I paced around his
tiny one-room apartment, spitting venom, devising his punishment.
"Either all this sleazy shit goes or I go."

He looked at me as if he were about to cry; his fingers ner-
vously picked at the edges of his flannel shirt. "I'll get rid of it all, I
promise," he whispered. Silence fell around the room like a metal
drape. "But first will you watch one—just one—video with me?"
The nerve. Here I am threatening to walk, and he's got the audacity
to ask me to watch a fuck film before I go. He prattled on about how
he just wanted a chance to show me why this stuff turned him on and
that it didn't mean he didn't love me and if I didn't like it, he would,
as agreed, torch everything in a purging bonfire. I crossed my arms
and chewed on the inside of my lip for a minute. If I was going to
make him destroy his life's collection of porn, I guess I could allow

him one last fling. So that evening we watched *Sleepless Nights*. It was the first dirty movie I ever saw. A seminal film.

I saw that movie when I was twenty years old, and now I'm twenty-nine. Since then I've watched hundreds of X-rated videos, patronized plenty of erotic theaters, put money down for live sex shows, and even run up a few phone-sex bills. Today I make my living making porn. I edit an erotic magazine titled *Future Sex* and recently produced the virtual-reality-based sex CD-ROM program *Cyborgasm*. I've always been a firm believer that if you want something done right, you've got to do it yourself.

Until I sat down and watched an adult film, the only thing I knew about porn was that I shouldn't be looking at it. Growing up female, I quickly learned that girls don't get to look at girlie magazines. Sure, you could take your clothes off for the camera (becoming, of course, a total slut and disgracing your family), but the pleasure is for *his* eyes only. The message to us girls was, Stay a virgin until you get married, procreate, and don't bother finding your clitoris. Whatever you do, stay away from porn, because it's a man's world, honey. Ironically certain strains of feminism gave a similar sermon: Pornography can only exploit, oppress, and degrade you. It will destroy any female in its path, unless you can destroy it first. And if you don't believe this, you've obviously been brainwashed by The Patriarchy.

If the truth be known, the forbidden aspect of pornography made me a little curious. However, I wasn't about to be caught renting a porn video. So when Greg challenged me to watch an X-rated movie, I decided to see for myself what all the fuss was about.

At the time, I thought of myself as an antiporn feminist. Before that I had identified as a rock-and-roll chick from Chicago. I grew up on the northwest side of the city, not too far from Wrigley Field: the last in a line of four Polish Catholic middle-class kids. My childhood was carved out of a loaf of Wonder bread: I went to church on Sundays, was Cinderella in the kindergarten play, got gold stars in spelling and math, took tap and ballet lessons, forged my troop leader's signature to get extra Girl Scout badges, read all the Judy Blume books (starting with the menstrual manifesto of the sixth grade: *Are You There God? It's Me, Margaret.*), scarfed down Swanson dinners while watching every episode of *The Brady Bunch,* cried when I got caught shoplifting a Bonne Bell Lipsmacker, played doctor with the kids in the neighborhood, and asked my older brothers why they didn't wipe when they peed. It was like, you know, normal.

"But how did you get so interested in sex?" I always get asked. I interpret this question to mean, "What terrible trauma did you experience as a child that made you so perverted?" The answer: I was a corrupted papist.

Catholic school was twelve long years of wool-plaid penance, confessing to empty boxfuls of sin, and silently debating whether Mary stayed a virgin even after Jesus was born. I'd stare up at the crucifix and wonder how much it must have hurt. Then I'd wonder what Jesus looked like naked. Because of my profane thoughts, I always had a fear that I'd become a nun—seriously. That would straighten me out but good. On Career Day, joining the convent was always presented as a fine choice. "But not everyone is chosen to do the Lord's work," the sisters would say, and go on to tell us how one day they just "got the calling" and that was that. "Please don't pick me," I would whisper to myself over and over, bowing my head. "Oh, please, oh, please, oh, PLEASE! Don't make me go!" Needless to say, I never got *that* calling. I chalked it up to the fact that God would never pick someone who mentally undressed his only Son.

Or perhaps I simply inherited a kinky gene. My brothers read *Playboy.* My dad read *Hustler.* I know that because I used to steal peeks at it every time I had the chance. Whenever I'd start to feel bored and like there was nothing to do, I'd find myself thinking, *Maybe I should go look at that* Hustler *magazine again.* My father had a couple of them hidden with his fishing tackle in the basement. On hot summer days when my mom was out mowing the lawn, I'd go downstairs, lie down on the cool concrete floor, and look at those bizarre naked pictures. The one I remember most was of an Asian woman smoking a cigarette out of her pussy. It was the weirdest thing I ever saw. These magazines fascinated me for a long time, and then one day they weren't there anymore. I think my mother found them and threw them out. I didn't look at any more sex magazines until I got to college.

I moved to Minneapolis in the early eighties and enrolled at the University of Minnesota. I really wanted to go to Berkeley, but the family leash would only stretch as far as the land of ten thousand lakes. My career choice: midwife. I applied to the school of nursing. I'd already completed one year of premed at Loyola University in Chicago, but I had to escape from the Jesuits—and my prosaic little existence. In our house, if you were smart, you picked a career that showed it in dollars and cents. Dad looked at college as one long training seminar for the occupation of your choice: business, medicine, or law—the trinity of success. After all, I had to recoup all that college tuition, so forget about majoring in psychology or getting some crummy art degree. If I didn't land a high-paying job when I graduated, I might as well flush my diploma down the toilet. This was the philosophy of the survivors of Operation Bootstrap, the camp that made my dad. I solemnly vowed to rise above my Hallmark-card life and get to know the edges of the world.

Most of my sophomore year was spent either studying, getting wasted, or undergoing some kind of mutation. I went from heavy-metal chick to New Wave punk (albeit about four years late), squeezing into leopard-skin leggings and low-cut sweaters trimmed with ostrich feathers. I spiked my hot-pink hair up with gobs of gel and swam all night in hot-pink heels. I turned on to Joy Division and said "gnarly" a lot. I went to gallery openings. Ronald Reagan bored me and Patti Smith thrilled me. The way things were going, I could handle the tough science it took to get a nursing degree, but I couldn't handle the outfits. White slacks and a tasteful perm were unconscionable. I dropped out and went to art school.

I came out as a film major. My roommate came out as a lesbian. She was the first dyke I ever knew. Suzie was from California and was totally rad. I met her when I was at the U, and we escaped dorm hell together. Together we ate our first mouthfuls of feminism.

I had never heard the word *feminist* before. My mother wasn't a feminist, my older sister didn't call herself a feminist. Yet feminism gave me the words to describe my own experience. I quickly learned that being treated with less respect simply because I was female was called sexism, and it was not okay. Feminism illuminated the offenses that I'd chalked up to being a girl: enduring public comments on the size of my breasts, being paid less for the same work than my male counterparts, putting up with shoddy contraception. This knowledge was power: the power to take control of my life and make my own choices about everything I did.

Armed with our new feminist thinking, Suzie and I resolved to be women, not girls. We tromped on every bit of sexism in pop culture. We marched for pro-choice. We resented having to be constantly on guard against the threat of rape. We mourned the plight of women all across the globe who lived in squalid cages. We turned into pink sticks of dynamite, the crackle and spit of our fast-burning fuse getting louder all the time.

Pornography of course was the big bang. At that time Minneapolis was a hotbed of radical antiporn politics. Catharine MacKinnon and Andrea Dworkin were teaching a class on porn at the U of M, and they drafted the very first feminist-inspired antipornography law, defining pornography as a form of sex discrimination. *The Story of O* was picketed on campus, with flyers denouncing S&M as just another bourgeois word for violence. *Not a Love Story,* a documentary about one woman's adverse experience in the adult business, become a women's-studies classic. One woman set herself on fire in Shinder's Bookstore on Hennepin Avenue, a martyr for the right to a porn-free society. The message was clear: This battle was as important as ending the Vietnam War.

Meanwhile the Meese Commission was in full swing, bringing *Deep Throat* star Linda "Lovelace" Marchiano's disturbing testimony of coercion into the living rooms of America and alleging a link between pornography and violence. Women Against Pornography toured the heartland with their slide show, featuring the infamous *Hustler* cover of a woman being fed through a meat grinder. The tenet seemed to be this: Get rid of porn and get rid of all injustice against women. All the battles feminists were fighting could be won by winning the war on porn. So I enlisted.

I didn't have any firsthand experience with porn. I had never watched an adult film, bought an explicit sex magazine, or known anyone who did. Aside from a few stolen glances at my father's collection, the only pornography I saw was in the classroom. This carefully selected group of pornographic images didn't appear very liberating: she's tied up and gagged, with clothespins biting down on her nipples; she's spreading her legs wide open showing pink, his come squirting all over her face. These images were described as inherently degrading and oppressive. No other interpretation was offered. I looked at these images (which were supposedly representative of all porn), added my own experience of being sized up as a piece of ass, and agreed that pornography was the reason women were oppressed. Pornography bred sexism. Like Justice Potter Stewart, I knew pornography when I saw it and I'd seen enough to swallow the rally cries of the antiporn movement. I chanted and marched and applauded the spray painting of LIES ABOUT WOMEN over Virginia Slims ads and across the fronts of XXX black-veiled bookstores. I learned the slogans like "Porn is the theory and rape is the practice" from older feminists like Robin Morgan.

But soon I began to wonder how it all fit in with what I was doing in my bedroom. I still liked men, even if I didn't like all their piggish behavior. And I liked sleeping with them even more. Since I was fifteen, I used my feminine charms to lure them in. They used their virility to seduce me. Did this constitute sexual objectification? I wasn't sure. I questioned the definition of pornography I'd been handed. Yes, the images I'd seen offended me, but surely there were sexual images that weren't sexist. Where were the erotic alternatives? If the bottom line here was that looking at images of people having sex was wrong, then I hadn't come very far from Catholic school after all. Plus, lumping all men under the heading Sexist Patriarchy seemed a little unfair. The guys I hung out with were caring, respectful, and intelligent—but could they suddenly turn into psychopathic rapists if I waved a porn mag in front of their faces?

Underneath it all, I had a lot of questions. And then my boyfriend's porn came tumbling out of the closet.

"Ready?" he said, looking at me with dark eyes full of some corrupt knowledge I didn't yet have. We were both nervous; he was afraid I was going to hate it, leaving him with a mound of prurient ashes and a dead relationship. My fear was more tangled.

"Yeah," my voice cracked like a dry twig. Greg slipped *Sleepless Nights* into the VCR.

Sitting on the floor in the TV room, my mind began churning up shame-filled scenarios: What if my roommate walked in and caught us watching this dirty movie? Or worse, what if I am so turned on by this hideous smut that I become a full-blown porno addict? I could hear the voice: *What a disgusting girl. No one's gonna want you once they find out about this.* Or what if I laugh?

My initial reaction was, *Boy is this stupid.* Everything was bad, bad, bad: lame script, lousy acting, garish lighting, crippled disco soundtracks, anachronistic garter belts, and repulsive leading men. As a film student I was appalled that the director of this cheap thing didn't even bother with the basics of good filmmaking. The plot was forgettable. I vaguely remember a contrived sex scene on a pool table. I was waiting for the violent rape scene, which never happened. "Is that all?" I asked when it was over. I expected my porno research to yield some kind of groundbreaking vision, the same way that my first glimpses of feminism did.

It's hard to remember exactly what made me want to watch another one. Part of it was like social anthropology, peeling back the layers to see what I could see. And the unladylike act of watching porn was piquantly rebellious. But as we watched other X-rated films, I noticed they suffered from the same plague of filmic badness. I spent my early viewing hours counting the pimples on performers' asses and mimicking the orgasmic fakery of the starlets. Some of the actors looked bored out of their minds; others looked painfully luckless. They fucked in unnatural positions for the sake of the camera. Sometimes they were so unemotional, they reminded me of Spock. Some were so skinny and so young, I felt like shouting

"Get out of porn and run for your lives!" I imagined myself in their place; I imagined what my father would think if I did such a thing. Wouldn't all these women rather be doing something else but just don't have the skill or means?

A paradox emerged that I didn't understand. Sometimes I'd see an image of a woman on all fours begging for his cock and think, how humiliating. Other times during scenes like that, the actress's eyes filled up with fire so genuine, and he stroked her hair so tenderly while she sucked him off . . . it seemed romantic, like an unfiltered moment of pleasure. I began separating the images, recognizing that all of them weren't the same. I began to have flashes of lust.

But I wanted to have what Greg was having. He was getting something out of these movies that I wasn't. The movies didn't turn me off, but they didn't completely turn me on either—he did; his sexual excitement. He was sharing a very intimate part of himself with me and trusting me not to reject him. I wanted to know the side of him he'd so painstakingly hidden from me. Watching him watch the screen, I got turned on by the fact that he was turned on. But this Pavlovian eroticism worried me. While he slipped into erotic wonderland, I stood outside, waiting.

Then I made an important decision: I decided I needed to be alone with pornography. I wondered what might turn me on—if anything. God only knows what could happen to a girl who got turned on by thinking of a naked Jesus. I wanted to perform an experiment, to watch it by myself without him, without talking. I could no longer scrutinize these images from an intellectual distance. I had to get a little dirty.

I made a date with an "all-lesbian" action feature called *Aerobisex Girls*. I tried not to care about the plot. I didn't wonder about the performers' family histories. I didn't think about anything. The movie featured an oiled-up orgy where the women shook with the fury of real, uncontrollable orgasms. I could feel the heat between my legs. As if my erotic imagination was being mapped to the screen, I fingered myself in sync with the women in the film. I opened and closed my eyes, imagining I was part of their scene, replaying certain close-ups over and over. Then my mind began moving back and forth between the real-time video and the frozen frames of cherished erotic memories. I fed the screen with my own fantasies, splicing together an erotic sequence that played only in my head. When I came, it was intense.

Now I knew firsthand what most women don't think about: what men do with all those sex magazines. Guys don't buy *Playboy,* turn to the centerfold, and think *I'd like to marry her,* then turn the page and go grab a burger. No, they masturbate to it. They jerk off. Masturbation is such a big part of every man's life, and to a much lesser extent every woman's, but nobody talks about it. Men do it and don't talk about it, while women don't talk about it and don't *do* it. This is a fact. Studies like *The Kinsey Report* and *The Hite Report* have documented the high percentage of women who do not masturbate. This statistic is further mirrored in our language: We don't even have the words to describe female self-stimulation. If there is any jerking, wanking, or beating off to be done, it involves a penis, not a clitoris. It's a testimony to how cut off women are from their sexuality, both physically and psychologically.

Despite the fact that seventies feminist liberation honored the female flower and encouraged women to talk more openly about sex, masturbation still remains a taboo. In addition women still aren't given any social encouragement to use erotic pictures to stimulate their sexual imagination. So when it comes to understanding how to use porn, they're in the dark. They don't get what it's for. Men, on the other hand, are very familiar with the concept of stroking, and since they've always had such easy access to sexual material, they can't understand why it's such a big deal for a woman to get off on porn. "So you masturbated to some porno, big deal," they say. "I did that when I was thirteen."

The truth is, I didn't masturbate until I was nearly twenty years old and a vibrator hit me on the head—literally. I was cleaning out a closet in my new apartment, when a battery-operated vibrator fell off a high shelf and bonked me. As if I were a cartoon character, a light bulb went off inside my brain and I decided to give myself a buzz. It was the first time I had an orgasm. Strange but true, I never really thought much about touching myself until then. Try to imagine a guy who doesn't masturbate until an appliance hits him on the head at the age of twenty.

Until this point I never felt in charge of my own pleasure. I was taught that sexual satisfaction was something I lay back and waited for. An orgasm was something my boyfriend gave to me—only he didn't. Although I'd been having penis-in-vagina sex since I was fifteen, I hadn't come from it. I heard plenty about the Big O, but clearly never had the feelings they described in *Cosmo*. I remember one time when an old lover asked me the inevitable question after sex: Did you come? Embarrassingly I said I didn't—ever. "Don't you masturbate to come?" he asked. I was bewildered.

At the beginning of my porn adventures, I was also confused. I was looking for a political theory instead of a sexual experience, and that's why it hadn't been working. Now I had the carnal knowledge that so few women possessed: how to use porn and come. What's important about this isn't just that I learned how to get physically aroused by pornography but that I became sexually autonomous. I was now in complete control of my own erotic destiny. My experience was sexual liberation in action. I now knew how to use my mind to turn a two-dimensional image into a flesh-and-blood erotic response and explore sexual fantasies.

Before I watched porn, my erotic imagination was groggy. I didn't know what a sexual fantasy was; I hadn't really had them. Even when I masturbated, I didn't think about anything except the physical sensations. When I had sex with my lovers, my thoughts were filled only with them, the way they were touching me, the immediacy of the act. And that was good. But there were all these other thoughts that I hadn't explored yet. Pornography dangled sexual fantasy in front of me. It made me aware that my sexual imagination wasn't limited to the heat of the moment or a sensual reminiscence. I could think about *anything*. I could use *anything*—books, magazines, videos—for erotic inspiration.

One of my most formative sources of inspiration was a journal titled *Caught Looking*. Written by a group of East Coast feminist activists, this book combined academic refutations of the antiporn argument with hard-core sex pictures. As its title implied, it gave women the rare opportunity to look at a wide variety of pornographic images. *Caught Looking* confirmed what I had been living: The censorship of pornography is unfeminist. The book represented a whole new breed of women who were reclaiming the power of female sexuality. I felt very much a part of that breed.

Soon I was reading *On Our Backs,* a lesbian sex magazine edited by a woman named Susie Bright. This was pornography created by women for women—how revolutionary! It not only challenged countless stereotypes about lesbian sex being boring and vanilla, but it also defied the myth that women weren't interested in erotic pictures. The magazine ripped apart the notion that porn was only for men. I uncovered Candida Royalle's series of feminist porn videos, *Femme,* and watched every one with fervent camaraderie. Other books, like Nancy Friday's *My Secret Garden,* which detailed women's wide-ranging sexual fantasies, and *Coming to Power,* edited by the lesbian S&M group Samois, further validated my position that female sexuality was a powerful force that could not be politically pigeonholed.

My newfound sexual freedom was sweet, but finding the pornography that waved it along was rare. Wading through the swamp of split beavers and raging hard-ons, I felt by turns critical, angry, depressed, pensive, embarrassed, and bored. I began a relentless search for the right stuff. Often I was surprised at the things that made me wet; things that would no doubt be labeled "male oriented" and "degrading" by any number of good feminist soldiers. But these "good parts" were so few and far between, I spent more time fingering the fast-forward button than anything else. I wanted lots of images that reflected my erotic desires and depicted authentic female sexuality. I scanned for cute guys with long hair, punk butchy women, plots with lots of psychosexual tension, come shots where he doesn't pull out and most of all, genuine female orgasms —most of the actresses' orgasms were so fake, they were laughable.

It seemed the biggest problem with pornography wasn't that it was evil smelling and immoral—it was artificial and predictable. But despite my exhaustive search through all the local dirty bookstores, I came up rather empty-handed. Finally I realized I couldn't wait around any longer for somebody else to give me what I wanted. I had to create it myself.

In 1986 during my senior year in college I created a two-page erotic fanzine called *Magnet School: A Sexographic Magazine.* I felt strongly that the problem with porn wasn't that it was inherently degrading but that it was, for the most part, an erotically retarded genre that needed to get real. I wanted to create something that aroused people sexually and intellectually, where the complexity of human sexuality had a voice. Because I so badly wanted to produce something different, I called it something different. In my first editorial column titled "Yeow!" I did away with those loaded language guns *erotica* and *pornography* and put *sexography* in their place.

Sexography was alternative sexual expression in all its lush and lusty glory. In Issue One, I defined sexography as "absolutely no writing about harlots, no getting off with big orchids, no high heels in bed, no masturbating to Lionel Richie, and no split beavers." (Okay, so I've changed my mind a bit since then.) There were other contenders for a newer, blue title—cliterature, lustography, climaxerox, and even Ovaria—but they didn't have the right egalitarian ring.

Although the Macintosh computer had already made its debut, this 'zine was still a cut-and-paste production. I hammered the first issue out on my typewriter, reprinting text from a Throwing Muses album, daring my best girlfriend to pen a porn story, and pirating any decent hard-core images I could find. I photocopied it for free during the middle of the night at the twenty-four-hour copy center, since I'd made friends with the anarchist punks who worked there. I handed it out in cafés and bars, and of course made distribution rounds to every dirty bookstore in town, telling every dildo clerk about the coming erotic revolution. It was very grassroots.

At the same time I was publishing *Magnet School,* I was completing my senior thesis at art school: a sixteen-millimeter color erotic film called *What You Want.* It was a dark and abstract narrative that dealt with issues of female sexuality, control, and erotic relationships. Basically it was my life turned porn drama with me as the star in a long red wig, since no one else auditioned. Greg and I got naked in a bathtub, toyed with oral sex, and even fabricated a nipple-piercing scene. I had intended deep introspection, but my unpolished direction made it corny. I was disappointed that my best intentions had turned camp because I was trying to make a very important point: Sexual images can be profoundly liberating, rather than oppressive.

During the making of this film we had student critiques in the screening room. Everyone in my class was always very opinionated until I showed *my* work in progress. Then there was dead silence, followed by, "God; what are your parents going to think?" Well, I wasn't making this film for my parents. I was making it for my peers, and I wanted to know what they thought. At first they were sort of . . . shocked. They didn't know what to say. The silence was uncomfortable and sometimes hurt me. But outside the classroom my colleagues had a lot to say.

Much to my relief my female friends were extremely supportive. They related to my journey from antiporn feminism to sex-positive feminism, because many of them were on the same trip. They, too, were fed up with everyone shouting, "Don't look!" when it came to porn. They wanted to see it and they wanted me to show it to them. My friend Bitsy even asked me to invite all the girls over for pizza and porno night.

As we talked, I realized that learning how to use porn is an option most women are never aware of. Too many women only react to pornography as a political debate. Pornography, erotica, sexography, whatever you choose to call it, is a tangled genre with a few razor-sharp sides. This complexity is a reflection of the mystery and depth of our own sexuality, where erotic conflict often makes for excitement. My investigation into the erotic world has resulted in a few mixed feelings. There were images that troubled me, and there still are. But I believe my initial knee-jerk reaction against porn was a result of my own misunderstanding and lack of sensitivity to erotic images.

Pornography as a whole is usually described as offensive. Yet I found that much of what is offensive about porn has to do with interpretations, not sexual acts. Take the controversial example of a woman sucking a man's cock until he comes all over her face. This image can be presented in a very crass and repellent way, or it can be depicted as sensuous and kind. To me the act itself isn't degrading; feeling my lover come all over me can be the most intimate gift. But no matter how artfully presented this image is, it is almost always interpreted as crass and repellent because people refuse to believe there can be other interpretations.

The words *degrading* and *oppressive* are often presented as absolute, objective terms. I found them to be vague and subjective. Was the very act of a woman spreading her legs and wanting sex degrading? Were photographs of her genitals outright demeaning? Why is the image of a woman's sexual appetite seen as oppressive rather than liberating? If we're going to talk about oppressive images of women, we'd better include laundry soap commercials. The depiction of women as vapid Stepford wives, valued only for their stain-removing talents is to me completely oppressive.

Another thing that really surprised me as I explored this erotic underworld was the lack of violent porn. I was taught to believe that all porn was violent. However, my own exploration quickly revealed that the majority of commercial porn is rather peacefully formulaic. No knives, no blood, no rape scenes. Instead there was a lick-suck-fuck formula that ended in orgasm, not murder.

Ultimately I felt the antiporn feminists viewed women as being without sexual self-awareness. Their arguments for the elimination of porn were shaky and flawed. Their claims denied women independence by refusing to acknowledge that women had rich sexual fantasies, powerful libidos, and the power to choose.

I chose to discuss sex in a way my older sister probably never did, particularly with my women friends. We traded vibrator tips, talked about our erotic fantasies—or the lack of them—and shared the secrets of our guilt-ridden, latent masturbatory experiences. We didn't waste time dissing men—we mainly focused on ourselves and figuring out how to power up our own orgasms—although we did agree that the general lack of male nudity was lame. Tits and ass flood our culture, but his bare body is nowhere in sight. We also found it interesting how pornography is usually discussed as the sexual depiction of women, although almost all heterosexual porn features women *and* men. We felt that if porn was going to come of age, not only would the images of women have to change, so would the images of men. Paunchy guys with overgrown mustaches who had little to offer except their big dicks weren't our idea of sexy. We wanted bad boys with angel faces who understood the meaning of seduction. We also wanted them to be a little, well . . . vulnerable.

Although what we said was significant, how we said it was also important. These conversations didn't take place behind closed doors, but in public. At parties, in cafés, and in living rooms across Minneapolis we talked about what turned us on. We didn't care who heard us. We had so many questions and we felt so powerful being able to ask them out loud.

Men, on the other hand, were less sure how to act. They were intrigued by my bold sexual independence. It struck a chord with them—they saw their own masculinity reflected in me. In other words they admired my balls. At the same time they were a bit confused by my overt sexuality. It conflicted with their understanding of feminism. A lot of men my age were raised to believe that if you respected women, you didn't look at naked pictures of them. So if I was a feminist, how could I like pornography? To them the concept of a loudmouthed, sexually self-governing woman was exciting, challenging, and sometimes a bit scary.

Surprisingly, or maybe not, I was never directly attacked by any antiporn feminists. People often expect me to tell horrifying tales of how I was branded a traitor and was run out of Wimmin's town on a rail. But the truth is the response to my work has always been overwhelmingly positive. I believe it's because more and more women are realizing that erotic images have a necessary place in their lives. Sexual freedom is an integral part of freedom and justice for all. If the basic tenet of feminism is giving women the freedom to choose, then it includes making choices about what we do sexually.

This freedom to go for the erotic gusto, however, exists because of the tremendous gains founding feminists have made. If it wasn't for social and economic battles won during the last few decades, female sexuality would still be chained up in ignorance and silence. The sexual revolution of the late sixties and early seventies paved the way for my generation's erotic liberation.

As a card-carrying feminist, I chose to pursue a career as a pornographer. With eight issues of my homegrown zine *Magnet School* completed, I gave in to my crush on California and headed west to San Francisco—Sin City. For two years I worked with my mentor, Susie Bright, as a senior editor at *On Our Backs* and as a freelance journalist.

In 1991 I was hired to edit *Future Sex,* a magazine for women and men that explores the intersection of sex, technology, and culture. I had written about so many aspects of sex, but not this one. What was the link between sex and technology anyway? Was it virtual-reality sex? Digital porn? Fucking robots? While these concepts were certainly futuristic, I hoped they weren't the only things the future of sex had to offer.

The fact that today's young women are able to think more critically about pornography is due in part to technology. The VCR brought a female audience to porn and gave them the unprecedented opportunity to see exactly what it is. Video porn allows both women and men to investigate sexual imagery in a more independent way. Moving X-rated images out of public, often unclean theaters and into the privacy and comfort of the bedroom gave women safe and direct access to this previously off-limits material. In fact women now represent the fastest-growing group of erotic consumers.

I now realize that technology may be this generation's key to taking control of our sexual identities. While computer technology may seem isolating rather than unifying at first, personal computers, modems, camcorders, and a host of other tools offer the potential for unparalleled communication, including erotic communication. In many ways high technology puts the means of production back in everyone's hands. We no longer have to depend on someone else's mass-produced idea of eroticism; we can create our own—easily, cost-effectively, often instantly. Moreover digital technology gives us the chance to transmit our ideas globally, not just locally.

Today we must also contend with something no other generation had to: AIDS. Since this devastating plague sends the message that sex can equal death, it forces us to talk publicly about sex in a straightforward way in order to save lives. Latex is vogue. Jerking off is in. Safe sex is hot. AIDS is a catalyst for rethinking our relationship to erotica. And the stigma of pornography is slowly being chipped away.

But this new-world pornography will suffer the same pitfalls of the old world if we don't take advantage of the possibilities. A naked babe on a computer screen is just the same old babe, unless we add change. Technology doesn't magically transform—or even replace —erotic traditions. People do. The depth of both female and male sexuality can't be explored if we don't break the mold of prefabricated turn-ons. We've got the power to turn the tired, piston-driven porn formula into a fluid reflection of modern erotic culture. What's hot isn't limited to high heels and big cocks. Gender-bending, multiracial eroticism, bisexuality, and a range of other polymorphous departures from the standard are all a part of the erotic spectrum, but we rarely see them presented as such. That's why the genesis of this new erotic entertainment must be influenced by people with more diverse points of view. And I intend to be influential right from the very start.

Since I watched *Sleepless Nights* almost nine years ago, I've learned a lot about myself and the power of being female. I've learned that the erotic impulse is a part of being human, that it can't be controlled through political warfare or replaced by a silicon chip. I've learned that pornography is a mirror reflecting our rosiest desires, our blackest fears. It catches us looking. And these days I like some of what I see—especially when I've created it.

I Never Called It Rape

Robin Warshaw

This testimonial is taken from the introduction of Robin War-shaw's 1988 book of the same name, which revealed the full scope of the results of the *Ms.* study on date rape on college campuses.

It was a low point in my life. The war in Vietnam, which I, along with hundreds of thousands of other college students, took to the streets to oppose, was becoming more bloody—at home and abroad. In unrelated violence a friend I loved was murdered that spring by a teenage gang. A few weeks after my friend's murder I ended a relationship with my boyfriend, whom I will call Carl. Carl and I parted on unpleasant terms—with me wanting a clean break, him wanting another chance. He left town and traveled for a while, with no clear plans.

One day, about two months after our breakup, Carl appeared at my apartment door entreating me to talk to him, to get back to-gether. I told him I wasn't interested in reviving the relationship. He began to shout that he would kill himself if I wouldn't speak with him.

I had loved this man once and felt guilty that I was making him so unhappy. I thought that he really might try to commit suicide. I agreed to go outside to talk with him. Once outside, he insisted that I go with him to a mutual friend's apartment where he was staying. According to Carl, that friend wanted to see me and had planned that we would all have dinner together. We could talk there, he said.

It never occurred to me that Carl was lying. I thought that maybe our friend could help me convince Carl that the relationship was really over. The friend's apartment was in a part of the city that I wasn't very familiar with. I can still remember climbing up the stairs to the apartment, thinking how glad I was that our friend would be there. I stepped into the apartment, calling out his name. Behind me I heard the thunk of a door bolt.

I turned, and Carl was standing, grinning. He held a large knife he must have retrieved from the kitchen as we walked in. Needless to say, our friend was not in the apartment—Carl had known that when he brought me there. I immediately believed that I could die. If I had any doubts, he removed them moments later by telling me that he was going to kill me.

As the night progressed, he continued to threaten to kill me and himself if I refused to renew our relationship. We talked around and around that subject for hours. He only let me out of his sight to use the bathroom, where I discovered the window had bars across it. I could have yelled out it for help, but I did not. My reasons are contradictory, yet very like the reasons I heard from many of the women I interviewed for this book: I didn't know where I was or who might come; I didn't want to embarrass Carl or myself; I still felt I could talk him out of the situation and I was afraid that my yelling would only make him angrier and put me in more danger.

When, late into the night, he motioned to the bedroom with the knife, I followed. In bed he draped his arm across me, holding the knife on the far side of the pillow all night. He had intercourse with me at least once, but I think it might have been more than that. It seemed to go on for a long time. I felt like I was in a corner of the room, watching the bed from a distance. Eventually he fell asleep. I did not move. I did not holler. I did not try to leave. In the morning Carl walked me back to my apartment. We parted company about a block from my door at my insistence, although now I think he agreed because he didn't want to risk running into my roommates. When I finally got inside, I stripped off my clothes and stood in the shower for an hour. I did not go to work that day.

Several times in the next week or two Carl intercepted me on the way to my job. My boss, who was also a friend, called the security office so I would have an escort. I had told no one about what happened, but she could tell that I was frightened by Carl's hanging around. After a few more weeks he was gone, but my fears that he would reappear were not. For months I dreaded going anywhere he might be—and that was everywhere.

It took me about three years to realize I had been raped. Before that all I focused on about the assault was the feeling that I could die. Since my attacker had been my boyfriend, with whom I had had sexual intercourse before, I never attached the word *rape* to what happened. Rape, after all, was what vile strangers did to you. Then one day, after a close friend became head of a local rape-crisis group, I was listening to her tell me about some of her group's recent cases. They were all rapes committed by strangers, but the stories evoked a rush of feelings about my own experience. Then I knew: I had been raped.

I'd like to say that naming it helped, but it didn't, not for a long time. The rape contributed to problems I had for the next several years. Eventually counseling helped overcome the cumulative effect of those years.

Ten years after the episode I finally felt that I had worked it all through. Of course I harbored my revenge fantasies—I daydreamed of encountering Carl in a public place and proclaiming him to be a rapist, which most certainly he would loudly deny—but I felt that at least I now understood what had happened, although I shared my story with very few people.

It was Christmas Eve, and I was home alone when the phone rang. I picked it up, and a man said, "I bet you don't know who this is. This is a voice from your past." I recognized Carl's voice immediately, which seemed to flatter him.

He then told me he had been reading the articles I was writing. I felt angry and afraid. Carl obviously knew where I lived and probably still lived in the area, since much of my writing at that time was for local publications. I asked him questions to try to figure out where he was and to determine how much of a danger he posed. He gave me little information about himself. I wanted to hang up, but I wanted to confront him even more. He had attacked me again, this time by telephone, and this would probably be my only chance to strike back. I steadied myself.

"Do you realize that the last time you saw me you raped me?"

There, I had said it to him, just as I always hoped I would. Now I braced myself for the outraged denial that I knew would come. I could feel my whole body tighten, waiting for the blow.

After a long pause his voice came over the line.

"Yes," he said, and then, after another pause he added, "but the statute of limitations is up."

I became enraged and warned him never to contact me again or I would call the police. Then I slammed down the phone. I couldn't believe it: I had confronted him and he had admitted that, yes, he *had* raped me.

When I finally calmed down, there was still anger. But most of it was anger at myself. I had really thought I was done with it. But after the phone call I realized that over the years I had still harbored some doubts: How could it be rape if you knew him? If you dated him? If you had had sex with him before?

By answering yes to my question, Carl gave a power to my belief in what happened that it had not had before. I was angry and disappointed in myself that his corroboration could mean so much.

That was seven years ago. When *Ms.* editor Ellen Sweet and I first talked about my writing this book, she did not know that I had been raped by a man I knew. I would not tell her that for several months. I needed time to think about the project. What would it be like for me to concentrate my efforts for more than a year on a subject that had already personally caused me pain, confusion, and anger? I realized, too, that my interviewing could dredge up pain for my subjects—much more than I, as a reporter, liked to stir. I am, after all, not a therapist or a rape-crisis counselor. Could I take women back over their experiences without causing more damage? I also knew I would have to write about my own acquaintance-rape experience. I could not ask other women to reveal what I was unwilling to show. As the book's author I knew I would be asked if I had ever been the victim of such rape. I could not imagine lying about that. Writing the book would also mean finally that I would have to tell my parents I had been raped.

When I decided to go ahead, I talked with and listened to date-rape and acquaintance-rape survivors around the country. To find a fuller range of women who had been raped by men they knew, I purchased advertisements in local newspapers, received some help from rape-crisis workers, and placed a small notice in *Ms.* seeking women willing to talk about their experiences. (It elicited scores of responses.) Some women I interviewed in person, others wrote eloquent narratives. In all I talked to or heard from more than 150 women. It is these women who are quoted throughout this book. For many of the women I interviewed it was the first time they had talked with anyone other than a counselor about their incidents. Most said they agreed to talk with me to educate other women and to encourage acquaintance-rape survivors who may be suffering in solitude to seek help. I also spoke with men who were sympathetic and unsympathetic about women's experiences with date and acquaintance rape as well as with male and female sociologists, psychologists, educators, and crisis workers who are looking for solutions to the problem.

When I began my research, I thought I understood my own rape experience fully. But, time and again, while working on this book I realized that I did not. Talking with other women who had been raped by men they knew, I learned much more about what happened to me. Nothing follows a formula, but I discovered how my experience—which I always thought to be one of a kind—was a typical acquaintance rape in many aspects (it was planned by the man, it happened in an isolated location, I didn't identify it as rape because I knew my attacker). Although most acquaintance rapes and date rapes don't involve a weapon as mine did, many of the women I interviewed spoke of how they feared for their lives during their assaults, how they truly believed that they were going to die. The tales of recovery that many women shared with me also helped me examine my own aftermath.

I mention all of this, in part, because it is a fondly held belief among journalists that we come to our subjects with no particular opinion or ax to grind. When we do have a bias, we like to make it clearly known up-front. I know that my having been raped makes a difference—not necessarily to my editors or to the experts I spoke with but to the women who shared their stories with me. Early on in each interview I mentioned briefly that I had been raped by a man I knew. Each time, my listener visibly relaxed. That piece of information was powerful enough to remove the ever-present fear among acquaintance-rape survivors—the fear of not being believed.

On Not Being a Victim

Mary Gaitskill

Mary Gaitskill is the author of the novel *Two Girls, Fat and Thin* and of *Bad Behavior,* a collection of short stories. This essay first appeared in the March 1994 issue of *Harper's* magazine.

In the early 1970s I had an experience that could be described as acquaintance rape. Actually I have had two or three such experiences, but this one most dramatically fits the profile. I was sixteen and staying in the apartment of a slightly older girl I'd just met in a seedy community center in Detroit. I'd been in her apartment for a few days when an older guy she knew came over and asked us if we wanted to drop some acid. In those years doing acid with complete strangers was consistent with my idea of a possible good time, so I said yes. When I started peaking, my hostess decided she had to go see her boyfriend, and there I was, alone with this guy, who, suddenly, was in my face.

He seemed to be coming on to me, but I wasn't sure. My perception was quite loopy, and on top of that he was black and urban-poor, which meant that I, being very inexperienced and suburban-white, did not know how to read him the way I might have read another white kid. I tried to distract him with conversation, but it was hard, considering that I was having trouble with logical sentences, let alone repartee. During one long silence I asked him what he was thinking. Avoiding my eyes, he answered, "That if I wasn't such a nice guy, you could really be getting screwed." The remark sounded to me like a threat, albeit a low-key one. But instead of asking him to explain himself or to leave, I changed the subject. Some moments later, when he put his hand on my leg, I let myself be drawn into sex because I could not face the idea that if I said no, things might get ugly. I don't think he had any idea how unwilling I was—the cultural unfamiliarity cut both ways—and I suppose he may have thought that all white girls just kind of lie there and don't do or say much. My bad time was made worse by his extreme gentleness; he was obviously trying very hard to please me, which, for reasons I didn't understand, broke my heart. Even as inexperienced as I was, I sensed that in his own way he intended a romantic encounter.

For some time afterward I described this event as "the time I was raped." I knew when I said it that the statement wasn't quite accurate, that I hadn't, after all, said no. Yet it *felt* accurate to me. In spite of my ambiguous, even empathic feelings for my unchosen partner, unwanted sex on acid is a nightmare, and I did feel violated by the experience. At times I even flat-out lied about what had happened, grossly exaggerating the violence and the threat—not out of shame or guilt but because the pumped-up version was more congruent with my feelings of violation than the confusing facts. Every now and then, in the middle of telling an exaggerated version of the story, I would remember the actual man and internally pause, uncertain of how the memory squared with what I was saying or where my sense of violation was coming from—and then I would continue with my story. I am ashamed to admit this, both because it is embarrassing to me and because I am afraid the admission could be taken as evidence that women lie "to get revenge." I want to stress that I would not have lied that way in court or in any other context that might have had practical consequences; it didn't even occur to me to take my case to court. My lies were told not for revenge but in service of what I felt to be the metaphorical truth.

I remember my experience in Detroit, including its aftermath, every time I hear or read yet another discussion of what constitutes "date rape." I remember it when yet another critic castigates "victimism" and complains that everyone imagines himself or herself to be a victim and that no one accepts responsibility anymore. I could imagine telling my story as a verification that rape occurs by subtle threat as well as by overt force. I could also imagine telling it as if I were one of those crybabies who want to feel like victims. Both stories would be true and not true. The complete truth is more complicated than most of the intellectuals who have written scolding essays on victimism seem willing to accept. I didn't understand my own story fully until I described it to an older woman many years later, as a proof of the unreliability of feelings. "Oh, I think your feelings were reliable," she returned. "It sounds like you were raped. It sounds like you raped yourself." I immediately knew that what she said was true, that in failing even to try to speak up for myself, I had in a sense raped myself.

I don't say this in a tone of self-recrimination. I was in a difficult situation: I was very young, and he was aggressive. But my inability to speak for myself—to *stand up* for myself—had little to do with those facts. I was unable to stand up for myself because I had never been taught how.

When I was growing up in the 1960s, I was taught by the adult world that good girls never had sex and bad girls did. This rule had clarity going for it but little else; as it was presented to me, it allowed no room for what I actually might feel, what I might want or not want. Within the confines of this rule I didn't count for much, and I quite vigorously rejected it. Then came the less clear "rules" of cultural trend and peer example that said that if you were cool, you wanted to have sex as much as possible with as many people as possible. This message was never stated as a rule, but, considering how absolutely it was woven into the social etiquette of the day (at least in the circles I cared about), it may as well have been. It suited me better than the adults' rule—it allowed me my sexuality at least —but again it didn't take into account what I might actually want or not want.

The encounter in Detroit, however, had nothing to do with being good or bad, cool or uncool. It was about someone wanting something I didn't want. Since I had been taught only how to follow rules that were somehow more important than I was, I didn't know what to do in a situation where no rules obtained and that required me to speak up on my own behalf. I had never been taught that my behalf mattered. And so I felt helpless, even victimized, without really knowing why.

My parents and my teachers believed that social rules existed to protect me and that adhering to these rules constituted social responsibility. Ironically my parents did exactly what many commentators recommend as a remedy for victimism. They told me they loved me and that I mattered a lot, but this was not the message I got from the way they conducted themselves in relation to authority and social convention—which was not only that I didn't matter but that *they* didn't matter. In this they were typical of other adults I knew, as well as of the culture around them. When I began to have trouble in school, both socially and academically, a counselor exhorted me to "just play the game"—meaning to go along with everything from school policy to the adolescent pecking order—regardless of what I thought of "the game." My aunt, with whom I lived for a short while, actually burned my jeans and T-shirts because they violated what she understood to be the standards of decorum. A close friend of mine lived in a state of war with her father because of her hippie clothes and hair—which were of course de rigueur among her peers. Upon discovering that she was smoking pot, he had her institutionalized.

Many middle-class people—both men and women—were brought up, like I was, to equate responsibility with obeying external rules. And when the rules no longer work, they don't know what to do—much like the enraged, gun-wielding protagonist of the movie *Falling Down,* played by Michael Douglas, who ends his ridiculous trajectory by helplessly declaring, "I did everything they told me to." If I had been brought up to reach my own conclusions about which rules were congruent with my internal experience of the world, those rules would have had more meaning for me. Instead I was usually given a series of static pronouncements. For example when I was thirteen, I was told by my mother that I couldn't wear a short skirt because "nice girls don't wear skirts above the knee." I countered of course by saying that my friend Patty wore skirts above the knee. "Patty is not a nice girl," returned my mother. But Patty *was* nice. My mother is a very intelligent and sensitive person, but it didn't occur to her to define for me what she meant by "nice," what "nice" had to do with skirt length, and how the two definitions might relate to what I had observed to be nice or not nice—and then let me decide for myself. It's true that most thirteen-year-olds aren't interested in, or much capable of, philosophical discourse, but that doesn't mean that adults can't explain themselves more completely to children. Part of becoming responsible is learning how to make a choice about where you stand in respect to the social code and then holding yourself accountable for your choice. In contrast, many children who grew up in my milieu were given abstract absolutes that were placed before us as if our thoughts, feelings, and observations were irrelevant.

Recently I heard a panel of feminists on talk radio advocating that laws be passed prohibiting men from touching or making sexual comments to women on the street. Listeners called in to express reactions both pro and con, but the one I remember was a woman who said, "If a man touches me and I don't want it, I don't need a law. I'm gonna beat the hell out of him." The panelists were silent. Then one of them responded in an uncertain voice, "I guess I just never learned how to do that." I understood that the feminist might not want to get into a fistfight with a man likely to be a lot bigger than she, but if her self-respect was so easily shaken by an obscene comment made by some slob on the street, I wondered, how did she expect to get through life? She was exactly the kind of woman whom the cultural critics Camille Paglia and Katie Roiphe have derided as a "rape-crisis feminist"—Puritans, sissies, closet-Victorian ladies who want to legislate the ambiguity out of sex. It was very easy for me to feel self-righteous, and I muttered sarcastically at my radio as the panel yammered about self-esteem.

I was conflicted, however. If there had been a time in my own life when I couldn't stand up for myself, how could I expect other people to do it? It could be argued that the grown women on the panel should be more capable than a sixteen-year-old girl whacked out on acid. But such a notion presupposes that people develop at a predictable rate or react to circumstances by coming to universally agreed-upon conclusions. This is the crucial unspoken presumption at the center of the date-rape debate as well as of the larger discourse on victimism. It is a presumption that in a broad but potent sense reminds me of a rule.

Feminists who postulate that boys must obtain a spelled-out yes before having sex are trying to establish rules, cut in stone, that will apply to any and every encounter and that every responsible person must obey. The new rule resembles the old good-girl/bad-girl rule not only because of its implicit suggestion that girls have to be protected but also because of its absolute nature, its iron-fisted denial of complexity and ambiguity. I bristle at such a rule, and so do a lot of other people. But should we really be so puzzled and indignant that another rule has been presented? If people have been brought up believing that to be responsible is to obey certain rules, what are they going to do with a can of worms like "date rape" except try to make new rules that they see as more fair or useful than the old ones?

But the "rape-crisis feminists" are not the only absolutists here; their critics play the same game. Camille Paglia, author of *Sexual Personae,* has stated repeatedly that any girl who goes alone into a frat house and proceeds to tank up is cruising for a gang bang, and if she doesn't know that, well, then she's "an idiot." The remark is most striking not for its crude unkindness but for its reductive solipsism. It assumes that all college girls have had the same life experiences as Paglia and have come to the same conclusions about them. By the time I got to college, I'd been living away from home for years and had been around the block several times. I never went to a frat house, but I got involved with men who lived in rowdy "boy houses" reeking of dirty socks and rock and roll. I would go over, drink, and spend the night with my lover of the moment; it never occurred to me that I was in danger of being gang-raped, and if I had been, I would have been shocked and badly hurt. My experience, though some of it had been bad, hadn't led me to conclude that boys plus alcohol equals gang bang, and I was not naive or idiotic. Katie Roiphe, author of *The Morning After: Sex, Fear, and Feminism on Campus,* criticizes girls who, in her view, create a myth of false innocence: "But did these twentieth-century girls, raised on Madonna videos and the six o'clock news, really trust that people were good until they themselves were raped? Maybe. Were these girls, raised on horror movies and glossy Hollywood sex scenes, really as innocent as all that?" I am sympathetic to Roiphe's annoyance, but I'm surprised that a smart chick like her apparently doesn't know that people process information and imagery (like Madonna videos and the news) with a complex subjectivity that doesn't in any predictable way alter their ideas about what they can expect from life.

Roiphe and Paglia are not exactly invoking rules, but their comments seem to derive from a belief that everyone except idiots interprets information and experience in the same way. In that sense they are not so different in attitude from those ladies dedicated to establishing feminist-based rules and regulations for sex. Such rules, just like the old rules, assume a certain psychological uniformity of experience, a right way.

The accusatory and sometimes painfully emotional rhetoric conceals an attempt not only to make new rules but also to codify experience. The "rape-crisis feminists" obviously speak for many women and girls who have been raped or have *felt* raped in a wide variety of circumstances. They would not get so much play if they were not addressing a widespread and real experience of violation and hurt. By asking, "Were they really so innocent?" Roiphe doubts the veracity of the experience she presumes to address because it doesn't square with hers or with that of her friends. Having not felt violated herself—even though she says she has had an experience that many would now call date rape—she cannot understand, or even quite believe, that anyone else would feel violated in similar circumstances. She therefore believes all the fuss to be a political ploy or, worse, a retrograde desire to return to crippling ideals of helpless femininity. In turn Roiphe's detractors, who have not had her more sanguine "morning after" experience, believe her to be ignorant and callous, or a secret rape victim in deep denial. Both camps, believing their own experience to be the truth, seem unwilling to acknowledge the emotional truth on the other side.

It is at this point that the "date-rape debate" resembles the bigger debate about how and why Americans seem so eager to identify themselves and be identified by others as victims. Book after article has appeared, written in baffled yet hectoring language, deriding the P.C. goody-goodies who want to play victim and the spoiled, self-centered fools who attend Twelve-Step programs, meditate on their inner child, and study pious self-help books. The revisionist critics have all had a lot of fun with the recovery movement, getting into high dudgeon over those materially well-off people who describe their childhoods as "holocausts" and winding up with a fierce exhortation to return to rationality. Rarely do such critics make any but the most superficial attempt to understand why the population might behave thus.

In a fussing, fuming essay in these pages ("Victims, All?" October 1991) that has almost become a prototype of the genre, David Rieff expressed his outrage and bewilderment that affluent people would feel hurt and disappointed by life. He angrily contrasted rich Americans obsessed with their inner children to Third World parents concerned with feeding their actual children. On the most obvious level the contrast is one that needs to be made, but I question Rieff's idea that suffering is one definable thing, that he knows what it is, and that since certain kinds of emotional pain don't fit this definition, they can't really exist. This idea doesn't allow him to have much respect for other people's experience—or even to see it. It may be ridiculous and perversely self-aggrandizing for most people to describe whatever was bad about their childhood as a "holocaust," but I suspect that when people talk like that, they are saying that as children they were not given enough of what they would later need in order to know who they are or to live truly responsible lives. Thus they find themselves in a state of bewildering loss that they can't articulate, except by wild exaggeration—much like I defined my inexplicable feelings after my Detroit episode. *Holocaust* may be a grossly inappropriate exaggeration. But to speak in exaggerated metaphors about psychic injury is not so much the act of a crybaby as it is a distorted attempt to explain one's own experience. I think the distortion comes from a desperate desire to make one's experience have consequence in the eyes of others and that such desperation comes from a crushing doubt that one's own experience counts at all.

In her book *I'm Dysfunctional, You're Dysfunctional,* Wendy Kaminer speaks harshly of women in some Twelve-Step programs who talk about being metaphorically raped. "It is an article of faith here that suffering is relative; no one says she'd rather be raped metaphorically than in fact," she writes, as if not even a crazy person would prefer a literal rape to a metaphorical one. But actually I might. About two years after my "rape" in Detroit I was raped for real. The experience was terrifying: my attacker repeatedly said he was going to kill me, and I thought he might. The terror was acute, but after it was over, it actually affected me less than many other mundane instances of emotional brutality I've suffered or seen other people suffer. Frankly I've been scarred more by experiences I had on the playground in elementary school. I realize that the observation may seem bizarre, but for me the rape was a clearly defined act, perpetrated upon me by a crazy asshole whom I didn't know or trust; it had nothing to do with me or who I was, and so, when it was over, it was relatively easy to dismiss. Emotional cruelty is more complicated. Its motives are often impossible to understand, and it is sometimes committed by people who say they like or even love you. Nearly always it's hard to know whether you played a role in what happened, and if so, what the role was. The experience *sticks* to you. By the time I was raped, I had seen enough emotional cruelty to feel that the rape, although bad, was not especially traumatic.

My response may seem strange to some, but my point is that pain can be an experience that defies codification. If thousands of Americans say that they are in psychic pain, I would not be so quick to write them off as self-indulgent fools. A metaphor like "the inner child" may be silly and schematic, but it has a fluid subjectivity, especially when projected out into the world by such a populist notion as "recovery." Ubiquitous recovery-movement phrases like "We're all victims" and "We're all codependent" may not seem to leave a lot of room for interpretation, but they are actually so vague that they beg for interpretation and projection. Such phrases may be fair game for ridicule, but it is shallow to judge them on their face value, as if they hold the same meaning for everyone. What is meant by an "inner child" depends on the person speaking, and not everyone will see it as a metaphor for helplessness. I suspect that most inner-child enthusiasts use the image of themselves as children not so that they can *avoid* being responsible but to learn responsibility by going back to the point in time when they *should* have been taught responsibility—the ability to think, choose, and stand up for themselves—and were not. As I understand it, the point of identifying an "inner child" is to locate the part of yourself that didn't develop into adulthood and then to develop it yourself. Whether or not this works is an open question, but it is an attempt to accept responsibility, not to flee it.

When I was in my late teens and early twenties, I could not bear to watch movies or read books that I considered demeaning to women in any way; I evaluated everything I saw or read in terms of whether it expressed a "positive image" of women. I was a very P.C. feminist before the term existed, and, by the measure of my current understanding, my critical rigidity followed from my inability to be responsible for my own feelings. In this context being responsible would have meant that I let myself feel whatever discomfort, indignation, or disgust I experienced without allowing those feelings to determine my entire reaction to a given piece of work. In other words it would have meant dealing with my feelings and what had caused them, rather than expecting the outside world to assuage them. I could have chosen not to see the world through the lens of my personal unhappiness and yet maintained a kind of respect for my unhappiness. For example, I could have decided to avoid certain films or books because of my feelings without blaming the film or book for making me feel the way I did.

My emotional irresponsibility did not spring from a need to feel victimized, although it may have looked that way to somebody else. I essentially was doing what I had seen most mainstream cultural critics do—it was from them that I learned to view works of art in terms of the message they imparted and, further, that the message could be judged on the basis of consensual ideas about what life is and how it can and should be seen. My ideas, like most P.C. ideas, were extreme, but they were consistent with more mainstream thought—they just shifted the parameters of acceptability a bit.

Things haven't changed much: At least half the book and film reviews that I read praise or condemn a work on the basis of the likability of the characters (as if there is a standard idea of what is likable) or because the author's point of view is or is not "life-affirming"—or whatever the critic believes the correct attitude toward life to be. The lengthy and rather hysterical debate about the film *Thelma and Louise,* in which two ordinary women become outlaws after one of them shoots the other's rapist, was predicated on the idea that stories are supposed to function as instruction manuals, and that whether the film was good or bad depended on whether the instructions were correct. Such criticism assumes that viewers or readers need to see a certain type of moral universe reflected back at them or, empty vessels that they are, they might get confused or depressed or something. A respected mainstream essayist writing for *Time* faulted my novel *Two Girls, Fat and Thin* for its nasty male characters, which he took to be a moral statement about males generally. He ended his piece with the fervent wish that fiction not "diminish" men or women but rather seek to "raise our vision of" both—in other words that it should present the "right" way to the reader, who is apparently not responsible enough to figure it out alone.

I have changed a lot from the P.C. teenager who walked out of movies that portrayed women in a demeaning light. As I've grown older, I've become more confident of myself and my ability to determine what happens to me, and, as a result those images no longer have such a strong emotional charge. I don't believe they will affect my life in any practical sense unless I allow them to do so. I no longer feel that misogynistic stories are about me or even about women (whether they purport to be or not) but rather are about the kinds of experience the authors wish to render—and therefore are not my problem. I consider my current view more balanced, but that doesn't mean my earlier feelings were wrong. The reason I couldn't watch "disrespect to women" at that time was that such depictions were too close to my own experience (most of which was not unusual), and I found them painful. I was displaying a simplistic self-respect by not subjecting myself to something I was not ready to face. Being unable to separate my personal experience from what I saw on the screen, I was not dealing with my own particular experience—I think, paradoxically, because I hadn't yet learned to value it. It's hard to be responsible for something that isn't valuable. Someone criticizing me as dogmatic and narrow-minded would have had a point, but the point would have ignored the truth of my unacknowledged experience, and thus ignored me.

Many critics of the self-help culture argue against treating emotional or metaphoric reality as if it were equivalent to objective reality. I agree that they are not the same. But emotional truth is often bound up with truth of a more objective kind and must be taken into account. This is especially true of conundrums such as date rape and victimism, both of which often are discussed in terms of unspoken assumptions about emotional truth anyway. Sarah Crichton, in a cover story for *Newsweek* on "Sexual Correctness," described the "strange detour" taken by some feminists and suggested that "we're not creating a society of Angry Young Women. These are Scared Little Girls." The comment is both contemptuous and superficial; it shows no interest in *why* girls might be scared. By such logic, anger implicitly is deemed to be the more desirable emotional state because it appears more potent, and *scared* is used as a pejorative. It's possible to shame a person into hiding his or her fear, but if you don't address the cause of the fear, it won't go away. Crichton ends her piece by saying, "Those who are growing up in environments where they don't have to figure out what the rules should be, but need only follow what's been prescribed, are being robbed of the most important lesson there is to learn. And that's how to live." I couldn't agree more. But unless you've been taught how to think for yourself, you'll have a hard time figuring out your own rules, and you'll feel scared—especially when there is real danger of sexual assault.

One reason I had sex with strangers when I didn't really want to was that part of me wanted the adventure, and that tougher part ran roughshod over the part of me that was scared and uncertain. I'll bet the same thing happened to many of the boys with whom I had these experiences. All people have their tough, aggressive selves as well as their more delicate selves. If you haven't developed these characteristics in ways that are respectful of yourself and others, you will find it hard to be responsible for them. I don't think it's possible to develop yourself in such ways if you are attuned to following rules and codes that don't give your inner world enough importance. I was a strong-willed child with a lot of aggressive impulses, which, for various reasons, I was actively discouraged from developing. They stayed hidden under a surface of extreme passivity, and when they did appear, it was often in a wildly irresponsible, almost crazy way. My early attraction to aggressive boys and men was in part a need to see *somebody* act out the distorted feelings I didn't know what to do with, whether it was destructive or not. I suspect that boys who treat girls with disrespectful aggression have failed to develop their more tender, sensitive side and futilely try to regain it by "possessing" a woman. Lists of instructions about what's nice and what isn't will not help people in such a muddled state, and it's my observation that many people are in such a state to a greater or lesser degree.

I am not idealistic enough to hope that we will ever live in a world without rape and other forms of sexual cruelty; I think men and women will always have to struggle to behave responsibly. But I think we could make the struggle less difficult by changing the way we teach responsibility and social conduct. To teach a boy that rape is "bad" is not as effective as making him see that rape is a viola-tion of his own masculine dignity as well as a violation of the raped woman. It's true that children don't know big words and that teen-age boys aren't all that interested in their own dignity. But these are things that children learn more easily by example than by words, and learning by example runs deep.

A few years ago I invited to dinner at my home a man I'd known casually for two years. We'd had dinner and comradely drinks a few times. I didn't have any intention of becoming sexual with him, but after dinner we slowly got drunk and were soon floundering on the couch. I was ambivalent, not only because I was drunk but because I realized that although part of me was up for it, the rest of me was not. So I began to say no. He parried each no with charming banter and became more aggressive. I went along with it for a time because I was amused and even somewhat seduced by the sweet, junior-high spirit of his manner. But at some point I began to be alarmed, and then he did and said some things that turned my alarm into fright. I don't remember the exact sequence of words or events, but I do remember taking one of his hands in both of mine, looking him in the eyes, and saying, "If this comes to a fight, you would win, but it would be very ugly for both of us. Is that really what you want?"

His expression changed and he dropped his eyes; shortly afterward he left.

I consider that small decision to have been a responsible one because it was made by taking both my vulnerable feelings and my carnal impulses into account. When I spoke, my words came from my feeling of delicacy as well as from my capacity for aggression. And I respected my friend as well by addressing both sides of his nature. It is not hard for me to make such decisions now, but it took me a long time to get to this point. I only regret that it took so long, both for my young self and for the boys I was with, under circumstances that I now consider disrespectful to all concerned.

Two Good People

Stephen L. Carter

Stephen L. Carter, a professor of law at Yale University, is the author of *Culture of Disbelief* and *Reflections of an Affirmative Action Baby*. This essay, about his personal dilemma in the Hill-Thomas hearings, first appeared on the op-ed page of *The New York Times* on October 13, 1991.

As a longtime student of the confirmation process, I usually reserve my comments until after the battle ends. In this bitter year, however, sitting on the sidelines has not been so easy.

I spent much of the summer watching in horror as many opponents of Clarence Thomas's nomination to the Supreme Court raised nasty and offensive charges, the worst of which rested on the ridiculous proposition that as a black person, he has an obligation to hold a particular set of political views. I at once leaped to his defense, for I could not allow such calumnies to go unanswered.

I have never had the privilege of meeting Clarence Thomas, but I admire him for what he has overcome. I admire much of what he stands for, and even where we disagree—and we do, on many issues —I believe that his is an important voice in the black community and in national affairs. His ostracism as a traitor, an enemy, an Uncle Tom, reflects no credit on those who have sought to cast him out.

And yet when Professor Anita Hill's allegations of sexual harassment became public knowledge, accusations that now threaten Judge Thomas's confirmation, I at once defended her against attacks on her character and subsequently supplied the Judiciary Committee with a written character reference. Had I been asked, I would have testified to her integrity at the committee's reopened hearings.

Nevertheless, when the controversy erupted, I found the situation awkward and not a little painful because I so admired both Judge Thomas and Professor Hill. But I could make no other choice. I have been a friend of Anita Hill for fourteen years and I find what some of Judge Thomas's supporters are saying about her simply incredible.

Yes, there was a despicable national effort to gather dirt on Judge Thomas. Yes, there are people who would stop at nothing to defeat him who are delighted that Anita Hill turned up—and that she is willing to take the heat that they deserve.

But all of this proves only that there are dishonest, mean-spirited people in the world. It does not prove that Anita Hill is among them.

I understand the anger and bewilderment of Judge Thomas's allies. I can scarcely imagine the pain that his family and closest friends—and Judge Thomas himself—must now be enduring. A week ago his confirmation to the Supreme Court was a near certainty. Today, after two days of hearings, its outcome is in question. The situation must surely seem impossible and deeply, deeply unfair.

Consequently I empathize with the desire on the part of his supporters to lash out. The Clarence Thomas described by Anita Hill, they say, is not the Clarence Thomas they know. This must, they insist, be the long-awaited October surprise, the desperate last-ditch effort by his opponents to fling lots of mud and hope that some will stick. Anita Hill, in this vision, is an enemy or a pawn. But for the fact that I happen to know Anita Hill, this might have been my view too.

The trouble is that just as Professor Hill's allegations do not describe the Clarence Thomas known to his friends, the cruel depictions of Anita Hill by her detractors do not describe the Anita Hill whom I have known since we were law students together more than a decade ago.

The Anita Hill I know—and the Anita Hill who testified before the committee—is a person of integrity, compassion, and deep spiritual substance. She is not a political activist. She is not vindictive. She is not a publicity hound. She does not seek controversy. She is warm. She is smart. She is thoughtful. She is funny. She is perhaps a little shy.

The Anita Hill I know would not join any sort of smear campaign. She came forward reluctantly and then tried very hard to have her allegations handled by the committee out of public view. When the committee decided—wrongly, in my view—to take no action beyond the cursory FBI investigation, Professor Hill never pressed for more. A leak from Capitol Hill—not her action—brought her story to the public's attention. The attacks on her character that immediately followed brought her friends to her side.

Judge Thomas's friends have also rallied to his side, weighing in with testimonials of their own. Indeed, what has made the Judiciary Committee's task so difficult is that neither Judge Thomas nor Anita Hill can simply be dismissed. Both are serious people who have earned the intense loyalty of those who know them well.

With the Judiciary Committee leak, Anita Hill's name became a household word, and the battle line hardened. Both before and during the reopened hearings, many of Judge Thomas's supporters in and out of the Senate made the choice to answer the allegations by attacking Professor Hill's credibility. Given the anguish they must feel and the widespread sense that the allegations, if true, are disqualifying, this decision is understandable. Judge Thomas's own response, under oath, was a forceful and categorical denial.

Perhaps the allegations as finally made public were too serious to have been answered in a more conciliatory way, although I'm not quite sure of that. Yet, even had they been less severe, I suspect that the response of Judge Thomas's strongest partisans would have been similar.

The problem is that the confirmation process has become absurd. Long before Clarence Thomas's nomination our strange politics of confirmation had somehow reached a point at which no nominee is allowed any mistakes, and therefore no nominee is allowed any change or learning or growth. Nowadays honor seems to be found only in never having done anything wrong—a standard impossible to meet.

Now we face a double tragedy, one that might have been avoided had the committee held a closed hearing on Anita Hill's allegations weeks ago. The committee chose to do otherwise and what we have seen on television over the past two days is a clear signal that the process failed.

Although she never sought this confrontation, Anita Hill has had the courage and strength of character to stand publicly behind her allegations. She has done so at considerable personal cost, which only increases my admiration for her. The unknown leaker has none of the strength of character and will probably remain free to leak again. But perhaps politics is simply the art of sacrificing others for one's cause.

No matter what the outcome of Tuesday's vote, what is needed now is a time of healing; the bitter political wounds that have now been opened will not easily be closed. But close them we must, as the careers of two very fine people are on the line, and there is no reason that either of them has to be destroyed.

Appendix A

The Dworkin-MacKinnon Antipornography Civil Rights Ordinance* (Minneapolis)

An Ordinance of the City of Minneapolis
Amending Title 7, Chapter 139 of the Minneapolis Code of
Ordinances relating to Civil Rights: In General.

The City Council of the City of Minneapolis do ordain as follows:

Section 1. That Section 139.10 of the above-entitled ordinance be
amended to read as follows:

139.10 <u>Findings, declarations of policy and purpose.</u>

(a) <u>Findings.</u> The council finds that discrimination in employment,
labor union membership, housing accommodations, property rights,
education, public accommodations and public services based on race,
color, creed, religion, ancestry, national origin, sex, including sexual
harassment AND PORNOGRAPHY, affectional preference,
disability, age, marital status, or status with regard to public
assistance or in housing accommodations based on familial status
adversely affects the health, welfare, peace and safety of the
community. Such discriminatory practices degrade individuals, foster
intolerance and hate, and create and intensify unemployment, sub-

---

* For other versions of the ordinance, see *Pornography and Civil Rights: A New
Day for Women's Equality,* Andrea Dworkin and Catharine A. MacKinnon,
Organizing Against Pornography, 1988. Later versions include defamation as a
cause of action.

standard housing, under-education, ill health, lawlessness and poverty, thereby injuring the public welfare.

(1) SPECIAL FINDINGS ON PORNOGRAPHY: THE COUNCIL FINDS THAT PORNOGRAPHY IS CENTRAL IN CREATING AND MAINTAINING THE CIVIL INEQUALITY OF THE SEXES. PORNOGRAPHY IS A SYSTEMATIC PRACTICE OF EXPLOITATION AND SUBORDINATION BASED ON SEX WHICH DIFFERENTIALLY HARMS WOMEN. THE BIGOTRY AND CONTEMPT IT PROMOTES, WITH THE ACTS OF AGGRESSION IT FOSTERS, HARM WOMEN'S OPPORTUNITIES FOR EQUALITY OF RIGHTS IN EMPLOYMENT, EDUCATION, PROPERTY RIGHTS, PUBLIC ACCOMMODATIONS AND PUBLIC SERVICES; CREATE PUBLIC HARASSMENT AND PRIVATE DENIGRATION; PROMOTE INJURY AND DEGRADATION SUCH AS RAPE, BATTERY AND PROSTITUTION AND INHIBIT JUST ENFORCEMENT OF LAWS AGAINST THESE ACTS; CONTRIBUTE SIGNIFICANTLY TO RESTRICTING WOMEN FROM FULL EXERCISE OF CITIZENSHIP AND PARTICIPATION IN PUBLIC LIFE, INCLUDING IN NEIGHBORHOODS; DAMAGE RELATIONS BETWEEN THE SEXES; AND UNDERMINE WOMEN'S EQUAL EXERCISE OF RIGHTS TO SPEECH AND ACTION GUARANTEED TO ALL CITIZENS UNDER THE CONSTITUTION AND LAWS OF THE UNITED STATES AND THE STATE OF MINNESOTA.

(b) Declaration of policy and purpose. It is the public policy of the City of Minneapolis and the purpose of this title:

(1) To recognize and declare that the opportunity to obtain employment, labor union membership, housing accommodations, property rights, education, public accommodations and public services without discrimination based on race, color, creed, religion, ancestry, national origin, sex, including sexual harassment AND PORNOGRAPHY, affectional preference, disability, age, marital status, or status with regard to public assistance or to obtain housing accommodations without discrimination based on familial status is a civil right;

(2) To prevent and prohibit all discriminatory practices based on race, color, creed, religion, ancestry, national origin, sex, including sexual harassment AND PORNOGRAPHY, affectional preference, disability, age, marital status, or status with regard to public assistance with respect to employment, labor union membership, housing accommodations, property rights, education, public accommodations or public services;

(3) To prevent and prohibit all discriminatory practices based on familial status with respect to housing accommodations;

(4) TO PREVENT AND PROHIBIT ALL DISCRIMINATORY PRACTICES OF SEXUAL SUBORDINATION OR INEQUALITY THROUGH PORNOGRAPHY;

(5) To protect all persons from unfounded charges of discriminatory practices;

(6) To eliminate existing and the development of any ghettos in the community; and

(7) To effectuate the foregoing policy by means of public information and education, mediation and conciliation, and enforcement.

Section 3. That Section 139.20 of the above-entitled ordinance be amended by adding thereto a new subsection (gg) to read as follows:

(gg) Pornography. Pornography is a form of discrimination on the basis of sex.

(1) Pornography is the sexually explicit subordination of women, graphically depicted, whether in pictures or in words, that also includes one or more of the following:

(i) women are presented dehumanized as sexual objects, things or commodities; or

(ii) women are presented as sexual objects who enjoy pain or humiliation; or

(iii) women are presented as sexual objects who experience sexual pleasure in being raped; or

(iv) women are presented as sexual objects tied up or cut up or mutilated or bruised or physically hurt; or

(v) women are presented in postures of sexual submission; or

(vi) women's body parts - including but not limited to vaginas, breasts, and buttocks - are exhibited, such that women are reduced to those parts; or

(vii) women are presented as whores by nature; or

(viii) women are presented being penetrated by objects or animals; or

(ix) women are presented in scenarios of degradation, injury, abasement, torture, shown as filthy or inferior, bleeding, bruised, or hurt in a context that makes these conditions sexual.

(2) The use of men, children, or transsexuals in the place of women in (1) (i-ix) above is pornography for the purposes of subsections (l) - (p) of this statute.

Section 4. That section 139.40 of the above-mentioned ordinance be amended by adding thereto new subsections (l), (m), (n), (o), (p), (q), (r) and (s) to read as follows:

(l) <u>Discrimination by trafficking in pornography.</u> The production, sale, exhibition, or distribution of pornography is discrimination against women by means of trafficking in pornography:

(1) City, state, and federally funded public libraries or private and public university and college libraries in which pornography is available for study, including on open shelves, shall not be construed to be trafficking in pornography but special display presentations of pornography in said places is sex discrimination.

(2) The formation of private clubs or associations for purposes of trafficking in pornography is illegal and shall be considered a conspiracy to violate the civil rights of women.

(3) Any woman has a cause of action hereunder as a woman acting against the subordination of women. Any man or transsexual who alleges injury by pornography in the way women are injured by it shall also have a cause of action.

(m) <u>Coercion into pornographic performances.</u> Any person, including transsexual, who is coerced, intimidated, or fraudulently induced (hereafter "coerced") into performing for pornography shall have a cause of action against the maker(s), seller(s), exhibitor(s) or distributor(s) of said pornography for damages and for elimination of the products of the performance(s) from the public view.

(1) <u>Limitation of action.</u> This claim shall not expire before five years have elapsed from the date of the coerced performance(s) or from the last appearance or sale of any product of the performance(s), whichever date is later;

(2) Proof of one or more of the following facts or conditions shall not, without more, negate a finding of coercion;

(i) that the person is a woman; or

(ii) that the person is or has been a prostitute; or

(iii) that the person has attained the age of majority; or

(iv) that the person is connected by blood or marriage to anyone involved in or related to the making of the pornography; or

(v) that the person has previously had, or been thought to have had, sexual relations with anyone, including anyone involved in or related to the making of the pornography; or

(vi) that the person has previously posed for sexually explicit pictures for or with anyone, including anyone involved in or related to the making of the pornography at issue; or

(vii) that anyone else, including a spouse or other relative, has given permission on the person's behalf; or

(viii) that the person actually consented to a use of the performance that is changed into pornography; or

(ix) that the person knew that the purpose of the acts or events in question was to make pornography; or

(x) that the person showed no resistance or appeared to cooperate actively in the photographic sessions or in the sexual events that produced pornography; or

(xi) that the person signed a contract, or made statements affirming a willingness to cooperate in the production of pornography; or

(xii) that no physical force, threats, or weapons were used in the making of the pornography; or

(xiii) that the person was paid or otherwise compensated.

(n) <u>Forcing pornography on a person.</u> Any woman, man, child, or transsexual who has pornography forced on him/her in any place of employment, in education, in a home, or in any public place has a cause of action against the perpetrator and/or institution.

(o) <u>Assault or physical attack due to pornography.</u> Any woman, man, child, or transsexual who is assaulted, physically attacked or injured in any way that is directly caused by specific pornography has a claim for damages against the perpetrator, the maker(s), distributor(s), seller(s), and/or exhibitor(s), and for an injunction against the specific pornography's further exhibition, distribution, or sale. No damages shall be assessed (A) against the maker(s) for pornography made, (B) against distributor(s) for pornography distributed, (C) against seller(s) for pornography sold, or (D) against exhibitors for pornography exhibited prior to the enforcement date of this act.

(p) <u>Defenses.</u> Where the materials which are the subject matter of a cause of action under subsections (l), (m), (n), or (o) of this section are pornography, it shall not be a defense that the defendants did not know or intend that the materials were pornography or sex discrimination.

(q) <u>Severability.</u> Should any part(s) of this ordinance be found legally invalid, the remaining part(s) remain valid.

(r) Subsections (l), (m), (n), and (o) of this section are exceptions to the second clause of Section 141.90 of this title.

(s) <u>Effective date.</u> Enforcement of this ordinance of December 30, 1983, shall be suspended until July 1, 1984 ("enforcement date") to facilitate training, education, voluntary compliance, and implementation taking into consideration the opinions of the City Attorney and the Civil Rights Commission. No liability shall attach under (l) or as specifically provided in the second sentence of (o) until the enforcement date. Liability under all other sections of this act shall attach as of December 30, 1983.

Amending Title 7, Chapter 141 of the Minneapolis Code of Ordinances relating to Civil Rights: Administration and Enforcement.

The City Council of the City of Minneapolis do ordain as follows:

Section 1. That Section 141.50 (l) of the above-entitled ordinance be amended by adding thereto a new subsection (3) to read as follows:

(3) Pornography: The hearing committee or court may order relief, including the removal of violative material, permanent injunction against the sale, exhibition or distribution of violative material, or any other relief deemed just and equitable, including reasonable attorney's fees.

Section 2. That Section 141.60 of the above-entitled ordinance be amended as follows:

141.60 Civil action, judicial review and enforcement.

(a) Civil actions.

(1) AN INDIVIDUAL ALLEGING A VIOLATION OF THIS ORDINANCE MAY BRING A CIVIL ACTION DIRECTLY IN COURT.

(2) A complainant may bring a civil action at the following times:

(i) Within forty-five (45) days after the director, a review committee or a hearing committee has dismissed a complaint for reasons other than a conciliation agreement to which the complainant is a signator; or

(ii) After forty-five (45) days from the filing of a verified complaint if a hearing has not been held pursuant to Section 141.50 or the department has not entered into a conciliation agreement to which the complainant is a signator. The complainant shall notify the department of his/her intention to bring a civil action, which shall be commenced within ninety (90) days of giving the notice. A complainant bringing civil action shall mail, by registered or certified mail, a copy of the summons and complaint to the department and upon receipt of same, the director shall terminate all proceedings before the department relating to the complaint and shall dismiss the complaint.

No complaint shall be filed or reinstituted with the department after a civil action relating to the same unfair discriminatory practice has been brought unless the civil action has been dismissed without prejudice.

GOV'T OPS - Your Committee, to whom was referred ordinances amending Title 7 of the Minneapolis Code of Ordinances, to add pornography as discrimination against women and provide just and equitable relief upon finding of discrimination by hearing committee of the Civil Rights Commission, and having held public hearings thereon, recommends that the following ordinances be given their second readings for amendment and passage:

a. Ordinance amending Chap 139 relating to <u>Civil Rights: In General;</u>

b. Ordinance amending Chap 141 relating to <u>Civil Rights: Administration and Enforcement.</u>

Appendix B

Selected Results from the *Ms.* Magazine Campus Project on Sexual Assault

One quarter of women in college today have been the victims of rape or attempted rape, and almost 90 percent of them knew their assailants. These are two of the more startling statistics to emerge from the *Ms.* Magazine Campus Project on Sexual Assualt, the most far-reaching study to date on patterns of sexual aggression at America's institutions of higher learning. Funded by a grant from the National Center for the Prevention and Control of Rape, and under the direction of Kent State University psychologist Mary P. Koss, the survey reached more than seven thousand students at thirty-five schools. Preliminary results of the three-year study show:

- Fifty-two percent of all the women surveyed have experienced some form of sexual victimization.
- One in every eight women were the victims of rape, according to the prevailing legal definition.
- One in every twelve men admitted to having fulfilled the prevailing definition of rape or attempted rape, yet virtually none of those men identified themselves as rapists.
- Of the women who were raped, almost three-quarters did not identify their experience as rape.
- Forty-seven percent of the rapes were by first or casual dates, or by romantic acquaintances.
- Three-quarters of the women raped were between the ages fifteen and twenty-one; the average age at the time of the rape was eighteen.

- More than 80 percent of the rapes occurred off-campus, with more than 50 percent on the man's turf: home, car, or other.
- More than one-third of the women raped did not discuss their experience with anyone; more than 90 percent did not tell the police.

—ELLEN SWEET

Appendix C

Excerpt from the Antioch College Sexual-Offense Policy

1. For the purpose of this policy, "consent" shall be defined as follows: the act of willingly and verbally agreeing to engage in a specific sexual contact or conduct.

2. If sexual contact and/or conduct is not mutually and simultaneously initiated, then the person who initiates sexual contact/conduct is responsible for getting the verbal consent of the other individual(s) involved.

3. Obtaining consent is an ongoing process in any sexual interaction. Verbal consent should be obtained with each new level of physical and/or sexual contact/conduct in any given interaction, regardless of who initiates it. Asking "Do you want to have sex with me?" is not enough. The request for consent must be specific to each act.

4. The person with whom sexual contact/conduct is initiated is responsible to express verbally and/or physically his/her willingness or lack of willingness when reasonably possible.

5. If someone has initially consented but then stops consenting during a sexual interaction, she/he should communicate withdrawal verbally and/or through physical resistance. The other individual(s) must stop immediately.

6. To knowingly take advantage of someone who is under the influence of alcohol, drugs, and/or prescribed medication is not acceptable behavior in the Antioch community.

ABOUT TH

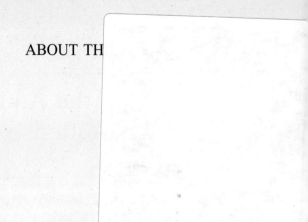

Adele M. Stan is a freelance journalist whose work has appeared in a number of publications, including *The New Republic, The Nation, The Village Voice,* and the op-ed pages of *The New York Times,* the *New York Daily News,* and the *Los Angeles Times.* She is a former member of the *Ms.* editorial staff and lives with her husband, Barry Morgan Thomas, in Weehawken, New Jersey.